WARRANT AND
PROPER FUNCTION

*To Barbara
with more best wishes*

— Al

WARRANT AND PROPER FUNCTION

Alvin Plantinga

New York   Oxford
OXFORD UNIVERSITY PRESS
1993

Oxford University Press

Oxford   New York   Toronto
Delhi   Bombay   Calcutta   Madras   Karachi
Kuala Lumpur   Singapore   Hong Kong   Tokyo
Nairobi   Dar es Salaam   Cape Town
Melbourne   Auckland   Madrid

and associated companies in
Berlin   Ibadan

Published by Oxford University Press, Inc.
200 Madison Avenue, New York, New York 10016

Oxford is a registered trademark of Oxford University Press

Library of Congress Cataloging-in-Publication Data
Plantinga, Alvin.
Warrant and proper function / Alvin Plantinga.
p.   cm.   Includes index.
ISBN 0-19-507863-2; ISBN 0-19-507864-0 (pbk)
1. Knowledge, Theory of. 2. Belief and doubt. 3. Cognition.
I. Title.
BD161.P57   1993   121'.6—dc20   92-408

2 4 6 8 9 7 5 3 1

Printed in the United States of America
on acid-free paper

Preface

In *Theaetetus*, Plato sets the agenda for Western epistemology: What is knowledge? More exactly, What is it that distinguishes knowledge from mere true belief? What is this elusive quality or quantity enough of which, together with truth and belief, is sufficient for knowledge? Call that quantity, whatever it is, 'warrant'; in *Warrant: The Current Debate,* the first volume in this series, I considered some of the main contemporary views of warrant. You may not be surprised to learn that I found them all wanting. Now it is time to take the next and more dangerous step, leaving the safety of the philosophical bunker from which one snipes at other views for the more risky business of exposing my own views on the subject. (My plan was to call this volume *Warrant: the Sober Truth,* but wiser heads prevailed.) Before taking that precarious step, however, I wish to recapitulate briefly the main themes of the first volume. Its principal aim was to take a careful and critical look at some of the main contemporary accounts of warrant, trying to understand them, noting where they go wrong or are inadequate, seeing what can be learned from them, and trying to figure out where to look for a better account.

In the first chapter of *Warrant: The Current Debate* I noted that twentieth-century British and American epistemology has been heavily *internalist.* Internalism is really a loosely related set of views about epistemic *access*—access to whatever it is that makes for warrant. According to the internalist, the knower can know, and know in some special way, that a certain proposition or belief has warrant or justification for her; alternatively, she can know that the condition constituting the ground of warrant is present, or that she has the property that makes it true that a belief has warrant for her, or something else in that neighborhood. But this epistemic access must be special in some way. I have access to the distance from Vienna to Prague (I own an atlas); but that kind of access doesn't count. The access in question must be *privileged* in some way: perhaps it is *certain* for the epistemic agent that the condition in question holds, or perhaps she can determine *by reflection alone* that it holds, or perhaps there is a certain kind of mistake she can't nonculpably make; however precisely she puts it, the internalist claims that a knower has special epistemic access to the conditions of warrant.

Internalism in epistemology, so I argued, goes hand in hand with the idea that warrant is really *justification.* More exactly, what it goes with is the thought that justification is necessary for warrant and *nearly* sufficient for it: what is required in addition is only a fillip to mollify Gettier. I noted that twentieth-century epistemology displays a vast and confusing diversity. The major movements, however, unite in declaring that there is an intimate connection between justification and *warrant,* between justification and *internalist constraints,* between justification and *evidence,* and between justification and the *satisfaction of epistemic duty.* Twentieth-century epistemology also displays, however, great diversity with respect to the question what, exactly, justification *is.* Some say it is intimately connected with duty and responsibility—a matter of aptness for epistemic duty fulfillment (Chisholm) or perhaps a matter of pursuing one's epistemic goals responsibly (BonJour). Others say that justification crucially involves having evidence for a belief (Alston, Conee, Conee and Feldman, many others). Others see the degree of justification enjoyed by a belief as a measure of how well you have fulfilled your epistemic goals (Lehrer); still others see a belief's being justified as a matter of everything's going right with respect to the knower as knower; yet others say it is a matter of a belief's being produced by a reliable belief-producing mechanism.

I argued that this blooming buzzing confusion with respect to justification can be reduced to order by going back to the fountainheads of contemporary theory of knowledge, those twin towers of Western epistemology, Descartes and Locke. What is crucial to Descartes and (perhaps even more important) Locke, is *epistemic deontologism:* the view that there are epistemic duties and obligations. According to Descartes, the central epistemic duty is that of abstaining from any belief that isn't clear and distinct; according to Locke, it is that of proportioning degree of belief to degree of evidential support by what is certain. Justification itself, however, is just the condition of having done your duty and satisfied the requirements: the condition of doing no more than is permitted, going contrary to no duty or obligation. The main contemporary conceptions of justification can all be understood in terms of this deontological tradition—either as explicitly carrying it on, or as diverging from it to one or another degree, and thus using the term 'justification' in a sense analogically related to this aboriginal sense.

It is therefore easy to see the historical roots of contemporary concern with epistemic justification. Further, as I pointed out, deontology generates internalism; so it is also easy to see the roots of contemporary internalism. Finally, given Locke's view that the prime epistemic duty just is that of proportioning degree of belief to the evidence (evidence from what is certain for me), it is equally easy to see the origin of the contemporary stress on the importance of *evidence* with respect to justification.

I turned next to some prominent internalist construals of warrant. First there is the powerful and powerfully influential work of Roderick Chisholm. According to the classical Chisholm, warrant is aptness for epistemic duty fulfillment. We all have a duty to get into the right relation to the truth: the better you can fulfill that duty by believing a certain proposition, the more warrant that belief has for you. This is an attractive view (and for many years I followed Chisholm in accepting it); closer examination, however, shows that it can't possibly be correct. First, the very notions of duty and obligation don't apply at all directly to the formation and sustenance of belief; for the most part these things are not within our direct control. But concede as much control as Chisholm needs: it is still wholly obvious that epistemic dutifulness is nowhere nearly sufficient for warrant. I may be doing my level best, I may be trying my hardest to get into the right relation to the truth, but, by virtue of epistemic malfunction, may still fail miserably—and fail in such a way that my beliefs have little or no warrant. And therefore I may be magnificently dutiful in forming or maintaining a given belief, but still be such that it has no warrant for me. The moral is that justification strictly so-called is nowhere nearly *sufficient* for knowledge or warrant. I also argued, though less vociferously, that justification isn't *necessary* for warrant either.

Turning to the post-classical Chisholm, the Chisholm of "The Place of Epistemic Justification"[1] and Chisholm's "Self-Profile"[2] we find quite a different view. Here the idea is that warrant, for a belief, is a matter of a certain *fittingness* between that belief and a person's "evidence base," that is, "the conjunction of all the purely psychological properties that that person has at that time." (Purely psychological properties are "those properties to which we have privileged access. Every such property is necessarily such that, if a person has it and if he attributes it to himself, then his attribution is evident in the strongest sense of the term."[3]) This is a much more general view than classical Chisholmianism; one gets different specifications of it by differently specifying that relation of fittingness. Taking the view broadly, it includes coherentism; taking it still more broadly, it might even encompass the externalist theory I mean to propose. Taken Chisholm's way, however, this view seems clearly mistaken, as I argue in chapter 3 of *Warrant: The Current Debate*.

I turned next to coherentism *überhaupt* (chapter 4), then to the coherentism of Laurence BonJour (chapter 5), and then to Bayesian coherentism (chapters 6 and 7) a recent and very interesting coherentist entry in the lists. Coherentism *überhaupt* is unsuccessful because it sees warrant as involving only the relation between beliefs; but the fact is the relation between experience and belief and between environment and belief is also crucial to warrant. BonJour's articulate version of coherentism (so I argue, but BonJour might conceivably disagree) suffers from that problem, as well as some others specific to it. Bayesian coherentism isn't really an answer to the question of warrant (and if addressed to it would be a wholly unsatisfactory response); it is directed, instead, to the question of *rationality*. Rationality is protean and 'rationality' is multiply ambiguous; thinking about Bayesianism gives us a chance to disentangle some of the main varieties of the former and some of the main meanings of the latter. There is *Aristotelian* rationality, which goes with being a rational animal; there is means-end rationality and Foley rationality, an epistemic special case of it;

---

[1]*Philosophical Topics*, ed. Roberta Klein, vol. 14, number 1, p. 85.

[2]In *Roderick M. Chisholm*, ed. Radu Bogdan (Dordrecht: D. Reidel, 1986) p. 52ff.

[3]This is not an official analysis or definition; if it were, the account of reasonability would be circular. It is instead simply a means to enable the reader to identify the class of properties he proposes to discuss.

there is the sort of rationality that amounts to sanity, to epistemic proper function; and there is the rationality that is really a matter of believing in accord with the dictates of reason. Satisfying the Bayesian constraints, I argue, is neither necessary nor sufficient for any of these kinds of rationality. Bayesianism, so I argue, really describes the mental life of a certain kind of ideally rational agent—one who, like us, holds beliefs, reasons, learns, and the like, but is also unlike us in certain crucial respects. As such, Bayesian constraints aren't really conditions on *our* rationality (so one who violates them isn't necessarily irrational); but in some special cases these constraints may function as ideals to which we can appropriately strive to conform.

So internalist accounts of warrant go awry. Moving toward externalist accounts, I turned next in chapter 8 to the work of John Pollock, who offers, so I claimed, a sort of uncomfortable halfway house, an uneasy compromise between externalism and internalism. Pollock argues, fundamentally, that a belief is justified for a person if she arrives at it in conformity with her own norms. His discussion of norms is subtle and penetrating, but (so far as I can see) it does not yield a successful account of warrant. The reason is that it seems perfectly possible for my epistemic norms to be *incorrect* norms, and incorrect in such a way that my carrying on my epistemic life in conformity to them is nowhere nearly either necessary or sufficient for warrant. My beliefs could therefore be Pollock-justified, but have no warrant; Pollock-justification, therefore, is deficient as an account of warrant.

I turned finally to reliabilist and paradigmatically externalist accounts of warrant; here I examined the proposals of Fred Dretske, William Alston and Alvin Goldman in chapter 9. Reliabilism marks a real advance—or better, it represents a fortunate retreat, a happy return to the externalist perspective occupied much earlier by Thomas Reid, and earlier yet by Aquinas and Aristotle. Still, reliabilism does not offer a correct account of warrant. The early Goldman offers a stylized and paradigmatic reliabilism: A belief has warrant if and only if it is the product of a reliable belief producing mechanism (or process or faculty). But there are two problems here: first how can the reliabilist account for the fact that warrant comes in degrees? Attempts to follow Goldman by doing this in terms of degree of reliability lead straight to the generality problem, the reef on which the early Goldman founders. And second, a belief may be the product of a reliable belief producing mechanism, but if the mechanism in question malfunctions (the agent is drunk, or ill, or under attack by a shark) the resulting belief has little or no warrant, despite its respectable source. This problem bedevils both the early and the later Goldman. Reliabilists, as I see it, call attention to one of the four conditions characterizing paradigm cases of knowledge; reliabilism is therefore an approximation to the truth. But reliabilists also neglect the other three traits of paradigm cases of knowledge; reliabilism is therefore (at best) a zeroeth approximation to the truth.

Can we do better? Indeed we can (so I claim, anyway). As I see it, a belief has warrant if it is produced by cognitive faculties functioning properly (subject to no malfunctioning) in a cognitive environment congenial for those faculties, according to a design plan successfully aimed at truth. In the first couple of chapters of the present volume I fill out, develop, qualify and defend this view, exploring along the way some of the convoluted contours of the notion of proper function. In the next seven chapters I consider how the proposed account works in the main areas of our cognitive design plan: memory, introspection, knowledge of other minds, testimony, perception, *a priori* belief, and probability. Then in chapter 10 I consider broader, structural questions of coherentism and foundationalism. My account of warrant meets the conditions for being a *naturalistic* account; but in chapters 11 and 12 I claim that naturalism in epistemology flourishes best in the context of supernaturalism in metaphysics; for (as I argue in chapter 11) there appears to be no successful naturalistic account of the notion of proper function. Finally in chapter 12 I argue that metaphysical naturalism when combined with contemporary evolutionary accounts of the origin and provenance of human life is an irrational stance; it provides for itself an ultimately undefeated defeater.

Here I must acknowledge a complication with respect to my way of thinking of warrant. I aim at something in the neighborhood of an *analysis* of warrant: an account or exploration of our concept of warrant, a concept nearly all of us have and regularly employ. (As we all know, desperate difficulties beset any attempt to say precisely what analysis *is*.) Thus at the least I should be looking for necessary and sufficient conditions. But I very much doubt that there *is* any short and elegant list of conditions at once severally necessary and jointly sufficient for warrant. This is a way in which philosophy differs from mathematics; and epistemology differs more from mathematics, along these lines, than, for example, philosophy of logic or the metaphysics of modality. Our concept of warrant is too complex to yield to analysis by way of a couple of austerely elegant clauses. The structure of this concept, I believe, involves a central picture, a group of central paradigms—clear and unambiguous cases of knowledge—surrounded by a penumbral belt of analogically related concepts, concepts related by different analogies and standing in different degrees of closeness to the aboriginal paradigms. Between the central core area and this penumbral belt there is a more shadowy area of borderline possible cases, cases where it isn't really clear whether what we have is a case of warrant in the central sense, or a case of one of the analogically extended concepts, or neither of the above; and beyond the penumbral belt we have another area of borderline cases.

Hence perhaps a good way to characterize our system of analogically related concepts of warrant is to give first, the conditions necessary and sufficient for the central paradigmatic core. (Even here, as we shall see, there is no stylishly sparse set of necessary and sufficient conditions: various qualifications, additions and subtractions are necessary.) Second, what is needed is an exploration of some of the analogical extensions, with an explanation of the analogical bases of the extensions. This way of proceeding is less elegant and pleasing and more messy than the analysis we learned at our mother's knee: it is also more realistic.

In the preface to *Warrant: The Current Debate* I acknowledged my indebtedness to many (embarrassingly many) from whom I have learned and who have helped in various ways with these books. Here I want to single out for special thanks Bill Alston, Tom Senor, Dean Zimmerman, and Robin Collins. I should also point out that there are points of contact between the position I develop and the work of Ernest Sosa, Marshall Swain, and Hector Castañeda. Still another kind of intellectual debt: the position I shall develop is broadly Reidian; the global outline of Thomas Reid's epistemology seems to me to be largely correct.

Of course the fundamental style of Reidian epistemology with its externalist emphasis didn't originate with Reid; it can be traced back to Aquinas and indeed all the way back to Aristotle. A more proximate precursor is Claude Buffier (1661–1737),[4] in his *First Truths, and the Origin of Our Opinions, Explained: with an Inquiry into the Sentiments of Modern Philosophers, Relative to our Primary Ideas of Things* (Paris, 1724). There is an anonymous English translation (1780) which adds as it were another subtitle, *"To which is Prefixed A Detection of the Plagiarism, Concealment, and Ingratitude of the Doctors Reid, Beattie, and Oswald."* The author complains that "Of later years the *Transtweedian* regions have swarmed with a new species of men, different from their itinerant peddlers in the wares they sell, but familiar in the manner of packing them together from the labours of others . . . " (p. vi). These Transtweedians, furthermore, "persevere in collecting materials from other authors, and, industrious to conceal their plagiarism, compile and assume them as their own" (p. vii); they have "clandestinely taken the principles and opinions of Pere *Buffier*, converted them to their own purposes of acquiring fame, and concealed the theft by ungratefully unacknowledging the person to whom they are obliged . . . " (p. viii). The most dangerous (because ablest) of these Transtweedian ingrates is Reid himself: "Dr. Reid, in his *Enquiry*, has carefully avoided *literally* transcribing the passages relative to *DesCartes*, *Malebranche*, *Locke* and *Berkeley*, and the observations on them, which are to be found in *Buffier*; but he has with no less care adopted his sense, and modestly affirmed it as his own" (p. xi). Naturally I hope to avoid Reid's offenses. I therefore concede in advance that what follows has been influenced to any degree you please by Reid and hence, by the transitivity of *influences*, Buffier himself.

Notre Dame, Indiana   A.P.
April 1992

---

[4]Called to my attention by Kelly Clark.

Contents

WARRANT AND
PROPER FUNCTION

1

Warrant: A First Approximation

One thought emerging from our canvas of contemporary accounts of warrant in *Warrant: The Current Debate* is that there are many different valuable epistemic states of affairs—epistemic *values,* we might call them, giving that oft-abused word a decent sense; and different conceptions of warrant appeal to different epistemic values. For example, there is doing one's subjective epistemic duty, doing one's objective epistemic duty, and doing both; these figure prominently in classical internalism. There is having a set of beliefs that is coherent to one or another degree; there is also the *disposition* to have coherent beliefs; these things are what the coherentist is quite naturally enthusiastic about. There is having adequate evidence or good reasons for your beliefs; this goes with the evidentialism that has been a dominant feature of the epistemological tradition and is presently represented in different ways by Conee and Feldman,[1] and William Alston.[2] There is having a reliable set of faculties or belief-producing mechanisms, which of course goes with reliabilism of various sorts. There is also knowing that you have a reliable set of epistemic faculties. There is also Foley rationality; and there are the several varieties of Foley rationality, such as believing what you *think* would contribute to your attaining your epistemic goal, believing what on reflection you *would* think would contribute to your attaining that goal, believing what *really would* contribute to your doing so, and so on. There is having a set of beliefs that contributes to your nonepistemic goals such as happiness, or living the good life, or living the moral life. There is having the *right* goals; there is *aiming* to have the right goals; and there is *knowing* that you have the right goals. There is believing what is true, and there is having true beliefs on important topics; there is accepting a given belief to the right degree. There is knowing that you know; there is being able to prove to the skeptic that you know. And there are a thousand other epistemic virtues.

---

[1] "Evidentialism," *Philosophical Studies* (1985), p. 15.
[2] See his "Concepts of Epistemic Justification," *Monist* (January 1985), and "An Internalist Externalism," *Synthese* 74, no. 3 (1988); see also several of the articles collected in *Epistemic Justification* (Ithaca: Cornell University Press, 1989).

I. Proper Function

Now the notion of warrant is clearly connected with all of these epistemic values and more besides. (The problem here is to come up with a conception of warrant that gives to each its due and describes how each is connected with the others and with warrant.) As a first step toward developing a satisfying account of warrant, I should like to call attention to still another epistemic value: having epistemic faculties that *function properly*. The first thing to see, I think, is that this notion of proper function is the rock on which the canvassed accounts of warrant founder. Cognitive malfunction has been a sort of recurring theme. Chisholm's dutiful epistemic agent who, whenever he is appeared to redly, always believes that nothing is appearing redly to him, Pollock's cognizer who by virtue of malfunction has the wrong epistemic norms, the Coherent but Inflexible Climber, Dretske's epistemic agent whose belief that Spot emits ultraviolet radiation has been caused by the fact that Spot does indeed emit such radiation, Goldman's victim of the epistemically serendipitous lesion: all are such that their beliefs lack warrant for them. In each case the reason, I suggest, is *cognitive malfunction*, failure of the relevant cognitive faculties to function properly, to function as they ought to. Chisholm's agent meets Chisholm's conditions for warrant; his beliefs lack warrant, however, because they result from cognitive dysfunction due to a damaging brain lesion, or the machinations of an Alpha Centaurian scientist, or perhaps the mischievous schemes of a Cartesian evil demon. Something similar must be said for each of the others. In each case the unfortunate in question meets the conditions laid down for warrant by the account in question; in each case her beliefs fail to have warrant because of cognitive malfunction. Hence each of these accounts misfires, at least in part by virtue of its failure to take appropriate account of the notion of proper function.

I therefore suggest initially that a necessary condition of a belief's having warrant for me is that my cognitive equipment, my belief-forming and belief-maintaining apparatus or powers, be free of such malfunction. A belief has warrant for you only if your cognitive apparatus is functioning properly, working the way it ought to work, in producing and sustaining it. (Of course this isn't nearly sufficient, and I shall try to supply some of what is necessary to achieve sufficiency.)

The notion of proper function is one member of a connected group of interdefinable notions; some of the other members of the group are *dysfunction, design, function* (simpliciter), *normality* (in the normative nonstatistical sense),[3] *damage,* and *purpose.* There is initial reason to doubt, I think, that this circle of concepts can be broken into from the outside—that is, reason to doubt that any of them can be defined without reference to the others. Here we have a situation like that with modality: possibility, contingency, necessity, entailment, and their colleagues form a circle of properties or concepts that can be defined or explained in terms of each other but cannot be defined in terms of properties

---

[3]See p. 9, and see the discussion of Pollock's account of proper function in chapter 11, pp. 199ff.

outside the circle. (Of course that is nothing against these modal concepts.) The same goes here, I think; but I shall consider (in chapter 11) attempts to define or explain these terms by way of terms outside the circle.

You may nonetheless think there is a serious problem with this notion right from the start. Isn't the idea of proper function an extremely unlikely idea to appeal to in explaining the notion of warrant? Isn't it every bit as puzzling, every bit as much in need of explanation and clarification, as the notion of warrant itself? Perhaps so; but even if so, at least we can reduce our total puzzlement by explaining the one in terms of the other; and we can see more clearly the source and location of some of our perplexities about warrant. Further, the idea of proper function is one we all have; we all grasp it in at least a preliminary rough-and-ready way; we all constantly employ it. You go to the doctor; he tells you that your thyroid isn't functioning quite as it ought (its thyroxin output is low); he prescribes a synthetic thyroxin. If you develop cataracts, the lenses of your eyes become less transparent; they can't function properly and you can't see well. A loss in elasticity of the heart muscle can lead to left ventricular malfunction. If a bird's wing is broken, it typically won't function properly; the bird won't be able to fly until the wing is healed, and then only if it heals in such a way as not to inhibit proper function. Alcohol and drugs can interfere with the proper function of various cognitive capacities, so that you can't drive properly, can't do simple addition problems, display poor social judgment, get into a fist fight, and wind up in jail.

And it isn't just in rough-and-ready everyday commonsense contexts that the notion of proper function is important; it is deeply embedded in science.

> We are accustomed to hearing about biological functions for various bodily organs. The heart, the kidneys, and the pituitary gland, we are told, have functions—things they are, in this sense *supposed to do*. The fact that these organs are supposed to do these things, the fact that they have their functions, is quite independent of what *we* think they are supposed to do. Biologists *discovered* these functions; they didn't invent or assign them. We cannot, by agreeing among ourselves, *change* the functions of these organs. . . . The same seems true for sensory systems, those organs by means of which highly sensitive and continuous dependencies are maintained between external, public events and internal, neural processes. Can there be a serious question about whether, in the same sense in which it is the heart's function to pump the blood, it is, say, the task or function of the noctuid moth's auditory system to detect the whereabouts and movements of its archenemy, the bat?[4]

According to David Baltimore, "many instances of blood disorders, mental problems, and a host of other disabilities are traceable to a malfunctioning gene."[5] According to the great Swiss child psychologist Jean Piaget, a seven-year-old child whose cognitive faculties are functioning properly will believe that everything in the universe has a purpose in some grand overarching plan or design; later on a properly functioning person, he said, will learn to "think

[4]Fred Dretske, *Explaining Behavior* (Cambridge: MIT Press, 1988), p. 91.
[5]"Limiting Science: a Biologist's Perspective," *Daedalus* (Summer 1988), p. 336.

scientifically" and realize that everything has either a natural cause or happens by chance.[6]

Biological and social scientists, furthermore—psychologists, medical researchers, neuroscientists, economists, sociologists, and many others—continually give accounts of how human beings or other organisms or their parts and organs function: how they work, what their purposes are, and how they react under various circumstances. Call these descriptions (following John Pollock)[7] *functional generalizations*. For example, whenever a person is appeared to redly under such and such conditions, she will form the belief that there is something red present; whenever a person considers an obvious *a priori* truth such as $2 + 1 = 3$, she will find herself firmly believing it; whenever a person desires something and believes so and so, he will do such and such. To strike a more sophisticated if no more enlightening note: whenever an organism of kind K is in state S_i and receives sensory input P_i, then there is a probability of r that it will go into state S_j and produce output O_j. Pollock makes the important point that if these functional generalizations are taken straightforwardly and at face value, as universal generalizations about people and other organisms and their parts, they are nearly always false. They don't hold of someone who is in a coma, having a stroke, crazed by strong drink, or has just hit the ground after a fall off a cliff. Clearly these functional generalizations contain something like an implicit restriction to organisms and organs that are *functioning properly,* functioning as they ought to, subject to no malfunction or dysfunction. The notion of proper function, therefore, is presupposed by the idea of functional generalizations.

So the notion of proper function is a notion we have and regularly employ; I may therefore appeal to it in explaining warrant. Still, it needs exploration, clarification, and explication if it is to serve as the key notion in an account of warrant. I shall have more to say about this notion below and in the next chapter; for the moment, let us provisionally entertain the idea that a belief has warrant for me only if the relevant parts of my noetic equipment—the parts involved in its formation and sustenance—are functioning properly. It is easy to see, however, that proper function cannot be the whole story about warrant. You have just had your annual cognitive checkup at MIT; you pass with flying colors and are in splendid epistemic condition. Suddenly and without your knowledge you are transported to an environment wholly different from earth; you awake on a planet revolving around Alpha Centauri. There conditions are quite different; elephants, we may suppose, are invisible to human beings, but emit a sort of radiation unknown on earth, a sort of radiation that causes human beings to form the belief that a trumpet is sounding nearby. An Alpha Centaurian elephant wanders by; you are subjected to the radiation, and form the belief that a trumpet is sounding nearby. There is nothing wrong with your cognitive faculties; they are working quite properly; still, this belief has little by way of warrant for you. Nor is the problem merely that the belief is false; even

[6]*The Child's Conception of Physical Causality* (London: Kegan Paul, Trench, Trubner, 1930).

[7]"How to Build a Person," in *Philosophical Perspectives, 1, Metaphysics, 1987,* ed. James Tomberlin (Atascadero, Calif.: Ridgeview, 1987), p. 146.

if we add that a trumpet really *is* sounding nearby (in a soundproof telephone booth, perhaps), your belief will still have little by way of warrant for you.

To vary the example, imagine that the radiation emitted causes human beings to form the belief not that a trumpet is sounding, but that there is a large gray object in the neighborhood. Again, an elephant wanders by; while seeing nothing of any particular interest, you suddenly find yourself with the belief that there is a large gray object nearby. A bit perplexed at this discovery, you examine your surroundings more closely: you still see no large gray object. Your faculties are displaying no malfunction (you have your certificate from MIT); you are not being epistemically careless or slovenly (you are doing your epistemic best); nevertheless you don't know that there is a large gray object nearby. That belief has little or no warrant for you. Of course you may be justified, within your epistemic rights in holding this belief; you may be flouting no epistemic duty. Further, the belief may also be rational for you in every sensible sense of 'rational'.[8] But it has little warrant for you.

What this example is designed to show, of course, is that the proper function of your epistemic equipment is not (logically) sufficient for warrant: it is possible that your cognitive equipment be functioning perfectly properly but your beliefs still lack warrant for you. And the reason is not far to seek: it is that your cognitive faculties and the environment in which you find yourself are not properly attuned. The problem is not with your cognitive faculties; they are in good working order. The problem is with the environment—with your cognitive environment. In approximately the same way, your automobile might be in perfect working order, despite the fact that it will not run well at the top of Pike's Peak, or under water, or on the moon. We must therefore add another component to warrant; your faculties must be in good working order, and the environment must be appropriate for your particular repertoire of epistemic powers. It must be the sort of environment for which your faculties are designed—by God or evolution (or both). Perhaps there are creatures native to the planet in question who are much like human beings but whose cognitive powers fit that epistemic environment and differ from ours in such a way that Alpha Centaurian elephants are not invisible to them. Then their beliefs would have warrant where yours do not.

It is tempting to suggest that warrant *just is* (or supervenes upon) proper functioning in an appropriate environment, so that a given belief has warrant for you to the degree that your faculties are functioning properly (in producing and sustaining that belief) in an environment appropriate for your cognitive equipment: the better your faculties function, the more warrant. But this cannot be correct. Couldn't it happen that my cognitive faculties are working properly (in an appropriate environment) in producing and sustaining a certain belief in me, while nonetheless that belief enjoys less by way of warrant for me than some other belief? Say that a pair of beliefs are (for want of a better term) *productively equivalent* if they are produced by faculties functioning properly

---

[8]See my *Warrant: The Current Debate* (New York: Oxford University Press, 1993), chap. 6, sec. 1, "The Varieties of Rationality."

to the same degree and in environments of equal appropriateness. Then couldn't it be that a pair of my beliefs should be productively equivalent while nonetheless one of them has more by way of warrant—even a great deal more—than the other? Of course that could be; as a matter of fact it happens all the time. The belief that $7 + 5 = 12$, or the belief that I have a name, or the belief that I am more than seven years old—any of these has more by way of warrant for me than does the memory belief, now rather dim and indistinct, that forty years ago I owned a secondhand sixteen-gauge shotgun and a red bicycle with balloon tires; but all, I take it, are produced by cognitive faculties functioning properly in a congenial environment. Although both epistemic warrant and *being properly produced* come in degrees, there seems to be no discernible functional relationship between them: but then we can't see warrant as simply a matter of a belief's being produced by faculties working properly in an appropriate environment. We still have no real answer to the question *What is warrant?* That particular frog (with apologies to John Austin) is still grinning residually up from the bottom of the mug.

Fortunately there is an easy response. Not only does the first belief, the belief that $7 + 5 = 12$, have more by way of warrant for me than the second; it is also one I accept much more firmly. It seems *obviously* true, in a way in which the belief about the bicycle and shotgun do not. Among the things we believe, we believe some much more firmly than others. I believe that I live in Indiana, that $2 + 1 = 3$, that the sun is larger than the earth, that China has a larger population than India, and that Friesland used to be much larger than it is now; and I believe some of these things more firmly than others. Here I speak of full belief, not the partial beliefs of which Bayesians speak.[9] Following Ramsey, Bayesians sometimes suggest that my degrees of belief can be at least roughly determined by examining my betting behavior; the least odds at which I will bet on a proposition A measures the degree to which I believe A. If I am willing to bet at odds of 2:1 that the die will come up either 5 or 6 then I must believe to degree .667 that it will come up that way. This seems to me wrong. The truth is I believe it *probable* to degree .667 that the die will come up that way. And no doubt I fully believe *that;* that is, in this case I don't believe *anything* to degree .667 (strictly speaking, there is no such thing as believing something to degree .667), but I *do* believe (fully believe) that there is a .667 probability that the die will come up either 5 or 6. Suppose I buy a ticket in a thousand-ticket lottery I believe to be fair. Here it is false, I think, that I believe I will not win, or believe that to degree .999. What I do believe is that it is very *probable* (probable to degree .999) that I won't win.[10]

[9]See ibid., chap. 6, pp. 117ff.

[10]It is sometimes suggested that whenever I believe A no more firmly than not-A and not-A no more firmly than A, then I can be thought of as believing A (and not-A) to degree .5. This seems clearly mistaken. Consider a case where I have no idea at all whether the proposition in question is true. You ask me (a touch pedantically) "consider the proposition that the highest mountain on Mars is between ten and eleven thousand feet high and call it 'A'; do you think A is true? I have no idea about A and do not believe it more likely than its denial; I also do not believe its denial more likely than it. Then on the Bayesian view, I must believe A to degree .5. You then ask me the same

Return to the case in question, then: although I believe both $7 + 5 = 12$ and *40 years ago I owned a secondhand 16-gauge shotgun and a red bicycle with balloon tires,* I believe the former more strongly than the latter; this is correlated with the fact that the former has more by way of warrant for me than the latter. I therefore conjecture that when my cognitive establishment is working properly, then in the typical case, the degree to which I believe a given proposition will be proportional to the degree it has of warrant—or if the relationship isn't one of straightforward proportionality, some appropriate functional relationship will hold between warrant and this impulse. When my faculties are functioning properly, a belief has warrant to the degree that I find myself inclined to accept it; and this (again, if my faculties are functioning properly and nothing interferes) will be the degree to which I *do* accept it.

Initially, and to (at most) a zeroeth approximation, therefore, we may put it like this: in the paradigm cases of warrant, a belief B has warrant for S if and only if that belief is produced in S by his epistemic faculties working properly in an appropriate environment; and if both B and B^* have warrant for S, B has more warrant than B^* for S iff S believes B more firmly than B^*. And knowledge requires both true belief, and a certain degree of warrant (a degree that may vary from context to context, so that knowledge may display a certain indexical character).[11]

Putting the matter thus imports what is at this stage at best a wholly spurious pretense of precision and completeness; and the rest of this chapter and the next will be given over to some of the necessary qualifications, amplifications, and the like, including attention to the absolutely crucial notion of the design plan. To begin with some of the essential and obvious qualifications then: it is of first importance to see that this condition—that of one's cognitive equipment functioning *properly*—is not the same thing as one's cognitive equipment functioning *normally,* not, at any rate, if we take the term 'normally' in a broadly statistical sense.[12] Even if one of my systems functions in a way far from the statistical norm, it might still be functioning properly. (Alternatively, what we must see is that there is a distinction between a normative and statistical sense of 'normal'.) Carl Lewis is not defective with respect to jumping by virtue of the fact that he can jump much further than the average person.

---

question about B: the proposition that the highest mountain on Mars is between eleven and twelve thousand feet high. Again, I have no idea; so on the Bayesian view I am considering, I must also believe B to degree .5. Now A and B are mutually exclusive; according to the probability calculus, therefore, I should believe their disjunction to degree 1. But of course I do not; for I also have no idea whether the highest mountain on Mars is between ten and twelve thousand feet high. And the problem is not that I am desperately incoherent. The problem is that we can't properly represent ignorance of this sort as believing the proposition in question to degree .5. There is a vast difference between the situation in which I think A probable to degree .5 (perhaps A is the proposition that the die will come up side 1, 2, or 3) and the situation in which I have no idea what the probability of A's being true might be.

[11]See H. N. Castañeda's "The Indexical Theory of Knowledge," in *Midwest Studies in Philosophy* Vol. V, *1980,* ed. Peter French, Theodore E. Uehling, Jr., and Howard Wettstein (Minneapolis: University of Minnesota Press, 1980).

[12]See the discussion of Pollock's account of proper function, in my Chapter 11, pp. 199ff.

Perhaps most adult tomcats get into lots of fights and ordinarily move into late middle age with patches of fur torn out; it does not follow that an old tomcat with all of his fur suffers from some sort of tonsorial disorder. Perhaps most male cats get neutered; it does not follow that those that don't are incapable of proper function. If, by virtue of some nuclear disaster, we were nearly all left blind, it would not follow that the few sighted among us would have improperly functioning eyes. So your belief's being produced by your faculties working *normally* or in *normal* conditions—that is, the sorts of conditions that most frequently obtain—must be distinguished from their working *properly*.

Further, a belief has warrant for me only if my epistemic faculties are working properly in producing and sustaining it; but of course it isn't true that *all* of my cognitive faculties have to be functioning properly in order for a given belief to have warrant for me. Suppose my memory plays me tricks; obviously that does not mean that I can't have warrant for such introspective propositions as that I am appeared to redly. What must be working properly are the faculties (or subfaculties, or modules) involved in the production of the particular belief in question. And even they need not be working properly over the entire range of their operation. Suppose I cannot properly hear high notes: I may still learn much by way of the hearing ability I do have. Furthermore, a faculty that does not function properly *without outside aid* can nonetheless furnish warrant; I can have warrant for visual propositions even if I need glasses and can see next to nothing without them. Still further, even if my corrected vision is very poor, I can still have warrant for visual propositions; even if I can't perceive colors at all, I can still have warrant for the proposition that I perceive something round. Again, even if I can't perceive colors at all, I can still have visual warrant for the proposition that something is red; even if for me nothing appears redly (everything is merely black and white) I might still be able to see that something is red, in the way in which one can see, on a black and white television, which boxer is wearing the red trunks. And of course there will be many more qualifications of this sort necessary:[13] suppose my belief is based upon two different mechanisms and one but not the other is functioning properly; suppose the same process works properly over one part of its range of operation but not over another, and my belief is produced by its working over both of these parts of its range of operation; or suppose a process is not working properly over part of its range but produces in me in given circumstances the very same belief it would have if it were working properly; in these cases does my belief have warrant? These are good questions, but there isn't time to work out all the answers here.

Still further, proper functioning, of course, *comes in degrees;* or if it does not, then approximation to proper functioning does. Clearly the faculties relevant with respect to a given belief need not be functioning *perfectly* for me to have warrant for my belief; many of my visual beliefs may constitute knowledge even if my vision is not 20/20. Similarly, my faculties can function *properly* even if they do not function *ideally,* even if they do not function as well as

---

[13]Here I am indebted to Tom Senor.

those of some other actual or possible species (a point I discuss in chapter 6 of *Warrant: The Current Debate*). My locomotory equipment may be functioning properly even if I can't run as fast as a cheetah; my arithmetic powers may be in good working order even if I can't anywhere nearly keep up with a computer, or an angel, or an Alpha Centaurian. But how well, then, must such powers be functioning? Part of the answer here, of course, is that there is no answer; the ideas of knowledge and warrant are to some degree vague; hence there needs to be no precise answer to the question in question. What I hope is that the vaguenesses involved in my account of warrant vary with the vaguenesses we independently recognize in the notion of warrant. If warrant and proper function are properly tied together, then we may expect that they will waver together.

Similar comments and qualifications, of course, must be made about the environmental condition. For my beliefs to have warrant, the environment must be similar to that for which my epistemic powers have been designed; but just how similar must it be? Here, of course, we encounter vagueness; there is no precise answer. Further, suppose I *know* that the environment is misleading; and suppose I know in just which ways it is misleading. (I'm on a planet where things that look square are really round.) Then, clearly enough, the fact that my environment is misleading need not deprive my beliefs of warrant. And of course the same must be said for the requirement that my faculties be in good working order. Suppose (as in Castañeda's fantasy)[14] I suffer from a quirk of memory: whenever I read a history book, I always misremember the dates, somehow adding ten years to the date as stated: beliefs formed by way of reading history books—even beliefs about dates—can still have warrant for me; I can compensate for my erroneous tendency. What counts, of course, are uncorrected and uncompensated malfunctionings. Clearly there is need here for a good deal of chisholming; let me postpone it, however, in order to turn to other more pressing matters.

II. The Design Plan

But aren't there cases in which our faculties function perfectly properly in the right sort of environment but the resulting beliefs still lack warrant? Surely there are. Someone may remember a painful experience as less painful than it was, as is sometimes said to be the case with childbirth.[15] You may continue to believe in your friend's honesty long after evidence and cool, objective judgment would have dictated a reluctant change of mind. I may believe that I will recover from a dread disease much more strongly than is justified by the statistics of which I am aware. William James's climber in the Alps, faced with a life or death situation, believed more strongly than the evidence warrants that he could leap the crevasse. In all of these cases, there is no cognitive dysfunction or

---

[14]"The Indexical Theory of Knowledge," p. 202.

[15]"A woman giving birth to a child has pain because her time has come; but when her baby is born she forgets the anguish because of her joy that a child is born into the world." John 16:21.

failure to function properly; it would be a mistake, however, to say that the beliefs in question had warrant for the person in question.

I cannot forbear quoting a couple of Locke's examples:

> Would it not be an insufferable thing for a learned professor, and that which his scarlet would blush at, to have his authority of forty years standing wrought out of hard rock Greek and Latin, with no small expence of time and candle, and confirmed by general tradition, and a reverent beard, in an instant overturned by an upstart novelist? Can any one expect that he should be made to confess, that what he taught his scholars thirty years ago, was all errour and mistake; and that he sold them hard words and ignorance at a very dear rate?[16]

The professor's faculties may be functioning properly (there may be a properly functioning defense mechanism at work); but his belief that the young upstart is dead wrong would have little by way of warrant. Another of Locke's examples:

> Tell a man, passiounately in love, that he is jilted; bring a score of witnesses of the falsehood of his mistress, 'tis ten to one but three kind words of hers, shall invalidate all their testimonies. . . . What suits our wishes, is forwardly believed is, I suppose, what every one hath more than once experiemented; and though men cannot always openly gain-say, or resist the force of manifest probabilities, that make against them; yet yield they not to the argument. (*Essay*, IV, xx, 12)

Now it was widely believed in the eighteenth century that love was or induced a sort of madness, so that the lover's epistemic faculties are not functioning properly. Even if that isn't so, however, even if we are designed to act and believe in extravagant fashion when in love, the lover's belief that his mistress is true to him has little by way of warrant.

Still another case: according to Freud, religious belief is "the universal obsessional neurosis of mankind"; religious belief consists in "illusions, fulfillments of the oldest, strongest, and most insistent wishes of mankind."[17] Rather similar sentiments are expressed by Marx, who holds that religious belief is produced by an unhealthy, perverted social order: "This State, this society, produce religion, produce a perverted world consciousness, because they are a perverted world. . . . Religion is the sigh of the oppressed creature, the feelings of a heartless world, just as it is the spirit of unspiritual conditions."[18] Now neither Freud nor Marx would be mollified if we pointed out that religion is very widespread among human beings, that is, "normal" in the statistical sense; what is statistically normal may still be a disease, a matter of malfunction, in this case a cognitive dysfunction. But there is a further subtlety here;

---

[16]*An Essay concerning Human Understanding*, ed. A. C. Fraser (New York: Dover, 1953), IV, xx, 11, hereafter referred to as *Essay*.

[17]*The Future of an Illusion* (1927), trans. and ed. James Strachey (London: Norton, 1961), p. 30.

[18]K. Marx, *Introduction to a Critique of the Hegelian Philosophy of Right*, in *Collected Works*, by K. Marx and F. Engels (London: Lawrence & Wishart, 1975), 3:175.

Freud and Marx differ in a significant way. Marx seems to think that religion is a sort of perversion, something unhealthy; it is as if he says, "Let's call it an aberration and be done with it." Freud, on the other hand, is ambivalent. First, he says that religious belief is or stems from neurosis: that sounds like he thinks religious belief arises from a cognitive malfunction of some sort. But then he also says it is a matter of illusion, and arises from the "oldest and strongest and most insistent wishes of mankind." That suggests not that religious belief arises from malfunction or failure of some cognitive module to function properly, but instead by way of wish fulfillment. What one believes in *that* way isn't necessarily a product of malfunction; illusion and wish fulfillment also have their functions. According to Freud, they enable us to mask the grim, threatening, frightening visage of the world—a visage that would otherwise cause us to cower in terror or sink into utter and apathetic despair. On the second way of thinking, then, religious belief need not be a result of malfunction; it might be produced by faculties functioning just as they should. Even so, however—even if the wish fulfillment that produces religious belief does not result from cognitive malfunction—religous belief won't enjoy much by way of warrant.

So the proposed condition for warrant—proper function in an appropriate environment—isn't anywhere nearly sufficient for warrant. Why not? Well, consider the elements of our cognitive faculties responsible for beliefs of the above sorts—those produced by wishful thinking, or by the optimism that enables one to survive a deadly illness—one thinks that the purpose of *these* modules of our cognitive capacities is not to produce true beliefs. They are instead aimed at something else: survival, or the possibility of friendship, or (Freud thinks) the capacity to carry on in this bleak and nasty world of ours.

To get a better understanding of this matter, we must consider a notion of crucial importance: that of specifications, or blueprint, or *design plan*. Human beings are constructed according to a certain design plan. This terminology does not commit us to supposing that human beings have been literally designed—by God, for example. Here I use 'design' the way Daniel Dennett (not ordinarily thought unsound on theism) does in speaking of a given organism as possessing a certain design, and of evolution as producing optimal design: "In the end, we want to be able to explain the intelligence of man, or beast, in terms of his design; and this in turn in terms of the natural selection of this design."[19] We take it that when the organs (or organic systems) of a human being (or other organism) function properly, they function *in a particular way*. Such organs have a *function* or *purpose;* more exactly, they have several functions or purposes, including both proximate and more remote purposes. The ultimate purpose of the heart is to contribute to the health and proper function of the entire organism (some might say instead that it is to contribute to the *survival* of the individual, or the species, or even to the perpetuation of the genetic material itself).[20] But of course the heart also has a much more circumscribed and specific function: to pump blood. Such an organ, furthermore,

[19]*Brainstorms* (Cambridge: Bradford Books, 1978), p. 12.
[20]See Richard Dawkins, *The Selfish Gene* (Oxford: Oxford University Press, 1976).

normally functions in such a way as to fulfill its purpose; but it also functions to fulfill that purpose in just one of an indefinitely large number of possible ways. Here a comparison with artifacts is useful. A house is designed to produce shelter—but not in just any old way. There will be plans specifying the length and pitch of the rafters, what kind of shingles are to be applied, the kind and quantity of insulation to be used, and the like. Something similar holds in the case of us and our faculties; we seem to be constructed in accordance with a specific set of plans. Better (since this analogy is insufficiently dynamic) we seem to have been constructed in accordance with a set of specifications, in the way in which there are specifications for, for example, the 1992 Buick. According to these specifications (I'm just guessing), after a cold start the engine runs at 1,500 RPM until the engine temperature reaches 190°F; it then throttles back to 750 RPM.

Similarly, there is something like a set of specifications for a well-formed, properly functioning human being—an extraordinarily complicated and highly articulated set of specifications, as any first-year medical student could tell you. *Something* like such a set: a copy of these specifications does not come with every newborn child, and we can't write to the manufacturer for a new copy to replace the one we have carelessly lost. Suppose we call these specifications a 'design plan'. It is natural to speak of organisms and their parts as exhibiting design, and such talk is exceedingly common: "According to Dr. Sam Ridgway, physiologist with the US Naval Ocean Systems Center in San Diego, seals avoid the bends by not absorbing nitrogen in the first place. 'The lungs of marine mammals,' Dr. Ridgway explains, 'are designed to collapse under pressure exerted on deep dives. Air from the collapsed lungs is forced back into the windpipe, where the nitrogen simply can't be absorbed by the blood.'"[21] Of course the design plan for human beings will include specifications for our *cognitive* system or faculties. Like the rest of our organs and systems, our cognitive faculties can work well or badly; they can malfunction or function properly. They too work in a certain way when they are functioning properly—and work in a certain way to accomplish their purpose. The purpose of the heart is to pump blood; that of our cognitive faculties (overall) is to supply us with reliable information: about our environment, about the past, about the thoughts and feeling of others, and so on. But not just any old way of accomplishing this purpose in the case of a specific cognitive process is in accordance with our design plan. It is for this reason that it is possible for a belief to be produced by a cognitive process or belief-producing mechanism that is *accidentally* reliable (as in the case of the processes I have cited as counterexamples to Goldman's version of reliabilism).[22] Although such belief-producing processes are in fact reliable, the beliefs they yield have little by way of warrant; and the reason is that these processes are pathologically out of accord with the design plan for human beings.

Our design plan, of course, is such that our faculties are highly responsive to

[21]*National Geographic* 171, no. 4 (April 1987), p. 489.
[22]See my *Warrant: The Current Debate*, chap. 9.

circumstances. Upon considering an instance of *modus ponens,* I find myself believing its corresponding conditional; upon being appeared to in the familiar way, I find myself with the belief that there is a large tree before me; upon being asked what I had for breakfast, I reflect for a moment, and the belief that what I had was eggs on toast is formed within me. In these and other cases I do not *deliberate;* I do not total up the evidence (I am being appeared to redly; on most occasions when thus appeared to I am in the presence of something red; so most probably in this case I am) and thus come to a view as to what seems best supported; I simply find myself with the appropriate belief. Of course in *some* cases I may go through such a weighing of the evidence; for example, I may be trying to evaluate the alleged evidence in favor of the theory that human life evolved by means of such mechanisms as random genetic mutation and natural selection from unicellular life (which itself arose by substantially similar mechanical processes from nonliving material); but in the typical case of belief formation nothing like this is involved.

Chapters 3–9 are devoted to an exploration of the design plan of our epistemic faculties; but here I wish to note just a couple of its salient features. According to our design plan, obviously enough, *experience* plays a crucial role in belief formation. *A priori* beliefs, for example, are not, as this denomination mistakenly suggests, formed prior to or in the absence of experience. Thinking of the corresponding conditional of *modus ponens* somehow *feels* different from thinking of, say, the corresponding conditional of *affirming the consequent;* and this difference in experience is connected with our accepting the one and rejecting the other. Of course experience plays a different role here from the role it plays in the formation of perceptual beliefs; it plays a still different role in the formation of memory beliefs, moral beliefs, beliefs about the mental lives of other persons, beliefs we form on the basis of inductive evidence, and the like. In later chapters we shall look into these matters in more detail.

Further, our design plan is such that under certain conditions we form one belief *on the evidential basis* of others. I may form the belief that Sam was at the party on the evidential basis of other beliefs—perhaps I learn from you that Sam wasn't at the bar and from his wife that he was either at the bar or at the party. Of course (if our faculties are functioning properly) we don't form just *any* belief on the evidential basis of just any other. I won't form the belief that Feike is a Catholic on the evidential basis of the propositions that nine out of ten Frisians are Protestants and Feike is a Frisian—not, at any rate, unless I am suffering from some sort of cognitive malfunction. And here too experience plays an important role. The belief about Sam *feels like* the right one; that belief about Feike (in those circumstances) feels strange, inappropriate, worthy of rejection, not to be credited. Still further, the design plan dictates the appropriate *degree* or firmness of a given belief in given circumstances. You read in a relatively unreliable newspaper an account of a 53-car accident on a Los Angeles freeway; perhaps you then form the belief that there was a 53-car accident on the freeway. But if you hold that belief as firmly as, for example, that $2 + 1 = 3$, then your faculties are not functioning as they ought to and the belief has little warrant for you. Again, experience obviously plays an important role.

What we need is a full and appropriately subtle and sensitive description of the role of experience in the formation and maintenance of all these various types of beliefs; in the next chapters I shall try to do something (though not nearly enough) to meet this need. For the moment, we may rest satisfied simply to note the importance of experience in the economy of our cognitive establishment.

Now return to the examples that precipitated this excursus about the design plan—the cases of beliefs produced by wish fulfillment, or the optimism necessary to surviving a serious illness, or willingness to have more children, or the like. In these cases, the relevant faculties may be functioning properly, functioning just as they ought to, but nevertheless not in a way that leads to truth, to the formation of true beliefs. But then proper function in a right environment is not sufficient for warrant. Different parts or aspects of our cognitive apparatus have different purposes; different parts or aspects of our design plan are aimed at different ends or goals. Not all aspects of the design of our cognitive faculties need be aimed at the production of true belief; some might be such as to conduce to survival, or relief from suffering, or the possibility of loyalty, or inclination to have more children, and so on. What confers warrant is one's cognitive faculties working properly, or working according to the design plan *insofar as that segment of the design plan is aimed at producing true beliefs.* But someone whose holding a certain belief is a result of an aspect of our cognitive design that is aimed not at truth but at something else won't be such that the belief has warrant for him; he won't properly be said to know the proposition in question, even if it turns out to be true.

So there are cases where belief-producing faculties are functioning properly but warrant is absent: cases where the design plan is not aimed at the production of true (or verisimilitudinous) beliefs but at the production of beliefs with some other virtue. But then there will also be cases where cognitive faculties are not functioning properly, but warrant is present; these will be inverses, so to speak, of the cases of the preceding paragraph. Suppose our design demands that under certain special circumstances our ordinary belief-producing mechanisms are overridden by a mechanism designed to deal with that specific case: perhaps there is a sort of optimistic mechanism that cuts in when I am seriously ill, causing me to believe more strongly than the evidence indicates that I will survive the illness, thereby enhancing my chances to survive it. Suppose I am taken seriously ill, and suppose through some malfunction (induced, perhaps, by the illness itself) the operation of the optimistic mechanism is inhibited, so that, believing just in accord with the evidence, I form the belief that I probably will not survive. Then the relevant segment of my cognitive faculties is not functioning properly; that is, it is not functioning in accordance with the design plan; but doesn't my belief have warrant anyway?[23] Might I not have the degree of warrant that goes with the degree to which I believe that I probably won't survive, despite the fact that if my faculties were functioning properly, I would believe (to one or another degree of firmness) that I *will* survive? The answer, of course, is as before: those segments of my cognitive faculties (those

[23]I owe this example to Caleb Miller.

modules, we might say) that are aimed at *truth* are functioning properly; my cognitive faculties are functioning in accord with the design plan insofar as the design plan is aimed at the production of true beliefs. There is malfunction only with respect to those cognitive modules aimed at something other than truth; so in this case the belief that I will not survive has the degree of warrant normally going with the degree of belief I display.

Many questions remain,[24] but I must leave them to the reader.

III. Reliability

According to the zeroeth approximation, a belief has warrant for me, speaking roughly, if it is produced by my cognitive faculties functioning properly in a congenial environment. We have just seen that these two together are insufficient: the segment of the design plan governing the production of the belief in question must also be aimed at truth. (In the next chapter I shall say a bit more by way of explaining just what this "being aimed at truth" comes to.) But this is still insufficient. For suppose a well meaning but incompetent angel—one of Hume's infant deities,[25] say—sets out to design a variety of rational persons, persons capable of thought, belief, and knowledge. As it turns out, the design is a real failure; the resulting beings hold beliefs, all right, but most of them are absurdly false.[26] Here all three of our conditions are met: the beliefs of these beings are formed by their cognitive faculties functioning properly in the cognitive environment for which they were designed, and furthermore the relevant modules of the design plan are aimed at truth (the relevant modules of their cognitive equipment have the production of true beliefs as their purpose). But the beliefs of these pitifully deceived beings do not have warrant.[27] What must we add? That the design plan is a *good* one—more exactly, that the design governing the production of the belief in question is a good one; still more exactly, that the objective probability[28] of a belief's being true, given that it is produced by cognitive faculties functioning in accord with the relevant module of the design plan, is high. Even more exactly, the module of the design plan governing its production must be such that it is objectively highly probable that a belief produced by cognitive faculties functioning properly according to that module (in a congenial environment) will be true or verisimilitudinous. This is the reliabilist constraint on warrant, and the important truth contained in reliabilist accounts of warrant.

It is easy to overlook this condition. The reason is that we ordinarily take it

[24]Some of which were forcibly brought to my attention by Dean Zimmerman.

[25]*Dialogues Concerning Natural Religion*, Part V (1779), ed. N. K. Smith (Bobbs-Merrill, 1947), p. 169.

[26]Some (Donald Davidson, for example) apparently hold that it is impossible that there be a sizeable community of believers most of whose beliefs are false; I disagree and explain why (see pp. 80–81).

[27]This counterexample was called to my attention by Richard Swinburne, Ian Foster, and Thomas Senor.

[28]See chapter 9 for a gesture at an account of objective probability.

for granted that when our cognitive faculties—at any rate, those whose function it is to produce true beliefs—function properly in an appropriate environment, then for the most part the beliefs they produce are true. When our faculties function in accord with our design plan (in an appropriate environment), the beliefs they produce are for the most part true. Certainly we think so with respect to memory, perception, logical and arithmetical beliefs, inductively based beliefs, and so on. Further, we take it for granted that these faculties are *reliable;* they not only *do* produce true beliefs, but *would* produce true beliefs even if things were moderately different. (They produce true beliefs in most of the appropriately nearby possible worlds; that is, most of the appropriately nearby possible worlds W meet the following condition: necessarily, if W had been actual, then our cognitive faculties would have produced mostly true beliefs.) Still another way to put it: we take it for granted that the statistical or objective probability of a belief's being true, given that it has been produced by our faculties functioning properly in the cognitive environment for which they were designed, is high. Perhaps more specifically our presupposition is that in general (for a person S with properly functioning faculties in an appropriate environment, and given the cited qualifications) the more firmly S believes p, the more likely it is that p is true. Of course, we think some faculties more reliable than others, and think a given faculty is more reliable under some conditions than others. This assumption on our part is a sort of presumption of reliability. Of course, it *is* a presumption or an assumption; it isn't or isn't obviously[29] entailed by the notion of proper function itself. So the account of proper function must include it as another condition: if one of my beliefs has warrant, then the module of the design plan governing the production of that belief must be such that the statistical or objective probability of a belief's being true, given that it has been produced in accord with that module in a congenial cognitive environment, is high.

How high, precisely? Here we encounter vagueness again; there is no precise answer. It is part of the presumption, however, that the degree of reliability varies as a function of degree of belief. The things we are most sure of—simple logical and arithmetical truths, such beliefs as that I now have a mild ache in my knee (that indeed I have knees), obvious perceptual truths—these are the sorts of beliefs we hold most firmly, perhaps with the maximum degree of firmness, and the ones such that we associate a very high degree of reliability with the modules of the design plan governing their production. Even here, however, we are not immune from error: even what seems to be self-evident can

[29]I suppose it might sensibly be held that it is impossible that there be rational beings (beings capable of reasoning or belief) whose cognitive faculties function properly but who nonetheless hold predominantly false beliefs. Perhaps there are purposes or ends necessarily built into certain kinds of creatures. Then if a malevolent Cartesian demon were to design a race of rational creatures whose beliefs were nearly always mistaken, their cognitive faculties would not be functioning properly, even if they were functioning just as they were designed to. Instead, we should have to say that what this demon wanted to do was to design a race of cognitive beings that did not function properly.

be mistaken, as Frege learned to his sorrow.[30] It may be worth noting, however, that Frege did not believe the offending 'axiom' to the maximal degree; if he had, then he would have been no more likely to give up that 'axiom' than to conclude that there really *is* a set that is and is not a member of itself.

I say the presupposition of reliability is a feature of our usual way of thinking about warrant; but of course this presupposition is not inevitable for us. The skeptic, for example, can often best be seen as questioning this presupposition. She may agree that there is indeed a perfectly proper distinction between cognitive proper function and malfunction, but be agnostic about the question whether there is any correlation at all between proper function and truth. Or she may think there is indeed such a correlation, but think it far too weak to support our ordinary claims to knowledge. Or she may think that since the long-run purpose of our beliefs, as she sees it, is to enable us to move about in the environment in such a way that we do not come to grief (or do not come to grief until we have had a chance to reproduce), there is no interesting correlation between a belief's being produced by faculties functioning properly and its being true.[31] Of course one can be a skeptic about one particular area as opposed to others: a rationalist may think sense perception less reliable than reason and may thus maintain that it is only reason, not perception, that gives us knowledge; an empiricist may see things the other way around. Philosophy itself is a good candidate for a certain measured skepticism: in view of the enormous diversity of competing philosophical views, one can hardly claim with a straight face that what we have in philosophy is *knowledge;* the diversity of views makes it unlikely that the relevant segments of the design plan are sufficiently reliable. (In a properly run intellectual establishment, therefore, most philosophical views will not enjoy anywhere nearly the maximal degree of belief.)

To return to warrant then: to a first approximation, we may say that a belief *B* has warrant for *S* if and only if the relevant segments (the segments involved in the production of *B*) are functioning properly in a cognitive environment sufficiently similar to that for which *S*'s faculties are designed; and the modules of the design plan governing the production of *B* are (1) aimed at truth, and (2) such that there is a high objective probability that a belief formed in accordance with those modules (in that sort of cognitive environment) is true; and the more firmly *S* believes *B* the more warrant *B* has for *S*. This is at best a first approximation; it is still at most programmatic, a suggestion, an idea, a hint. Furthermore, it might be suggested (in fact, it *has* been suggested) that while it may be

---

[30]Frege produced a set of axioms for set theory, including the famous or infamous proposition that for any property *P* there exists the set of just those things that have *P*. Russell showed him that this axiom (together with the others) yields a contradiction: if it is true, there will be a set of nonselfmembered sets, which both will and will not be a member of itself.

[31]Thus Patricia Churchland: "Boiled down to essentials, a nervous system enables the organism to succeed in the four F's: feeding, fleeing, fighting and reproducing. The principle chore of nervous systems is to get the body parts where they should be in order that the organism may survive. . . . Truth, whatever that is, definitely takes the hindmost" (*Journal of Philosophy* 84 [October 87], p. 548). See my chapter 12, sec. 3, for discussion of this suggestion.

difficult to find counterexamples to the view, that is only because it is vague and imprecise. I have sympathies with both complaints, although I would implore those who make the second to heed Aristotle's dictum and seek no more precision than the subject admits. Maybe there isn't any neat formula, any short and snappy list of conditions (at once informative and precise) that are severally necessary and jointly sufficient for warrant; if so, we won't make much progress by grimly pursuing them. But in the next chapters I shall try to respond to both complaints by providing more detail. In chapter 2, I shall make some refinements and respond to some objections; and then in the next seven chapters I shall investigate each of a number of areas of our epistemic functioning, asking how our faculties function when they function properly in that area, and applying the view of warrant to that area of the cognitive domain.

2

Warrant: Objections and Refinements

I. The Design Plan

As we saw in chapter 1, the notion of warrant involves the notion of proper function, which involves or presupposes the idea of a *design plan*. In order to achieve a deeper understanding of warrant (and in reply to some objections), we must look further into this idea of design: it is much richer and more complex than it initially looks. A thing's design plan is the way the thing in question is 'supposed' to work, the way in which it works when it is functioning as it ought to, when there is nothing wrong with it, when it is not damaged or broken or nonfunctional. Both human artifacts and natural organisms and their parts have design plans. Computers, automobiles, and linear accelerators have design plans, but so do plants, animals, hearts, livers, immune systems, digestive tracts, and the like. There is a way in which your heart is supposed to work: for example, your pulse rate should be about 55–80 beats per minute when you are at rest, and (depending on your age) achieve a maximum rate of some 180 beats per minute when you are exercising. If your resting pulse is only 10, or if it goes up to 250 upon walking slowly up a short flight of stairs, then your heart (or something in your circulatory system) is not functioning properly; it is not functioning according to the design plan for human circulatory systems.

We need not initially take the notions of *design plan* and *way in which a thing is supposed to work* to entail *conscious* design or purpose (see pp. 13ff.); it is perhaps possible that evolution (undirected by God or anyone else) has somehow furnished us with our design plans. But in the central and paradigm cases, design plans do indeed involve the thing's having been designed by one or more conscious designers who are aiming at an end of some sort, and design the thing in question to achieve or accomplish that end. In exploring the notion of design plan, therefore, we must keep close to the front of our minds the way things go in these central and paradigm cases. We must therefore bear in mind the way in which a radio, say, or a rope, or an airplane, or some other kind of artifact can be said to function properly, and what the connection in those cases is with a design plan. Here I shall explore the notion of proper function and design plan and shall do so with respect to the following five rubrics: the max plan versus the design plan, unintended by-products, functional multiplicity, the distinction between purpose and design, trade-offs and compromises, and defeaters and overriders.

A. Design Plan versus Max Plan

The design plan of an organism or artifact specifies how it works when it works properly: that is (for a large set of conditions), it specifies how the organism *should* work. When the coolant temperature of my car gets up to 200°F, the thermostat should open and the engine, if idling, should slow to the warm idling speed. When body temperature begins to rise, surface blood vessels will expand, pores will open, perspiration will begin, and so on—provided the organism is functioning properly. We might initially think of the design plan as a set of circumstance–response pairs; for each member of some class of circumstances it specifies what the appropriate response is, what the thing in question will do if it is functioning properly.

What makes that response appropriate, of course, is the fact that the thing in question is designed to accomplish an end or purpose; it has a function to perform. Perhaps it pumps the blood, or reduces the voltage, or turns the engine over in order to start it, or provides a shot of adrenalin. It would therefore be better to think of the design plan as a set of triples: circumstance, response, and purpose or function—and, of course, the latter could itself be complex in one way or another. Under ordinary conditions your kidneys function a certain way: they respond in a certain way to circumstances, and they do so in order to accomplish their purpose or function, which is the removal of metabolic waste products from the bloodstream. Of course a given system or organ may have both proximate and remote functions: its immediate or proximate function may be to remove metabolic waste from the blood, but its ultimate function is to contribute to the survival and well-being of the organism. (It may also have functions intermediate between proximate and ultimate functions.) What will be contained in a triple of the design plan will not be the ultimate function (since that will be the same for nearly all of the organs and systems of an organism) but some more proximate function.

Here we are thinking of the design plan as specifying how the thing works *now*, or at a given time: call this a *snapshot* design plan. But the design plan, at least in the case of organisms, may also specify how the thing will change over time. There is such a thing as maturation; and it can be thought of as involving a master design plan, which specifies a succession of snapshot design plans.

But the design plan of an organism or artifact does not say what it is supposed to do in just *any* old circumstance. I design a radio in such a way that it has certain fail-safe features: if there is an electrical surge of moderate voltage along the line, a circuit breaker will trip, thus forestalling damage. The design plan may say nothing, however, about how it will respond (or what will happen to it) when struck by lightning, or when it sinks to the bottom of the Mindanao Trench, or is run over by a steamroller. The design plan of my self-sealing tire says nothing about what it will do when it is 'punctured' by an object that leaves a hole six inches in diameter, or when it is blown to bits in a terrorist dynamite attack. The radio is supposed to work in a certain way when there is an electrical surge: the circuit breaker should trip. But there is no particular way in which it is supposed to work if subjected to a current strong enough to melt (or vaporize) it. The self-sealing tire is supposed to work a certain way if punctured by a nail; but there is no particular way in which it is supposed to work if it is blown up by a high-explosive device.

Tires and radios are artifacts, of course; but the same goes for organisms. My body is so designed that it will respond to attack by microbes: antibodies will be rushed to the scene, heart rate and temperature may be elevated, and all the rest. This is how things are supposed to work under those conditions. But there isn't any particular way in which my body is supposed to work if I am smashed by a huge boulder or crushed by a runaway steam-roller or vaporized in a nuclear explosion. My cognitive design plan says something about how I will respond (if my cognitive faculties are functioning properly) when appeared to redly: for example, under those conditions (properly filled out) I may be inclined to form the belief that what I see is red. But my design plan says nothing about how I will respond when I am appeared to redly, but am also suffering a massive heart attack, or have just ingested huge quantities of strychnine, or have just hit the ground after a 300-foot fall. So the design plan does not include a description of how the thing will work under just any or *all* circumstances, but under only *some*: those that in some sense (in the paradigm artifactual case) the designer(s) plan for, or have in mind, or intend.

Of course, radio, tire, and human body will indeed *respond* in a certain way (better, something will happen to them) under the conditions not catered for by the design plan. If run over by a steamroller, for example, each will lose its shape and structure, become very flat, achieve a new level of density, and cease to do much else of interest. If a squirrel is hit by a car, it will no longer respond (to the approach of a hungry fox, say) as before. So here we must distinguish the *design plan* of the thing in question from what we might call *the maximum plan* ('max plan' for short). The design plan is a set of triples; the max plan is a set of circumstances–response *pairs*. It is maximal in three ways. First, unlike the design plan, it is not a description of how the thing works under just those circumstances (as in the paradigm cases) the designer plans for or takes into account; it includes a much broader set of circumstances. How *much* broader? Well, not all logically possible circumstances, and not circumstances involving a change in the natural laws. Nor does it include circumstances involving an extensive change in the structure of the thing: it describes how the thing will work given its present structure and organization. What it describes is how the thing will work[1] so long as it retains its approximate present structure in circumstances involving the natural laws that do in fact obtain. (So perhaps we should refer to it as a mini-max plan.)

As a special case, therefore (and secondly) the max plan says how the thing will behave, what it will do (what will happen to it) when it is broken or

[1] I don't mean to espouse determinism; perhaps we could say, if we wish, that the max plan does not say *simpliciter* how the thing will work but assigns a certain (statistical or objective) probability to the response in question.

damaged or destroyed as well as what it will do when it is functioning properly. It also specifies the new max plans the thing would acquire as a result of change in its structure. Here we need a distinction like that between master and snapshot design plan: the master max plan says that if the thing is run over by a steamroller, it will get smashed and will acquire a new and less interesting snapshot max plan. And third, any given circumstance member M of a circumstance–response pair is maximal in the sense that it is a *complete* specification of relevant circumstances. That is to say, in any circumstance including M the organism or artifact will behave in the same way; it includes all that could be relevant to the response of the artifact or organism in question. Thus, for my radio or refrigerator, M will not specify, say, who won the battle of Marathon or whether the Continuum Hypothesis is true; but for any circumstance that could affect how it works, it will specify how things stand with respect to that circumstance. Cut down the design plan by removing the purpose from each triple, and add to the circumstance that the thing in question is functioning properly: the resulting set of circumstance-response pairs will be a subset of the max plan. It will be a set such that each circumstance member of a circumstance-response pair will both include proper function (that is, will include the circumstance that the thing in question is functioning properly) and also will be one of the circumstances that (in the paradigm cases) the designer plans for.

Functional generalizations (see pp. 270ff.) involve members of the design plan. A hungry cat will pounce on a mouse it sees emerging from a mouse hole—but only if it is not deranged, or crippled, or in the grip of an evil demon, or in some other way malfunctioning. A human being in my present circumstances being appeared to in the way I am will believe that she is sitting before a computer—but again, only with similar provisos.

B. Unintended By-products

There is another distinction intimately related to the design plan/max plan distinction: that between what the thing in question is designed to do and *unintended by-products* of the way it works. I design a refrigerator; one consequence of my design is that when a screwdriver touches a certain wire, the refrigerator will emit a loud angry squawk. I didn't *intend* for it to work this way; I have no interest in its doing that under those conditions and don't care whether it does so or not. Its working that way is no part of the design plan; there is no circumstance-response-purpose triple according to which it will do that. But of course its working that way is a consequence of how it is designed, and its working that way in those circumstances will be an element of the max plan. Although I did not intend it to work this way, the fact that it does is no indication of malfunction. This is an *accidental* or *unintended by-product* of the design. It is not accidental in the sense that it happens just by chance, or isn't *caused* to happen; its working that way is of course a causal consequence of the way the refrigerator is constructed. It is accidental, rather, from the point of view of the intentions of the designer; I designed the thing to do certain things, to work a certain way, and that way of working also has the unintended consequence that it makes that loud squawk. Of course it could be that a given bit of behavior or response has more than one purpose; then it might be an unintended by-product with respect to the one but not with respect to the other.

Again, this distinction is present for organisms as well as artifacts: that thumpa-thumpa sound the heart makes is (so we think) merely accidental, a by-product of how it works when it works in such a way as to fulfill its purpose or function of pumping the blood. The sound is accidental with respect to the design plan; it is no part of the design plan that it will make that sound; the circumstance-response-purpose triples that constitute the design plan will not include pairs where the response is making that sound. (I assume for purposes of illustration, that this thumping sound has no purpose.) My brain might be so constructed that pressure on a certain area (from a lesion or tumor, say) may cause headache, or bizarre beliefs—among which might be the belief that I have a lesion or tumor. That the lesion happens to cause me to form that true belief is no part of my cognitive design plan; it is either an unintended by-product of the design of my brain or else just a part of the max plan that is not involved in the design plan at all. As a result, this belief does not have warrant.

C. *Functional Multiplicity*

Different parts of the design plan may be aimed at different ends; different triples, obviously enough, may include different purposes. Indeed, the *same* bit of behavior or response can serve different purposes. What we have here is *functional multiplicity*. And different parts of the design plan governing the cognitive establishment may include different purposes. We took advantage of this fact in chapter 1 in noting that a given belief has warrant only if the part of the design plan governing the production of that belief is aimed at truth—only if, in other words, the relevant triples of the design plan include as purpose the production of true belief (rather than, say, the production of beliefs that by virtue of statistically unjustified optimism contribute to the survival of a dangerous illness or to the successful leaping of a wide crevasse).

There are other important kinds of functional multiplicity. The design plan of an organism, I say, specifies how it will function when it is functioning properly. But it may also specify how it will function when it is *not* functioning properly—when it has been damaged in some way, as when it has been invaded by a virus, or stung by a wasp, or cut or abraded. The design plan may include triples where the purpose or function is *damage control* or *recovery* and where the circumstance member includes malfunction elsewhere in the organism or artifact. (So the circumstance members of the triples include not only environmental circumstances *exterior* to the organism or artifact in question; they may also include the way some other part of it is functioning.) Upon being invaded by a virus, the organism (from one perspective) no longer functions properly: there is elevated temperature and pulse, dizziness, and inability to walk a straight line. But there are certain ways of responding to that invasion that constitute proper function and others that do not. You contract an influenza bug; your temperature rises. From one perspective your temperature-regulating mechanisms are functioning improperly, in that your temperature is not now the temperature of a healthy human being. But from another perspective they are functioning just as they ought; part of your body's defense against the invader involves your temperature's rising, and if it does not rise, there is malfunction (further malfunction).

Here we have another way in which different segments of the design plan may be aimed at different ends. Your normal temperature and the mechanisms for maintaining it are aimed at providing the best (or a good) temperature for the ordinary conduct of organic life for a creature of your sort; the higher temperature when attacked by the virus is a result of a part of the design plan aimed at damage control and healing. (Perhaps, for example, viruses and bacteria reproduce less rapidly at those higher temperatures.) Alternatively, this rise in temperature could be a by-product of defense and damage-control mechanisms.

This distinction too will be relevant to the cognitive case. When the organism is under attack, parts of the cognitive establishment may fail to work in the way they ordinarily do. This failure may be due to simple malfunction, as when a tumor pressing on a part of the brain may cause bizarre belief formation, or it may be due to the damage-control and defense mode of functioning, as when you optimistically believe that you will survive the disease, this belief itself helping you survive the disease. In still other cases, a certain mode of belief formation may be an accidental by-product of the damage-control and defense mode of function. So a belief can arise by way of proper function of a module of the design plan aimed at truth; it can arise by way of proper function of a module not aimed at truth; it can arise as an unintended by-product of a damage-control mode of function; and it can arise by way of simple malfunction. It is only in the first case that there is warrant.

One final kind of functional multiplicity: a thing can obviously acquire a *new* purpose and a new design plan. I construct my refrigerator and then make a minor adjustment; now the refrigerator works and is intended to work slightly differently. It has acquired a new design plan. Relative to its old design plan, it is not functioning properly; relative to the new, it is. More drastically, I turn my refrigerator into a food warmer by reversing a crucial circuit: then when it functions properly according to its new design plan, it works badly indeed according to the old. So suppose our cognitive faculties are redesigned by Alpha Centaurians, whose aims here are aesthetic rather than epistemic. Then it might be that our faculties work in accord with the *new* design plan and that the *old* design plan is aimed at truth; that would not be sufficient for warrant, however, since what is required is that your faculties work in accord with their current design plan and that *that* design plan be aimed at truth.

D. Purpose versus Design

Another important distinction is that between what a thing is *designed* to do (its *purpose,* say) and *how it is designed to accomplish that purpose* (its *design,* we might say).[2] (Computers, as programmers know, do what you *tell* them to do, not what you *want* them to do.) There is a sort of ambiguity in the notion of working properly. On the one hand, a thing works properly when it works in accordance with its design plan, when it works just the way in which it was designed to work. My radio works properly when there is nothing wrong with it and it works just as its designer designed it to. But what shall we say when it works as it was designed to, all right, but has a very poor design and won't receive stations more than 500 yards away? Then it does not work very well, despite its functioning precisely in accord with its design plan. I aim to make a refrigerator that will keep its contents at a constant temperature of 33°F; through incompetence and inattention, I fail; as a result of a lamentably inferior design, its internal temperature varies between 70° and 85° F. Then the thing works properly in one way: it works just as it was designed to work. But in another way it works badly: it does not do what it was designed to do. Paul designs a deicer for an airplane. As we might expect, his design is deficient; so while the device functions just as it was designed to, it never removes ice from the wings, and occasionally adds a bit of its own.[3] Then in one way it works properly and in another way it does not. I once owned an automobile with an air conditioner whose operation caused the automobile to overheat unless the outside temperature was below 70° F; this could have been due either to failure to work as it was designed to or to poor design. (One hopes it was the former.)

Again, the same distinction holds in the case of an animal or other organism. Perhaps you think the human knee is poorly designed; then you may think that a knee functioning in accord with its design plan is nonetheless not functioning very well. Someone might think the panda's thumb doesn't work well, even when the way it works does not deviate from its design plan. Evolution might not always or often hit on maximally apt design plans; in many cases, says Stephen Gould, a reasonably clever engineer could do a lot better. Clearly, something works properly in the fullest sense only when both conditions are met to an appropriate degree.

Subtleties arise here. For example, I might design my refrigerator, intending and expecting that it function a certain way. As it turns out, it functions in some wholly different way—not because it is broken, but only because I am mistaken with respect to how a thing with that kind of construction will in fact work. Is it then functioning in accord with its design plan? Here, clearly enough, a more complete account would make further distinctions; but perhaps they are not needed for present purposes. Another subtlety: if a large rock falls on my radio and it no longer does what it was designed to do, it is broken; it no longer works right. But suppose a small rock falls on it; now it no longer works the way it did before, but instead, by some wild chance, performs its function *better* than before so that it receives stations further away, with less static, more

---

[2] In this section I am indebted to a remark by William Ramsey.

[3] Of course if the thing works badly enough, then it is not a deicer: it isn't a failed deicer because it isn't a deicer at all. My computer isn't a deicer, even if some misguided soul designed it to deice and it works perfectly in accord with its design plan. Here I am indebted to a remark by Andrew Hsu.

fidelity, and so on. (Indeed, it goes so far as to correct errors in the performance of Beethoven sonatas.) Is my radio then malfunctioning, broken? That's not so clear; here one of the two conditions for working properly is met (and met magnificently) but the other is not. It works in such a way as to fulfill its purpose, but it does not work in accordance with its design plan. So is it working properly or not? In cases like this the answer is not always clear; here we reach that penumbral area of vagueness surrounding the central paradigm.

Is one of these conditions more important or central than the other? Well, if the radio does not perform the function it was designed to perform (it only emits a loud hum and does not receive any stations at all) it isn't working properly, even if it is functioning exactly as it was designed to function. On the other hand, one is inclined to some degree to believe that it is working properly if it performs its function, even if it is not functioning in accord with its design plan. Perhaps what we must say here is this: in the paradigm or central cases, a properly functioning device does what it is designed to do and does it the way it was designed to do it; there will be analogical extensions of the term to the sorts of cases where it does what it was designed to do but by some fortuitous circumstance doesn't do it the way it was designed to do it; but there are not analogical extensions to the sort of case where it functions in accord with its design plan, but doesn't at all perform the function the designer was aiming at.

The distinction between purpose and design is what occasions the addition (in chapter 1, pp. 17–19) of the fourth condition for warrant: that the design plan be a good one. Suppose our cognitive faculties had been designed by, say, one of Hume's infant deities or an incompetent angel. She intends that we have true beliefs on a wide variety of topics but botches the job: the fact is the design guarantees beliefs that are nearly always false. Then it looks as if our faculties would be functioning properly, functioning in accord with their design plan, but surely our beliefs would have very little by way of warrant for us. The occasional true belief we have would not constitute knowledge. But the answer is clear: under those conditions our cognitive faculties would be functioning properly in the sense that they would be functioning in accord with our design plan, but not functioning properly in the sense of enjoying good design. Both are necessary for proper function and both are necessary for warrant.

But if I am obliged to speak of distinct faculties or belief-producing mechanisms or processes, don't I then fall victim to the dreaded *generality problem* that afflicts Alvin Goldman's reliabilism (in particular in the earlier and in some ways more satisfactory formulation to be found in "What Is Justified Belief?"[4])? On that account, a belief has justification if and only if it is produced by a reliable belief-producing cognitive process: the more reliable the process, the more justification enjoyed by the belief. Such processes, says Goldman, are to be thought of as *types*, not tokens. Clearly enough, however, a given concrete process culminating in the production of a belief will be a token of many different types: which type is the one determining its degree of justification? But

---

[4]In *Justification and Knowledge: New Studies in Epistemology,* ed. George Pappas (Dordrecht: D. Reidel, 1979).

just here is the problem: take the relevant processes broadly, and the same process will have outputs of differing degrees of justification, so that—contrary to the theory—the degree of justification of a belief is not determined by the degree of reliability of the relevant associated process; take them narrowly enough so as to avoid this difficulty, and there will be or could be reliable belief-producing mechanisms—the tumor that causes several belief-producing processes, most of which produce absurdly false beliefs, but one of which causes you to believe that you suffer from a tumor—that produce beliefs that do not have warrant.[5]

Now Goldman suggests[6] that my account suffers from the same problem; he adds that "a little reflection should make it clear that cognitive faculty individuation is no trivial matter." Indeed it isn't, but how does that create a problem for my view? The fact that it is not easy to individuate faculties is not, by itself, much cause for alarm. It is also hard to individuate mountains and sentences; that does not mean that there is automatically a problem in talking about mountains and sentences; everything depends upon what you propose to *say* about them. I don't, of course, say that the degree of warrant of a belief is determined by the degree of reliability of the faculty or faculties that produce it; the analogue of *that* claim for processes is what creates the problem for Goldman; so at any rate I am not afflicted with the very *same* problem.

Is there a problem here at all? According to Goldman, "Plantinga owes us an answer to the question precisely what cognitive faculties are there, and which ones must be functioning properly for a given belief to be justified?" But why do I owe us an answer to that question? No doubt it would be nice to have one, and no doubt a really complete theory would include something like such an account. But this just means that without such an answer my account is incomplete—which of course it is. For Goldman, on the other hand, the problem is not incompleteness, but something much more debilitating: we can see that no matter which level of generality we select, the analysis will give us the wrong results. No analogue of that problem, so far as I can see, afflicts my account.

We can employ some of the above distinctions to respond to an objection by William Hasker, who asks us to consider

> Geoffrey, who as the result of a random genetic mutation, not directed or planned by anyone, finds himself in an unusual cognitive situation. On the one hand, Geoffrey is totally blind, and there is no hope of his ever regaining any

[5]See my "Positive Epistemic Status and Proper Function," in *Philosophical Perspectives, 2, Epistemology, 1988,* ed. James Tomberlin (Atascadero, Calif.: Ridgeview, 1988), pp. 24–31; and see my *Warrant: The Current Debate* (New York: Oxford University Press, 1993), chap. 9, pp. 199ff. It is no part of my cognitive design plan that my brain is so designed that when invaded by this tumor, the result is a belief-producing process causing me to form the true belief that I have a tumor. This feature is either an unintended by-product of the design of my brain, or else just a part of the max plan that is not involved in the design plan at all. Similar comments apply to some of the other counterexamples to reliabilism; from one point of view the problem with reliabilism is that it fails to distinguish design plan from max plan.

[6]Symposium on warrant at Central Division of the American Philosophical Association, St. Louis, 1986.

degree of vision. But the mutation which rendered Geoffrey blind also had another result. The portion of his brain which would normally be devoted to processing visual information has now acquired another ability: it registers, in an extremely sensitive way, the magnetic fields generated by the earth and by objects in the environment. Because of this, Geoffrey has the ability, hitherto verified only in certain marine organisms, to locate himself and to make his way around by magnetolocation. As he grows to maturity, he is able to determine his location in the neighborhood and to make his way about with considerable facility; automobiles are still a problem for him, to be sure, but so long as he stays on the sidewalk he is all right.

   Under the described circumstances I think we are obliged to say that Geoffrey's beliefs about his whereabouts are warranted, and indeed that he *knows* where he is. It seems, however, that Geoffrey's cognitive situation is by no means in accordance with his design plan; that plan calls for that portion of his brain to be devoted to visual perception. So there can be warranted belief even where there is not function according to the design plan, and TPEF [the Theory of Proper Function—that is, my account of warrant] is false.[7]

Hasker clearly intends that Geoffrey has acquired a new max plan, and has acquired it by chance. There is a way in which his cognitive faculties regularly work, a way different from that of the rest of us human beings; it is not the case, for example, that his cognitive responses are determined by Alpha Centaurians who decide what a given response will be by way of some chance device such as throwing dice. But if Geoffrey has acquired a new *max* plan by chance, what is to prevent his acquiring a new *design* plan by chance as well? If evolutionary theory is fundamentally correct, organisms acquire their design plans by way of random genetic mutation (or some other source of variation) and natural selection. Well, can't Geoffrey have acquired his new design plan by way of a sizable (and improbable) random genetic mutation? Then his cognitive faculties would be working properly according to the new design plan (even if improperly according to the old) and there would be no reason to deny his beliefs warrant.

   But perhaps you think it impossible that a creature should acquire a design plan, or a new design plan by random genetic mutation, or, indeed, by mere chance in any form. Hasker considers the possibility that Geoffrey has been given his new design plan by God or by someone else—some young and inept angel, perhaps—to whom God has delegated this task. True (as Hasker points out), you would not ordinarily expect God to revise Geoffrey's cognitive capacities in the direction of less rather than greater cognitive capacity, but of course that is by no means decisive. Perhaps there is some great good for Geoffrey that God can best achieve by making or permitting this revision.

   Of course, if God revises Geoffrey's cognitive design plan, then this new way in which his cognitive system works is not (contrary to the original stipulation) "the result of a random genetic mutation, not directed or planned by anyone." The example must be so understood, then, that Geoffrey has acquired a new and different *max* plan but not a new *design* plan; his cognitive faculties malfunction, and do not work in accord with his design plan. And we must stipulate that he has acquired his new max plan just by chance. Perhaps we must imagine God permitting an angel to determine the relevant part of his cognitive max plan by some random choice method. What then? Shall we say that Geoffrey knows? Our first thought might be that Geoffrey's beliefs are warranted, all right, but warranted by nothing more arcane than induction; he has learned of correlations between how he is (nonstandardly) appeared to or what he is nonstandardly inclined to believe and what his location (as he learns from those around him) is. According to Hasker, however, "the example can be redescribed (focusing on very early examples of Geoffrey's exercise of this faculty) so as to obviate this objection."

But is it at all clear that under these conditions (when we explicitly stipulate that his faculties are not functioning in accord with his design plan) those first exercises of this faculty *do* provide Geoffrey with warranted belief? I think not. Perhaps in those cases what he has is not warranted true belief, but beliefs true by lucky accident. But it is equally unclear, I think, that Geoffrey's beliefs *lack* warrant. What we have is a situation rather like that with the radio whose performance improves after being hit by a random rock (and perhaps we could make the example more striking by adding that Geoffrey's cognitive performance is *better* than that of the rest of us). One of the *purposes* involved in Geoffrey's design plan (that is, the provision of true beliefs about his location) is still served by his new max plan, although not in accord with the design plan. In a case like that we are pulled in two directions: on the one hand since that purpose is served, we are inclined to think that the relevant cognitive module is functioning properly; on the other hand since it is not functioning in accord with the design plan we are inclined to think that it is not functioning properly. This hesitation is mirrored, I think, by our hesitation as to whether or not the relevant beliefs have warrant. So the right answer is that the module in question is not functioning properly in the full or strict sense, but is functioning properly in an analogically extended sense; and in a corresponding analogically extended sense of 'warrant', his beliefs do have warrant, although they do not have warrant in the full or strict sense. Here we must follow Aristotle (who did not have Hasker in mind): "we should perhaps say that in a manner he knows, in a manner not."[8]

E. Gettier, Trade-offs, and Compromises

1. Gettier

Knowledge is justified true belief: so we thought from time immemorial. Then God said, "Let Gettier be"; not quite all was light, perhaps, but at any rate we learned we had been standing in a dark corner. Edmund Gettier's three-page paper[9] is surely unique in contemporary philosophy in what we might call 'significance ratio': the ratio between the number of pages that have been

[8]*Posterior Analytics*, I, 1, 71a 25, in *The Oxford Translations of Aristotle*, trans. G. R. G. Mure, ed. W. D. Ross (Oxford: Oxford University Press, 1928).
[9]"Is Justified True Belief Knowledge?" *Analysis* 23 (1963), pp. 121–23.

written in response to it, and its own length; and the havoc he has wrought in contemporary epistemology has been entirely salutary. Never have so many learned so much from so few (pages). What Gettier pointed out, of course, is that belief, truth, and justification are not sufficient for knowledge. Naturally, there have been many attempts to provide a "fourth condition," many attempts to add an epicycle or two to circumvent Gettier. Sadly enough, however, in most cases the quick response has been another counterepicycle that circumvents the circumvention—which then calls for a counter-counterepicycle, and so on, world without end.[10] I don't mean at all to denigrate this often illuminating literature; but what Gettier examples really show, as I shall argue, is that internalist accounts of warrant are fundamentally wanting; hence the added epicycles, so long as they appeal only to internalist factors, are doomed to failure. My aim in this section is to try to understand what really underlies Gettier situations, and then to see how Gettier looks from the vantage point of the present conception of warrant. It will become clear, I think, that Gettier problems do not in fact bedevil it; considering them will nonetheless enable us to deepen our analysis.

Gettier problems come in several forms. There is Gettier's original *Smith owns a Ford or Brown is in Barcelona* version: Smith comes into your office, bragging about his new Ford, shows you the bill of sale and title, takes you for a ride in it, and in general supplies you with a great deal of evidence for the proposition that he owns a Ford. Naturally enough you believe the proposition *Smith owns a Ford*. Acting on the maxim that it never hurts to believe an extra truth or two, you infer from that proposition its disjunction with *Brown is in Barcelona* (Brown is an acquaintance of yours about whose whereabouts you have no information). As luck would have it, Smith is lying (he does not own a Ford) but Brown, by happy coincidence, is indeed in Barcelona. So your belief *Smith owns a Ford or Brown is in Barcelona* is indeed both true and justified; but surely you can't properly be said to *know* it. In a similar example (due to Keith Lehrer), you see (at about ten yards) what you take to be a sheep in the field; acting again on the same principle, you infer that the field contains at least one sheep. As it turns out, what you see is not a sheep (but a wolf in sheep's clothing); by virtue of sheer serendipity, however, there is indeed a sheep in a part of the field you can't see. Your belief that there is a sheep in the field is true and justified, but hardly a case of knowledge.

In these cases you infer the justified true belief from a justified false belief (that Smith owns a Ford, that *that* is a sheep); your justification, we might say, goes through a false belief. Naturally enough, some of the early attempts at repairs stipulated that a belief constitutes knowledge only if it is true, and justified, and its justification does not go by way of inference from a false belief. But this is not the key to Gettier problems. Modify the sheep case so that you don't first form the belief that *that is a sheep,* but proceed directly to the belief that there is a sheep in that field. Or consider the following case, due originally

[10]For a penetrating and encyclopedic account of this literature, see Robert Shope, *The Analysis of Knowing* (Princeton: Princeton University Press, 1983).

to Carl Ginet. You are driving through southern Wisconsin, near Waupun. In an effort to make themselves look more prosperous, the inhabitants have erected a large number of fake barns or barn facades—three for each real barn. From the road, these facades are indistinguishable from real barns. You are unaware of this innocent deception; looking at what is in fact a real barn you form the belief *now that's a fine barn!* Again, the belief is true; you are justified in holding it; but it seems to many that it does not constitute knowledge. Continue the bucolic motif with the following case. The Park Service has just cleaned up a popular bridle trail in Yellowstone, in anticipation of a visit from a Department of the Interior bigwig. A wag with a perverse sense of humor comes along and scatters two bushels of horse manure on the trail. The official arrives and goes for a walk on the trail, naturally forming the belief that horses have recently been by. Once more, his belief is true and justified, but does not constitute knowledge. Still another Gettier example, this one, oddly enough, predating Gettier's birth by a good twenty years: consider a person who at noon happens to look at a clock that stopped at midnight last night, thus acquiring the belief that it is noon; this belief is true and (we may stipulate) justified, but clearly not knowledge.[11]

But why not, precisely? What is going on in these cases? One salient point: in each of these cases it is merely *by accident* that the justified true belief in question is true. It just *happens* that Brown is in Barcelona, that there is a sheep in another part of the field, that what you are looking at is a barn rather than a barn facade, that the clock stopped just at midnight (and you happened to look at it at exactly noon). In each of these cases, the belief in question could just as well have been false. (As a matter of fact, that's not putting it strongly enough; these beliefs could *much better* have been false. There are so many other places Brown could have been; there are many more barn facades than barns there in southern Wisconsin; wags don't often or ordinarily take the trouble to make the Park Service look bad; there are so many other times at which the clock could have stopped; and so on.) But what is the force, here, of saying that the beliefs are true by *accident*?

The basic idea is simple enough: a true belief is formed in these cases, all right, but not as a result of the proper function of the cognitive modules governed by the relevant parts of the design plan. The faculties involved are functioning properly, but there is still no warrant; and the reason has to do with the local cognitive environment in which the belief is formed. Consider the first example, the original *Smith owns a Ford or Brown is in Barcelona* example. Our design plan leads us to believe what we are told by others; there is what Thomas Reid calls "the Principle of Credulity,"[12] a belief-forming process whereby for the most part we believe what our fellows tell us. Of course credulity is modified by experience; we learn to believe some people under some circumstances and disbelieve others under others. (We learn not to form

[11]See Bertrand Russell, *Problems of Philosophy* (Oxford: Oxford University Press, 1912), p. 132.

[12]*An Inquiry into the Human Mind on the Principles of Common Sense* in *Inquiry and Essays*, ed. R. Beanblossom and K. Lehrer (Indianapolis: Hackett, 1983), VI, 24, p. 95.

beliefs about a marital quarrel until we have heard from both parties; we discount statements made by television salesmen and candidates for public office.) Still, credulity is part of our design plan. But it does not work well when our fellows lie to us or deceive us in some other manner, as in the case of Smith, who lies about the Ford, or the Wisconsinites, who set out to deceive the city-slicker tourists, or the wag aiming to hoodwink the Interior Department official. It does not work well in the sense that the result of its proper operation in *those* circumstances does not or need not result in true belief. More exactly, it's not that *credulity* does not work well in these cases—after all, it may be working precisely according to its specifications in the design plan. It is rather that credulity is designed, we might say, to work in a certain kind of situation (one in which our fellows do not intend to mislead us), and designed to produce a given result (our learning something from our fellows) in that situation. But when our fellows tell us what they think is false, then credulity fails to achieve the aimed at result.

But of course it isn't just our fellow's *intentions* that count; even if they are entirely well intentioned, we may still have a Gettier situation. Consider a child whose parents are seriously confused and therefore teach him a battery of falsehoods with only an occasional truth thrown in by accident: such a child does not know the occasional truths he is thus taught, despite the fact that there is nothing wrong with his cognitive equipment and despite the fact that his parents intend to teach him nothing but the unvarnished truth. Gilbert Harman has called our attention to increasingly subtle cases of this general sort, cases where it becomes increasingly difficult to tell whether there is or isn't warrant. CBS evening news reports that General X has been assassinated; you are watching the news and, naturally enough, form the belief that General X was assassinated; as it happens, there was a retraction on a later CBS newscast, but also a still later retraction of the retraction; and General X was in fact assassinated. You don't hear either the retraction or the retraction-retraction and so believe all along that he was assassinated: do you know that he was? What if the first retraction was due merely to the malicious actions of a prankster, so that no one in the know believed it? What if there wasn't a retraction of the assassination report, but only because of some communications malfunction (the courier carrying the report that the general is safe falls into a creek and his message is devoured by piranhas)? It can become monumentally difficult to say whether there is warrant, or sufficient warrant to constitute knowledge in such cases. But what is clearly at issue in these cases is a malfunction of some sort, a deviation from the norm, in the communications chain.

What counts, for the warrant of a belief you form on the basis of credulity, is not just *that* belief-forming mechanism and its virtues, but also the epistemic credentials the proposition you believe has for the person from whom you acquire it.[13] Credulity is designed to operate in the presence of a certain condition: that of our fellows knowing the truth and being both willing and able to

---

[13]For more detail about credulity and testimony, see chapter 4, sec. 2.

communicate it. In the absence of that condition, if it produces a true belief, it is just by accident, by virtue of a piece of epistemic good luck: in which case the belief in question has little or nothing by way of warrant.

Not nearly all Gettier examples involve credulity, of course: consider the sheep in the field case, or the clock that stopped at midnight. In these cases, just as in the case of the examples involving credulity, there is a sort of glitch in the cognitive situation, a minor infelicity, a small lack of fit between cognitive faculties and cognitive environment. The locus of the infelicity, in these cases too, is not the cognitive faculties of the person forming the justified true belief that lacks warrant; they function just as they should. The locus is instead in the cognitive environment; it deviates, ordinarily to a small degree, from the paradigm situations for which the faculty in question has been designed. (In brain-in-vat cases the cognitive environment is deceptive, but on a massive scale; hence brain-in-vat cases are not Gettier cases.) Thus the wolf is in sheep's clothing, or Smith is lying, or the Wisconsinites are deceptively giving the appearance of affluence, or the wag is having his little joke. Take it, for the moment, that this notion of a design plan is more than metaphor: imagine that we have in fact been consciously designed (by God perhaps): then the designer of our cognitive powers will have designed those powers for certain situations. They will be designed to produce mostly true beliefs in the main sorts of situations that (as the designer sees it) their owners will ordinarily encounter. What we have in Gettier situations is a belief's being formed in circumstances differing from the paradigm circumstances for which our faculties have been designed.

So the first thing to see about the Gettier situations is that the true beliefs in these situations are true by accident, not by virtue of the proper function of the faculties or belief-producing mechanisms involved. And the second thing to see is that in the typical Gettier case, the locus of the cognitive glitch is in the cognitive environment: the latter is in some small way misleading. The clock has unexpectedly stopped, the usually reliable Smith is lying, the wolf is dressed in sheepskin, and so on. (And here we might note that Gettier examples come in degrees, the degree in question being a function of the degree of departure from the paradigm circumstances for which our cognitive equipment is designed.)

But is this really an essential feature of Gettier situations—that is, is it really essential to Gettier situations that the glitch in question be a (misleading) feature of the cognitive *environment?* I think not. Consider the following Gettier example, attributed by Chisholm to Meinong (and again predating Gettier's birth). An aging Austrian forest ranger lives in a cottage in the mountains with his daughter. There is a set of wind chimes hanging from a bough just outside the kitchen window; when these wind chimes sound, the ranger forms the belief that the wind is blowing. As he ages, his hearing (unbeknownst to him) deteriorates; he can no longer hear the chimes. He is also sometimes subject to small auditory hallucinations in which he is appeared to in that wind-chimes way; and occasionally these hallucinations occur when the wind is blowing.[14] In these cases, then, he has justified true belief but not knowledge. The problem is not with the environment, however, but with his hearing. So it isn't right to think of Gettier situations as involving only cognitive *environmental* pollution; the problem can be with the agent's faculties rather than with the environment.

Well, what *is* essential here? First, of course, Gettier situations are ones in which the believer is justified[15] in her beliefs; she is within her rights; she has done all that could be expected of her, and the unfortunate outcome, the lack of warrant, is in no way to be laid to her account. But there is also something broader. In chapter 1 of my *Warrant: The Current Debate,* I argued that *internalism* essentially involves a view about cognitive accessibility: what constitutes or confers warrant, on internalist views, must be *accessible,* in some special way, to the agent. Note that in all these Gettier cases (including that of the aging Austrian forest ranger) the cognitive glitch has to do with what is *not* accessible to the agent in this way. In a Gettier case, it is as if everything connected with what is in this sense *internal* to the agent, is going as it ought; but there is a relatively minor hitch, a relatively minor deviation from the design plan in some *other* aspect of the whole cognitive situation—perhaps in the environment, but also, possibly, in some aspect of the agent's cognitive equipment that is not internal in this sense. What is essential to Gettier situations is the production of a true belief that has no warrant—despite conformity to the design plan in those aspects of the whole cognitive situation that are internal, in the appropriate sense, to the agent. In these Gettier situations there is conformity to the design plan on the part of the *internal* aspects of the cognitive situation, but some feature of the cognitive situation external (in the internalist's sense) to the agent forestalls warrant.

Gettier problems afflict internalist epistemologies, and they do so essentially. The essence of the Gettier problem is that it shows internalist theories of warrant to be wanting. What Gettier problems show, stated crudely and without necessary qualification, is that even if everything is going as it ought to with respect to what is internal (in the internalist sense), warrant may still be absent. The real significance of Gettier problems, therefore, is not that they are relatively minor technical annoyances that prevent us from getting a counterexample-proof analysis of knowledge; their real significance is that they show justification, conceived internalistically, to be insufficient for warrant. We

---

[14]Says Meinong, "Assume now that someone who has lived in the vicinity of such an apparatus has become hard of hearing in the course of time and has developed a tendency to have auditory hallucinations. It could easily happen that he hallucinates the familiar sounds . . . at the very moment when these sounds are actually to be heard." Quoted in R. Chisholm, *Theory of Knowledge,* 3d ed. (Englewood Cliffs, N.J.: Prentice-Hall, 1989), p. 92. The quotation from Meinong is to be found in Meinong's *Gesamtausgabe* (Graz: Akademische Druck- und Verlagsanstalt, 1973), 5:398–99.

[15]Here I use 'justification' not as a synonym for warrant, but (a) to denote the condition of not having flouted one's epistemic duty and having done no more than is permitted by epistemic obligation, and (b) to denote that vaguer and analogically related condition of being such that everything 'downstream from experience' is going as it ought to go. See my *Warrant: The Current Debate,* p. 10ff.

should therefore expect that an externalist account such as the present account will enjoy a certain immunity to Gettier problems (unless, of course, we take the term 'Gettier Problem' so widely that any proposed counterexample to the sufficiency of a proposed account of warrant counts as a Gettier problem for that proposal). And, indeed, some of the Gettier cases—the Case of the Aging Ranger, for example—are immediately ruled out on the grounds that the beliefs in question are not formed by faculties functioning properly.

Still, thinking about Gettier cases enables us to see more of the shape and complexity of the design plan and to learn more about the conditions under which a belief acquires warrant. Different Gettier cases must be treated differently. First, consider again the original *Smith owns a Ford or Brown is in Barcelona* case, the sort of case that involves testimony and the operation of credulity. Here what we see is that we need an addition to the official account of warrant; more exactly, something implicit in it must be made explicit. Some cognitive mechanisms or faculties take as input other beliefs: inference is the obvious example, but something similar goes on with respect to credulity. In the latter case, it isn't that you necessarily form the belief *Paul says so and so* when forming the belief that so and so on the basis of Paul's saying it; *that* belief—that *Paul says* so and so—may never come to consciousness. Still, you are in some way aware that Paul (or someone) says so and so, and it is on the basis of that awareness that you form the belief that so and so. Now in the case of inference, it is clear that the status, with respect to warrant, of the inferred belief depends upon the status, with respect to warrant, of the belief from which the inference is drawn. But something similar is true for testimony. The status of the belief you form on the basis of testimony depends upon the status of this proposition in the noetic structure of her from whom you get it. I say 'proposition' rather than 'belief', because, of course, in some of the Gettier cases the person from whom you acquire your belief by testimony does not himself hold it—Smith bragging about his Ford, for example, or the proud but impecunious Wisconsinites. In the case of such second-level belief-forming mechanisms (or faculties) as inference and credulity, then, the notion of proper function must include the input proposition's having the right sort of credentials: it must be a *belief* on the part of the testifier, and it must be a belief that has warrant for her. In the central and paradigm cases, you will have warrant for a belief that you acquire by way of testimony only if the person from whom you acquire the belief himself holds the belief and has warrant for it.[16]

There is another way in which reflection on Gettier examples can give us a deeper understanding of warrant. Consider the other Gettier cases—the case of the fake barns, or the wag in Yellowstone, or the clock that stopped at midnight. In each of these cases, what we saw was that the local cognitive environment deviated in some more or less moderate fashion from the paradigm situations for which the faculty was designed. But can we get a deeper grasp of the situation here? I think so, but to do so we must turn to trade-offs and compromises.

[16]See chapter 4, pp. 83ff.

2. Trade-offs and Compromises

Suppose we begin by adding to the Gettier cases the following sorts of situations: straight sticks look bent in water; it can falsely appear that there is an oasis just a mile away; a dry North Dakota road looks wet on a hot summer day; an artificial apple among the real apples in the bin can deceive almost anyone (at least so long as she doesn't touch it); a hologram of a ball looks just like a ball and can confuse the unwary perceiver; in those famous Müller-Lyer illusions, the shorter line looks the longer because of the direction of the arrow heads. There seems to be no perceptual malfunction in these cases. Still, if you are a desert tyro and, due to a mirage, form the belief that there is an oasis about a mile away, your belief will have little warrant. Even if it happens to be true (by happy coincidence there is an oasis a mile away in a different direction), you don't know it. The same goes in the other cases; so here we have proper function in what certainly appears to be the environment for which our faculties are designed; but the result is not warrant. Why not?

The answer involves *trade-offs and compromises*. You want to minimize the time you spend mowing your lawn; you therefore want a mower that cuts a wide swath; this requires a large mower, and the larger the better. (Perhaps one that cuts a forty-foot swath will mow your entire lawn in two passes.) On the other hand, you want to be able to maneuver the mower, you want to keep its cost down, and you want to be able to park it in your garage; these requirements place limitations on its size. The mower you want, therefore, will be a result of trade-offs and compromises between large size and those other desiderata. You are designing an automobile; you want it to be fast (and the faster the better, at any rate up to two-hundred miles per hour) but you also want to maximize safety. The former calls for light construction, but the latter for substantial bumpers and a strong and heavy frame; the design plan you adopt, therefore, will have to be a result of trade-offs and compromises.

But the same goes in the cognitive case. A belief has warrant for you (so I say) only if it is formed by your faculties functioning properly in an appropriate epistemic environment, only if the right statistical probabilities hold, and only if the cognitive processes that produce that belief have the production of true beliefs as their purpose—that is, only if the segment of the design plan governing its production is aimed at the production of true beliefs. But now consider these perceptual illusion cases, and for definiteness imagine that our faculties have actually been designed; and then think about these matters from an engineering and design point of view. The designer aims at a cognitive system that delivers truth (true beliefs), of course; but he also has other constraints he means or needs to work within. He wants the system to be realized within a certain sort of medium (flesh, bone and blood rather than plastic, glass, and metal), a humanoid body (and one of a certain relatively modest size), in a certain kind of world, with certain kinds of natural laws or regularities. This means that cognition will be mediated by brain and neural activity. He also wants the cognitive system to draw an amount of energy consonant with our general type of body, and to require a brain of only modest size (given too large a brain, we might have to support our heads with both hands, so that moun-taineering or tennis or basketball would be utterly out of the question). No doubt there are reasons why he wants to do things this way (that is, in accord with these constraints), but we need not try to guess what they might be. From an evolutionary perspective, we can see these constraints originating not in the conscious design of God, but in the way evolutionists are fond of; and evolu-tion, like God, is obliged to make certain trade-offs. (A cognitive system deliv-ering truth most of the time could be adaptively advantageous: on the other hand, too large a brain will reduce mobility and make a creature easy prey to predators.)

So the designer's overall aim is at truth, but within the constraints imposed by these other factors; and this may require trade-offs. It may not be possible, for example, to satisfy these other constraints and also have a system that (when functioning as it is designed to function) produces true beliefs in *every* sort of situation to be encountered in the cognitive environment for which it is designed. There are an enormous number of different situations arising within the cognitive environment for which the system is designed; and it might be impossible, given the constraints, to handle them all in the most desirable way.

Thus consider the straight stick in water. A visual system like ours works well (that is, fulfills its function, produces true belief nearly all the time) in a wide variety of circumstances, but not when (for the first time, or without other knowledge) someone is looking at a straight stick partly immersed in water: such a stick has a misleading bent look to it. Now it might be possible to design an epicycle that would circumvent this problem—perhaps it could correct the way the stick looks by taking advantage of the way in which light is reflected from water and other similar liquids. (Or maybe it would be possible to cir-cumvent the problem *partially:* maybe with the partially corrected system there would still be situations that lead to false beliefs, but fewer of them.) And of course this is only one of many such situations: there are all of the other sorts of perceptual illusions cases, as well as many cases (false testimony, say) that do not involve perception. Perhaps a system could be designed in which there would be nothing misleading in any of these situations: but only at a price, and perhaps the price was not right.

Then the thing to do would be to trade-off some accuracy for efficiency (and the satisfaction of these other constraints). You would want to design a system that worked well (that is, produced true beliefs) over as large a proportion as possible of the situations in which its owners will find themselves, consistent with satisfying those other constraints. (The other constraints could be abso-lute and nonnegotiable, or they might also be subject to negotiation.) In this way you will wind up with a system that works well in the vast majority of circumstances; but in a few circumstances it produces false belief. (Of course, you add the important feature of learning from experience in order to mitigate the doleful effects of the compromises: after a couple of trials you no longer believe that the road is wet, that there is an oasis just a mile away, that the stick is bent, or what Paul, that habitual deceiver, says; you learn to be on the lookout for fake fruit and holograms.)

And now think about those triples of the design plan where the cognitive response *R* is misleading: cases where the circumstance member *M* involves the conditions under which the perceiver is subject to mirages or other perceptual illusions. Why does the perceptual system work this misleading way in these circumstances? Well, the answer is not that its working this way contributes directly to the main goal or purpose of the whole perceptual system, namely, the provision of true perceptual beliefs. Instead, its working this way is a trade-off or compromise between fulfilling that purpose and satisfying those other constraints. The designer does not join the circumstance member *M* with the response member *R* because this contributes to the formation of true beliefs (it doesn't), but because organizing the whole system this way, though misleading in a few situations, helps enable the system as a whole to satisfy those constraints. We might say that in the misleading cases, *R* is joined with *M* not in order to satisfy the main purpose of the perceptual system but in order to satisfy those other constraints. Or perhaps more accurately (since, in a way, the aim at truth on the part of the whole system is also the reason for *R*'s being joined with *M*) the thing to say is that *R* is joined with *M* not in order to serve *directly* the main purpose of providing true beliefs (it doesn't do that) but to do so *indirectly*. It indirectly serves that purpose by being a locus of a best compromise of the overall purpose, on the part of the perceptual system, of producing true beliefs.

So what shall we say about warrant, with respect to these misleading responses? Just this: a belief has warrant for you only if the segment of the design plan governing its production is *directly* rather than indirectly aimed at the production of true beliefs (and an addition to that effect must be made to the official account of warrant). If a given response is present only because it is a part of the best compromise and not because it directly serves the purpose of producing true beliefs, then the belief in question does not have warrant.

This is how to think of beliefs produced by perceptual illusions; but the idea can be generalized to a wider class of cases including, for example, false testimony. In all these cases there seems to be proper function but little warrant. If we add that the belief in question is true, then we have 'quasi-Gettier cases'. (*Quasi*-Gettier cases, because Gettier cases properly so-called have to do with *justification,* as the alleged source of warrant, rather than with proper function.) Take a perceptual illusion or false testimony case and add that the belief produced is true (but by accident): then what you have is a quasi-Gettier case. The belief in question has little warrant and, though true, does not constitute knowledge; for a belief has warrant for you only when it is produced by a segment of the design plan directly aimed at truth.

F. Defeaters and Overriders

Pollock and Chisholm emphasize the importance of *defeaters.* You read in a usually reliable guidebook that the University of Aberdeen was founded in 1405 A.D.; you form the belief that it was founded then; that belief has a certain degree of warrant for you. You later read in an authoritative history of Aberdeen that the university was founded in 1495; you now no longer believe that it was founded in 1405, and (as we may put it) the warrant that belief had for you has been defeated. If things are going properly, you will no longer believe the first proposition, and will perhaps not believe the second as firmly as you would have, had you not first believed the first. Here the first belief gets defeated, and its warrant disappears by virtue of your getting warrant for another belief inconsistent with it. Following John Pollock,[17] call such defeaters *rebutting* defeaters: the paradigm case of rebutting defeat occurs when you first have evidence for a certain proposition, and then get evidence for its denial. But there are also (following Pollock) undercutting defeaters. You visit a factory: the items coming down the assembly line look red and you form the belief that they are indeed red, a belief that has warrant by virtue of the way you are appeared to. You are then told by a local authority that this part of the assembly line is a quality control module, where the items are irradiated by red light in order to make it easier to detect a certain kind of flaw. You then no longer believe that the items you are looking at are red—not because you have reason to believe that they are some other color, but because your belief that they are red has been undermined by what you were told.

The basic idea here is that the design plan is such that (for example) when you are appeared to a certain way you will form a certain belief: when you are appeared to redly, you will (*ceteris paribus*) form the belief that you see something red. But the design plan also specifies circumstances under which, even though you are appeared to redly, you won't or don't form that belief. These circumstances would include, for example, your learning that the thing in question, despite appearances, is not red (rebutting defeater), or your coming to believe that the thing would have looked that way even if it were not red (undercutting defeater). Again, following Pollock, we may note that defeaters of either kind are themselves sometimes defeated by further defeaters (of either kind): 'defeater-defeaters', as Pollock calls them. The basic idea is clear enough; but there are many subtleties, much to be said by way of development and qualification, much to explore.[18] This defeater structure is to be found across the length and breadth of our cognitive structure, and nearly any belief is possibly subject to defeat. I say *nearly* any belief; perhaps a few beliefs—such beliefs about my own mental life as that I am in pain or that I am being appeared to in some way, or that I exist, together with those that are wholly self-evident and accepted with maximal degree of belief, for example—are not thus subject to defeat. The defeater system works in nearly every area of our cognitive design plan and is a most important part of it; we must therefore explicitly understand the proper function condition of warrant as applying to the relevant portions of the defeater system.

---

[17]Pollock's work on this topic begins with *Knowledge and Justification* (Princeton: Princeton University Press, 1974), pp. 42ff, proceeds through *Contemporary Theories of Knowledge* (Totowa, N.J.: Rowman and Littlefield, 1986), pp. 48ff, and goes on to one of his most recent assaults on the topic, "Defeasible Reasoning," *Cognitive Science* 11 (1987), pp. 481–518. See also Stewart Cohen's "Knowledge and Context," *Journal of Philosophy* (October 1986), pp. 574ff.

[18]See the appendix of my *Warrant: The Current Debate*.

The defeater system seems to be aimed at the formation of true beliefs (and the avoidance of false beliefs). You no longer believe that the items coming down the line are red, after hearing that they are irradiated with red light. Presumably this reflects the fact that the statistical probability of a thing's being red, given that it appears red to you, is high, but the statistical probability of its being red, given both that it appears to you to be red and that you are told by an authority that it is irradiated by red light, is not high. But there are similar structures that do *not* seem to be aimed at truth. To return to a previous example, you might be much more optimistic about your recovery from a serious illness than the statistics in your possession would warrant; here this excessive optimism, presumably, is aimed at survival rather than truth. And here, of course, proper function and warrant do not go together. You know the statistics: nine out of ten cases of the disease are fatal; if it were someone else who had the disease, you would form the belief that his chances were about one out of ten. But there is the optimistic overrider; so you are much more sanguine about your own recovery than the statistics warrant. We might say that your statistical evidence is 'defeated' by the optimistic overrider; it might be better, however, to say that it is *overridden,* reserving 'defeat' for the activity of structures of this kind that are aimed at true belief.

This optimistic overrider, of course, is part of the design plan; there is no dysfunction here, and the belief in question is formed by the relevant faculties functioning properly. Nevertheless, of course, the belief that you are very likely to recover has little by way of warrant; indeed, if by some chance the optimistic overrider failed to function and, by virtue of that dysfunction you formed that belief that your chances were about one out of ten, it is *that* belief that would have warrant. What confers warrant is the proper function of faculties aimed at the production of true beliefs; when such beliefs are overridden by beliefs that are the result of the proper function of modules not aimed at truth (wishful thinking, for example) the resulting beliefs do not have warrant.

II. Two Concluding Comments

We should pause for a moment to marvel at the enormously articulate, subtle, and complex nature of our cognitive faculties. These faculties produce beliefs on an enormously wide variety of topics—our everyday external environment, the thoughts of others, our own internal lives (someone's internal musings and soliloquies can be complex and interesting enough both to him and others to be worth an entire novel), the past, mathematics and logic, what is probable and improbable, what is necessary and possible, beauty, right and wrong, our relationships to God, and a host of other topics. They work with great subtlety and in a thousand ingeniously different ways. As we shall see in more detail in the next chapters, we believe on the basis of sense experience, testimony, memory, mathematical and logical intuition, philosophical intuition, introspection, extrospection (whereby we come to know the thoughts and feelings of others), induction, evidence from other beliefs, and (so I say, anyway) Calvin's *sensus divinitatis*. Our faculties work so as to produce beliefs of many different degrees of strength ranging from the merest shadow of an inclination to believe all the way to complete certainty. Our beliefs and the strength with which we hold them, furthermore, respond with great delicacy to changes in experience—to what people tell us, to perceptual experience, to what we read, to further reflection, and so on. There is that elaborate and highly developed defeater system, and the overrider system. There is also the fact that while most of our belief formation goes on automatically, it is sometimes also possible for us to take a hand in it: realizing that I am too easily impressed by someone in a white coat, I make corrections for it.

I spoke of truth as what (most of) our cognitive faculties are aimed at; but often it is verisimilitude rather than the truth itself that is aimed at. Further, falsehood can be a vehicle for truth; a falsehood can lead us closer to the truth than the sober truth itself; thus when the truth is too difficult for us to grasp, we may nonetheless be able to get close to it via something that is strictly speaking false. And finally, there are both maturation and learning. Cognitive proper function at the age of three is quite different from cognitive proper function at the age of thirty; a small child will have bizarre beliefs but not necessarily by way of cognitive malfunction. There is that whole series of snapshot design plans, with a master design plan specifying which of them is appropriate at which age and under which circumstances. In addition there is also learning, which also, in a way modifies the design plan. More exactly, the design plan specifies how learning new facts and skills will lead to changes in cognitive reaction.

It is because of this complication, articulation, and fine detail that simple formulas for rationality, warrant, and their like inevitably fail. Is it suggested that it is irrational to believe an inconsistent set of propositions, a set from which it is possible to deduce a contradiction by, say, ordinary first-order logic? But (before he was corrected by Russell) was Frege irrational in believing his axioms for set theory? True enough, once he clearly *saw* the contradiction, then it would have been irrational for him to persist (although even this requires qualification); so shall we say that it is irrational to believe a set of propositions you know or believe to be contradictory? But what about the Paradox of the Preface (see my *Warrant: The Current Debate,* pp. 145 ff.): can't I perfectly sensibly believe, of some set *S* of propositions all of which are believed by me, that at least one of them is false? But then I believe all the members of *S**: the union of *S* with {*At least one member of S is false*}; *S** is inconsistent (there is no possible world in which all its members are true) and I know that it is; can't I nonetheless be perfectly rational, in so believing? Indeed, can't it be the case that each of these beliefs has a great deal of warrant for me? So sometimes it is quite rational to believe the members of an inconsistent set; and sometimes, indeed, it is rational to do so in the full knowledge that the set is inconsistent. Of course, other inconsistent sets are such that (if I am subject to no dysfunction) I could not come to accept all their members—for example, explicit contradictions; and one who succeeds in believing the members of such sets will indeed be irrational. But there is no simple formula to tell us which is which.

Another example. William Alston raises the following question. Suppose I believe *A* and do so on the basis of some ground *B*, which is in fact a reliable indicator of *A*: must I know or justifiably believe that indeed *B* *is* a reliable indicator in order to have warrant in believing *A*? If we insist on this as a general condition of justification, we fall into a nasty infinite regress; he therefore doesn't add it. Alston discusses this question with respect to justification; let's instead think about it with respect to warrant. Our noetic establishment is enormously varied and complex; it has many quite different sectors; in some of those sectors, warrant requires that you justifiably or warrantedly believe that *B* is a reliable indicator of *A* and in others it does not. Suppose, as Alston suggests, I believe $2 + 1 = 3$ on the basis of its just seeming utterly obvious to me; in such cases warrant does not require that I have any views at all as to whether its *seeming* that way to me is a reliable indication of its actually *being* that way. But in other cases things are quite different. I may believe that a bear has passed by on the basis of the way the brush looks; and to have warrant for *this* belief, I must know or warrantedly believe (or at any rate *have* known or warrantedly believed) that the brush's having that particular crushed sort of look is indeed a reliable indicator (in this particular kind of forest area and at this time of the year) that a bear has been by. I believe that an electron is sporting in the cloud chamber; I believe this on the basis of the trail I see in the cloud chamber. I believe that the child has measles, and so believe on the basis of certain symptoms. If these beliefs are to have warrant, I will warrantedly believe (or have believed) that the ground in question is a reliable indicator of the truth of the belief in question.

In many other cases, such a belief is not necessary for warrant. Consider memory beliefs, for example. The indication on the basis of which I believe is just its seeming so to me (see the next chapter); and I can have warrant for a memory belief even if I have never raised the question whether its seeming to be like that is a good or reliable indication of its being like that. (Of course, if I *do* think of or raise that question, then, perhaps, to have warrant I must believe that my being inclined toward such a memory belief is a reliable indication of its truth.) And suppose I know that I suffer from a certain kind of memory lapse, so that there are two noticeably different sorts of phenomenology accompanying my inclinations to memory beliefs, one of which usually accompanies inclinations to false beliefs: then too perhaps to have warrant for a given memory belief I must pay attention to the sort of phenomenology accompanying my inclination to that belief, and must believe or have believed that *that* phenomenology is the kind that goes with reliable inclinations. So there isn't anything at all like a simple, single answer to the question whether warrant for grounded beliefs requires that the subject know that the ground is an indicator of the belief; sometimes this is required and sometimes it is not. And the reason is not far to seek. In some cases it is perfectly in accord with proper cognitive function to believe *A* on the basis of *B* even if you have never had any views at all as to whether *B* is an indicator of *A*; in a wide variety of other cases a properly functioning human being will believe *A* on the basis of *B* only if she has first learned that *B* reliably indicates *A*; in certain cases where you are aware of partial malfunction, to have warrant you will have to believe of a ground that it is a reliable indicator, even though in the *absence* of such malfunction you would not have had to have any views at all on the subject. Of course there will be many other complications. And the point is that it is the complex, highly articulated nature of the human design plan that makes impossible simple generalizations of these sorts about rationality and warrant.

By way of concluding this initial overview, I wish to ask and briefly answer one final question. Is the view I have outlined an example of that 'naturalized' or maybe 'naturalistic' epistemology so much in contemporary vogue? This is a vexed question: it inherits its vexation from a prior question—namely, What is it for an epistemology to be naturalized or naturalistic? The question is difficult, but perhaps the essence of a naturalistic approach to epistemology has to do with *normativity*. Perhaps the mildest form of naturalism would be one in which it is denied that warrant is to be understood in terms of *deontology*. Mild as it is, this would still signal a radical break with the received epistemological tradition; as I argued in the first chapter of *Warrant: The Current Debate*, the dominant tradition in twentieth-century Anglo-American epistemology conceives warrant in terms of justification, which, in turn, is at bottom conceived in terms of the fulfillment or aptness for fulfillment of epistemic duty. At the other end, the most extreme version of naturalism in epistemology eschews normativity altogether, seeking to replace traditional epistemology (with its concern with justification, rationality, reasonability, and their normative colleagues) by descriptive psychology; this seems to be W. v. Quine's suggestion.[19] A more moderate version—stronger than the mildest but less radical than Quine's—is suggested by Hilary Kornblith, who says that according to the "naturalistic approach to epistemology," "Questions about how we actually arrive at our beliefs are thus relevant to questions about how we ought to arrive at our beliefs. Descriptive questions about belief acquisition have an important bearing on normative questions about belief acquisition."[20] We are to take it, I presume, that the 'ought' in the quotation need not be taken deontologically; the normativity involved is not necessarily that of duty and permission.

The view I mean to urge is, of course, naturalistic in that first and mildest sense. But it is also naturalistic in Kornblith's more moderate sense. For warrant is indeed a normative notion. The sort of normativity involved is not that of duty and obligation; it is normativity nonetheless, and there is an appropriate use of the term 'ought' to go with it. This is the use in which we say, of a damaged knee, or a diseased pancreas, or a worn brake shoe, that it no longer functions as it ought to. This is the use in which we say that a human heart ought to beat between forty and two-hundred times per minute, and that your car's choke ought to open (and the engine ought to throttle back to 750 RPM) when it warms up. Now will it be the case that "questions about how we actually arrive at our beliefs are relevant to questions about how we ought to

---

[19]See his "Epistemology Naturalized," in *Ontological Relativity and Other Essays* (New York: Columbia University Press, 1969), pp. 69ff. Reprinted in (for example) Hilary Kornblith's *Naturalizing Epistemology* (Cambridge: MIT Press, 1985).

[20]*Naturalizing Epistemology,* p. 3.

arrive at our beliefs?" Surely so: at any rate if we construe 'ought' as referring to the normativity going with warrant, and 'actually arrive at' as 'actually arrive at when there is no cognitive malfunction'. Indeed, thus construed the first question is maximally relevant to the second, being identical with it. So the present account is naturalistic in Kornblith's moderate sense.

But what about that more radical Quinian view according to which normative concerns in epistemology should give way to descriptive psychology? The first thing to see is that Quine's view imports more normativity than meets the eye. The descriptive psychologist typically delivers herself of functional generalizations: "when a human organism O is in state S and conditions C obtain," she says, "there is a probability p that O will go into state S^*." But these functional generalizations taken neat are false; they typically won't hold of human beings who have just been attacked by sharks, or transported to Alpha Centauri, or suffered a stroke. They should therefore be seen as containing an implicit qualification: when a *properly functioning* human organism *in an appropriate environment* is in state S, then . . . . The very sort of normativity involved in warrant, therefore, runs riot in descriptive psychology. Quine's radical naturalism is presumably the view that the only sort of normativity appropriate to epistemology is the sort to be found in natural science— descriptive psychology, perhaps. But then the question whether the view I advocate is naturalistic in the radical Quinian fashion is really the question whether a belief's having warrant *just is* its being produced by properly functioning faculties in the right sort of cognitive environment—or whether, on the other hand, a belief's having warrant *supervenes* upon such states of affairs. From Quine's perspective, this will no doubt be a distinction without a difference.

So the view I propose is a radical naturalism: striking the naturalistic pose is all the rage these days, and it's a great pleasure to be able to join the fun. The view I urge is indeed best thought of as an example of naturalistic epistemology; here I follow Quine (if only at some distance). Naturalistic epistemology, however, is ill-named. In the first place, it is quite compatible with, for example, supernaturalistic theism; indeed, the most plausible way to think of warrant, from a theistic perspective, is in terms of naturalistic epistemology.[21] And second (as I shall argue in chapters 11 and 12), naturalism in epistemology flourishes best in the context of a theistic view of human beings: naturalism in epistemology requires supernaturalism in anthropology. This claim is perhaps a bit less congenial to the spirit of Quine's enterprise.

By way of concluding recapitulation, therefore: as I see it, a belief has warrant for me only if (1) it has been produced in me by cognitive faculties that are working properly (functioning as they ought to, subject to no cognitive dysfunction) in a cognitive environment that is appropriate for my kinds of cognitive faculties, (2) the segment of the design plan governing the production of that belief is aimed at the production of true beliefs, and (3) there is a high statistical probability that a belief produced under those conditions will be

[21]See my "Justification and Theism," *Faith and Philosophy* (October 1987), pp. 403ff.

true. Under those conditions, furthermore, the degree of warrant is an increasing function of degree of belief. This is intended as an account of the central core of our concept of warrant; as we have seen, there is a penumbral area about the central core where there are a hundred analogical extensions of that central core; and beyond the penumbral area, still another belt of vagueness and imprecision, a host of possible cases and circumstances where there is really no answer to the question whether what we would have would be a case of warrant. What we need to fill out the account is not an ever-increasing set of additional conditions and subconditions; that way lies paralysis. What we need instead is an explanation of how the account works in the main areas of our cognitive life. It is to just such an explanation that we now turn.

3

Exploring the Design Plan:
Myself and My Past

Our project for the next six chapters or so is a whirlwind tour of some of the main modules of our epistemic establishment: self-knowledge, memory, perception, knowledge of other persons, testimony, *a priori* knowledge, induction, and probability. I make no claim to completeness; indeed, I claim incompleteness, and that in two different directions. First, I shall stick to modules about whose existence there is fairly wide agreement. As I see it, however, there are other main modules, modules whose existence is a matter of controversy: there is our way of knowing moral truths,[1] for example, as well as our means of perceiving beauty; and there is the *sensus divinitatis* of which John Calvin speaks, as well as what some theologians refer to as the Internal Testimony of the Holy Spirit.[2] Second, I shall make no pretense of completeness with respect to the modules I do discuss; such a pretense would in any case be all too easy to see through. An even reasonably complete account of self-knowledge, say, would require a book all by itself; and the same goes for the other main modules. Accordingly I do not aim at a systematic and complete account of these modules and their working: instead, I shall mention and emphasize those features of these modules that illustrate and elucidate the account of warrant I think correct, and those features of these modules about which it has something special to say. We may therefore take the next few chapters as suggestions for research programs.

I. Knowledge of Myself

When we think of self-knowledge, we often turn, in a Cartesian vein, to our knowledge that we *think* (for example, that we are appeared to a certain way, or that we hold certain beliefs, or that we are in pain [or not]) and that we exist. On many occasions we think we *know* that we are appeared to in a certain way (at the moment I know that I am appeared to in the way in which one is

[1]Here a most promising approach seems to me that of Michael DePaul in his "The Highest Moral Knowledge and the Truth Behind Internalism," forthcoming in *Southern Journal of Philosophy*, and "A Tragedy of Love, Not De Re," so far unpublished.

[2]I hope to give an account of these last two in the sequel, *Warranted Christian Belief*.

appeared to when looking at the screen of a computer); we think we know whether we are in pain (at the moment I know that I am suffering a mild eye-ache, no doubt induced by an excess of being appeared to in the way just mentioned) and we think we know at least something about what we believe. According to the Cartesian tradition, we have *privileged epistemic access* to these matters. Some say it is impossible to be mistaken about them; we have incorrigible knowledge of these matters, where S has incorrigible knowledge of a proposition *p* if and only if it is not possible that *p* be false and S believe it, and not possible that *p* be true and S believe −*p*. Others say, not that we have incorrigible knowledge here, but that we can have knowledge here by reflection alone; all you need to do to know whether you are in pain, for example, is think about it.

Here the tradition in question seems right. It is right, first, in holding that we have *knowledge* here. Some of our beliefs about how we are appeared to, or what we believe, or whether we are in pain have warrant, and indeed have about as much warrant as any beliefs we ever form. It looks to me as if there is a cup on my desk; I currently believe both that there is a cup on my desk and also that it looks to me as if there is. That latter belief, I think, has a great deal of warrant for me: I hold it with near maximal firmness, and (so at any rate I believe) it is formed by my faculties working properly in a congenial epistemic environment, with the triples of the design plan governing its production both aimed at truth and *successfully* aimed at truth. This tradition is also right in seeing some of this knowledge as incorrigible, or at any rate *nearly* so,[3] although the extent of incorrigible knowledge is meager at best.

The tradition is right, furthermore, in holding that we also know that we do indeed exist (although in order to know that welcome fact we need not infer it from our knowledge that we think). But do we know what sort of thing we are? Well, what sort of thing do we *think* we are? First, each of us finds himself with the belief that he has existed for quite some time (for most of us, at least several years; for some of us more years than we like to think). Second, each of us thinks (more accurately, takes it for granted) that he is conscious—more exactly, *intermittently* conscious. That is, I, this very being who I am, am now conscious, was earlier unconscious (as in deep sleep), before that was conscious, before that unconscious, and so on. (Here we are contradicted by David Hume, who says "When my perceptions are removed for any time, as by sound sleep, so long am I insensible of *myself* and may truly be said not to exist.")[4] Each of us, furthermore (and perhaps this is what is most remarkable about

[3] "Nearly so": perhaps it is not quite impossible to believe (attentively) that you are not in pain when you are; perhaps you are just barely in pain, so that your condition is hard to distinguish from a tickle. But it isn't possible when you are in *severe* pain to believe that you are not in pain. And perhaps it is possible to believe (attentively) that you are being appeared to redly when you are not; perhaps it isn't quite *redly* that you are being appeared to, but (say) pinkly or mauvely. But it couldn't be that you should believe that you are being appeared to redly when, say, you aren't being appeared to visually at all, but are instead being appeared to in some other sense modality—aurally, say.

[4] *A Treatise of Human Nature,* ed. L. A. Selby-Bigge (Oxford: Oxford University Press, 1978) Bk I, Part IV, Sec. vi, p. 252 (Hume's emphasis).

nd has been *aware of* himself, as well as of many other things; and it is
...is very being, who is now aware of the sun shining on the lilacs in my
backyard, who a moment ago was thinking instead about a Yosemite rock
climb, and who yesterday was paying attention to the student who wanted to
postpone his examination (pleading mental anguish due to failure to win the
Illinois lottery). Awareness (awareness of) is at the root of *intentionality,* the
property of being *of* or *about* something, of being *directed* at or upon or toward
something, of *intending* something. This property is displayed by belief, but
also by many other mental states: for example, anger, love, hatred, contempt,
admiration, worship, delight, amusement, lust.

What I believe on this head, of course, is that I myself, this very self, this
very person, have existed for quite some time and done these things. Here it is
hard to match the eloquence of Thomas Reid:

> I take it for granted that all the thoughts I am conscious of, or remember, are
> the thoughts of one and the same thinking principle, which I call *myself* or my
> *mind.* Every man has an immediate and irresistible conviction, not only of his
> present existence, but of his continued existence and identity as far back as he
> can remember. If any man should think fit to demand a proof that the thoughts
> he is successively conscious of, belong to one and the same thinking
> principle—if he should demand a proof that he is the same person today as he
> was yesterday or a year ago—I know no proof that can be given him: he must
> be left to himself, either as a man that is lunatic or as one who denies first
> principles, and is not to be reasoned with.[5]

He adds that "The conviction which every man has of his Identity, as far back
as his memory reaches, needs no aid of philosophy to strengthen it; and no
philosophy can weaken it, without first producing some degree of insanity."[6]
Part of Reid's point, I take it, is this. Any well-formed adult human being who
is in an epistemically congenial environment and whose intellectual faculties
are in good working order will typically take utterly for granted at least three
things: that she has existed for some time (for some years, say), that she has had
many thoughts and feelings, and that she herself is not a thought or feeling or
congeries of thoughts and feelings. ("Typically"; perhaps a person who comes
to reject these commonsense views by way of philosophical reflection need not
be subject to cognitive dysfunction.) Surely Reid is right here. Accordingly, if,
as seems likely, the modules of the design plan governing the production of such
beliefs are successfully aimed at truth, then (on the present account) such
beliefs will have warrant; if true and held with sufficient conviction, they will
constitute knowledge.

But might it not be, as Derek Parfit suggests, that "We Are Not What We
Believe"?[7] Perhaps people aren't at all what we ordinarily think they are. It is
logically possible that I should exist for a very brief time—a microsecond, for

[5]*Essay on the Intellectual Powers of Man.* From *Thomas Reid's Inquiry and Essays,* ed. Keith
Lehrer and Ronald Beanblossom (Indianapolis: Hackett Publishing Co., Inc., 1983), p. 154.
[6]*Ibid.,* p. 212.
[7]*Reasons and Persons* (New York: Oxford University Press, 1985). (Chapter 11 is entitled
"Why We Are Not What We Believe".)

example—displaying all the temporally specific properties I do in fact display at the present moment. (Of course I wouldn't then have such properties as being over fifty years old, or being responsible for something that happened ten minutes ago.) So say that a *person slice* is a person who exists for a micro-second or so. Perhaps there aren't any enduring persons, but only successions of person slices linked by appropriate causal relations and overlapping series of apparent memories. Perhaps a person slice is what (strictly speaking) thinks, believes, feels, and so on; perhaps what I refer to, when I refer to the appropriate thing that thinks, is a person slice, a thing that exists but for a moment. There is I, and all my successors, and all my predecessors; each of us exists just for a moment, the later slices often involving apparent memories: memories apparently of earlier properties of an enduring self, but actually of slices earlier in the series to which the given slice belongs. Or perhaps there aren't even person slices, if a person slice is a thing distinct from thoughts and feelings that *has* thoughts and feelings; perhaps there are only the thoughts and feelings, linked by relations of causality and resemblance. Couldn't these things be the case? More to the point, couldn't it be *both* that our experience be as it is *and* these things be the case?

Let us suppose for the moment that these things are possible, and compatible with our experience being as it is. (For the record, it seems to me quite impossible that there be thoughts without a thinker, though possible that there be person slices.) It is also possible that I am not a member of any such series of person stages but have popped into existence this very instant, complete with a complement of insistent but wholly false memory beliefs; it is also possible that I have existed for a thousand centuries but suffer from a peculiar sort of amnesia with respect to all but the last few years of this time; it is also possible that it is really your body that is mine, and that I am unaccountably deceived about the connections between me and this body, and so on. These things are indeed possible, and (in a way I shall explain) compatible with my experience's being as it is. But if these things are possible, and consistent with my experience's being as in fact it is, then should we not conclude that those common-sense views about ourselves have little warrant? Indeed, shouldn't we give them up? If we wish to be philosophically responsible, shouldn't we say, with Lichtenberg, "Es denkt"[8] rather than with Descartes (and the rest of us) "Je pense"?

Parfit thinks so. Considering the view that what I am is a persisting Cartesian ego, he says

> As Locke and Kant argued, there might be a series of such entities that were psychologically continuous. Memories might be passed from one to the next like a baton in a relay race. So might all other psychological features. Given the resulting psychological continuity, we would not be aware that one of these entities had been replaced by another. We therefore cannot know that such entities continue to exist. (p. 223)

---

[8]"*Es denkt* sollte man sagen, so vie man sagt: *es blitzt.*" Quoted in J. P. Stern, *Lichtenberg: A doctrine of Scattered Occasions* (Bloomington: Indiana University Press, 1959), p. 270. Clumsily translated: "One should say 'It thinks', just as one says 'It lightnings.'" (Of course one *doesn't* say 'It lightnings'; this epigram (like most) resists translation.)

And,

> We could not tell, from the content of our experiences, whether we really are aware of the continued existence of a separately existing subject of experiences. The most that we have are states of mind. . . . when we have had a series of thoughts, the most that we are aware of is the psychological continuity of our stream of consciousness. Some claim that we are aware of the continued existence of separate existing subjects of experiences. As Locke and Kant argued . . . such awareness cannot in fact be distinguished from our awareness of mere psychological continuity. Our experiences give us no reason to believe in the existence of these entities. Unless we have other reasons to believe in their existence, we should reject the belief. (p. 224)

A few lines down he adds, "My claim is merely like the claim that, since we have no reason to believe that water nymphs or unicorns exist, we should reject these beliefs." (p. 224)

How shall we understand Parfit here? He puts his point variously:

> We could not tell, from the content of our experiences, whether we really are aware of the continued existence of a separately existing subject of experiences. . . . when we have had a series of thoughts, the most that we are aware of is the psychological continuity of our stream of consciousness. . . . such awareness [of a persisting subject of experience] cannot in fact be distinguished from our awareness of mere psychological continuity.

Clearly there is sense to these claims; from one perspective they seem no more than the simple truth. I am now being appeared to in that tiger-lily way; and I *believe* that I am being thus appeared to. But I also believe something else, which perhaps we can approach as follows. Parfit speaks here of *experiences;* he speaks as if, among the furniture of the world, there are, in addition to (say) persons and material objects, experiences. So, for example, if I am now being appeared to in that tiger-lily way, then there is in this situation a tiger-lily appearance or experience. Now the idea that there are such things as *appearances* is problematic along several dimensions (dimensions that were extensively explored earlier this century); perhaps the truth of the matter is not that there exists a tiger-lily appearance but simply that I am being appeared to tiger-lilyishly, in a tiger-lily way. But suppose for simplicity we concede Parfit's point. Then I can state a further belief I have: I believe that I am being appeared to tiger-lilyishly, that I am aware of a tiger-lily appearance, but also that there is something—I myself—that is both aware of that tiger-lily appearance and that is *distinct* from it. (I am not identical with that tiger-lilyish experience.)[9]

Now consider this last belief. The point made by Locke, Hume, Kant, Parfit, and others is that there is a certain way in which this belief is not supported by my experience, or by the appearances I am now aware of, or by the succession of ways in which I am being appeared to. Hume is right: "For my part, when I enter most intimately into what I call *myself,* I always stumble on some particular perception or other, of heat or cold, light or shade, love or

---

[9]To put it in terms of the theory of appearing, there is something present (namely I myself) that is being appeared to in that way and that is distinct from that way (and any other way) of being appeared to.

hatred, pain or pleasure. I never can catch *myself* at any time without a perception, never can observe any thing but the perception" (*A Treatise of Human Nature,* p. 252; Hume's emphasis). Say that I am *directly* aware of something if I am aware of it and am not aware of it by way of being aware of something else; and again suppose for present purposes that when I am appeared to thus and so, then typically there is something, a thus and so appearance, of which I am aware. Then when I perceive the tiger lilies I am directly aware of a tiger-lilyish appearance; but I am not directly aware of myself.[10] My belief that there is a tiger-lily appearance is supported by my being directly aware of a tiger-lily appearance; but my belief that I am distinct from that tiger-lily appearance is not supported by way of my being directly aware of myself. I am also being appeared to in the way that goes with perceiving a squirrel; I also believe that the tiger-lily appearance is distinct from that squirrel appearance; and this belief is supported by my being directly aware of both of these appearances and noting that one is distinct from the other. But not so for my belief that I myself am distinct from each of these appearances. It is not the case that I am directly aware both of the appearance and of myself and note that one is distinct from the other.

We might perhaps suppose that it is *memory* by virtue of which I know that I am not identical with the present appearance. I remember being aware a moment ago of a squirrel appearance, and am now aware of a tiger-lily appearance. I reason as follows: if I were identical with the present appearance, then I would have been identical with that past appearance; but in that case the present appearance would be identical with the past experience; but that could be the case only if the squirrel experience had somehow *turned into* the tiger-lily appearance, which certainly did not seem to happen. So (the suggestion goes), even if I am not directly aware of myself, I *am* directly aware of some things such that propositions reporting those awarenesses immediately entail that I am not identical with present appearances.

But this reasoning is flawed. What I am directly aware of, at the moment, is the tiger-lily appearance and (at best) my *memory belief* that I was aware of a squirrel experience; from propositions reporting these things it doesn't relevantly follow[11] that I am not identical with the tiger-lily appearance. First, from the fact that I can't be identical both with that squirrel appearance and

---

[10]Perhaps we can put this same point in terms of the theory of appearing as follows: while there is such a thing as being appeared to redly, (or tiger-lilyishly), there is no such thing as being appeared to 'myselfly'. Of course the fact that one doesn't in this way stumble on oneself (when "entering most intimately into myself") doesn't give me the slightest reason for thinking there is no such substantial self of the sort Hume didn't stumble upon: such a substantial self would not be an item of consciousness, a bit of phenomenal imagery, like a mental image of a triangle, a way of being appeared to, or anything of that sort. And if we are (as I think we are) aware of ourselves, it is not by way of introspecting a bit of mental imagery; rather, I am aware of myself by forming the belief that it is I who am aware of the mental imagery, I who am being thus appeared to.

[11]I believe that the proposition *I am not identical with a tiger-lily appearance* (taken *de dicto* with respect to me) is a necessary truth; therefore it is strictly implied by every proposition and in that sense follows from every proposition. Of course this is not the relevant sense of 'follows from'; perhaps a first approximation at a more relevant sense for '*p* follows from *q*' would be '*p* follows from *q* by way of first-order logic' or '*p* follows by way of first-order logic from *q* together with utterly obvious additional premises'. This isn't quite correct, but this is not the place to go into the matter.

with this tiger-lily appearance, it just does not relevantly follow that I am not identical with the tiger-lily experience. Second, any appearance of plausibility for the claim that it *does* follow arises from the fact that one who offers the argument takes it for granted that it is I, this very thing, who am *now* aware of the one appearance and was *then* aware of the other appearance. In so doing she is of course doing no more than following nature's promptings; the memory belief (that I was aware of the squirrel appearance) already comes with a subject-experience structure; it comes as the memory that one thing—I—was aware of another thing: that experience. I don't merely believe by way of memory that there was a squirrel appearance: what I remember is that *I* was aware of such an appearance. But if I can't take my present belief—that I am aware of but distinct from a tiger-lily experience—at face value, how will it help to appeal to a memory belief that has the same structure? The second is no better off than the first. If I agree that what I should say about my present experience is "There is a tiger-lily experience," then I will find it hard to deny that what I should say about my past experience is "there *was* a squirrel experience"; but then my memory gives me no independent grounds for sup-posing that there is a persisting thing which (who) *was* aware of the squirrel experience and *is* (now) aware of the tiger-lily experience.

So Parfit is right: "the most that we are aware of is the psychological continuity of our stream of consciousness." More exactly, that is the most we are *directly* aware of. And of course we are not at any one time directly aware even of this; for we must rely upon memory for our awareness of past elements of our stream of consciousness and hence for our awareness of the continuity of that stream. But Parfit (along with his illustrious predecessors) draws a fateful inference from this fact. He concludes that we don't know and cannot justifia-bly believe that there is such a thing as a persisting subject of experience that is distinct from any of those experiences (and any aggregations of them):

> Some claim that we are aware of the continued existence of separate existing subjects of experiences. As Locke and Kant argued . . . such awareness cannot in fact be distinguished from our awareness of mere psychological continuity. Our experiences give us no reason to believe in the existence of these entities. Unless we have other reasons to believe in their existence, we should reject the belief.

Here, however, we obviously need additional premises. You might as well argue that since we are not directly aware of tiger lilies but only tiger-lily appearances, our experience gives us no reason to believe in the existence of tiger lilies; and unless we can come up with some other evidence we should reject the belief. You might as well argue that since a Cartesian demon could arrange things so that I would believe a false proposition with the same fervor that I believe $2 + 1 = 3$, I don't know that latter proposition; and if I can't find some other evidence, I should try to give it up. You might as well argue that since my experience could be just what it is even if I were the unlucky brain-in-vat victim of an Alpha Centaurian cognitive experimenter, I don't really know any of the things I think I know; so if I have no other evidence (and how could I?) I should reject those beliefs.

All of these inferences are regrettably hasty. Those arcane possibilities are indeed possibilities; they are also consistent with my experience's being as it is; but it doesn't follow that the commonsense beliefs in question have little warrant. It is entirely possible *both* that what Locke, Hume, Kant, and Parfit say here is true *and* that the commonsense beliefs in question have much by way of warrant—enough, even, to constitute knowledge. It is entirely possible both that what Parfit and his mentors say is true, and that we nonetheless *can* "tell, from the content of our experiences, whether we really are aware of the continued existence of a separately existing subject of experiences." I *can* tell "from the content of my experience" that there is a squirrel in my backyard, even if my experience could be just what it is and there be no squirrel there. My experience could be as it is and the belief in question false: but that is nowhere near sufficient to show that the belief has little or no warrant for me, or that it does not constitute knowledge for me. *Most* of my contingent beliefs are such that my experience could be just what it is but the belief false; how is it supposed to follow that these beliefs don't constitute knowledge? How does it follow that (even more alarmingly) I should try to give them up unless I can find some other evidence? We know that there are trees and flowers, even though our experience could be just what it is and there be no trees and flowers; we know that the world has existed for more than five minutes (and even that there was such a land as ancient Greece) despite the fact that our experience could be just what it is and those beliefs false.

On an adequate account of warrant, what counts is not whether my experience somehow *guarantees* the truth of the belief in question (and how *could* it do a thing like that?), but whether I hold it with sufficient confidence and whether it is produced in me by cognitive faculties successfully aimed at truth and functioning properly in an appropriate environment. If so, it has warrant; and if it is also true it constitutes knowledge—and this even if what Parfit and his mentors say is true. These conditions certainly seem to be met for such beliefs as that I have existed for some substantial stretch of time, and that I am neither an experience nor an aggregation of experiences. Therefore the question whether we know that we are persisting subjects of experience (distinct from those experiences) reduces to the question whether these beliefs are *true*. It would be of great interest to go into the question whether there is reason to doubt what we ordinarily believe here (I can't myself see that any of the usual arguments have any force at all); but I shall resist the temptation to make an excursion from the firm dry ground of epistemology into the misty miasmic morasses of metaphysics.

I conclude this section with a brief excursus in a different direction. We are all inclined to think that we are subjects of experience, distinct from those experiences; but we are also inclined to think that we are not identical with our bodies or even our brains. More exactly, what we are inclined to think are things from which it obviously *follows* that we are not identical with our bodies or brains. Thus we think it possible, in the broadly logical sense, that we should survive a rapid series of transplants in which each of our bodily organs—arms, legs, liver, stomach, lungs—should be replaced by a prosthesis, one made of some more durable and thus more suitable material, perhaps. And the same goes even for our brains; for it is natural to think it possible, in the broadly logical sense, that I should survive the following sort of brain transplant. First, the left half of my brain is very rapidly replaced by another left half that is in the same functional (computational?) state; then the right half is replaced in the same way; and the original right and left halves are destroyed. It is possible, in that broadly logical sense, that I should survive this operation, and indeed that I should remain fully clothed, conscious, and in my right mind (perhaps reading a current text on neurobiology) throughout the entire process. (It is also natural to think that it is logically possible that I survive the sort of operation in which the neurons are rapidly replaced, neuron by neuron, by other neurons in the same functional state, and similarly for rapid molecule-by-molecule and atom-by-atom replacements.) Further, these beliefs of ours—that the preceding scenarios are broadly logically possible—don't arise (so at any rate we ordinarily think) by way of cognitive malfunction or disorder, or because of wishful thinking or other cognitive processes not aimed at truth, or because of trade-offs and compromises. But then they have warrant; and if they do, then so does the consequent belief that I am not identical with my brain or with my body.[12] So when *I* think, what thinks is not a brain or a body. That is, *I* think, and I am not either my body or my brain; it could be, for all I can prove, that my brain or body *also* thinks. What is clear is that *I* think and (by the preceding argument) am not identical with brain or body, so if either of *them* also thinks, then there are at least two of us in the neighborhood who think.

Accordingly, I am not a body or a brain or part of a brain. Am I perhaps something more like a computer program? Many seem to take it utterly for granted that we stand to our brains and nervous systems as a computer program does to a computer. Various different computers can realize (run) the same program; and in the same way I could be realized in various different brains or bodies. Of course I would not be *identical* with any of those brains, any more than the program for my Macintosh SE is identical with that machine; what I am is a program suited to be realized in a variety of appropriate media.

But what, after all, is a computer program? Well, it seems to be a *series* of some kind, perhaps a series of instructions or, more abstractly, perhaps a series of zeros and ones. Of course a computer program *need not* be a series of zeros and ones: it could be a series of other shapes; and perhaps it need not be a series of shapes at all: perhaps it could be instead a series of properties or of still other objects. But at any rate a computer program is ordinarily thought to be a series of one sort or another; on the present suggestion, therefore, what each of us really is, is a series. But what is a series? Well, according to current mathematics, a series is best thought of as an ordered set—an n-tuple, in the finite case. There is some choice as to just which sets would be the members of a

---

[12]This is not to deny the possibility that we should discover powerful evidence, broadly speaking scientific evidence, for the conclusion that we really *are* identical with brain or body. At present there is nothing like even reasonably strong evidence for such a belief; but that is not my present concern.

series (there are various set theoretical constructions available here), but if we are computer programs, then presumably each of us is a *set* of some sort. In a widely quoted passage, David Lewis once said that he couldn't believe that he and his surroundings were a set of sentences.[13] I can go him one better: I can't speak for others, but I can't for a moment bring myself to believe I am a set of *any* kind.[14] People can be aware of trees and flowers; sets cannot. I know that $7 + 5 = 12$; no set knows any such thing. A person can decide to go to Chicago; no set can do that. (No doubt our mental life—like the natural numbers or Greek history—can be *modeled*[15] in various set theoretical structures; but that is not to say that what I really *am* is one of those set theoretical structures.) These beliefs, therefore—the beliefs that we are neither our brains nor our bodies nor computer programs—have a good deal of warrant for us.[16]

II. Memory

A. Phenomenology

"Memory," said Aristotle, in a flash of inspiration, "is of the past."[17] Fair enough, but how does it work and how shall we understand it? In one respect memory is wholly familiar, closer to us than hands and feet; in another it is puzzling *in excelsis*. How does it come that each of us has this window on the past? We will no doubt be told that present experience modifies the appropriate neuronal networks, storing patterns that can later be activated.[18] Indeed, some go so far as to say that nothing of what has happened to me is lost; all could be recalled to memory by the appropriate cerebral stimulation. Well, suppose this is true; how does it relieve the puzzlement or reduce the wonder? So the passage of time leaves traces in my brain; it does the same for the trees in my backyard, but *they* don't remember. What is the connection between these traces and my

[13]*Counterfactuals* (Cambridge: Harvard University Press, 1973), p. 86.

[14]And this would also dispose of the suggestion that what I really am is a series of *events*—neural or psychological events, perhaps.

[15]See my "How to Be an Anti-Realist," Presidential Address to the Central (then Western) Division of the American Philosophical Association, in *Proceedings and Addresses of the American Philosophical Association, 1982,* and "Two Concepts of Modality: Modal Realism and Modal Reductionism," in *Philosophical Perspectives, I, Metaphysics, 1987,* ed. James Tomberlin (Atascadero, Calif.: Ridgeview, 1987), pp. 213ff., in particular p. 218.

[16]Could it be that what I am is not a set, but (as Simmias suggests in the Plato's *Phaedo*) something more like a melody, perhaps a *pattern* of some sort? Perhaps a pattern of computational activity? I can't see how. First, patterns are no better than sets when it comes to knowing things, believing things, making decisions, and the like. And second, if I am such a pattern, then presumably I am the pattern exemplified in the computational activity of my brain. But I could have been associated instead with a wholly different pattern; that is, I could have existed, but been such that my brain exemplified a wholly different pattern of computational activity. (My mental or intellectual life could have been very different from what it has been.) But then I can't just *be* the pattern of computational activity my brain does in fact exemplify.

[17]*De Memoria et Reminiscentia,* 449 a 15, in *The Complete Works of Aristotle,* ed. Jonathan Barnes (Princeton: Princeton University Press, 1984), p. 714.

[18]See, for example, Daniel L. Alkon, "Memory Storage and Neural Systems," *Scientific American* (July 1989), pp. 42ff.

having or forming memory beliefs about the past? How do those traces so much as enable me to grasp or apprehend the notion of the past? And by what alchemy do they get transmuted into the beliefs I have about what has happened to me?

The *phenomenology* that goes with memory is remarkable and puzzling. I now believe that yesterday a friend gave me a box of raspberries. What there is here by way of phenomenology is a few scraps of sensuous mental imagery, something like a rudimentary and fragmentary case of being appeared to in the way in which one is appeared to upon perceiving a box of raspberries, or perceiving one's friend's face. But why should *that* incline me to form a belief about the past? There is nothing past-directed about imagery of raspberries or friends. Could it be (in a quasi-Humean vein) that it is precisely that scrappiness of the image, its lack of vivacity, wholeness, vividness, that makes it a memory, makes it refer in this way to the past? Surely not; under certain conditions of lighting or in a movie theater I can have that very sort of fragmentary, unvivacious imagery but form no beliefs whatever about the past. I can imagine getting a box of berries tomorrow; and this imagination is accompanied, so far as I can see, by the same sort of fragmentary, scrappy, indistinct sensuous imagery as my memory that I got one yesterday.[19]

Let's think a bit further about the sensuous imagery involved in the phenomenology of memory. I remember having seen Paul a year ago in California; there are scraps of imagery here, as of a wall he was standing before, as well as bright sunshine and blue sky. But I can't now clearly think what he looks like, and certainly don't have before my mind anything like a clear image or mental snapshot of him. I certainly don't remember that it was *he* I saw then on the basis of anything like recognizing Paul in some part of the sensuous imagery, perhaps noting that the imagery contains a part that looks a lot like an image of Paul. I certainly don't note the phenomenal imagery, and then see the resemblance to Paul, thus forming the belief that it is *Paul* I saw there in California. I no more do this than look into a given proposition to see that it is Paul

---

[19]Speaking of Hume, Reid says,

Now I would gladly know of this author, how one degree of vivacity fixes the existence of the object to the present moment; another carries it back to time past; a third, taking a contrary direction, carries it into futurity; and a fourth carries it out of existence altogether. Suppose, for example, I see the sun rise out of the sea. . . . One is apt to think, that this idea might gradually pass through all possible degrees of vivacity without stirring out of its place. But, if we think so, we deceive ourselves; for no sooner does it begin to grow languid than it moves backward into time past. Supposing this to be granted, we expect, at least, that, as it moves backward by the decay of its vivacity, the more that vivacity decays it will go back the farther, until it removes quite out of sight. But here we are deceived again; for there is a certain period of this declining vivacity, when, as if it had met an elastic obstacle in its motion backward, it suddenly rebounds from the past to the future, without taking the present in its way. And now, having got into the regions of futurity, we are apt to think that it has room enough to spend all its remaining vigour; but still we are deceived; for, by another sprightly bound, it mounts up into the airy region of imagination. . . . This article of the skeptical creed is indeed so full of mystery, on whatever side we view it, that they who hold that creed are very injuriously charged with incredulity; for to me, it appears to require as much faith as that of St. Athanasius. (*An Inquiry into the Human Mind*, VI, 24, pp. 99–100.)

that the proposition is about. The memory in question has a sort of intrinsic intentionality or aboutness; it *already comes* as the memory of Paul; it isn't that it is a phenomenal image that I then somehow *identify* as being of Paul and of him in California. (Remembering having seen Paul in California isn't *phenomenally* different from remembering having seen Paul in Arizona.) It is exceedingly hard to focus one's mind on this imagery, fleeting and fitful as it is. Furthermore, it seems to vary widely from person to person; and, as Wittgenstein never tired of insisting, it isn't essential to remembering. That is, there is no phenomenological imagery of that sort such that, necessarily, one remembers seeing Paul in California only if one undergoes that phenomenology. The imagery may be nothing more than irrelevant scraps of color, maybe the color of the orange shirt Paul always wears, or perhaps a half-formed image of his face: obviously that imagery is not necessary to memory. Neither, of course, is it sufficient: I may have the very same imagery when I don't remember seeing him at all, but simply think about him. In some people, indeed, memory seems to work with no sensuous phenomenology at all; it is more like a matter of feeling strongly inclined, upon being asked whether you saw Paul yesterday (or in some other way prompted), to believe a certain proposition: that you did see him.

What is more important than the accompanying sensuous imagery is a sort of sense of *pastness;* a memory comes as of something past. What is that sense of pastness, and how shall we understand it? Is there something about the memory—some phenomenal or more precisely *sensuous* feature—that I can note and on the basis of which I can tell that it is indeed a memory, and that it is about the past? I don't think so. A memory *comes* as about the past, or about something past (a past event, perhaps) in something like the way in which a belief about Sam comes as a belief about Sam. It has a sort of *past tinged* feel about it. This past tinged feel, however, is not something sensuous. It isn't at all like a mental image; it doesn't fall under the modality of any of the senses. This is of course at best a very unsatisfactory description: but what more can I say? Here I have no answer, nor any suggestion as to how to try to explain our grasp of this mysterious notion of the *past* in other terms.

Of course, there is more to a memory than a past-tinged belief. Your belief that North Dakota became a state in the late nineteenth century also has a past-tinged feel about it, but it isn't a memory. (It is no doubt right to say that you remember that North Dakota became a state in the late nineteenth century; but you don't remember that event in the way in which you remember that your friend brought you the box of raspberries.[20]) There is something more in the case of memory, something one can only call a distinctively memorial feel about it. One recognizes it as a *memory*, not something learned by testimony or in

---

[20]This is another of those analogical connections: you remember that North Dakota entered the Union in the nineteenth century (or that the capital of North Dakota is Bismarck); but all that is required for your remembering in *that* sense is your once having been told or otherwise learned the thing in question. It isn't necessary for you to have witnessed the event yourself. For memory in the primary sense you have to have perceived the event in question yourself, not learned of it by testimony.

some other way. There is something about the thought or belief in question that identifies it as a memory thought or belief: but it is exceedingly hard to describe it or say more than that about it. At any rate I am not succeeding in doing so.

So there is sensuous imagery, a sense of pastness, an aboutness with respect to the subject of the memory, and something like a recognition that it is indeed a memory. These are all part of the phenomenology of memory. But further, when I form a memory belief—that, for example, I had an orange for breakfast—I do not take the belief to be a part of myself; that is, I do not believe that I am a thing somehow composed of such things as this memory belief. I do not believe that I am an aggregate of such things, or a set of them, or a mereological sum of them. Not only do I not believe these things: I believe their denials; I take it utterly for granted that I am one thing and this memory another. Still further, what I remember is that *I* tasted that orange: that is, what I remember is that I, the very being now aware of the memory, earlier on tasted the orange. Here I suppose I could (in some sense of 'could') be wrong. It could be that it wasn't I but one of my predecessors in some series of person slices who tasted that orange; it could be that a mischievous Alpha Centaurian experimenter implanted this 'memory' in me. Still (rightly or wrongly), my memory comes as a memory that *I* did thus and so; *pace* Lichtenberg, it comes not as *es hat sich daran erinnert* but as *ich habe mich daran erinnert*. I don't remember just that there was tasting, but that *I* tasted; the memory comes as a memory of something *I* did, something done by the very person who is the subject of the present thought *I did that*. Finally, there is still another phenomenological feature of memory beliefs, as of other sorts of beliefs: the sense of rightness or fittingness of that belief on that occasion. There is a kind of attractiveness about the belief, or just possibly a feeling of being inclined, impelled toward it; it has a different feel from some other proposition you might try on in the circumstances. I entertain the proposition that it was a box of plums, not raspberries my friend gave me; entertaining this proposition somehow *feels* different from entertaining the true proposition that it was a box of raspberries, but about all we can say is that it just doesn't seem right. It lacks that sort of seeming to be right or acceptable or *true* enjoyed by the belief in fact delivered by memory.

I have been speaking of propositional memory, memory as a source of beliefs about the past. Of course, there are other sorts of memory, and these other sorts are connected, in interesting ways, with propositional memory. You remember how to do something—how to ride a bicycle, for example; you don't, even in exercising this memory, need to remember any particular proposition. The smell of sun screen or oranges can trigger memories of mountaineering, although not necessarily propositional memories. Instead you may remember what it looked like at a particular place on a particular climb, or you may instead remember a given mountain—Mount Baker, perhaps—without explicitly remembering any particular proposition about it. You also remember moods, emotions, ambiences. You can remember feeling lost and desolate when you were benighted on the lower saddle with no tent or bivouac sack, the temperature at 15° F. and a cold, ominous wind blowing in from Idaho; to remember that feeling you need not remember any particular proposition. A whiff of perfume can trigger a sudden, sharp, almost painful stab of awareness of someone you haven't seen for 20 years; but again, there need be no particular propositions involving her that you then remember. Naturally there will be many interesting and subtle connections between propositional memory and these nonpropositional varieties: to do the phenomenology of memory properly would require a whole chapter or a whole book; even if I were capable of giving such an account, there is no space for it here.[21]

Finally, there is of course an important connection between memory and my sense of my self as an enduring subject of experience. My thought of myself is of someone who has done and thought many things; and, of course, it is by virtue of memory that I know that I have done and thought these things. Says Reid, "The remembrance of a past event is necessarily accompanied with the conviction of our own existence at the time the event happened. I cannot remember a thing that happened a year ago, without a conviction as strong as memory can give, that I, the same identical person who now remembers that event, did then exist." It is of course my memory that is the source of my belief that I am a being that thus persists through time. I couldn't have anything like this sense of myself as a persisting object without memory. It is equally clear, however, that I couldn't have the sense of other objects—trees and houses, for example—as objects that endure through time without memory; for without memory I would not have the notion of time and its passage at all.

B. Memory Beliefs as Basic

Clearly my memory beliefs are typically formed in the *basic* way; that is, I do not reason to them from other propositions, or accept them on the evidential basis of other propositions.[22] If I see a blackbird in my backyard, I may form beliefs about its past by virtue of knowing something about how it usually goes with blackbirds: no doubt this one, like most, was hatched from an egg. But that is not how I come to the belief that what I had for breakfast this morning was an orange. I don't form this belief on the basis of such beliefs as that I often or always have an orange for breakfast; instead I just remember it. I do not ordinarily believe that I remember so and so (or that so and so occurred) on the evidential basis of the fact that it *seems* to me that I remember so and so. (Of course in special circumstances I could do something like that.) But while I do not form my memory beliefs on the evidential basis of beliefs acquired from other sources of belief, I may very well learn to *correct* my memory, in part on

[21]For an effort in this direction, see Edward S. Casey, *Remembering: A Phenomenological Study* (Bloomington: Indiana University Press, 1987).

[22]Tom Senor points out that memory beliefs depend, for their warrant, upon the warrant of *earlier* beliefs. I have an orange for breakfast; I *believe* that this is what I have for breakfast even as I am having breakfast; if this belief has no warrant, then my later belief that I *had* an orange for breakfast will also have no warrant. Memory beliefs are like testimonial beliefs (see pp. 83ff.): the warrant they have is dependent upon the warrant enjoyed by an earlier belief. But it does not follow that memory beliefs are not basic; they are not formed on the *evidential basis* of those earlier beliefs.

the basis of what I learn from other sources of belief. Perhaps you seem to remember that the fence surrounding the elementary school you attended was at least six feet high; you return years later, noting that the fence is only three feet high; you also learn by way of testimony that the fence has not been replaced; putting these things together with your belief (acquired partly by induction and testimony) that fences do not shrink with the passage of time, you conclude that you remembered that fence as higher than it was. Of course, even in thus correcting my memory I must rely upon memory: the testimony of memory is an essential element of my grounds for the belief that the fence I see before me is the same fence that I remember.

So I don't ordinarily accept memory beliefs on the evidential basis of beliefs solely about the present. This is fortunate, since it is exceedingly hard to see how there could be anything like an even reasonably decent noncircular argument, for me, from present phenomena to the truth of my memory beliefs. Bertrand Russell is right: it is surely possible, in the broadly logical sense, that the world should have popped into existence five minutes ago, complete with all its apparent traces of the past—all its dusty books, decaying buildings, mature oaks, crumbling mountains, and apparent memories. This is possible; more, it is compatible with my present experience's being as in fact it is.

No doubt someone will propose that the *best explanation* of these present phenomena is that there has been the sort of past I think there has been. Here I am, confronting present phenomena, including my inclinations to form these memory beliefs; and the best explanation, so the claim goes, of these present phenomena is that there has indeed been a past and that these memory beliefs are in fact true. So I have an argument for the conclusion that these memory beliefs are indeed true.

But can we take such explanations and inferences seriously? It will be agreed on all sides that we don't *in fact* make any such inference; young children apparently form memory beliefs in the ordinary way long before they have any ideas about explanations at all. But more important, the strength of such an argument is at best exceedingly doubtful. First, how do I know, prior to my knowing anything by way of memory, that these present phenomena *have* an explanation? By way of my knowledge that most phenomena (or most similar phenomena?) do? But so to think is to rely upon memory. Furthermore, one important question here (important with respect to this argument from apparent memory to memory) is whether I am *idiosyncratic* in these memory beliefs; if there are lots of other people, and only *I* have these alleged memory beliefs allegedly about the past, a better explanation might be that I suffer from some kind of pathology. But in answering this question about others I will also rely upon my memory: my memory of the claims and behavior of other.

Finally, how can I hold that whole explanation and argument in my mind at once? Descartes observed that for any but the simplest kinds of argument, one must rely upon memory for knowledge of the conclusion. You clearly and distinctly see that the present step follows from earlier steps S_4–S_n; but you have only your memory to testify to such facts as that earlier on you were able to see that S_4–S_n themselves followed from prior steps. This dependence upon memory holds even for such simple arithmetical calculations as that $24 \times 32 = 768$. (Of course you can record the steps of the argument in your notebook; but then you will rely on memory for the belief that it was *you* who wrote them down and that you intended them to be an accurate written record of the argument.) And the same goes here for this purported argument to the best explanation. It isn't possible (for most of us, anyway) to hold in mind at one time the relevant phenomena to be explained, the most salient half dozen or so alternative explanations, the reasons (if any) why these explanations aren't as good as the favored candidate, the reasons (if any) for thinking that there must be (or probably is) a good explanation of those phenomena, and finally the inference from the alleged bestness of the explanation in question to the truth of the memory beliefs in question. So an argument of this sort will have at most very little force. Perhaps it isn't necessary to declare it *totally* without force; perhaps it has a modicum of cogency; what is utterly apparent, however, is that the strength of such an argument is vastly incommensurate with the serene and unruffled confidence with which we hold memory beliefs.

Memory beliefs are therefore typically taken in the basic way, and that is nothing whatever against them. It is not as if they would have more warrant if they were inferred from beliefs about the present. So far, memory beliefs resemble perceptual beliefs (see pp. 93ff.). But there is a crucially important difference between memory and perception here; for perceptual beliefs are typically formed *on the basis of* the phenomenal imagery, the appearances. There will typically be a detailed mapping from the way in which one is appeared to, to the perceptual beliefs one forms. When I look at my backyard, I am appeared to in a highly detailed and modulated way; and the detail and modulation is reflected in the perceptual beliefs I form. Appeared to in one way, I form the belief *that plant's leaves are about six inches long;* appeared to in another way I form the belief *the lilacs are now long past their prime;* and so on. My beliefs are also responsive to changes in the imagery in a variety of complicated and subtle ways. I look in a certain direction, am appeared to in a certain highly detailed and articulated fashion, and form certain perceptual beliefs: I look in another direction, am appeared to in a different highly detailed and articulated fashion, and form other perceptual beliefs. We can go further: there is a similar mapping from the way in which one is appeared to, to the beliefs one *would* form in the perceptual situation in question, were they occasioned in one way or another. I am appeared to in a rich and variegated way; I may not be paying much attention and may not form much by way of explicit beliefs about what looks like what, which flowers are which colors, and so on; nevertheless there is a detailed mapping from the way in which I am now appeared to, to the beliefs I *would* form if for some reason I were to pay more attention. (Perhaps we could say that these beliefs or some of them are *virtual.*) But the same, obviously enough, is not true for memory. Many of us, apparently, don't display much phenomenal imagery in connection with memory at all; and in hardly anyone's case is there that detailed mapping from sensuous imagery to belief that goes with perception.

So we don't in fact form memory beliefs on the basis of beliefs about the present—beliefs about how I am being appeared to, for example; and there isn't available much by way of a decent inference from present phenomena to the truth of memory beliefs. But on an adequate view of warrant, this does not so much as slyly suggest that memory beliefs don't have or can't have a high degree of warrant for us. On the contrary: what counts for warrant is whether memory beliefs typically result from the proper function of our cognitive faculties in an appropriate environment, whether the function of memory is to give us true belief about the past, and whether the design plan in this area is a good one. But the fact is (as we all believe) these conditions are all fulfilled. Memory beliefs, therefore, have warrant. Furthermore, they are often held with great firmness. (There are few things I believe more firmly than that I had an orange for breakfast a couple of hours ago.) I conclude that memory beliefs often have warrant and often have a great deal of warrant; many of them, if true, constitute knowledge.

4

Other Persons and Testimony

I. Other Persons

Consider our beliefs about other persons. Consider, in particular, beliefs ascribing specifically personal states to them: being appeared to redly, or believing that Moscow, Idaho, is smaller than its Russian namesake, or intending to go to graduate school, or being confident about the outcome of a biopsy. My general questions are, Do these beliefs have warrant for us, and if so, How do they get it? As a matter of fact I am less interested in the first question than the second; like the rest of us, I take it for granted that they do indeed have warrant for us, warrant that is sometimes sufficient for knowledge. So the question is, How does this warrant acquisition work? How do our beliefs ascribing mental states to others acquire warrant? There are substantially three answers lurking in the contemporary woods: that they get warrant by virtue of (1) an analogical argument, (2) being or being like scientific theories or hypotheses for each of us, and (3) Wittgensteinian criteria. I shall consider each of these in turn, arguing that none is correct and suggesting an answer that is both closer to the truth and more in line with the general theory of warrant I propose.

A. *The Analogical Position*

1. *Mental State Ascribing Beliefs as Basic*

Now the traditional answer in the dominant epistemological tradition going back to Descartes and Locke is this: warrant acquisition works *via* some kind of analogical argument. Roughly speaking, I note correlations between my own bodily behavior (broadly construed) and my own inner or mental states; I therefore suppose that these correlations hold for others as well, thus ascribing mental states to them; this conclusion therefore has for me the warrant enjoyed by any proposition that is the conclusion of an inductive argument.

Thus John Stuart Mill:

> By what evidence do I know, or by what considerations am I led to believe, that there exist other sentient creatures; that the walking and speaking figures which I see and hear, have sensations and thoughts, or in other words, possess Minds? . . . I conclude it from certain things, which my experience of my own states of feeling proves to me to be marks of it. . . . I am conscious in myself of

a series of facts connected by an uniform sequence, of which the beginning is modifications of my body, the middle is feelings, and the end is outward demeanour. In the case of other human beings I have the evidence of my senses for the first and last links of the series, but not for the intermediate link. . . . Experience, therefore, obliges me to conclude that there must be an intermediate link.[1]

Mill apparently believes that as a matter of fact human beings (or at any rate Mill himself) are "led to believe" in others by analogical arguments. Here he might have done well to heed an anticipatory scoff by Thomas Reid:

No man thinks of asking himself what reason he has to believe that his neighbour is a living creature. He would be not a little surprised if another person should ask him so absurd a question: and perhaps could not give any reason which would not equally prove a watch or a puppet to be a living creature. But, though you should satisfy him of the weakness of the reasons he gives for his belief, you cannot make him in the least doubtful. This belief stands upon another foundation than that of reasoning and therefore, whether a man can give good reasons for it or not, it is not in his power to shake it off.[2]

Surely Reid is right: surely none of us actually comes to these beliefs in this sort of way. I look at Paul and say to myself "Oh, oh, he's furious again—what have I done this time?" thus forming the belief that he is furious again. Do I form this belief by way of a quick but tacit induction, an application of an analogical argument from premises involving the proposition that he looks a certain way, and when *I* look that way I am ordinarily furious? Clearly not. First (in analogy with the perceptual case [see pp. 93ff.]), it seems that I don't ordinarily form any belief (any explicit belief, anyway) at all as to how Paul is looking: I move directly to the view that he is furious. Perhaps I *could* form such a belief: but typically I don't. Obviously I don't form a belief consisting in a *qualitative*[3] description of how Paul looks and sounds ("his brow is knit; his eyes are narrowed to slits; his mouth is wide open; loud noises of such and such timber and pitch emanate therefrom"). And even if I did form such a belief, it would be far too crude to play the role of a premise in a decent analogical argument: any such description would fail to distinguish the way he looks from a thousand other ways that do not warrant the belief that he is furious. Of course, I could form what we could call for want of a better term a *haecceitistic* or *quidditative*[4] belief: I take a quick look at you; you look out of sorts; I look again, quickly but carefully, and form a belief I express to myself by saying, "Look out, she's got *that* look again" (where what I believe is not a qualitative proposition describing a certain look, but instead the sort of proposition that gets expressed by a sentence containing a demonstrative term); but in the typical case I don't do so.

[1]*An Examination of Sir William Hamilton's Philosophy* (London: Longmans, Green, Reader, and Dyer, 1878), p. 243.
[2]*Essays on the Intellectual Powers of Man*, in *Thomas Reid's Inquiry and Essays*, ed. R. Beanblossom and Keith Lehrer (Indianapolis: Hackett, 1983) VI, 5, pp. 278–79.
[3]See my "On Existentialism," *Philosophical Studies* (July 1983).
[4]Again, see "On Existentialism."

Furthermore, I ascribe to others a wide variety of mental states, making fine and subtle discriminations between rather similar states, often ascribing to them states I have seldom if ever experienced myself; how could I do this on the basis of simple analogical reasoning from correlations between behavior and mental states in my own case? As a matter of fact, much of the relevant behavior is such that I *can't* observe it in my own case: facial expression, for example, is extremely important,[5] and I typically can't observe what sort of facial expressions I am presenting to the world. Of course we have mirrors: but our ancestors, prior to the advent of mirrors, no doubt sometimes knew that someone else was angry or in pain. And we ourselves form these beliefs without adverting to mirrors; who among us carries one with him, or (when in the grip of strong emotion) remembers to consult it in order to establish correlations between his mental states and his facial expressions?

Accordingly, even if we do form beliefs about the mental states of others on the basis of what we know or see about their bodies and behavior, we clearly don't do so by way of an ordinary inductive inference from what we have observed in the past about the connection between such bodily states and such mental states in our own case. We don't form such beliefs on the basis of an analogical argument. None of us remembers ever having done that; small children apparently form beliefs about the mental states of their parents long before they come to the age at which they make inductive inferences. The capacity for this sort of belief formation is not something one gains by inductive learning but is part of our native and original cognitive equipment.[6] Of course, it is always open to someone to claim that the inferences in question are there, all right, but carried on at a subconscious level—just as the Freudian can claim, your indignant protests to the contrary notwithstanding, that you have always hated your father for preventing you from enjoying your mother's sexual favors. There is about as much plausibility in the one suggestion as in the other; but in any event I am willing to scale my claim down to the claim that we don't form beliefs about others on the basis of conscious inferences from conscious beliefs about their bodies and behavior. If our mental-state-ascribing judgments are not basic, if we do form beliefs ascribing mental states to others on

---

[5]Reid goes on:

> That many operations of the mind have their natural signs in the countenance, voice and gesture, I suppose every man will admit. . . . The only question is, whether we understand the signification of those signs, by the constitution of our nature, by a kind of natural perception similar to the perceptions of sense; or whether we gradually learn the signification of such signs from experience, as we learn that smoke is a sign of fire. . . . It seems to me incredible, that the notions men have of the expressions of features, voice, and gesture, are entirely the fruit of experience. (*Essays,* VI, 5, pp. 278–79)

[6]Indeed, tiny babies, presumably at an age at which they form little by way of beliefs of any sort, respond to human-face-like figures differently than to figures made of the same parts but scrambled. Fantz notes that "It also appears that some of the capacity to establish spatial relations is manifested by the visual system from a very early age. For example, infants of 1–15 weeks of age are reported to respond preferentially to schematic face-like figures, and to prefer normally arranged face figures over 'scrambled' face patterns. Shimon Ullman, "Visual Routines," in *Visual Cognition,* ed. Steven Pinker (Cambridge: MIT Press, 1985), p. 99, citing R. L. Fantz, "The Origin of Form Perception," *Scientific American* 204, no. 5 (1961), pp. 66–72.

the basis of beliefs about their bodily states, then at any rate it is not by way of ordinary inductive reasoning; there will be some other connection between the beliefs ascribing behavior and the beliefs ascribing mental states.

2. Analogical Arguments Examined

Here, no doubt, the analogical arguer will remind us that the genetic issue isn't the issue. The question is not, Are these beliefs typically taken the basic way? That is as may be; the question is whether these beliefs have warrant; and if they do, how do they get it? And the analogical position is that these beliefs have warrant because analogical arguments are *available* to us, even if in fact hardly anyone takes the trouble to form beliefs about others on the basis of such arguments. The analogical argument for other minds is not nowadays discussed with the fervor it was a couple of decades back. It is widely accepted (and accepted by first-rate epistemologists[7]), however, and, as we shall see in the next section, the sort of position that seems to have assumed its mantle is no improvement; so suppose we briefly look into its credentials.[8] It seems immediately apparent, first, that the *strength* of our convictions about the mental states of others is entirely out of proportion to the strength of the available analogical arguments. We all firmly believe, for example, that childbirth is often extremely painful, whether we have borne children or not; and the strength of our conviction is nowhere nearly matched by the strength of the relevant analogical arguments.

But do those analogical arguments have any appreciable degree of strength at all? A version of the argument may perhaps be stated initially as follows. First, I note a correlation between certain states of my body and certain of my mental states; then I argue as follows:

(1)   Whenever *this* body (that is, my body) is in state *S*, there is a person whose body it is and who is (for example) angry.

I then observe that

(2)   *B* over there (a human body distinct from mine) is in state *S*

and conclude that

(3)   *B* is a body of some person who is angry.

[7] For example, John Pollock: "Our knowledge of the mental states of others is based upon something like the traditional argument from analogy." He adds that "There can be no question of observing confirming instances of the correlation in the case of other people. The only basis I can have for extending the correlation to other people is that they are like me in many respects and hence it is reasonable to expect them to be like me in this respect as well." See Pollock's "How to Build a Person," in *Philosophical Perspectives, I, Metaphysics, 1987*, ed. James Tomberlin (Atascadero, Calif.: Ridgeview, 1987), pp. 137, 138. Pollock notes some of the shortcomings of the analogical argument (specified with respect to qualitative sensory states such as *being appeared to redly*). Sadly enough, he concludes that he never knows or has good reason to believe that other persons undergo such states.

[8] This section is a summary of a more extended discussion of these matters in my book *God and Other Minds* (Ithaca: Cornell University Press, 1967, reprint, 1991), chap. 10, esp. pp. 251–53, 262–67; for more detail, consult that work.

Since I am not angry, I conclude there is a person whose body is *B*, who is distinct from me, and who is angry.

Now the initial problem with this argument, of course, is that it appears to have an appallingly small sample class: its only member is my own body. According to a popular response, however, this objection is hasty:

> The objection that one is generalizing from a single instance can perhaps be countered by maintaining that it is not a matter of extending to all other persons a conclusion which has been found to hold for only one, but rather of proceeding from the fact that certain properties have been found to be conjoined in various circumstances. So the question that I put is not: Am I justified in assuming that what I have found to be true only of myself is also true of others? but: Having found that in various circumstances the possession of certain properties is united with the possession of a certain feeling, does this union continue to obtain when the circumstances are still further varied? The basis of the argument is broadened by absorbing the difference of persons into the difference of the situation in which the psycho-physical connections are supposed to hold.[9]

But this reply doesn't really help; if anything, it exacerbates matters. The chief problem with the argument thus revised is that there are parallel arguments of the same apparent strength for the *denials* of many of our most cherished beliefs about other minds.

We can see the problem as follows. As an analogical arguer, I don't initially know much about the general connections between bodies, behavior, and mental states. I don't know such things, for example, as that I feel pain only in this body, that no one else feels pain there, and that pain in bodies other than my own need not be connected with my behavior; these are the sorts of things I am supposed to learn from an analogical argument. The premises of a proper analogical argument, therefore, will be limited to what I know from introspection about my own mental states, what I know by perception about bodily states on the part of my body and other bodies, certain necessary truths, and what I can deduce from propositions of those sorts. As for such propositions as *when a person feels pain, her body will ordinarily display pain behavior* or *each person ordinarily has just one body*, these must be established by way of analogical arguments. Now it is obvious that I cannot determine by introspection or observation that a certain area of *your* body—your arm, for example—is free from pain, is such that no sentient creature feels a pain in it. The best I can do is note that *I* feel no pain there; but that does not show that *no one* does. And the same really goes for *my own* arm. As Wittgenstein quite properly observed, it is possible (in the broadly logical sense) that someone else should feel pain in my arm. Of course, we don't ordinarily think that others *do* feel pain in my arm, but that is precisely the sort of contingent truth that (on the analogical position) must be established by way of analogical arguments. I therefore cannot determine by introspection that no one feels a pain in my arm: as in the case of your arm, all I can do, along these lines, is to determine that *I* don't feel a pain there.

[9]A. J. Ayer, *The Problem of Knowledge* (London: Macmillan, 1956), p. 249.

The unfortunate fact, however, is that there is an analogical argument for the conclusion that every pain is in my body! For every pain such that I have determined (by introspection and perception), whether or not it was in my body, *was* in fact in my body. (I have never felt a pain in any other body.) I therefore conclude, and conclude quite properly, that probably every pain is in my body. You might object that as a matter of fact we don't think it possible that I should feel pain anywhere but in my body, so that the fact that I don't feel pain elsewhere doesn't prove much. No doubt you are right; on the analogical position, however, this fact is one we must learn by virtue of analogical argument; we therefore cannot use it to impugn *this* use of an analogical argument. Further, there is an analogical argument, for me, for the conclusion that every case of pain is accompanied by pain behavior on the part of my body (whenever there is pain, I engage in pain behavior): for (supposing, anyway, that I am a demonstrative sort) every case of pain such that I have determined whether it was accompanied by pain in my body *was* thus accompanied. I also have an argument for the proposition that whenever my body displays pain behavior, I feel pain; putting these two together, I conclude that whenever *any* sentient being feels pain, *I* feel pain—a nasty state of affairs indeed. I therefore have analogical arguments for such conclusions as that every pain is felt in my body and is accompanied by pain behavior on the part of my body, as well as for the doleful conclusion that whenever any sentient being feels pain, so do I. Of course, there will be similar arguments for such other mental states as anger, belief, and the like.

True, there will also be analogical arguments for the *denials* of these conclusions: but that just points up the weakness of the analogical position. Thus, for example, I have observed (in my own case) that pain behavior on the part of a body is accompanied by pain in that body: I note that B (a body other than my own) is displaying pain behavior; I conclude that this behavior is accompanied by pain in B (that is, that some sentient being is feeling a pain in B); since I feel no pain there, I conclude that sometimes there are pains that I don't feel. The problem is that there are analogical arguments *both* for the views we ordinarily hold about the general connections between mental and bodily states and other persons and their mental states, *and* for the *denials* of these views. The problem is that if the analogical position supports those ordinary views, it also supports their denials; hence it does not support those views. More irenically and more moderately, it does not support those views nearly strongly enough to justify the strength of our convictions with respect to them.

B. Beliefs about Others as Scientific Hypotheses

At present the analogical position is less popular than a sort of generalization of it: the view that our beliefs about other persons and their mental states are, or are like, *scientific hypotheses* for each of us. Each of us believes a host of propositions about other persons and about the connections between mental states, bodies, and behavior; and the idea is that these beliefs acquire the warrant they have by way of being, for each of us, elements of scientific theories. Each of us observes bodily behavior on the part of his own body and that of others; each of us also observes some of his own mental states.[10] Then, remarkably enough, each of us forms the conjecture (perhaps by way of a sort of inference to the best explanation) that perhaps there are other persons with mental states more or less like his own.

Now as an account of how we actually come to or form our beliefs about others, this is no more plausible than the claim that we come to such beliefs by way of analogical arguments. A child's belief, with respect to his mother, that she has thoughts and feelings, is no more a scientific hypothesis, for him, than the belief that he himself has arms or legs; in each case we come to the belief in question in the basic way, not by way of a tenuous inference to the best explanation or as a sort of clever abductive conjecture. A much more plausible view is that we are constructed ('hardwired' to use the current buzz word) in such a way that these beliefs naturally arise upon the sort of stimuli (being spoken to in 'motherese', for example) to which a child is normally exposed. But perhaps here, as in the case of the analogical position, the claim is not a broadly scientific claim about the genesis of these beliefs, but an epistemological claim about their warrant; and the claim is that they get the warrant they have by way of abductive inference, by way of being, for each of us, part of such a scientific theory.

But this can't be right—not, at any rate, if we *know*, as we think we do, that there are other persons who hold beliefs, are depressed, angry, exultant, who suffer pains, make plans, hope for the best, believe in God and a thousand other things. For clearly any such inference to the best explanation would be extremely tenuous. There are plenty of other explanatory hypotheses equally simple or simpler: for example, that the only minds or selves are mine and that of a Cartesian demon who, for reasons of his own, gives me these strong inclinations to believe in the existence of others. Alternatively, the only mind is mine; but by way of wishful thinking or projection or some other mechanism I come to believe that there are many other centers of consciousness like myself. These suggestions seem utterly fantastic; only a madman would believe them. But that is not because they are enormously inferior as scientific hypotheses to the views we do in fact hold; they are not. It is instead because, again, we are so constructed that the natural view, for us, is that there are others like ourselves. This view, then, is also mistaken; if our beliefs about others acquired the warrant they have by way of this abductive inference, they would have little warrant indeed.

C. *Criteria*

But of course there is no real reason to assume that if we do have knowledge of other minds, it must be by way of the traditional analogical argument or else by way of a sort of scientific inference to the best explanation. (Such an assumption is no more warranted than the corresponding assumption that if we have

---

[10]On a more radical version of this view, one's views about one's own mental states are also part of the same or another scientific theory.

knowledge of ordinary physical objects—tables, chairs, houses, mountains—it must be by way of some sort of inference from propositions about our own mental states to these conclusions.) There are other possibilities: for example, there is the Wittgensteinian suggestion that "inward processes stand in need of outward criteria."

Wittgenstein's notion of criterion has not wanted for critical scrutiny over the past three or four decades; it remains uncomfortably murky. I don't here have the space to examine the notion with the requisite care[11] or recapitulate the critical scrutiny; let us simply note its most prominent features. "If Mill has no criterion for the existence of feelings other than his own," said Norman Malcolm, "then in that sense he does not understand the sentence 'That human figure has feelings.'" On the other hand, "If he had a criterion he could apply it, establishing with certainty that this or that human figure does or does not have feelings (for the only plausible criterion would lie in behavior and circumstances that are open to view) and there would be no call to resort to tenuous analogical reasoning that yields at best a probability."[12] Here the suggestion is that (1) if behavior of a certain sort (call it pain behavior) is indeed a criterion for pain, then my observing pain behavior on the part of a person S tends to make evident for me the proposition that S is in pain. (*Tends* to make this evident—this tendency could be overridden by other circumstances.) (2) Although pain behavior on the part of S tends to make evident for me the proposition that S is in pain, this is not by way of analogical or inductive reasoning on my part. (3) My grasping that pain behavior is in this way a criterion for pain is a necessary condition of my understanding the sentence 'That human figure has feelings'; more generally, it is only because of this criterial connection, whatever exactly it is, that we are able to grasp the idea of others' having mental states, and can ascribe those mental states to them.

In explaining the "sense of 'criterion' which has become current through the influence of Wittgenstein's late work," Sydney Shoemaker suggested something similar:

> If so and so's being the case is a criterion for the truth of a judgment of identity, the assertion that it is evidence in favor of the truth of the judgment is necessarily (logically) rather than contingently (empirically) true. We know that it is evidence, not by having observed correlations and discovered empirical generalizations, but by understanding the concept of a ϕ. . . . The search for the criteria for the truth of a judgment is the search for necessarily true propositions asserting that the existence of certain phenomena or states of affairs is evidence of the truth of that judgment.[13]

Here the idea, I think, is as follows: where we come to learn *via* induction or abduction that As are associated with Bs, then we quite properly take the presence of an A as evidence that a B is present. We take smoke as evidence of

---

[11]See my *God and Other Minds*, pp. 212–44.

[12]*Journal of Philosophy* (1958), pp. 969–78; reprinted in *The Philosophy of Mind*, ed. Vere Chappell (Englewood Cliffs, N.J.: Prentice-Hall, 1962), p. 152.

[13]*Self-Knowledge and Self-Identity* (Ithaca: Cornell University Press, 1963), pp. 3–4.

fire; or to use an example of Reid's, on the basis of past experience we take a certain crunching gravelly sound to be evidence that a coach is coming up the drive. But of course it would be wrong to take smoke as evidence of fire if (ignoring testimony for the moment) we had not observed this connection between smoke and fire. We might say, here, that it is only *contingent* that smoke is evidence of fire; it is evidence only because (as we have discovered) there is a correlation (a correlation that is itself contingent) between the presence of the one and the presence of the other; in the absence of such a correlation the one would not be evidence for the other. Where the connection between the phenomena is *criterial,* however, things go differently: the criterion is evidence for that of which it is a criterion, *whether or not* we have discovered any such correlations. Indeed, in the typical case, there will not be any way of discovering such a correlation without using the criterion. So, says Shoemaker, that the criterion is evidence for the relevant proposition is a necessary truth rather than a contingent truth.[14]

Malcolm and Shoemaker (and Albritton and Strawson) apparently concur on the following. (1) For many mental states S, there are behavior-and-circumstances B that together constitute criteria: good (but defeasible) evidence for the mental states in question, so that in many cases we ascribe S to someone, and have warrant for so doing, on the basis of our awareness of B. (2) This evidence does not proceed by way of our observing a correlation between B and S. More generally, the warrant these ascriptions have for us is not by way of induction or abduction or analogical argument. Even if it is not possible to learn of the existence of these correlations without making use of these criteria, these ascriptions of mental states to others still have warrant for us.

So far Malcolm et al. seem to be quite correct; there *are* criteria or something like them, and the connection between them and the mental states for which they are evidence is not merely inductive or theoretical. They go on to claim, however, that the connection between B and S must somehow be *logical.* It must somehow be a *necessary* truth that B is evidence for S, that is, that someone who is aware of B has evidence for S; that is, that someone who is aware of B and forms the relevant belief about S (and has no undefeated defeaters for that belief) is such that the belief in question has warrant for him. And here there is a most interesting confluence between the Wittgensteinian criteriology rampant thirty years ago and post-classical Chisholmianism (see chapter 3 of my *Warrant: The Current Debate*): the former is best seen as a special case of the latter. The essence of post-classical Chisholmianism is the suggestion that warrant is to be explained in terms of the fact that certain epistemic pairs (that is, pairs whose first member is a belief B and whose second member is an evidence-base, a maximal psychological property diminished with respect to B[15]) simply have more by way of intrinsic value than others; and the greater this intrinsic value, the greater the degree of warrant

---

[14]See also Rogers Albritton, "Wittgenstein's Use of 'Criterion,'" *Journal of Philosophy* (1958), and P. F. Strawson, *Individuals: An Essay in Descriptive Metaphysics* (London: Methuen, 1959), pp. 105–6.

[15]See *Warrant: The Current Debate* (New York: Oxford University Press, 1993), pp. 48ff.

enjoyed by B for a person whose total evidence is the second member of the pair. Chisholm (and Brentano) hold, plausibly enough, that these relations of greater and less value among the pairs will be necessary: $<B_i, P_x>$ *has more intrinsic value than* $<B_j, P_y>$ will be necessarily true if true at all. The criteriological suggestion can be seen as a special case of this post-classical Chisholmian position. Put initially and crudely, the criteriological position goes as follows: consider those epistemic pairs whose evidence bases include awareness of pain behavior (and no undefeated defeaters for the ascription of pain) and where the first member of the pair is a mental-state-ascribing belief S: such epistemic pairs have a great deal of intrinsic value—so much that S has a good deal of warrant. And because this is really a claim about the relative intrinsic values of various evidence pairs, it is a necessary truth.

But isn't this a dubious contention? Why suppose it *necessary* that someone who is aware of pain behavior has evidence for the relevant ascription of pain? Perhaps those who make this claim are thinking along the following lines. Suppose we deny that the warrant-inducing connection between the behaviorial state of affairs B that serves as the criterion and the mental state ascribing belief S is *inductive* or *analogical* (or *abductive*); that is, suppose we deny that there is a good inductive or analogical or abductive argument for S from B; but suppose we also hold that we do believe S on the basis of B (and that when we do so, our mental state ascribing belief S has warrant). How can this be unless there is a logically necessary connection between B and S? If the connection is not inductive or analogical or abductive, what other possibilities are there?

Whatever the reason, however, the claim seems wrong. It is in fact true of *us human beings* that beliefs ascribing mental states to others have warrant for us, and don't have it simply by way of analogical or inductive or abductive evidence; it is in fact true that there are mental state ascriptions and behavior-cum-circumstance pairs such that the latter constitute evidence, for us, for the former. That is, I may have warrant for the ascription of a given mental state S by way of being aware of a certain behavior-cum-circumstance B even if it isn't possible to make a good (noncircular) analogical or inductive or abductive argument from B to S. But it isn't a *necessary* truth that B and S are correlated. We can see this as follows. First, quite different sorts of behavior could have been correlated with pain (or with anger or fear). When afflicted with pain, human beings cry out, or moan, or whine, or stoically grit their teeth; but no doubt we could have been so constructed that we would instead smile, or do a little dance, or stand on our heads. So suppose first that these correlations had in fact been quite different. Now of course properly functioning human beings find themselves inclined, when aware of B, to make the S ascription; but suppose further that we had been so constructed that (when functioning properly) we did *not* find ourselves inclined to make the S ascription upon being aware of B. Then, surely (under those conditions), it would not have been the case that someone who was aware of B had evidence for S. So it isn't necessary that anyone who is aware of B has evidence for S.

D. *Other Minds and Warrant*

But if the connection between *B* and *S* isn't either inductive or deductive, what is it? If neither the Millian analogical position nor the abductive scientific hypothesis position nor the Wittgensteinian criterial position is right, what is left? What other possibilities are there? From the present perspective on the nature of warrant, the answer is simplicity itself. The answer, first, is just that a human being whose appropriate cognitive faculties are functioning properly and who is aware of *B* will find herself making the *S* ascription (in the absence of defeaters). There is nothing in the least unjustified about such ascriptions; nor is there anything strange, odd, nonstandard about making them quite independently of any analogical or inductive or abductive arguments. Indeed, the pathology is on the other foot: it is the person who believes in others only on the basis of analogical arguments (and believes with a strength that matches the strength of those arguments) who is weird or nonstandard. It is part of the human design plan to make these ascriptions under those circumstances. It is part of the human design plan, in fact, to make such ascriptions with very considerable firmness; I may believe very firmly indeed that someone who has just suffered a shoulder dislocation and is holding his shoulder and moaning in that characteristic way is in pain. So if the part of the design plan governing these processes is successfully aimed at truth, then ascriptions of mental states to others will often have high warrant for us; if they are also true, they will constitute knowledge. This is so despite the fact that the epistemic connection between pain behavior and pain is neither inductive nor abductive nor deductive.

This is not to say, of course, that analogy plays no role at all in my knowing that someone else is in pain, or wishes he were home watching television, or is thinking about Vienna, or means *rabbit* by 'gavagai' rather than rabbit stage or undetached rabbit part or whatever.[16] Obviously we aren't born with the full

---

[16]Although it would take us too far afield to enter this area in detail, it is in this neighborhood that we can find a response to those, like Quine and Davidson, who endorse "indeterminacy of translation" and "inscrutability of reference." I learn the word 'rabbit'; the behavior and circumstances of my elders are compatible with that word's referring to *rabbits* or to *rabbit stages*, or *undetached rabbit parts*, or *either rabbits or elephants born after the year 2050*, or other whimsical Goodmanian constructions. What I learn, however, is that the word refers to *rabbits;* and my forming this belief has warrant despite that compatibility. That belief is the one a properly functioning human being in those circumstances would form. (See my chapter 7, pp. 130ff. for the parallel with induction.) If the belief is true, and if the parts of the design plan governing its production are successfully aimed at truth, then I *know* that 'rabbit' refers to rabbits, and that my elders and peers so use it. (There is no reason at all to accept the assumption that I could know this only if their behavior and circumstances are *not* compatible with the word's referring to those other things.) But then I can learn a foreign language in a substantially similar way; and the fact that the native's behavior and circumstances are compatible with their meaning all those variously different things by 'gavagai' doesn't show that I can't learn what it is that they do mean by it.

There is an interesting irony with respect to Quine's claims here. Roughly put, Quine holds that all there is, to meaning, is correlations between external stimuli and dispositions to verbal behavior. (See his *Word and Object* [Cambridge: MIT Press, 1960], chap. 2, pp. 72ff.) It then follows that we

complement of our highly subtle and sophisticated belief-forming procedures about the minds of others. The belief-forming procedures of an adult human being arise from a native complement of belief-forming mechanisms that (1) change and mature with time and (2) are modified by way of experience and learning—including, of course, learning by way of analogy with my own case. Precisely how this works—just what our inborn belief-forming mechanisms here are like, precisely how they are modified by maturation and by experience and learning, precisely what role is played by nature as opposed to nurture— these matters (fortunately enough) are not topics for this study. I mean only to argue that we can (and do) have warrant for beliefs ascribing mental states to others even if there aren't any good inductive or abductive arguments from premises of the sort to which the analogical arguer must confine himself to conclusions ascribing mental states to others.

A lurking skeptic may ask: isn't it possible that we should all be deceived here? Isn't it possible that I should have the very experience I do have and there be no other minds, or perhaps only one other mind, or many other minds, but not at all the sorts of minds I think there are? Couldn't I be a brain in a vat, the only survivor of an Alpha Centaurian intergalactic attack, kept alive by my captors for scientific purposes, and completely deceived about what sorts of other minds there are? Might I not be the victim of a Cartesian evil demon who delights in deception? Perhaps she and I are the only persons in the universe; she takes malicious pleasure in seeing what an elaborate and absurdly mistaken set of beliefs she can induce in me, how articulate and detailed a 'world' she can create for me; she delights in my naive simplicity, my thoughtless acquiescence in my natural belief impulses; and perhaps she sometimes adds a certain subtle piquancy by inducing in me the merest, most tenuous suspicion that in fact I *am* such a victim.

There is no need to declare these things impossible; indeed, they seem perfectly possible (in the broadly logical sense), if a bit farfetched. But nothing much follows. In particular it does not follow that no warrant is enjoyed by my beliefs ascribing mental states to other persons or my belief that there are many other human beings. Nor does it follow that I am unjustified in these beliefs, or that there is something irrational in my holding them. All that follows is that I don't have the sort of certainty Descartes sought. I don't have the sort of certainty (if indeed there could be any such thing) in which I can simply see (in a way that is somehow beyond the possibility of doubt or mistake) that things could not be otherwise than thus and so. In the present case, of course, my beliefs can be false, despite my best efforts. But that doesn't mean I don't have

---

can't distinguish the native's meaning *rabbit* by 'gavagai', from her meaning *rabbit state,* or *undetached rabbit parts.* But then of course we can't make these distinctions in our own case either; we can't distinguish *our* meaning *rabbit* by 'rabbit' from our meaning *rabbit part* or *rabbit stage,* or *either a rabbit or alien born after 2050.* As a matter of fact, if Quine's view were correct we would be unable to *see any difference* between meaning these things. But then how could we so much as state the thesis of the indeterminacy of translation? That thesis involves the claim that there are mutually exclusive and hence *different* (but nonetheless equally satisfactory) translations of the native's utterances.

knowledge of them; for while knowledge requires *psychological* certainty—or at any rate a high degree of belief—it is not the case that knowledge requires *Cartesian* certainty.

II. Testimony

A. *Testimony Characterized*

Another important source of belief is testimony, or teaching, or (to use Reid's name for the mechanism whereby we come to assimilate testimony) *credulity:*

> The wise author of nature hath planted in the human mind a propensity to rely upon human testimony before we can give a reason for doing so. This, indeed, puts our judgment almost entirely in the power of those who are about us in the first period of life; but this is necessary both to our preservation and to our improvement. If children were so framed as to pay no regard to testimony or authority, they must, in the literal sense, perish for lack of knowledge.
>
> I believed by instinct whatever they [my "parents and tutors"] told me, long before I had the idea of a lie, or a thought of the possibility of their deceiving me. Afterwards, upon reflection, I found they had acted like fair and honest people, who wished me well. I found that, if I had not believed what they told me, before I could give a reason for my belief, I had to this day been little better than a changeling. And although this natural credulity hath sometimes occasioned my being imposed upon by deceivers, yet it hath been of infinite advantage to me upon the whole; therefore, I consider it as another good gift of Nature.[17]

Reid's points here are worth emphasizing. First, the importance of credulity, testimony, to our entire intellectual enterprise is seldom sufficiently recognized. Testimony is the source of an enormously large proportion of our most important beliefs; it is testimony and learning from others that makes possible intellectual achievement and culture; testimony is the very foundation of civilization. The Enlightenment looked down its rationalistic nose at testimony and tradition, comparing them invidiously with science; but, without learning by testimony, clearly, science would be impossible. Newton stood on the shoulders of giants; indeed, every scientist must stand on the testimonial shoulders of others. Nearly all of what we know of the history of humanity or the structure of the universe we know by virtue of testimony; but it is also by virtue of testimony that I know such homelier items as what my name is and that I live in Indiana. You visit Armidale: you believe that it is indeed Armidale you are in, and that Armidale is in New South Wales. I have never visited Armidale and indeed have never ventured beyond the borders of Königsberg; but you rely upon testimony for your knowledge of those items as much as I do. You are also dependent upon testimony for your knowledge that New South Wales is in Australia (a fact you perhaps learned from a map or encyclopedia) and that there is such a nation as Australia.

[17]*Essay on the Intellectual Powers of Man,* in *Thomas Reid's Inquiry and Essays,* ed. R. Beanblossom and K. Lehrer (Indianapolis: Hackett, 1983), VI, 5, pp. 281–82.

Sigmund Freud, that Enlightenment figure born out of due time, offers an account of *religious belief* that, oddly enough, includes testimony as a special case: "Religious ideas are teachings and assertions about facts and conditions of external (or internal) reality which tell one something one has not discovered for oneself and which lay claim to one's belief." (Obviously testimony involves "teachings and assertions about facts and conditions of external [or internal] reality which tell one something one has not discovered for oneself and which lay claim to one's belief.") He immediately goes on to contradict this account of 'religious ideas' by claiming that what distinguishes religious ideas from testimony is that what you learn by way of testimony you can always check or verify for yourself, thus finding out whether what you were told is true.[18]

But surely this is Enlightenment optimism run amuck. Can I really discover, in a way independent of testimony, that in the fifth century B.C. there was a war between the Athenians and Spartans? Can I discover in this way that Plato was a philosopher? Or that the woman I take to be my mother really was? Or that I was given the name I think I was? Or that there is such a country as Australia? Indeed, the mayor of Armidale himself depends upon testimony for his knowledge that it is *Armidale* of which he is the mayor; and though a lifelong resident of Australia, he too depends upon testimony for his knowledge that Australia is the continent of which Armidale is a tiny part. You say: perhaps he just thinks to himself: "Armidale is a part of _____," where the blank is to be filled by his own name of the land he sees around him, land on which Armidale is obviously to be found. But if _____ is his name for Australia and is bestowed or introduced by way of the description 'the land around here' or 'the land I now see', the proposition *he* expresses by 'Armidale is a part of _____' is not the one *we* express by 'Armidale is in Australia'. To express the same or an equivalent proposition, his sentence would have to contain a name of *Australia;* and it is not easy to acquire a name of Australia on one's own. He might try to name Australia by picking it out with a definite description: 'the continent of which where I stand is a part' or 'the country to which this land belongs'; but of course it is only by testimony that he knows there *is* such a continent or country, or indeed any continents or countries at all.

We are therefore dependent upon testimony for most of what we know. Further, it is likely that most of our beliefs are such that the very possibility of our forming them is dependent upon testimony. For if there were no such thing as testimony, as a source of belief, then, in all likelihood, there would be nothing but the most rudimentary sorts of language. I don't mean to endorse Wittgenstein's enigmatic suggestions to the effect that it is impossible (in something like the broadly logical sense) that any person have a private language; that is as may be. (And the way it may be, I think, is at best inconclusive.) But it seems likely, as a matter of contingent fact, that language and testimony are mutually dependent phenomena in such a way that apart from testimony, there would be no language. And without the resources conferred by language we

[18]*The Future of an Illusion* (1927), trans. and ed. James Strachey (London: Norton, 1961), pp. 25, 26.

should have been unable to form any but a small proportion of the beliefs we do in fact hold.

Second, Reid is surely right in thinking that the beliefs we form by way of credulity or testimony are typically held in the basic way, not by way of inductive or abductive evidence from other things I believe. I am five years old; my father tells me that Australia is a large country and occupies an entire continent all by itself. I don't say to myself, "My father says thus and so; most of the time when I have checked what he says has turned out to be true; so probably this is; so probably Australia is a very large country that occupies an entire continent by itself." I *could* reason in this way and in certain specialized circumstances we do reason that way. But typically we don't. Typically we just believe what we are told, and believe it in the basic way. Of course, as Reid says, we learn to modify, qualify, modulate our native tendency to believe what others tell us: we believe certain people on certain topics but are skeptical of others on others. I believe you when you tell me about your summer vacation, but not when you tout on television the marvelous virtues of the deodorant you have been hired to sell. We learn not to form beliefs about a domestic quarrel until we have heard from both parties; we learn to mistrust pronouncements of campaigning politicians, lawyers arguing a case, and people with a strong financial interest in our believing what they tell us. Here, as in other cases, there is a complex and subtle interaction among sources of belief.

I say I *could* reason in the inductive way to what testimony testifies to; but of course I could not have reasoned thus in coming to the *first* beliefs I held on the basis of testimony. As Reid says, "if I had not believed what they told me, before I could give a reason for my belief, I had to this day been little better than a changeling." Perhaps the occasional great genius—a Leibniz, say, or an Augustine—could do better; but even they could do only a little better. Someone might say: "True, as a matter of contingent psychological and historical fact I can't learn what we learn by testimony by relying on induction and analogical reasoning; but now that I have reached the years of discretion with the help of others, I can reconstruct my noetic structure in such a way that I can retain all my knowledge but free it from reliance upon testimony. For example, I note that when I say 'That is a house' I express a proposition and express the proposition *that is a house*. So probably the same goes for others; they too express propositions when they utter sentences, and they too express the proposition *that is a house* when they utter the sentence 'That is a house'. But this is feckless; here the problems that bedevil the analogical argument for other minds return in spades. First, it is doubtful that I can know that my sentence expresses the proposition it does without already knowing something about how others use it. Second, supposing I could, there will be the same problem here as with the other conclusions the analogical arguer means to argue for: there will be similar analogical arguments for such dismal conclusions as that every sentence that has been used to express a proposition has been uttered or written by me, that anyone who asserts any proposition uses my body to do so, and so on.

So the warrant furnished by testimony isn't and couldn't be furnished by induction, analogy, and abduction. Testimony is an independent source of warrant for me; testimonial evidence is a basic sort of evidence for me. Is it, as Richard Swinburne thinks, *necessarily* evidence?[19] That is, is it a necessary truth that if I know that someone else has told me thus and so, then I have evidence (defeasible evidence) for that proposition, am such that (in the absence of undefeated defeaters) the proposition has at least some warrant for me? I don't think so. It is part of our design plan to learn from testimony; your telling me thus and so in fact gives me evidence for thus and so; but that this is so is not necessarily true. We, or to beg no questions, creatures like us, could have been so constructed that testimony would not furnish evidence at all. For example, we could have been constructed by a whimsical creator according to the following plan: (a) testimony is mostly false; and (b) we have an inclination to believe the denials of what we are told by others, and when we function properly, we do so. Then someone who believed *P* on the basis of testimony to *P* would be such that *P* has little or no warrant for him.

Or *is* this possible? Donald Davidson thinks it is "impossible correctly to hold that anyone could be mostly wrong about how things are."[20] He argues that in trying to understand the utterances of another human being, we must make the assumption that most of what she says is true; otherwise we will have no way at all of beginning the task of trying to understand her. Of course this doesn't show that most human beliefs are true; at best it shows something much weaker: that *in order to understand* someone, I must *make the assumption* that most of what she says is true. And (as Davidson asks) "couldn't it happen that speaker and interpreter understand each other on the basis of shared but erroneous beliefs?" The answer is this "couldn't be the rule":

> For imagine for a moment an interpreter who is omniscient about any sentence in his (potentially) unlimited repertoire. The omniscient interpreter, using the same method as the fallible interpreter, finds the fallible speaker largely consistent and correct. By his own standards, of course, but since these are objectively correct, the fallible speaker is seen to be largely correct and consistent by objective standards. We may also, if we want, let the omniscient interpreter turn his attention to the fallible interpreter of the fallible speaker. It turns out that the fallible interpreter can be wrong about some things, but not in general; and so he cannot share universal error with the agent he is interpreting. Once we agree to the general method of interpretation I have sketched, it becomes impossible correctly to hold that anyone could be mostly wrong about how things are.

Richards Foley and Fumerton point out that this argument has its problems: the premise appears to be

(1)   If there were an omniscient interpreter using Davidson's methods of interpretation, he would believe that most of what *S* believes is true,

[19]*The Existence of God* (Oxford: Oxford University Press, 1979), pp. 260, 272.
[20]"A Coherence Theory of Truth and Knowledge," in *Kant oder Hegel?*, ed. Dieter Henrich (Stuttgart: Klett-Cotta Buchhandlung, 1983), p. 535.

but the conclusion appears to be

(2)   Most of what S believes is true;

which does not follow from the premise.[21] (Of course, it *would* follow if, as the ontological argument concludes, it is a necessary truth that there is an omniscient being.) Foley and Fumerton conjecture (very plausibly, in my estimation) that Davidson is relying upon a further but unspoken premise:

(3)   Any proposition that is such that any omniscient being would believe it, is true.

They then point out that (3) is surely true if indeed there *is* an omniscient being, but need not be true if there isn't. Here they are right. Indeed, more can be said; as they point out, (3) is *necessary* for the proposition that there is an omniscient being, but in fact it is also *sufficient*. Clearly (and necessarily) one proposition any omniscient being worth its salt would believe is that there is an omniscient being. Hence Davidson's premises for his conclusion that most human beliefs are true also entail, as an unexpected bonus, that there is an omniscient being. This conclusion won't much disturb a theist, but there will be those (and possibly Davidson is among them) who may find it unsettling.[22]

No doubt there are better ways of arguing for the conclusion that it must be the case that most human beliefs are true; if so, I leave them to others. Reid makes a much more modest and more plausible claim. There is in us, he says,

> a propensity to speak truth, and to use the signs of language so as to convey our real sentiments. This principle has a powerful operation, even in the greatest liars; for where they lie once, they speak truth a hundred times. Truth is always uppermost, and is the natural issue of the mind. It requires no art or training, no inducement or temptation, but only that we yield to a natural impulse. Lying, on the contrary, is doing violence to our nature; and is never practised, even by the worst men, without some temptation. Speaking truth is like using our natural food, which we would do from appetite, though it answered no end; but lying is like taking physic, which is nauseous to the taste, and which no man takes but for some end which he cannot otherwise attain.[23]

Reid perhaps overlooks the fact that a habitual liar may come no longer to be able to distinguish truth from falsehood or to tell whether he speaks the truth or a lie; our natural tendency to tell the truth can be smothered by sufficient determination and practice. But surely there is in us a tendency of the

---

[21]"Davidson's Theism?" *Philosophical Studies* (1985), p. 84.

[22]This sort of problem is more widespread than you might have guessed. Following Peirce, Hilary Putnam takes *truth* to be what an Ideally Rational Scientific Community (IRS) would believe (*Proceedings and Addresses of the American Philosophical Association,* 1977, p. 485); but this entails that in fact there is (and indeed necessarily is) an IRS. See my "How to Be an Anti-Realist," *Proceedings and Addresses of the American Philosophical Association,* 1982, pp. 64ff. for details.

[23]*An Inquiry into the Human Mind on the Principles of Common Sense,* in *Inquiry and Essays,* ed. R. Beanblossom and K. Lehrer (Indianapolis: Hackett, 1983) VI, 24, p. 95.

sort of which Reid speaks. Equally surely, its presence is an essential part of the design plan for the human cognitive situation; were it not present, credulity or testimony could not properly perform its function of producing in us beliefs that are for the most part true. So when you tell me what your name is or that you are thirsty, then (if things are going according to the design plan) you believe that you are thirsty, you will indeed be thirsty, you will be telling me this in the hope and expectation that I will believe you, and I will in fact believe you. Here it is of the first importance, once more, to see that the design plan for our cognitive system does not involve us merely as individuals; our cognitive systems are designed to work together in a certain way. The human design plan is oriented toward a certain kind of cognitive environment: the sort of cognitive environment in which our faculties originally arose, whether by the hand of God or of evolution (or both). But from the point of view of the individual person, other people are part of the cognitive environment; the design plan does not cover my cognitive faculties in isolation from yours or yours from mine: as it applies to my faculties it presupposes that you and *your* faculties will function and react in certain ways.[24] So the design problem set God or evolution was less like that of designing a rocket ship for travel through as yet uncrowded interstellar space than that of designing an automobile for use in Mexico City, say, or Bangkok—except, of course, that the reciprocal reaction and interrelation is vastly subtler and more intimate in the case of our cognitive faculties than with automobiles, no matter how nasty the traffic.

On the present account of warrant, therefore, if you tell me what your name is or that you have just returned from Australia or that you own a Ford, I may thus acquire evidence for this belief and it may have warrant for me: it may be produced by my faculties functioning properly in an appropriate environment, with the segment of the design plan covering this belief acquisition successfully aimed at truth. Testimonial evidence is indeed evidence; and if I get enough and strong enough testimonial evidence for a given fact—for example, that there was such a thing as the American Civil War, or that London, England, is larger than London, Ontario—the belief in question may have enough warrant to constitute knowledge.

B. Testimony and Gettier Problems

But doesn't this interrelation and interdependence make trouble for my account? Being of a whimsical turn of mind, my parents intend to teach me mainly falsehoods about the geography of Scotland; fortunately for me, however, they suffer from a rare but well-defined malady that causes them to believe the denials of what *they* were taught about British geography, so that most of what they believe on that head is false. Although they wind up teaching me mainly truths about Scottish geography, these are not truths I know. You come into my office, show me the bill of sale and title made out to you for a new Ford, explain to me in confident and convincing tones that you now own a new Ford,

---

[24]Sartre was thus unduly pessimistic when he claimed that "Hell is other people." What he really meant, no doubt, was "The cognitive environment is other people."

take me for a ride in what you say is your new Ford, and all the rest; I form the belief, on the basis of your testimony, that you own a new Ford. The sad fact of the matter is that you don't believe for a moment that you own a new Ford; you are misinforming me as part of an initiation into the Elks Club. Unbeknownst to you, however, your uncle has just died and left you a brand new Ford. Then my faculties may be working perfectly in an acceptable environment in producing in me a true belief that I hold very firmly; but I surely don't know that you own a Ford.

In these two cases there is intent to deceive on the part of the testifier: but of course that isn't essential to these cases. Consider the young tribesman whose elders fill him with wildly false beliefs about the stars—the stars, they say, are pinholes in a giant canvas pulled over the sky every night to enable us to get a good night's sleep—with a few true beliefs tossed in (for example, that the stars are not made of wood). These true beliefs do not constitute knowledge for him. In these cases we may suppose that the cognitive faculties of the testifiee are functioning properly in the very sort of environment for which they were designed, and the segments of the design plan governing the formation of those beliefs on the part of the testifiee are in fact aimed at truth (rather than psychological comfort or survival of a disease or the possibility of loyalty and friendship); so why don't the beliefs formed have warrant? Why can't they have enough warrant for knowledge?[25]

What we have here are semi-Gettier problems.[26] (*Semi* because what Gettier problems really show is that *justification* is not sufficient for knowledge.) But just as the interrelatedness and interactions of our cognitive systems seems to provide the problem, so it provides the solution. The cognitive design plan, as I argued, applies not only to the individual cognizer and her faculties, but also to the whole cognitive situation in which she finds herself, including the cognitive functioning of other persons. In these cases the testifiee's beliefs lack warrant, not because of malfunction in *his own* cognitive system, but because of lack of warrant elsewhere in the chain leading to the belief he forms on the basis of testimony. The last item in this sort of epistemic chain has warrant only if the preceding items are formed in a way that accords with the design plan for the whole chain.

There is a sort of recursive structure here. Consider a chain of length two: you communicate to me a belief B by way of testimony. If B arises in you by way of cognitive malfunction, then B has little or no warrant for you and little or no warrant for me (although as I shall explain, I may be entirely justified in accepting it). Similarly, if B arises in you by way of proper function of cognitive processes not aimed at truth, then the belief has little or no warrant for either of us. (You are certain you will survive this disease; this belief arises in you not because of a sober and reasoned calculation of the odds but because of the

[25]Although the enormous complexity and articulation of the design plan for human beings is again brought out by the fact that in the case of testimony, the design plan appears to be aimed both at truth and also other states of affairs, such as the possibility of cooperative effort and psychological well-being.

[26]See chapter 2, pp. 31ff.

operation of the Optimistic Overrider (see p. 42); this belief has little warrant for you, and if you communicate it to me by way of testimony, it will have little for me.) Again, a belief may arise in you by way of perceptual illusion: I have come to North Dakota for the first time; the road ahead looks wet; I announce that it has recently rained a half mile up the road; you (who are otherwise occupied and don't look) believe me. Under these conditions my belief arises by way of perceptual illusion and hence by way of cognitive trade-off (pp. 38ff.); thus it has little or no warrant for me; and the same then holds for your belief acquired from me by way of testimony. In the chain of two members, therefore, the testifiee's belief has warrant only if the testifier's belief does.

Here we have the base case for a fanciful application of mathematical induction: and clearly enough, for a chain of greater length, the $n + 1$st member will have warrant only if the nth member does. But that means then, that the last item in such a chain has warrant only if the preceding items do. In some varieties of natural deduction logics, there is a form of inference some-times called 'Repetition': from A to infer A. Testimony, we might say, is a kind of interpersonal Repetition; and clearly there will be no warrant for the second occurrence of the belief unless there is for the first. It is also true, I think, (although I won't argue it here) that in the simplest sorts of cases the testifiee's belief has no more warrant than the testifier's. (I won't stop to explore what happens when I believe A on the basis of the testimony of *several* people, for whom A has widely different degrees of warrant, or where some tell me A and others not-A, or where some tell me not-A and others merely express doubts about A, and so on.) This exemplifies an important principle: to put it tech-nically, testimonial warrant, like water, rises no higher than its source. (Alter-natively: a testimonial chain is no stronger than its weakest link.)

Now we can return to the semi-Gettier cases. If, by virtue of cognitive malfunction, you form some belief or other and communicate this belief to me by way of testimony, then the belief has for me no more warrant than it has for you, despite the fact that there is nothing wrong with my cognitive faculties. In the case of the young tribesman, we may suppose that somewhere back along the cognitive chain this belief arose in such a way that it had little by way of warrant. Perhaps it arose out of sheer guess work, or perhaps it began its career in an imaginative bedtime story and its youthful auditor mistook it for intended sober truth, passing it on as such. As it was passed on, perhaps it was believed ever more strongly, gradually assuming the status of established and unques-tioned lore. But if it didn't originally have much by way of warrant, then it doesn't in the case of the young tribesman.

The Gettier cases involving lying and deception are slightly different and require slightly different treatment. Here the testifier doesn't accept the belief involved at all, but nonetheless testifies to it, the testifiee thus acquiring it. But obviously here too the belief in question (if it has no other source of warrant) will have little or no warrant; the belief in question has no warrant for the testifier, for the testifier does not so much as accept that belief. When the testimonial situation is going according to design plan, the testifier testifies to what he believes is true. The purpose of our cognitive nature is to furnish us with appropriate truths; one module or aspect of the design plan involves our learning from others, from our parents when we are young and from various appropriate others throughout our lives. But of course this plan will be successful only if those from whom we learn teach us truths.[27] And in the typical case, they will teach us truths only if they intend to do so, an intention sadly lacking in cases of deception.

The design plan for the whole situation, therefore, is such that things are proceeding according to the plan only if those from whom I learn by way of credulity intend to teach me the truth—and we must add, are not themselves deceived in some wholesale way incompatible with the design plan of the whole cognitive situation. The lack of warrant, however, is not (or need not be) by way of *malfunction* in the testimonial chain. When I lie to you, my cognitive faculties may be functioning properly (that is, there need be no cognitive malfunction)—just as the strangler's hands display no dysfunction in being used for that evil purpose. But then how shall we account for the lack of warrant? It is not a matter of malfunction; nor is it like the sort of case where the segment of the design plan governing the relevant modules of the system is aimed at something other than truth. Perhaps we must say something like this (at least for the simplest cases of lying): although the natural aim or purpose of our faculties is to produce true beliefs, certain aspects of the cognitive situation are under our control; some of our cognitive faculties are such that we can aim them in a different direction, use them for a different purpose. (In the same way, I can use my car as a battering ram, or an anchor, or a large paperweight.) When this happens, when the testifier employs the relevant segments of the cognitive system for, say, deceit or subterfuge, then on that occasion the testifier's intentions override the natural purpose of the cognitive modules in question. On that occasion their use is not (as it ordinarily is) aimed at the production of true beliefs but at something else—in this case, indeed, the production of false beliefs. And hence the belief formed by the testifiee has little or no warrant for him.[28] If it happens that when she lies, the testifier nonetheless unawares and unintentionally speaks the truth, the testifiee still does not know. Richard Foley points out that here there is something like a corrective to Cartesian individualism in epistemology; Cartesianism is skewed from the start by its focus on the solitary knower. *Justification* may be a solitary matter; it may be such that I can achieve it without reliance upon others; whether I am justified depends solely upon my own efforts. The same is not true for warrant.

[27]Here (as elsewhere) I of course oversimplify. My teacher tells me something she knows isn't strictly speaking true because I can't yet understand the strictly spoken truth and this is the best way to get me moving toward the condition of being able to understand it; her procedure, clearly, is not at all out of accord with the design plan. Here again, the design plan is exceedingly complex; an effort to state exactly how it goes in detail would take us very far afield.

[28]From a theistic perspective: God gives us cognitive faculties, but allows us to take a hand in their operation, and gives us the freedom to employ them for purposes other than their intended uses. (Of course, there are many perfectly proper uses of our cognitive equipment in addition to that of producing true beliefs: there is the whole realm of storytelling, poetry, fiction, art, play, humor, and the like.)

But doesn't it seem a bit peculiar to say that the warrant of your present belief (when it is acquired by way of testimony) may depend upon the degree of warrant that belief had for someone else, perhaps someone long dead, someone such that you have no way at all of discovering anything about his noetic structure? Can the degree of warrant your belief has depend in this way upon something by now wholly inaccessible to you? But where, exactly, is the problem? The warrant a belief has for you, after all, depends upon whether your faculties are functioning properly, a condition that may be equally inaccessible to you. A belief may fail to have warrant for you by failing to meet a condition of warrant, even if there is no way in which you could discover that that condition is not met. By virtue of cognitive malfunction, I believe I am Napoleon; this belief has little warrant for me, even though there may be no way in which I could find out that I am subject to cognitive malfunction.

So a belief on the part of the testifiee has warrant only if that belief has warrant for the testifier. There are further subtleties, some of which have been brought to our attention by Gilbert Harman. What if you acquire a belief by way of testimony but fail to note, later on, that the relevant experts have given it up? Does it still have warrant for you? Suppose you are a simple believer in Darwinian evolution. Suppose the experts become doubtful about Darwinian evolution, due to reflection on the spotty character of the fossil record. (It presents so few intermediate forms as to make it unlikely that anything much like Darwinian evolution occurred.) Suppose these doubts get communicated to nearly everyone around you, but by some fluke you continue to believe, somehow not hearing or heeding the doubts of the skeptics. Suppose, as it turns out, Darwinian evolution is indeed the truth. Did you know all along? Or was the warrant that belief held for you reduced by the fact that others (mistakenly) doubted? Here we must say, I think, that the answer is not clear; this is one of those penumbral borderline areas.

Where you lack warrant because of conditions in a part of the epistemic chain far removed from you, it is clear, of course, that you may nonetheless have *justification*. You may be perfectly within all of your rights; you may have been flouting no duties whatever; you may have been doing your level best to achieve the truth. (Given the semideontological tang of ordinary uses of 'warrant', we could put it paradoxically like this: you are entirely warranted in the belief in question, even though the belief has little warrant for you.) You may therefore have justification: you may have much more. For example, you may have post-classical Chisholmian justification: that is, the relation between your purely psychological properties and the belief in question may have as high a degree as you please of intrinsic value. More generally, you may be such that everything is going splendidly with respect to everything that is cognitively accessible to you in the way in which, according to the internalist, what confers warrant must be cognitively accessible.[29] Still more generally, everything involving your own cognitive faculties and your use of them may be going prop-

[29]See pp. 36ff.

erly. You may also be entirely rational and that in a fourfold sense: (a) in the sense that contrasts with someone's irrationally believing that he is Napoleon or that his head is a gourd or made of glass, (b) in the sense of Foley rationality, so that upon sufficient reflection you would think that forming this belief in these circumstances is a good way to achieve your epistemic goals, (c) in the sense that forming this belief in this way is following the dictates of reason, and (d) in the deontological sense of being entirely within your intellectual rights. All of this is compatible with the belief's having little or no warrant for you.

Testimony or credulity, therefore, is a crucially important part of our noetic arsenal; it is the foundation of culture and civilization. I conclude by pointing out two ways in which it is nonetheless a second-class citizen of the epistemic republic. First, testimony is ordinarily parasitic on other sources of belief so far as warrant goes. We have already seen a special case of this phenomenon: if you tell me what you think is false, then I don't know it even if you are mistaken and I meet the other conditions of knowledge. More generally, if you tell me something and I believe it on your say-so, I have warrant for it only if you do. To take an example of Steve Wykstra's: most of us who believe in quantum mechanics do so on the say-so of others; most of us have no independent evidence (independent of testimony) for the results of, say, double slit experiments. I may be entirely justified in believing as I do, on the basis of testimony, and in some cases (though perhaps not in this case) when I believe what I read in science textbooks I *know* what I come thus to believe. But I wouldn't have this knowledge if there weren't others in the neighborhood (that is, in the cognitive chain) who had nontestimonial evidence for the fact in question. As Wykstra says, if no one has nontestimonial evidence for the claim in question, then the whole epistemic community is in "big doxastic trouble." (And the kind of trouble is this: if no one has nontestimonial evidence for the facts in question, then none of our beliefs on this head has warrant, even though we are both justified in forming the beliefs and such that our faculties are functioning properly.)

In the typical case, therefore, if I know something by testimony, then someone else must have known that proposition in some other way. Of course, this condition isn't *always* met. Perhaps you and I and many others together map the coast of Australia: then I know by nontestimonial means that *this* bit has *this* shape; you know similarly that *that* bit has *that* shape, and so on for the rest of the members of our crew; we all know what shape the whole continent has, even though none of us has nontestimonial knowledge of the fact that it has that shape. The principle has to be stated more carefully to be correct; I leave this as a homework problem.

Second, in many situations, while testimony does indeed provide warrant, there is a cognitively superior way. I learn by way of testimony that first-order logic is complete, or that the continuum hypothesis is independent of ordinary set theory; I may thus come to know these things. I do even better, however, if I come to see these truths for myself, by understanding an appropriate argument, let's say.[30] You tell me that So and So was at the corner of Fifth and Broadway at midnight last night; I then have warrant for this belief, but not as much warrant as if I had seen him there and then myself. An eyewitness report carries more weight than a report from someone to whom the eyewitness told what he saw. Thus Sigmund Freud:

> I was already a man of mature years when I stood for the first time on the hill of the acropolis in Athens, between the temple ruins, looking out over the blue sea. A feeling of astonishment mingled with my joy. It seemed to say: "So it really *is* true, just as we learnt at school!" How shallow and weak must have been the belief I then acquired in the real truth of what I heard, if I could be so astonished now![31]

Testimonial evidence is indeed evidence; it is not always the evidence of choice.

---

[30]Although Charles Stevenson once remarked that beliefs about logic that he formed on the basis of testimony by W. v. O. Quine had a good deal more warrant, for him, than beliefs he formed on the basis of proofs he constructed himself.

[31]*The Future of an Illusion*, p. 25.

5

Perception

Much has been written about perceptual knowledge, and much of it is both penetrating and insightful. I have little to add; as a result, this will be the shortest chapter in the book. I shall simply point out a couple of salient features of the present account of warrant, as it applies to perceptual warrant.

I. Perceptual Belief as Knowledge

How shall we think about perception? And do we have perceptual knowledge, that is, do our perceptual judgments sometimes constitute knowledge? Well, from the present perspective on warrant, a perceptual judgment—that there is a squirrel running across my backyard, for example—constitutes knowledge if and only if (roughly speaking) that belief is true, sufficiently strong, and produced by cognitive faculties that are successfully aimed at truth and functioning properly in an epistemic environment that is right for a creature of my perceptual powers. Most of us take it utterly for granted, with respect to many occasions and many perceptual judgments, that these conditions are in fact met. If we are right, then on those occasions the perceptual judgment in question constitutes knowledge. It is not necessary that I *know* or *believe* that the above conditions obtain, in order for the judgment to constitute knowledge; I need not so much as consider that question in order to have knowledge. (Thus you can know that A without knowing that you know that A.) Nor is it necessary that the judgment in question be *certain* for us, or *infallible* for us; nor need it be *deducible* from what is certain or infallible. All that is required is that it meet the above conditions. Like nearly everyone else, I think many of our perceptual judgments do indeed meet those conditions: I therefore believe that many of these judgments have warrant, and have enough warrant to constitute knowledge.

Some have claimed, of course, that these conditions are rarely if ever met. Now I don't know how to prove to someone intent on denying perceptual knowledge that we really do have it. I don't know of any arguments that start from premises the perceptual skeptic already accepts sufficiently firmly (and

accepts more firmly than he accepts perceptual skepticism)[1] and proceed by
argument forms he also already accepts, to the conclusion that we do have such
knowledge. Prior to philosophical reflection, however, most of us assume that
many of our perceptual judgments do constitute knowledge and thus meet
whatever conditions are necessary for knowledge; this assumption is one of
those natural starting points for thought of which Richard Rorty says there
aren't any; and the rational stance is to accept it unless there are sufficiently
powerful arguments against it. As far as I can see, however, the arguments
against it are nowhere nearly sufficiently powerful. I don't here have the space
to canvass these arguments; let me say only that they invariably employ premises whose claims on us (as G. E. Moore pointed out) are vastly more tenuous
than the claims of the denials of their conclusions. Accepting perceptual skepticism on the basis of these arguments is a little like rejecting *modus ponens* on
the grounds that it figures in the derivation of the contradiction in the Russell
paradoxes: it does indeed so figure, but so do premises (for example, that for
every condition there exists the set of just those things that meet that condition)
that have vastly less claim on us than does *modus ponens*. The sensible route,
therefore, is to continue to take it for granted that many of our perceptual
judgments do indeed have warrant, and warrant that ranges all the way from
the minimum to near the maximum degree. I perceive a horse at 50 yards
through a fairly heavy fog; I form the belief that what I see is a horse; my belief
may have at best a moderate degree of warrant. The horse comes trotting up so
that I get a good clear look at him from 8 feet away: my belief that it is a horse I
see may then have a great deal more warrant, no doubt enough for knowledge
of that proposition.

   So the basic idea is that a perceptual belief constitutes knowledge (roughly)
if and only if the preceding conditions are met. But of course there are many
qualifications to be added. As we saw in the first chapter, I can have perceptual
knowledge—visual knowledge, let's say—even if my vision does not in fact
function entirely properly. For example, I can learn much about my environment even if I am extremely farsighted and can see next to nothing less than
three feet from me; I can have visual knowledge even if I can see only with the
help of outside aids that, as we say, "correct" my vision. What such aids
typically do is restore my visual system to the condition of proper function—
although what now functions properly is not (except in an analogical sense)
just my visual system, but my visual system together with these corrective
devices. And it need not be true that the prosthetic devices do no more than
restore my vision to proper functioning. Suppose my distance vision is bad;
suppose (by virtue of medical techniques not now available) a prosthesis is

---

[1] We can see that this condition is necessary as follows. Suppose it were not met; that is, suppose
I present the skeptic with an argument whose premises he accepts but accepts less firmly than he
accepts perceptual skepticism. Wouldn't he then quite properly use *modus tollens* rather than
modus ponens, rejecting one of those premises rather than his perceptual skepticism? Indeed, even
if he *knows* the premises he might still reject them, once he sees the connections between them and
perceptual skepticism; thus it is possible to reduce someone from a state of knowledge to one of
ignorance by giving him an argument he sees to be valid from premises he knows to be true.

implanted that improves my vision in such a way that I can focus on a distant scene and see it as clearly and in as much detail as through eight-power binoculars: the judgments I then form would of course have warrant for me. We can think of such cases as ones in which my visual system is extended and mildly redesigned: it now has a slightly different design plan; but the conditions for warrant are all still met.

Furthermore, I can compensate for what I know to be quirks or glitches in my perceptual system, so that even if I am color-blind, I may be able to tell what color the stop light is: a red light looks different from a green light, although neither looks red or green to me. (In neither case am I appeared to either redly or greenly.) In such a case, of course, it is clear that vision is not the only module involved; induction is certainly also involved, as (very likely) is testimony. I now have the power to tell what color the light is by taking a look at it; but I have had to learn by way of induction and testimony that when it looks like *that*, it is red. In the same way, I can have knowledge of this sort even if my cognitive environment isn't of the sort for which my faculties are designed. I take a trip to another planet; there elephants (or their analogues) are invisible but cause human beings to be appeared to in the trumpet-sounding way (see chapter 1, pp. 6ff.); but once I learn this fact, I can have perceptual knowledge (or something very much like perceptual knowledge) of the presence of those creatures.

II. Perceptual Experience

Experience, clearly enough, plays a crucial role in sense perception and in perceptual knowledge. First and most obviously, there is what we might call, appropriately enough, *sensuous* experience: in looking out at my backyard, perceiving grass, trees, sky, flowers, I am *appeared to* a certain way—greenly, or more accurately, greenly, brownly, bluely, redly, yellowly, and so on. Of course it is notoriously difficult to describe sensuous experience; in particular, the adverbial 'appeared to thus and so' locutions permit no more than a laughably inadequate description of it. My experience, upon looking at my backyard, is as of a complicated, reticulated, variegated, highly detailed three-dimensional manifold, with many different hues, shadings, and degrees of brightness, many different shapes and forms. There are degrees of salience, and of light and dark, there is foreground and background, there are degrees of distinctness and much else. It takes skill and training to describe how one is appeared to (skill and training I lack, as the previous couple of sentences demonstrate). Indeed, it takes skill and training to focus attention on one's sensuous experience, abstracting from beliefs about what is experienced, and paying attention only to that experience as opposed to the objects one perceives.

But there is also a different sort of experience involved. Upon being appeared to a familiar way, I may form the belief that I perceive a branch of a certain peculiarly jagged shape. Here there is, of course, sensuous experience;

but there is a sort of nonsensuous experience involved as well, an experience distinct from that sensuous experience but nonetheless connected with the formation of the belief in question. That belief has a certain felt attractiveness or naturalness, a sort of perceived fittingness; it feels like the *right* belief in those circumstances.[2] I try on a different belief: that what I see is, say, a small walrus. That belief *feels* different, somehow; it feels strange, inappropriate, wrong, wholly ridiculous. Is it that I feel a kind of *inclination* or *impulsion* or disposition to form that jagged branch belief, as opposed to the belief that I am perceiving a walrus, or the ocean?[3] That's not quite right: the belief is formed much too quickly and automatically for that; I don't experience anything like a push or impulsion. Indeed, is it the case that there is *any* experience that can properly be described as 'finding the belief in question attractive'? Perhaps not; perhaps that is not the way to describe the matter; still, there is *something* like that there, however hard to describe. (Where are the phenomenologists, now that we need them?) There is *something* in addition to the sensuous experience, some kind of an experiential reflection of the acceptance of the belief in the question. Is it just an experience of actually *having* or forming that very belief?

Alternatively, perhaps what we should say is not that there is an experience *of* forming or holding the belief in question, but rather a sort of phenomenal *accompaniment* of forming or having the belief in question. What is most important to see here, however, is that there is both sensuous experience and nonsensuous experience present in the typical perceptual belief situation—as, indeed, with memory beliefs, *a priori* beliefs, and others. There is at least the sensuous experience, the nonsensuous experience, and the belief formed.

Further (when things go right), certain kinds of sensuous and nonsensuous phenomena go with certain kinds of beliefs; others go with others. The phenomena accompanying perception are different from those accompanying memory, which in turn are different from those accompanying *a priori* belief. (*Remembering* that the Notre Dame cathedral in Paris has two towers *feels* different from *seeing* that it does.) And the connections between experience and belief are multiply contingent. First, one can have the sensuous experience without forming the perceptual belief at all: one can simply look at the scene and enjoy the play of sensuous experience, forming no perceptual belief at all, or forming what are at best partial or incipient beliefs.[4] Second, when I form a belief in response to experience, it isn't necessary that I form the belief I do in fact form, or any belief *like* that one. I look at my backyard and form the belief that the tiger lilies are now blooming. By virtue of cognitive malfunction,

---

[2]Recall that the same holds for memory; see pp. 58ff.

[3]As I said in "Positive Epistemic Status and Proper Function," in *Philosophical Perspectives, 2, Epistemology, 1988,* ed. James Tomberlin (Atascadero, Calif.: Ridgeview, 1988), p. 38.

[4]The idealistic coherence theorists of the last century (and they are joined by Brand Blanshard and Wilfrid Sellars of this) were inclined to deny that this sort of distinction could be drawn between perceptual belief and perceptual experience. Indeed, this is the only way to parry the otherwise crushing objection to a coherence theory of warrant, for *coherence* is a *doxastic* relation among *beliefs,* but *warrant* requires as well the right sort of relation between belief and *experience.* See my *Warrant: The Current Debate* (New York: Oxford University Press, 1993), chap. 4, pp. 81ff.

however, I could have the same sensuous experience but form a perceptual belief of a wholly different sort—that there are tigers in my backyard, for example. (We need not limit ourselves thus unimaginatively to *perceptual* beliefs: upon being appeared to in that way, I might, by virtue of malfunction, form the belief that the Taj Mahal is in Australia or that Goldbach's Conjecture is true.) Third, we could have such a thing as perception (or at any rate something like perception) without being appeared to in *any* sensuous way; we could have it without having perceptual experience at all. Indeed, this is not merely possible. There is the phenomenon called "blindsight," which "delivers true belief in—capacity to point to—the position of visual stimuli without either assent [that is, conscious belief] or visual sensation."[5]

Accordingly, logic (that is, broadly logical necessity) dictates little by way of what sort of sensuous and nonsensuous experience goes with what sort of belief. Proper function, of course, dictates much more. If (in my cognitive circumstances) I form the belief that I see a tiger in my backyard in response to being appeared to in that tiger-lilyish way, I display cognitive dysfunction. Cognitive health dictates a relatively narrow range of doxastic response to given sensuous experience (for a given epistemic context). When I am appeared to in the familiar way, I form the belief that I see a tiger lily; when appeared to in another familiar way, I form the belief that there are heavy and dark thunderclouds; it is only cognitive malfunction that would permit these two beliefs to be interchanged in those circumstances.

III. Perceptual Beliefs as Basic

When I am appeared to in that characteristic and familiar way, I form the belief that I see a tiger lily; but of course I don't ordinarily *infer* that I see a tiger lily from the belief that I am being appeared to in that way (together with other beliefs I hold); nor do I hold the former belief on the evidential basis of the latter. I do not first note that I am being thus appeared to, and then *reason* to the belief that I see a tiger lily—perhaps by virtue of a causal argument, or an inductive or abductive argument, or an argument of some other kind. Indeed, in the typical case I do not form a belief about my experience at all. It is wholly obvious, I suppose, that under these conditions we do not form beliefs describing the experience in question in 'qualitative' terms—thinking, for example, such a thing as that I am now being appeared to by way of a highly reticulated pattern of such and such a nature, color, hue, or shape: most of us who lack artistic training are quite incapable of forming such beliefs, or at least of forming beliefs of this sort with any sort of accuracy or completeness. (Although we can easily recognize our friends and distinguish them from each other on the basis of how we are appeared to, we can't give a qualitative description of the differences in those ways of being appeared to.)

[5]H. D. Miller, quoted in Thomas Natsoulas' "Conscious Perception and the Paradox of 'Blind-Sight,'" in *Aspects of Consciousness,* Vol. 3, *Awareness and Self-awareness* ed. Geoffrey Underwood (London: Academic Press, 1982), p. 91. For a book-length study, see L. Weiskrantz, *Blindsight: A Case Study and Implications* (Oxford: Oxford University Press, 1986).

Of course, I *could* form beliefs of the sort: *I am appeared to like that.* I see a mountain goat at four-hundred yards; I form the belief that I see the goat; I could also form the belief that I am being appeared to like *that,* where 'that' refers to the way in which I am then appeared to. I *could* form such a second-order, reflective belief; but in fact we don't ordinarily do so, being content with forming beliefs about the goat or the crag or ourselves. Some will suggest that I have a *virtual* or *dispositional* belief that I am being appeared to like *that,* meaning, perhaps, that if you had asked me or I had asked myself how I was being appeared to, I would have turned my attention to my phenomenal field and formed such a belief. Perhaps this is correct; but it doesn't follow that in fact I already had that belief at the time in question. (If you were to ask me whether someone was asking me something, I would form the belief that someone was asking me something; it does not follow that I believe, implicitly or dispositionally or in any other way, that someone is asking me something.) There is a difference between a dispositional belief that *p* and a disposition to believe that *p.* So we don't ordinarily form beliefs describing our experience when we form perceptual beliefs; *a fortiori,* therefore, we don't form the perceptual belief on the basis of a belief about experience. Instead, the belief in question is held in the *basic* way.[6]

Of course, if you ask me *why* I believe that I see a tree, I may cite my experience by way of reply; but it does not follow that I accept that belief on the evidential basis of the propositions I affirm by way of reply, that is, the proposition that my experience is of such and such a nature. For first, your question is ambiguous: I may take it as a request for my reason for thinking it is a *tree* that I see, rather than, for example, a large cactus. I could then respond by saying that it looks to me like a tree, not a cactus. (I could even report that the way I am appeared to is *treely,* not cactusly.) Alternatively, perhaps I interpret your question as a request for my reasons for thinking that I *see* a tree rather than, say, hear or smell one (perhaps it is a eucalyptus tree that is at issue). Still further, perhaps I take you as requesting that I give *you* a reason for believing that a tree is there. You can't see the tree; you have lost your contact lenses, or are sitting behind a large rock that obscures the tree, or perhaps you have adopted the folk remedy for hiccups and have put a brown paper bag over your head; I know that you believe that when I am appeared to treely, then there is nearly always a tree nearby. But of course in none of these cases does it follow that I believe the perceptual proposition on the evidential basis of a proposition about my experience.

Perceptual beliefs taken in the basic way, furthermore, have or may have very high degrees of warrant. I now believe that there are a couple of books on

---

[6]Basic beliefs, of course, are not necessarily incorrigible, or certain, or held more firmly than nonbasic beliefs. Having just calculated the product of 78 by 36, I believe it to be 2,808; I believe this on the evidential basis of such other propositions as that $6 \times 8 = 48$, $7 \times 3 = 21$, and the like. This belief, therefore, is not basic for me; nevertheless, I hold it more strongly than the belief that I once owned a red bicycle with balloon tires, a memory belief that I do not accept on the evidential basis of other beliefs and that is accordingly basic for me.

my desk, and I believe this nearly as firmly as anything else I believe; given the other conditions of warrant, this is something I know. The belief is a basic one, hence the warrant it has is not conferred upon it by way of an argument or inference from other propositions—propositions about how I am appeared to, for example; it gets its warrant, we might say, directly from the circumstances, including in particular my being appropriately appeared to. My being appeared to in that way under those circumstances (including the circumstance of proper function, and the other conditions necessary for warrant) is what confers warrant. My *having* that sort of experience in those circumstances helps confer warrant upon the belief in question; it does not acquire its warrant by being believed on the basis of propositions *reporting* that experience.

Here there is an important difference between classical foundationalism and the sort of Reidian view I mean to defend. According to the classical foundationalist, my perceptual belief has warrant only if it is accepted on the basis of *beliefs* about my experience, and only if those beliefs support it—deductively (as Descartes thought) or, more moderately, inductively (with Locke) or, still more moderately, abductively, with Peirce and others. But Reid's claim here— correct, as I see it—is that the belief can perfectly well have warrant even if it is not accepted on the basis of other beliefs at all; it can have warrant even if it is taken in the basic way. Furthermore, this belief can have warrant for me—even very high degrees of warrant—*whether or not it is evidentially supported by propositions about my immediate experience*. For it can be the case that my faculties are functioning properly (in the right sort of environment, and so forth) when I form that belief in the basic way, even if there is no good argument, deductive, inductive or abductive, from the character of my experience to the truth of the perceptual judgment in question.

Philip Quinn argues that if indeed I *do* have warrant for this perceptual belief taken the basic way, then I could as well have had warrant for it taken nonbasically, taken as an inference from a proposition specifying how I am being appeared to. He considers

(8)   I see a hand in front of me

and

(9)   It seems to me that I see a hand in front of me

and remarks that

> If the proposition expressed by (8) were indirectly justified by being properly based on the proposition expressed by (9), it would be no less well justified than if it were directly justified by being directly grounded in visual experience. Since, by hypothesis, my visual experience in those conditions suffices to confer a certain degree of justification on the proposition expressed by (8), the amount of justification that reaches the proposition expressed by (8) from that experience will not be less in those conditions if it passes by way of the

proposition expressed by (9) than if it is transmitted directly without inter-mediary.[7]

I venture to suggest Quinn has uncharacteristically erred. Our epistemologi-cal tradition going back to Descartes and Locke offers two quite different suggestions as to how a belief like (8) can receive warrant. On one of these suggestions (the majority opinion), such a belief gets warrant only if it is accepted on the evidential basis of other beliefs, in particular beliefs like (9) about immediate experience. On this view the warrant a perceptual belief acquires is conferred, so to speak, by virtue of warrant transfer from experien-tial beliefs. On the other view (the minority opinion) such a belief gets warrant for me just by virtue of being formed in the right circumstances; these circum-stances crucially include my *having* the experience in question (being appeared to in the way in question), but they need not and ordinarily do not include my *believing* that I have the experience in question. Furthermore, even if, in those circumstances, I *do* believe that I am being appeared to in that way—even if I do believe (9)—it isn't necessary, in order for (8) to have warrant for me, that I believe (8) *on the evidential basis* of (9). This is Reid's view, and (as I see it) the correct view. Our design plan permits and indeed calls for the immediate formation of those beliefs in those circumstances; it does not call for the formation of those beliefs on the basis of other beliefs about immediate experi-ence. If that part of the design plan is (as most of us believe) successfully aimed at truth, then these beliefs have warrant for us.

Now Quinn's suggestion, as far as I understand it, is that if a belief acquires warrant in the *second* way, that is, by virtue of being taken as basic in the right circumstances, then it could have acquired *equal* warrant in the *first* way—that is, by virtue of being believed on the evidential basis of other propositions recording the experiences involved in those circumstances. Of course, one who held this view would not suppose that (8) is believed *solely* on the basis of (9), but on the basis of (9) together with other propositions constituting back-ground beliefs: perhaps such beliefs as,

> (10)   Most of the time, when it seems to me that there is a hand present, there is indeed a hand present;

or

> (11)   My perceptual faculties are working properly and, most of the time, when someone whose perceptual faculties are working properly is ap-peared to in that way, she sees a hand.

And the suggestion is then that (8) could have received its warrant by virtue of being believed on the evidential basis of propositions like (9), (10), and (11).

---

[7]"On Finding the Foundations of Theism," *Faith and Philosophy* 2, no. 4 (October 1985), p. 478. The numbering of propositions (8) and (9) is from this article.

But this suggestion is true only if such propositions as (9), (10), and (11) are in fact good propositional evidence—inductive, deductive, or abductive—for such propositions as (8). More poignantly, the suggestion is true only if those propositions *themselves* have warrant for me; believing (8) on the evidential basis of propositions that *lack* warrant for me would confer no warrant on (8) for me. And how would these propositions—in particular, (10) and (11)—acquire warrant for me? The classical modern foundationalist suggestion, of course, is that such propositions get their warrant by being believed, ultimately, on the evidential basis of *other* propositions like (9)—other propositions relevantly about my experience—together with self-evident propositions. But then (8) can get warrant, by this route, only if there are some propositions that are either self-evident or appropriately about my immediate experience, and (together) evidentially support such propositions as (8), (10) and (11). Proposition (8) can get warrant, by this route, only if there are good arguments—deductive, inductive, abductive—from self-evident propositions together with propositions like (9) to propositions like (8), (10), and (11). But, as the history of modern philosophy up through Thomas Reid makes abundantly plain, it is at best extremely unlikely that there are any decent (noncircular) arguments—inductive, deductive, abductive—whose premises are self-evident propositions together with the appropriate experiential propositions, and whose conclusions are propositions entailing the existence of such things as tables, chairs, trees, and houses.[8] Reid was correct, I take it, in agreeing with Hume (as he understood Hume) that such beliefs as (9) do not in fact constitute (noncircular) evidence for such propositions as (8); if the latter get the warrant they have by virtue of being believed on the evidential basis of the former, then they have no warrant.

On the current view of warrant, however, it does not follow that such propositions as (8) have little or no warrant if taken as basic. For it could be that human beings subject to no cognitive dysfunction will typically form beliefs of the sort exemplified by (8) when they are in the sort of circumstances reported by (9). (Indeed, this not only *could be* the case; it *is* the case.) The other conditions of warrant, obviously enough, could also be met; but then the belief in question could have a good deal of warrant, even if it could not have had much by way of being believed on the evidential basis of such propositions as (9). But then (*contra* Quinn) (8) accepted on the basis of (9) might very well have vastly less warrant than (8) accepted in the basic way.

Quinn, indeed, has a sort of argument for thinking that (8) could have as much warrant if believed on the basis of (9) as if believed in the basic way: "Since, by hypothesis, my visual experience in those conditions suffices to confer a certain degree of justification on the proposition expressed by (8), the amount of justification that reaches the proposition expressed by (8) from that experience will not be less in those conditions if it passes by way of the proposi-

---

[8]In *Perceiving God* (Ithaca: Cornell University Press, 1991), chap. 3, William P. Alston gives a detailed and penetrating argument—the most detailed and penetrating I've seen—for the conclusion that it is impossible to give a noncircular argument from experience to ordinary perceptual judgments.

tion expressed by (9) than if it is transmitted directly without intermediary."
But here I think we must demur. The suggestion seems to be that if a proposition gets a certain degree of warrant by way of being formed in certain circumstances, then it would have the same degree of warrant if formed on the evidential basis of the belief that those circumstances do in fact hold. But why think that's true? Couldn't it be both that (a) propositions like (9) don't offer much by way of inductive, deductive, or abductive evidence for propositions like (8), so that if (8) were accepted on the evidential basis of (9) it would have little warrant, and (b) properly functioning human beings typically believe propositions like (8) when their experience is as (9) specifies, so that if the other conditions for warrant are satisfied, such propositions as (8) have much warrant for them when taken in the basic way? I say this could be the case; indeed, this *is* the case.

IV. Perceptual Beliefs Formed on the Basis of Experience

My perceptual beliefs are not ordinarily formed on the basis of *propositions about* my experience; nonetheless they are formed on the basis of my experience. You look out of the window: you are appeared to in a certain characteristic way; you find yourself with the belief that what you see is an expanse of green grass. You have *evidence* for this belief: the evidence of your senses. Your evidence is just this way of being appeared to; and you form the belief in question *on the basis of* this phenomenal imagery, this way of being appeared to. Here perception differs from memory. Phenomenal imagery accompanies memory as it does perception; but (as I argued—see pp. 63ff.) it would be wrong to say that memory beliefs are formed *on the basis of* such imagery. The imagery is more like an irrelevant accompaniment; the same imagery may go with a wide variety of different memory beliefs, and in some cases of memory, phenomenal imagery is absent. Not so, however, for perceptual beliefs. There is that detailed and highly articulate mapping from the character of perceptual experience to the relevant perceptual beliefs mentioned previously; and perceptual belief is minutely responsive to change in perceptual experience. I am appeared to in a certain way and form the belief that it is Paul I see before me; appeared to in a slightly different way (a way so slightly different that I can't describe the difference in qualitative terms) I form the belief that it isn't Paul but Peter who is there. You recognize your son's voice on the phone and can easily distinguish it from that of his friends; on the basis of being appeared to in that way you form the belief that your son is speaking to you. Again, appeared to in a slightly different way (a way such that you can't describe in qualitative terms what the difference is) you form instead the belief that it is your department chairman who is speaking to you.

But what makes it the case that a particular way of being appeared to—being appeared to greenly, say—is evidence for the proposition that I see something green? That is, why does *that* particular way of being appeared to confer warrant upon that belief? Why does my being appeared to in that way (as opposed to other ways) make that proposition evident for me? Is it a matter of probability, construed objectively in terms of frequencies or chances? Is it because on most occasions (in α, the actual world, as well as in appropriate nearby possible worlds) when I or someone like me is appeared to in this way, she is appeared to by something that is green? I don't think so; that's not sufficient. Suppose that whenever I am appeared to greenly, I am appeared to by something that is admired by the angel Gabriel: I would not automatically have evidence for the proposition that the thing before me is admired by the angel Gabriel. I would not have evidence for that proposition unless I had learned of the connection between something's appearing green to me and its being admired by Gabriel. But we don't have to learn of the connection between being appeared to greenly and there being something green present in order for the former to be evidence, for us, for the latter. This evidential connection is, as it were, built in; the other one must be learned.

Is my being appeared to in this way evidence for something green's being present because (as Fred Suppe suggests) it is *necessary in the circumstances* that I wouldn't be appeared to in that way if there weren't anything green present? Suppose we ignore the problems with this notion of necessity in the circumstances and pretend we have a firm grasp of it: we can easily see, I think, that this is also insufficient, and for similar reason. Perhaps it is necessary, in the circumstances, that I would not be appeared to in this way unless there were quarks present, quarks with a certain indefinable charm. It does not follow that I have evidence for the proposition that there are charming quarks present; for me to have that sort of evidence I should have to know something about the connections between being appeared to in the way in question with the presence of quarks.

Well then, what *does* make it the case that being appeared to greenly in this way provides me with evidence for the proposition that I see something green? How does it happen that this belief gets warrant for me under those circumstances? The answer is clear: this sort of belief formation under that sort of circumstance is dictated by our design plan. When our perceptual faculties function properly, when they function in accordance with our design plan, we form *that* sort of belief in response to *that* way of being appeared to. Given an appropriate epistemic environment and given that the module of the design plan governing perception is successfully aimed at truth, such beliefs will have warrant; when held with sufficient firmness, they constitute knowledge.

V. Nature, Nurture, and Perceptual Judgments

I turn finally and much too briefly to a topic already broached. Clearly there is much one must *learn* to perceive. It is not part of our original noetic endowment to be able to perceive that something is a tree, or an orange, or an automobile, or a human being; these are things we must learn to do. Perhaps it is part of my native noetic equipment (given sufficient maturity) to be able to see that something looks a certain way, that *that* thing looks so and so. But an orange, clearly enough, is not simply something that *looks* a certain way; it is not just something that looks the way oranges look. The fake orange in the supermarket bin (placed there by a wag with a juvenile sense of humor) looks like the real article, but it isn't. In order to be able to see that something is an orange, in order to be able to form the judgment *I see an orange* in the usual way, I must also know or take it for granted that *things that look like that* are oranges. A Maasai tribesman can't see that something is a 1986 Chevrolet, and someone just off the plane from Chicago can't see that a rhinoceros has recently passed by: in each case because a proposition of the form *Something that looks like that is a Y* is unknown to the unfortunate in question but known to those who *can* see those things. In the same way one must learn how to make perceptual judgments about things at a distance: at the age of six or so you learn that airplanes in flight and people viewed from the top of a high tower are not, contrary to appearances, much smaller than things nearby.

Our belief-forming processes and faculties, therefore, get modified by what we learn. The design plan specifies *how* they are to get modified; upon having the course of experience the Maasai tribesman has, he acquires the disposition to form the belief, when he sees that the underbrush has that peculiar crushed look, that a rhinoceros has recently passed by; he does not instead acquire the disposition to form the belief that a frog has hopped by. For my current beliefs to have warrant it is necessary that they be formed by faculties functioning properly, where this includes their having been modified in the way dictated by the design plan for the course of experience I have undergone.

But suppose you learn that something that looks like *that* is a dolphin, so that you can see that something is a dolphin: when you are then appeared to in that way and form the belief that you see a dolphin, do you then form it in the basic way? In order to be able to form the judgment that I see a dolphin, I must know such things as *Something that looks like that is a dolphin;* so do I really form the belief in question in the basic way? Or do I form it instead on the evidential basis of this knowledge that something that looks like *that* is a dolphin? Should we say that the perceptual judgments that are really basic for us are only ones like *There's something red* (*I see something that's red*) or *There's something that looks like that?* Consider what we might call 'perceptible' qualities: for example, being red, or in motion, or hot, or pointed, or smooth, or having such and such a shape: must we say that the perceptual judgments that are *really* basic are those that predicate such properties of objects, rather than ones like *That's a tree* or *That's a tractor?* And must we say that judgments of the latter sort are formed on the evidential basis of propositions of the form *Something that looks like that is a tree?* (or a tractor?)

Perhaps as a child you begin by seeing something that looks like *that*—that looks the way a tree ordinarily looks. Your mother (adopting the tone of feigned excitement mothers use) exclaims, "Tree!! That's a tree!!!" Perhaps you then associate with the word 'tree' the concept *something that looks like that.* (Of course, it isn't *necessary* that you associate that concept with 'tree'; it could be, for example, that you should instead associate with it the concept *something that looks like that and is perceived by me,* thus refusing to countenance the possibility that someone else should perceive a tree when you don't; but unless you are subject to some sort of cognitive dysfunction, you won't.) However, you don't yet have the concept *tree;* no particular way of looking is sufficient for being a tree; to be a tree a thing must not be made of papier-mache, for example, and must have the right sort of insides. Precisely what the concept of tree *is*—what properties it includes, for example—is a vexed question that I can't go into here; but in any event it includes more than looking a certain way. Later on perhaps you apply the word 'tree' to a papier-mache mock-up; you are then corrected; and the concept you associate with that word is then closer to the right one. In this way you acquire the concept in question in stages. And in this way you finally come to know that what looks like *that* is a tree. Similarly for perceiving an airplane, or people from a tower: at first (as a young child) perhaps I think they are very small; later I learn that they aren't, but just *look* small from that distance. And I learn this by way of a complicated interplay between testimony, perception, and induction.

Of course this does little to answer the question with which I began: do I, once I have learned how to perceive a tree or a dolphin or a mountain goat on a distant crag, make those perceptual judgments in the basic way? Or do I make them on the evidential basis of propositions about what such things as trees, dolphins, and mountain goats look like? Well, perhaps it isn't important to have an answer. Perhaps the thing to say is that such judgments as *That tree is at least 100 feet tall* are *partially* basic; they aren't formed *solely* on the evidential basis of other beliefs, but are formed partly on the basis of present perception and partly on the basis of beliefs about what trees at least 100 feet tall look like.

6

A *Priori* Knowledge

We know such items as

> 7 + 5 = 12,
> If all men are mortal and Socrates is a man, then Socrates is mortal,
> Whatever is red is colored,
> No one is taller than herself,

and (more contentiously)

> There are no things that do not exist,
> No object could have had a property without existing,
> No sets are either true or false.

But what is the nature of this knowledge? *How* do we know these things? A traditional answer is that we know them *a priori;* that sort of knowledge is to be contrasted with the way in which we know, for example, that

> It is now raining outside,
> The average annual rainfall in the Sonoran desert is about ten inches,

and

> I had an orange and oat bran for breakfast.

which we know *a posteriori.*

The distinction between these two kinds of knowledge and belief has a long and illustrious history; it goes far back in Western philosophy: back, of course, to Kant, and before him to Descartes, Locke, Leibniz, and other giants of early modern philosophy, but also much further back to Aquinas and Aristotle. The twentieth century, by contrast, has been distinctly inhospitable to the notion of *a priori* knowledge. It has decried this notion in a dozen ways, casting up many objections to it, many efforts to downplay its importance or in some other way disparage or belittle it. There is, for example, the linguistic theory of the *a*

102

priori, according to which, oddly enough, what we know *a priori* is somehow created by or dependent upon our linguistic behavior—"true by definition," perhaps, or such that "we won't permit it to be false."[1] There is also the view that all propositions we know *a priori* are analytic;[2] and there is the recrudescence of the Millian view that there really is not any *a priori* knowledge at all. These views have the glamor and allure of novelty; but when it comes time to tell the sober truth, they seem merely Quixotic—long on flash and panache, but short on good sense. There is no reason to look unfavorably upon that part of our cognitive nature that instructs us in necessities and possibilities. Or if there is, it is unusually well concealed. I don't have the space, here, to canvass these strictures; in what follows, therefore, I shall take it for granted both that there really is such a thing as *a priori* knowledge, and that it is important. Here I side with Aristotle: "Thinking and understanding are regarded as akin to a form of perceiving; for in the one as well as the other the soul discriminates and is cognizant of something which is."[3]

I. *A Priori* Knowledge Initially Characterized

But what *is* it for *S* to know *A a priori?* First of all, of course, it is for *S* to *believe A* and believe it *a priori.* Well then, what is it for *S* to *believe* something *a priori?* The tradition has characterized *a priori* knowledge negatively; what is known *a priori* is known, somehow, prior to or independently of experience. What is believed *a priori,* therefore, is believed (in that same way) prior to or independently of experience. But this needs qualification and clarification in at least two respects. First, the idea is not, of course, that a person could have *a priori* knowledge or belief prior to or without having any experience *at all.* The

---

[1]But how could it sensibly be thought that whether such propositions are true is up to us? No doubt it is up to us which proposition is expressed by, for example, 'if all men are mortal and Socrates is a man, then he's mortal', so that it is up to us whether that sentence expresses a true proposition. But how could anything we do be responsible for the truth of the proposition that sentence does in fact express?

[2]Again, analyticity on most construals seems to be a property of *sentences:* for example, according to Quine, a sentence is analytic if it can be reduced to a truth of logic by the substitution of synonyms for synonyms. If this is what analyticity is, however, the notion of an analytic *proposition* will not be coherent. (There's no such thing as substituting synonyms for synonyms in a proposition.) Of course we could say, with Kant, that an analytic proposition was one in which the subject contains the predicate. But (a) this view presupposes a certain way of thinking of propositions—a way in which they all have subject-predicate form; and even if some propositions do have subject-predicate form, there are many propositions known *a priori* that are not of that form. And (b) consider those that *are* of that form, and are alleged to be such that their subjects include their predicates: what is this *inclusion?* Here it is hard to find an account that is both plausible and not such that it simply reduces to (or is equivalent to) the claim that the propositions in question are necessarily true. But the original claim that all *a priori* propositions were analytic was supposed to be something of a *derogation* or *denigration* of *a priori* knowledge; the suggestion is that the importance of *a priori* knowledge is at best limited; if that claim turns out to be no more than the suggestion that propositions known *a priori* are necessarily true, the traditionalist can accept it with equanimity.

[3]*De Anima,* III, 3 427a 21.

initial idea, rather, is this: in order to know, for example, *If there were five passengers in the car and only three of them survived the crash, then two of them did not* one needs only the experience necessary to *grasp* or *understand* that proposition. One needs only the experience necessary to grasp the concepts or properties it involves, such as the properties of being a car, being a crash, survival, and the like. In the same way, to *believe* this proposition *a priori* one need only consider it. One need not be told it by another; and no particular experience is required, beyond experience sufficient to be enabled to *grasp* the proposition. This is in contrast with your believing the *antecedent* of that proposition. To believe *that,* in the typical case, merely considering it is not enough; ordinarily you will believe it only as a result of some perceptual experience, or the sort of experience that goes with learning it by testimony.

Second qualification: here we are speaking of *sensuous* experience. The idea is that the only sensuous experience necessary to know the proposition is the sensuous experience necessary to grasp it. In exploring memory and perception, we noted that there is more than one kind of experience lurking in the neighborhood. First, of course, there is sensuous experience: being appeared to redly, or roundly, or loudly, or fragrantly, and so on; when I remember that I met Paul in California, there is a sort of indistinct, hard-to-focus sensuous experience as of a fragmentary image—perhaps of Paul's orange shirt, or his orange hair, along with a similarly fragmentary image of bright California sunshine. But there is another kind of phenomenology that goes with memory: indeed, there are two other kinds. First, there is something like a sense of pastness; a memory comes with a kind of phenomenological feel to it, a feel that can only be described, unhelpfully, as a feeling of pastness. And second, there is that other kind of phenomenology that is equally hard to describe: the belief that it was Paul you met there in California somehow *feels like* the right belief. (You consider the proposition that it wasn't Paul but Eleanor you met there then: as a candidate for belief, that proposition feels strange, improper, incorrect, wholly wrong.)

The phenomenology of *a priori* knowledge or belief displays a similar structure. First, it is typically accompanied by a certain sensuous experience, even if that experience is not necessary to the formation of the belief. I consider the proposition *If all men are mortal and Socrates is a man, then Socrates is mortal.* There are bits of sensuous imagery present: perhaps auditory or visual representations of snatches of a sentence that expresses the proposition in question, or perhaps imagery associated with mortality and with being human. This imagery is not essential to the formation of the belief; it is more like a sort of decoration, and apparently it varies widely from person to person. Second, there is that feeling of rightness or correctness: considering or entertaining *If all men are mortal and Socrates is a man, then Socrates is mortal* feels different, somehow, from considering, say, *If all men are mortal and Lassie is mortal, then Lassie is a man.* The one belief seems right, compelling, acceptable; the other seems wrong, off-putting, and eminently rejectable; and this difference in experience is surely connected with our accepting the one and rejecting the other. This second kind of phenomenology or experience is not *sensuous* experience; it is not a matter of being appeared to in a certain way; it is instead a nonsensuous phenomenology that goes with all belief.

Is there still another kind of phenomenology distinct from sensuous imagery? Locke speaks in this connection of an "evident luster"; a proposition one knows *a priori*, he thinks, displays a kind of "clarity and brightness to the attentive mind." Descartes, as we learned at our mother's knee, speaks instead of "clarity and distinctness." He and others have carried the visual metaphor still further, speaking (as, for example, Aquinas, Descartes, and Locke do) of the *natural light of reason*. Indeed, we all employ such metaphors in this context: we find a comment *illuminating* or *enlightening;* we see the point of an argument; we see such truths as that every first-order theory with an infinite model has models of every infinite cardinality. What shall we make of this 'seeing'? Is there really a sort of semisensuous phenomenology, a sort of luminous glow, an evident luster (as Locke says) connected with seeing (for example) that *Socrates is mortal* follows from *All men are mortal and Socrates is a man?* The authority of tradition as well as our visual metaphors make it plausible to think so. When *I* introspect, however, trying to focus on the phenomenology involved in such cases, I do not find anything like a luminous glow, or brightness, or luster.[4] I note nothing phenomenologically like, say, clearly seeing the color of Paul's shirt (seeing it in sunlight, from up close, with an unobstructed view), or seeing sunshine on the grass or water. There is no actual luminosity or gleam. Assuming that I am not idiosyncratic, I suggest what goes on here is not really a matter of sensuous brightness, clarity, luminosity, or luster at all.

There is *something* phenomenological going on: but it isn't that sort of phenomenology; it isn't or isn't just a matter of sensuous imagery. You see that if every first-order theory with an infinite model has models of every cardinality, then any theory of the real numbers is bound to have nonstandard models; you see that first-order logic is complete; you see something much simpler and more evident, as that no dog is both an animal and a nonanimal: what does this 'seeing' consist in? It consists, first (I suggest), in your finding yourself utterly convinced that the proposition in question is *true*. It consists second, however, in finding yourself utterly convinced that this proposition is not only true, but *could not have been false*. When you see that $2 + 1 = 3$, you don't merely form the belief that this is indeed so; you also believe that it *must* be so, could not be otherwise. To *see* that a proposition *p* is true—in the way in which we see that *a priori* truths are true—is to apprehend not only that things *are* a certain way but that they *must* be that way. Reason is the faculty whereby we learn of what is possible and necessary.

But even this is not enough; clearly I might be convinced that a proposition is necessarily true without *seeing* that it is true. (Maybe I can't follow the argument, but believe you when you tell me that there can't be a set of all sets.) So what is it, then, to *see* that a proposition *p* is true? All I can say is this: it is

---

[4]This corrects what I said in *Faith and Rationality: Reason and Belief in God,* ed. A. Plantinga and N. Wolterstorff (Notre Dame: University of Notre Dame Press, 1983), p. 57.

(1) to form the belief that p is true and indeed necessarily true (when it *is* necessarily true, of course), (2) to form this belief immediately, rather than as a conclusion from other beliefs, (3) to form it not merely on the basis of memory or testimony (although what someone tells you can certainly get you to see the truth of the belief in question), and (4) to form this belief with that peculiar sort of phenomenology with which we are well acquainted, but which I can't describe in any way other than as the phenomenology that goes with seeing that such a proposition is true. We must add one further qualification. Suppose I suffer from a certain sort of malfunction, so that with respect to each of the first 25 natural numbers greater than 15, I form the belief that it is prime, also form the belief that it is necessary that it is prime, and in forming these beliefs am subject to the right kind of phenomenology. Then clearly I wouldn't really be *seeing* that, say, 23 is prime, despite the fact that it is true and meets the other conditions mentioned. One sees that p is true only if the relevant cognitive module is functioning properly.

I am sorry to say this is the best I can do by way of describing what it is to see that a proposition is true. To return to *a priori* belief, then: *one* way to believe p *a priori* is to see that it is true. That isn't the only way, however; for I can also believe p *a priori* if I can see that it *follows from* some proposition q that I see to be true—that is, see that it is necessarily true that if q is true, then so is p. To believe p *a priori*, therefore, it suffices to see that it is true, or to see that it follows from what you see to be true. But this isn't necessary: for you also believe p *a priori* when you only (and mistakenly) *think* you see that it is true. Before Russell showed him the error of his ways, Frege believed that for every property there is the set of just those things that display the property; and he believed that *a priori*. But he didn't see that it is true; it *isn't* true. So what is it to believe p *a priori*? Take the conditions severally necessary and jointly sufficient for seeing that p is true; to believe p *a priori* is to meet the set of those conditions minus the *truth* conditions—that is, the condition that p be true (in the case of seeing directly that p is true) and the condition that p follow from q (in the case of seeing indirectly that p is true).

All (so I assume, at any rate)[5] of what we know *a priori* is necessarily true.[6] Is this a necessary truth? Here we must make a distinction. God could certainly create (there could certainly be) creatures who knew contingent truths but did not come to know them by experience. Perhaps at a certain age they inevitably find within themselves a conviction that the velocity of light is an upper limit on velocities, or that there were 276 comets in the solar system in 1392; there is no reason why this belief could not constitute knowledge. Perhaps Alpha Centaurian superscientists (or God) have designed or redesigned their cognitive

---

[5]In "Naming and Necessity," in *Semantics of Natural Language,* ed. Donald Davidson and Gilbert Harman (Dordrecht: D. Reidel, 1972), p. 253, Saul Kripke argues that we can know *a priori* such contingent truths as *Stick S is one meter long.* Here I think he is mistaken; see my *The Nature of Necessity* (Oxford: Oxford University Press, 1974), p. 8.

[6]It is of course possible for *me* to know *a posteriori* what *someone else* knows *a priori*: this is how most of us know most of what we know about the more recondite reaches of mathematics— for example, that the continuum hypothesis is independent of ordinary set theory.

creatures in such a way that (when they are subject to no cognitive dysfunction) upon maturation they form powerful convictions of this sort. But would this be *a priori* knowledge of contingent truths? That depends. It could be knowledge with the right sort of independence of experience; and it could also exhibit two of the three kinds of phenomenology that go with our knowing something *a priori*—that is, it could display that faint and scrappy sensuous phenomenology, together with that sense of rightness or correctness. Perhaps it could also display the phenomenology that Descartes and Locke (incorrectly, as I said previously) describe in terms of luminosity, brightness, and luster. It would presumably lack, however, one important feature of *our a priori* knowledge in that it would not involve the conviction that the proposition known could not be false.[7] Whether it would be *a priori* knowledge, then, depends upon whether that notion includes having that conviction. More exactly, the question here is whether the term '*a priori* knowledge' expresses the concept of knowledge independent (in the right way) of experience, or whether it expresses a stronger concept: the concept of knowledge independent of experience accompanied by the conviction that what is known is necessary.[8] This is the sort of question to which there may be no answer; the thing to do is to note both concepts but bracket the question which concept is expressed by the term.

According to the tradition, the faculty or power by which one knows propositions of this sort is *reason*. The tradition was also inclined to distinguish two parts or aspects to reason, two subfaculties. First, there is *intuition,* by which one knows the truth of such simple propositions as $2 + 1 = 3$ and *If all men are mortal and Socrates is a man, then Socrates is mortal.* Intuition so thought of is not a sort of last ditch resort when you have nothing better to go on. It is not hunch or shaky guess. On the contrary; the fact is intuition is the source of what we know best. It is by intuition that we know that *modus ponens* is valid, that there aren't any things that don't exist, that if both of these two propositions are true, then at least one is, that $7 + 5 = 12$, and so on. An appeal to intuition of this sort is not a *weak* appeal; in many cases there isn't anything stronger one *could* appeal to. An *argument,* after all, would only transfer intuitive warrant from its premises to its conclusion.

The other subfaculty is *deduction,* by which one sees that one proposition—for example, *Something is wise—follows from* another, for example, *Socrates is wise.* Intuition, therefore, gives us the truth of certain simple propositions together with logical relations among them such as that one of them entails (or is consistent or inconsistent with) another. And the deliverances of reason include, in the first instance, both the propositions one sees to be true by intuition, in this *a priori* way, together with the logical relations one sees to

---

[7]Here I am indebted to Aron Edidin and Dean Zimmerman. God or Alpha Centaurian super-scientists could design cognizers that *did* undergo that phenomenology in connection with (true) contingent propositions: would such creatures have *a priori* knowledge of those contingent propositions, despite their mistakenly thinking them necessary? I should think so: no doubt I know that $2 + 1 = 3$ even if, contrary to what I believe, Mill is right in supposing that proposition contingently true.

[8]Here I am indebted for correction to Dean Zimmerman and Aron Edidin.

hold among propositions. But the deliverances of reason extend further: there is also what can be seen to follow from what one sees to be true, as when you follow a complicated proof or argument. We might say (recursively) that the deliverances of reason consist of those propositions we can know by way of intuition together with propositions that follow by deduction from deliverances of reason—that is, are such that by way of the subfaculty of deduction we can see that they are entailed by them. Of course you might not be able to know *all* the deliverances of reason by reason alone. As Descartes pointed out, if you can't keep the whole argument—premises, conclusion, and the connections between them—in mind at once, then the conclusion is not something you know just by reason; you also depend at least upon memory.[9]

II. *A Priori* Knowledge Is Knowledge

On the account of warrant I propose, what we believe *a priori* often constitutes knowledge, as in the case of simple arithmetic, elementary logic, and the like. For here, as I assume, our cognitive faculties are indeed functioning properly in producing these beliefs in us, the purpose of the faculties or powers involved is to produce true beliefs, and so on for the remaining conditions of warrant. The proper functioning clause is essential here. I come to believe a necessarily true proposition and enjoy an accompanying phenomenology of the sort that goes with my grasping the truth of, say, the corresponding conditional of *modus ponens*. Will that be sufficient for my knowing that it is true, for that belief's having a substantial degree of warrant for me? No. Suppose my cognitive faculties are redesigned by an Alpha Centaurian superscientist in an experimental mood; he modifies them in such a way that when I consider any proposition of the sort *n is prime* (where *n* is any of the first 10,000 natural numbers), it has for me the very appearance of necessity enjoyed by even the most elementary of elementary truths of arithmetic. I form the belief that *n* is prime, for some fairly large number *n* less than 10,000; chances are I form a false belief; but even if it happens to be true, I don't *know* that it is. Here the problem is that this belief, though necessarily true, is not formed in me by virtue of faculties functioning properly and successfully aimed at truth.

According to the tradition, propositions known by intuition are self-*evident*: such that they are indeed evident, and are not made evident by way of their evidential relationships to other propositions. Fair enough; but the tradition also held that self-evident propositions—simple truths of arithmetic and logic, for example—are such that we can't even grasp or understand them without seeing that they are true. But is the idea that it is *logically* impossible (in the broadly logical sense) that I understand such a proposition and fail to

[9]In *The Man Who Mistook his Wife for a Hat* (New York: Harper and Row, 1985), Oliver Sacks recounts the story of Jimmy, the "Lost Mariner," who suffered from a case of Korsakov's syndrome so severe that he could remember for only a few seconds: "He was superb at arithmetical (and also algebraic) calculations, but only if they could be done with lightening speed. If there were many steps, too much time, involved, he would forget where he was, and even the question" (p. 27).

see that it is true? There seem to be some such propositions, but surely there aren't many—not nearly as many as, according to the tradition, there are self-evident truths. A better position, I think, is that a self-evident proposition is such that a *properly functioning* (mature) human being can't grasp it without believing it. This makes self-evidence a species-relative notion; there may be angels or Alpha Centaurians for whom quite different propositions are self-evident in this sense. Perhaps, furthermore, the maximum degree of warrant—*certainty,* as we may call it—is enjoyed for us by those propositions that a properly functioning human being can't entertain without believing.

There are two further points on which the tradition has erred, or at least displayed considerable infelicity. First, it has displayed an unhappy penchant for the view that intuition is *infallible*—at least in the sense that *all* of its deliverances are true. Second (and consequently), it has tended to hold (at least implicitly) that *a priori* or intuitive warrant does not come in degrees. We can see that each of these is mistaken by considering the Russell paradoxes. It seems intuitively obvious that there is such a property as self-exemplification; it seems intuitively obvious that every property has a complement; and we all know the rest of the sorry tale.[10] But then intuition isn't infallible; at least one proposition has a good deal of intuitive support but is nonetheless false. Further, intuitive warrant comes in degrees. No one, confronted with such a paradox, proposes to rest in the conclusion that there is a property that both does and does not exemplify itself; nor does anyone propose to solve the problem by giving up *modus ponens,* even though the latter is essentially involved in the argument. Instead, we pick some premise that seems less certain, one that has less warrant. Perhaps we deny that every property (or condition) has a complement; perhaps we deny that there is such a property as self-exemplification (or such a condition as self-satisfaction); or perhaps we take some other course. The point, however, is that we (initially) believe the propositions involved to different degrees; hence (given the satisfaction of the other conditions for warrant) they have different degrees of intuitive warrant.

Intuitive warrant, therefore, comes in degrees. I see that the corresponding conditional of *modus ponens* is true; I also see (*pace* David Lewis and others) that no set could be true or false: but I see the former more clearly than the latter. I see (*pace* Meinong and Castañeda) that *actualism* is true: it is not possible that there be nonexistent objects. I also see that *serious* actualism—that no object has a property in a world in which it does not exist—is true. I see the former more clearly than the latter, however, because the argument from actualism to serious actualism involves a premise—that (necessarily) for any

---

[10]Perhaps you doubt that every property has a complement—on the ground, no doubt, that there aren't any negative properties. Then think instead in terms of *conditions:* a condition C is a function from objects to propositions whose value for a given object x is the proposition that x meets C. (Thus the condition *is wise* takes Socrates to the proposition *Socrates is wise.*) Because propositions clearly have denials or negations, conditions will have complements: the complement of C will be the condition that for any object x takes x to the denial of $C(x)$. Then say that an object x satisfies a condition C if $C(x)$ is true, and conduct the argument in terms of the condition *non-self-satisfaction.*

property *P,* if *P* had been exemplified, there would have been something that exemplified it—which I see (as I think) to be true, but do not see to be true as clearly as actualism itself. According to Aquinas, the existence of truth is self-evident. I think he is right; but one sees this less clearly than that it is false that there both is and is not such a thing as truth. These differences in seeing are typically accompanied by differences in degree of belief: the more clearly I see a proposition to be true, the more firmly I believe it.[11] But then, given that the other conditions of warrant are satisfied, those that I believe more firmly will have more warrant, for me, than those I believe less firmly.

III. Fallibilistic A Priorism

The fact that *a priori* warrant is fallible and comes in degrees makes trouble for otherwise plausible conceptions of *a priori* knowledge. Hilary Putnam asks the following question: "Are there *a priori* truths? That is, are there true statements which (1) it is rational to accept (at least if the right arguments occur to me) and (2) which it would never subsequently be rational to reject no matter how the world turns out (epistemically) to be?"[12] But why should an *a priori* truth be such that I could never rationally reject it, no matter how the world turned out to be? Some *a priori* statements will be ones for which I have much less than the maximal degree of warrant. Perhaps I am originally inclined to believe *a priori* that no object has a qualitative essence; perhaps you then present me with a powerfully convincing but subtly fallacious argument for the denial of this proposition;[13] then my original belief was both rational and accepted *a priori,* but my subsequent rejection of it was (or could have been) equally rational. A belief that has *a priori* warrant need not be *incorrigible*. No doubt Putnam accepts many philosophical views on *a priori* grounds; it does not follow that if, perchance, he were to change his mind, then he was either irrational in originally holding the belief in question or else irrational in later rejecting it. No doubt Frege was rational in believing *a priori* that for every condition there is the set of just those things that satisfy that condition; but no doubt he was equally rational in rejecting that proposition later on, upon seeing where it led.

---

[11] *Typically,* but not always: it might seem to me to be necessarily true that no function could be everywhere continuous but nowhere differentiable; you, a mathematician for whom I have great respect, smile indulgently and correct me, but don't produce the argument. Then I may wind up in the following condition: the proposition still seems to me to be necessarily true (when I consider it, I still have at least some of the phenomenology that goes with a proposition's being intuitively evident) but I fail to believe it, expecting that you will produce some recondite construction to show that intuition has failed me.

[12] Hilary Putnam, "Analyticity and A Priority: Beyond Wittgenstein and Quine," in *Midwest Studies in Philosophy,* Vol. IV, *Studies in Metaphysics,* ed. Peter French, Theodore E. Uehling, Jr., and Howard Wettstein (Minneapolis: University of Minnesota Press, 1979), p. 435.

[13] See John Pollock's "Plantinga on Possible Worlds," in *Alvin Plantinga,* ed. James Tomberlin and Peter van Inwagen (Dordrecht: D. Reidel, 1985), pp. 126–30.

According to Philip Kitcher,

> X knows a priori that *p* if and only if X knows that *p* and X's belief that *p* was produced by a process which is an a priori warrant for it.

Furthermore,

> α is an a priori warrant for X's belief that *p*, if and only if
> α is a process such that, given any life *e* sufficient for X for *p*,
> (a) some process of the same type could produce in X a belief that *p*
> (b) if a process of the same type were to produce in X a belief that *p*, then it would warrant X in believing that *p*
> (c) if a process of the same type were to produce in X a belief that *p*, then *p*.[14]

A life sufficient for X for *p*, is, nearly enough, a course of sensuous experience such that having that course of experience is sufficient (given the powers of understanding human beings in fact have) for grasping or understanding *p*. And the basic idea of the definition is that I know a proposition *p*—the corresponding conditional of *modus ponens,* for example—*a priori* if and only if the belief that *p* is produced in me by a process α which (a) produces only true beliefs and (b) is such that, no matter what the course of my experience had been, (1) α (or another process of the same type) could have produced the belief that *p* in me, and (2) if α (or another process of the same type) *had* produced the belief that *p* in me, then *p* would have had warrant for me.

There are problems, here, with the notion of the same *type* of process, and with the counterfactual notions employed. Furthermore, if, in clause (a) we are to think of process *tokens,* actual concrete psychological processes or mechanisms rather than *types* of processes,[15] then we can't sensibly suppose *a priori* that there *is* any process α of the relevant type. We can't suppose *a priori* that there is a process that produces, for example, belief in the corresponding conditional of *modus ponens* and also produces no false beliefs (as according to (c) there must be if my belief in the corresponding conditional of *modus ponens* is to have warrant for me). How could we know *a priori* that the process or processes that produced Frege's mistaken belief didn't also produce some belief that had an *a priori* warrant? And must we suppose that no process that sometimes produces false philosophical beliefs also sometimes produces beliefs that have *a priori* warrant? Questions about the identity and individuation of such processes seem to be broadly speaking *scientific,* and are at present vastly beyond us. (Of course if it is process *types* of which we speak, there will be such processes, but then condition (c) will be idle in that it is much too easily met.)

But suppose we temporarily ignore these small annoyances: the chief problem still looms. Kitcher's view is that if I have an *a priori* warrant for a proposition *p*, then the process α that produces *p* in me must meet the following condition: it must be such that no matter what the course of my experience had been (provided it was sufficient for me to grasp *p*) if α had produced that

---

[14]*The Nature of Mathematical Knowledge* (New York: Oxford Univ. Press, 1983), p. 24.

[15]See the discussion of Goldman in my *Warrant: The Current Debate* (New York: Oxford University Press, 1993), pp. 208ff.

belief in me, then I would have been warranted in believing *p*. Now he doesn't say much about what he takes warrant to be (Is it *justification,* of one of the several sorts we noted in chapter 1 of *Warrant: The Current Debate?* Is it instead some version of rationality?) But suppose we take the term in the rough-and-ready spirit in which it is offered. The problem is much like Putnam's: according to Putnam, roughly speaking, if you have an *a priori* warrant for *p*, then it will never be rational to change your mind about it, no matter what the course of your experience; according to Kitcher, if you have an *a priori* warrant for *p*, then you will be warranted in believing *p* no matter what the course of the rest of your experience. As we have seen, the Putnamian condition is much too strong; but the same goes for Kitcher's weaker condition. Can't I have *a priori* warrant for a philosophical view—that there aren't any things that do not exist, let's say—but come to be no longer warranted in so believing? You offer me an extremely subtle but fallacious argument for the contrary conclusion from premises I believe more strongly than the proposition in question: the argument looks wholly cogent to me, and even after much thought and reflection I can see no difficulties in it at all. Then, I should think, I would no longer be warranted in believing that proposition. And it isn't only other *a priori* arguments that can defeat my warrant. I am a philosophical tyro and you a distinguished senior practitioner of the art; you tell me that those who think about these things are unanimous in endorsing Meinong and rejecting my view that there aren't any things that don't exist: then too, I should think, my view would no longer have warrant (or *much* warrant) for me. Intuitive warrant comes in degrees (and hence in less than maximal degrees); that makes it possible for the intuitive warrant for a given proposition to be defeated.

The central notion of *a priori* warrant or knowledge is of warrant or knowledge that is independent of experience—in the sense that the only experience it requires is the experience necessary for grasping or understanding the proposition involved. But it doesn't follow that what has *a priori* intuitive warrant is indefeasible, or infallible, or rationally unrevisable or indubitable, or anything of that Cartesian sort. Nor does it even follow that beliefs formed *a priori* are independent of experience in that they can't be corrected or defeated by beliefs from other sources—testimony, for example. It may be, of course, that the very highest degrees of warrant are occupied only by *a priori* beliefs; but (given the wide range of warrant in which *a priori* beliefs come) it does not follow that every *a priori* belief has more warrant than any *a posteriori* belief.[16] Indeed, *a*

---

[16] In "Y-a-t'il une Philosophie Chretienne?" *Revue de Metaphysique et de Morale* (1931), Emile Brehier argues that the Thomist conception of Christian philosophy is bankrupt; the reason, says Brehier, is that on this conception, reason can properly be *corrected* by other sources of belief (in this instance, faith); but, says Brehier, if reason is subject to correction from other sources, then "even when it is exercised in a perfectly correct manner, it can never be sure of its conclusions" (p. 149). The result, he says, is that "all systematic and rational investigation becomes completely futile," and "there is a quasi-absolute impossibility of founding a coherent and systematic philosophy" (p. 150) (my translation). Put in Putnamian or Kitcherian terms, his point would be that philosophy properly includes only the deliverances of reason; but a deliverance of reason can't properly be corrected by any other source, on pain of complete skepticism about the deliverances of reason. Like Putnam and Kitcher, he seems to ignore the fact that the deliverances of reason come in

priori beliefs display the same defeasibility structure displayed by perceptual beliefs, inductive beliefs, and so on. I seem to see a fine barn: you tell me that it is only a barn facade left over from a Hollywood production; if things are going properly I will no longer believe that what I see is a barn. But similarly: it seems to me impossible that a function should be both everywhere continuous and nowhere differentiable; you, a habitually authoritative mathematician, tell me about the demonstrations that there are such functions; if things are going properly, I will no longer hold the belief in question.

IV. *A Priori* Knowledge and the Causal Requirements

We have *a priori* knowledge (so I claim) if we have true *a priori* beliefs that are held with sufficient firmness and produced in us by cognitive faculties functioning properly and successfully aimed at truth. According to a currently fashionable view, however, knowledge requires the satisfaction of still another condition, a condition that some think makes trouble for *a priori* knowledge. The view in question is seldom stated with precision: the rough idea, however, is that any objects of which we have knowledge must be such that we stand in an appropriate *causal relation* with them. An object that stood in no causal relation to us would be one of which we could have no knowledge at all. The reason, presumably, is not that we can perfectly well form *beliefs* about such an object, but cannot know that these beliefs are true; what the causal requirement requires is that any object about which we can so much as *form beliefs* be one to which we stand in some causal relation.[17]

This causal requirement is thought to be particularly poignant with respect to such alleged varieties of *a priori* knowledge as that of mathematics and set theory. On straightforward construals, such knowledge appears to be knowledge of numbers and sets; numbers and sets, however (along with properties, propositions, possible worlds, and their ilk), are *abstract* objects;[18] but abstract objects, so the claim goes, are causally inert and therefore cannot stand in causal relations with us or anything else. Hence if there are such things, we cannot so much as *think* about them, let alone *know* anything about them. Thus according to Paul Benacerraf, "a typical 'standard' account (at least in the case of number theory or set theory) will depict truth conditions in terms of conditions on objects whose nature, as normally conceived, places them beyond the reach of the better understood means of human cognition (e.g., sense perception and the like)." He adds that "If, for example, numbers are the kinds of entities they are normally taken to be, then the connection between the truth

---

different degrees of warrant; perhaps beliefs with the *highest* degrees of warrant can't be corrected by beliefs from other sources (on pain of skepticism), but the same need not hold for *a priori* beliefs in general.

[17]See, for example, Richard Grandy, "Reference, Meaning and Belief," *Journal of Philosophy* 70 (1973), p. 446.

[18]On David Lewis's view, possible worlds are concrete rather than abstract; the problem (if there is one) remains, however, for on his view worlds other than the actual world are also spatiotemporally and hence causally unrelated to us.

conditions for the statements of number theory and any relevant events connected with the people who are supposed to have mathematical knowledge cannot be made out."[19]

Stated thus vaguely, of course, this is less an objection than a sort of worry; and perhaps the first response to the worry must be that since *a priori* knowledge is as good an example of knowledge as we have, if a theory (or worry) implies that there is no such knowledge, then so much the worse for the theory. But perhaps there is a less imperious response; suppose we briefly look into this alleged causal requirement. At first glance, the problems it creates might seem especially pressing with respect to mathematics, set theory, and other examples of *a priori* knowledge; at second glance, however, its depredations extend much further. For consider *propositions*. We have been assuming that when I believe, for example, that all men are mortal, then there is something I believe: the proposition *All men are mortal*. To make this assumption more explicit, say that propositions are the things (whatever precisely their nature) that are fundamentally[20] capable of being believed or disbelieved, that are true or false, and that stand in logical relations (such as entailment) to each other. (And for present purposes, let us suppose that it is the *same* things that meet each of these conditions.) Propositions, whatever exactly they may be, are often and ordinarily taken to be paradigmatically abstract. Now Benacerraf is relatively inspecific about which cognitive relationships R are such that if I stand in R to an object x, then I must also stand *causally* related to x. One supposes, however, that the idea is this: if the causal relationship is absent, then I can't have any cognitive contact (to keep things at that inspecific level) at all with the thing in question; in particular I can't think about such a thing, or have a cognitive grasp of it—or, of course, *believe* it. Accordingly, if in fact propositions *are* abstract objects, and if it is impossible to stand in a causal relationship to an abstract object, then the causal requirement seems to imply that we can't know any propositions at all, because we can't *believe* any propositions at all, no matter what their subject matter. An extraordinary skeptical argument indeed!

Perhaps the causal theorist will object that what is proscribed by his requirement is only *de re* belief, with respect to some specific abstract object(s), that it (or they) has some property or other—and that this doesn't obviously preclude *believing* it. If so, however, then we might know or have reason to believe that there *are* such things as propositions, that they are in fact abstract, and that they stand in various relationships to each other, and that they are the things we believe, doubt, question, hope, and the like. We might have *theoretical* reason to believe these things; perhaps, according to our best theory, there are abstract objects, and some of them are the things to which we take proposi-

---

[19]"Mathematical Truth," *Journal of Philosophy* (November 8, 1973), pp. 667–68, 673.

[20]"Fundamentally": propositions, whatever they are, are expressed by sentences. (To speak more carefully and close no options, we should say that propositions either are identical with or are expressed by sentences.) Even if it is false that they *are* sentences, therefore, nevertheless they are *expressed by* sentences, and it will be natural to speak of a sentence that expresses a true proposition as true—derivatively or analogically true. In the same way we might say that a *set* of true propositions is true.

tional attitudes, the things that are true or false, that stand in logical relations, and so on. We might also know in this way that there is just one of these objects that meets a certain condition—being the thing one believes, for example, when one believes that snow is white; and we might know interesting facts about that thing. We might know further, in this way, that the thing in question is true if and only if snow is white, and that it is distinct from but logically equivalent to the proposition *If arithmetic is incomplete, then snow is white.* What is proscribed by the causal requirement is not knowledge by description (so to speak) of abstract objects, but only knowledge by acquaintance. We can't see, inspect, be acquainted with a given abstract object (the proposition *All men are mortal,* perhaps) and see that it has a certain property (for example, the property of being inconsistent with the proposition *Some men are immortal*); but that doesn't mean that we can't have theoretical knowledge that there are such propositions and that they stand in that relationship.

But if this is the way the wind blows, then the causal requirement does not have nearly the bite one initially thought—in particular, it doesn't raise much of a worry about mathematics and set theory. For if we can have theoretical knowledge of abstract propositions, we can do the same for abstract numbers and sets. True: given the causal requirement and the abstract nature of numbers and sets, perhaps we can't (contra Gödel) grasp a given number—the number 3, let's say—and see that it is prime; but we can have the theoretical knowledge that there is such a thing as the number 3 and that indeed it is prime. Perhaps we can't think *de re* about the null set and see that it has no members (and is therefore included in every set); but nothing here proscribes our having the theoretical knowledge that there is a unique set that has no members (and that it is therefore included in every set). And what more could the sensible arithmetician or set theorist ask for?

If the causal requirement is to raise a genuine worry for knowledge of numbers and sets, therefore, it will also have to imply that we can't *believe* objects with which we have no causal contact. So one who sees it as raising a genuine worry must suppose that if indeed there *are* such things as propositions (that is, if there are things to which we take propositional attitudes, which are either true or false, and which stand in logical relationships to each other), then they are *concrete objects* of some kind or other. She therefore cannot sensibly suppose that propositions are *sentences,* that is, sentence *types;* for a sentence type—perhaps a sequence or series of shapes or sounds—is no less abstract than a number. Nor, of course, can she suppose that they are *sets*—of possible worlds, perhaps, or synonymous sentences, or anything else; for sets too are abstract objects. If the causal requirement causes trouble for *a priori* knowledge of mathematics and set theory, then, it causes trouble in a much wider area as well; it exacts a much higher price than one might initially think.

Accordingly, what the causal requirement (if it causes trouble for *a priori* knowledge) really requires is that propositions be *concrete* objects of some sort—concrete sentence inscriptions or utterances, perhaps. I write the sentence '2 + 1 = 3' on the blackboard; what I believe or know is that concrete inscription. You utter the sentence 'Sam is on the way'; what I believe is the sound you utter. But that can't be right; if you erase the board after I leave you don't deprive me of my belief that $2 + 1 = 3$; and that can be so even if by chance there happens to be no inscription of '$2 + 1 = 3$' anywhere else. I can believe that Sam is coming long after the sound is no longer ringing in my ears, and even at a time when no one is uttering 'Sam is on the way'. Someone will suggest that our brains contain something like concrete inscriptions of such sentences, concrete representations or stand-ins of some sort, of all the sentences that we believe; and perhaps she will add that these concrete inscriptions are the things we really believe or fear, the things that are true and false, and so on. This is of course wholly speculative—armchair psychology at its most expansive. But that is far from the worst of its woes. For here we encounter familiar and paralyzing difficulties. First, it seems clear (to many of us, anyway) that there are propositions no one—no human being, at any rate—has so far entertained. For example, there is a truth about how many Frisians had herring for breakfast last Saturday; chances are no one knows or has even entertained that truth. But then (given that no *other* creatures with brains have entertained it) that proposition, whatever it is, presumably won't be a brain inscription. Take one of the leaves on the oak trees in my backyard: there will be many propositions about it that no creature with a brain has ever entertained or thought of: that it is less than 5 inches long, for example, that it is less than 5.5 inches long, that it is less than 5.55 inches long, and so on. These truths, too, presumably won't be brain inscriptions. On whose brains have they been inscribed?

Further, (monolingual) German and English speakers often believe, as we say, the same thing; how shall we understand that on the theory in question? You and I believe some of the very same truths—that $2 + 1 = 3$, for example. If what we know or believe is really a brain inscription, Aristotle's argument for the unicity of the intellect must be reinstated—but in appropriately modern guise as an argument for the unicity of the brain! We might try saying, by way of reply, that (strictly speaking) two people never do believe literally the same proposition: you believe the inscriptions in your brain, and I the ones in mine. Still (the reply goes on) what we say when we say that you and I believe the same thing is often true: you and I believe the same thing if we believe appropriately similar brain inscriptions. But how shall we understand this 'appropriately similar'? We can't say that appropriately similar brain inscriptions are ones that share a property—not, at least, if we take the usual view that properties are abstract. (If properties are abstract, then either we can't theorize about them, or, if we can, we can also theorize about abstract mathematical objects, in which case (once more) the causal requirement turns out more bark than bite.) Nor, of course, can we suppose that the similarity relation is a set of ordered pairs; nor can we say that a pair of brain inscriptions are relevantly similar if they play the same causal role; for causal roles are also abstract objects. How are we to understand this similarity?

There are other problems as well: propositions stand in logical relations; but can a concrete array of neural material entail the proposition that the North won the Civil War? I can't see how. (Of course a concrete array of neural material, like any other material, could *express* a proposition and hence in an analogically extended sense entail anything entailed by the proposition it expressed; my claim is that it is at best exceedingly hard to see how it could entail a proposition in the fundamental sense of 'entail'.) And this leads to the deepest problem; here I can only point to it.[21] Propositions, the things we believe and know, are true or false. Consider a simple proposition—7 *is prime,* let's say. This proposition is about something: the number 7. Further, it predicates a property of that object—the property of being prime. Such a proposition singles out a given object and says something about it: that it is prime. As a result, it is true or false: true if the object it is about has the property it predicates of that object, false otherwise. But this isn't the sort of thing that either a set or a concrete array of neural material can do. A brain inscription can't be about a given object and predicate a property of it. It can't pick out a given object—7, let's say—and say that it is prime. Of course we can *use* such a concrete array (a sentence, for example) to make a claim, to express a proposition. If we do, the sentence is true or false derivatively: true if the proposition it expresses is true, false otherwise. But in itself, apart from the connection we users of language forge between it and the proposition, the sentence predicates nothing of anything. And something similar goes for an array of neurons. I suppose such an array could be used like a sentence to express a proposition; it might be inconvenient, but that does not mean it couldn't be done. Furthermore, it is compatible with my present point that the array of neurons *be* a belief—that is, be a *believing.* For all I say here, it might be that what it *is* to believe that 7 is prime, is to have a brain in which some array of neurons displays the property that goes with its being a brain inscription. I don't for a moment believe that is true (for God, after all, has beliefs and knowledge but has no brain); but it isn't incompatible with my present point. My present point is only that what is believed—the thing that is true or false—couldn't just *be* that array of neurons. Concrete arrays, whether of neurons or graphite, can't be what we know or believe.

V. Why Propositions Cannot Be Concrete

I should next like to offer an argument for the conclusion that propositions (the things, whatever their nature, that can be believed or disbelieved, are true or false, and stand in logical relations) cannot be concrete objects of *any* sort—at any rate, they can't be concrete objects that do not exist necessarily. We can see this as follows. For definiteness, suppose propositions are human mental acts or perhaps brain inscriptions. It follows that if there had been no human beings, then there would have been no propositions. But doesn't that seem wrong? If there had been no human beings, one thinks, then it would have been true that there are no human beings—that is, *that there are no human beings*

[21]For a development of this objection, see my "Two Concepts of Modality," in *Philosophical Perspectives, 1, Metaphysics, 1987,* ed. James Tomberlin (Atascadero, Calif.: Ridgeview, 1987), pp. 206ff.

would have been true—in which case there would have been at least one truth (and thus one proposition): that there are no human beings.

The concretist, of course, will retort that as *she* sees the matter,

> (a)   If there had been no human beings, then it would have been true that there are no human beings—that is, *that there are no human beings* would have been true

is false. She will therefore have to reject

> (b)   Necessarily, there are no human beings if and only if it is true that there are no human beings;

more specifically, she will be obliged to reject the left-to-right conjunct of (b):

> (c)   Necessarily, if there are no human beings, then it is true that there are no human beings

for (c) entails (a). She is therefore committed to

> (d)   Possibly, (there are no people and it is not true that there are no people).

But here we strike a problem: what does she mean, here, by 'possibly'? Not, presumably, 'possibly true' or 'could have been true'. For consider the proposition (d) says is possible: if it is possible, then so is its first conjunct. But on the concretist position, the first conjunct, clearly enough, could not have been true. For if it had been true, there would have been no people, in which case there would have been no propositions, in which case the proposition *There are no people* would not have existed, in which case that proposition would not have had the property of being true.[22] So that proposition could not have been true after all. But what, other than 'could have been true', could the concretist possibly mean by 'possible'?

This leads us to a more general problem. Most of us think that among the true propositions, there are some that are necessary: true, and such that they could not have failed to be true. But the concretist cannot concur; she cannot agree that there are propositions that could not have failed to be true. For propositions, on her view, are contingent beings: that is, they are contingently *existing* beings; they could have failed to exist. But then any given proposition could have failed to be true, for it could have failed to exist, in which case it would have failed to be true. Not that it would have been *false,* of course; if a

---

[22]Here I assume *serious actualism:* the view that no object could have had a property without existing. Serious actualism is a consequence of actualism *tout court:* the view that it is impossible that there be things that do not exist. See *Alvin Plantinga,* pp. 130–34 and 316–23.

proposition—*Socrates is wise,* let's say—had not existed, then there simply would have *been* no such proposition at all; so it would not have had the property of being false. (If you had failed to exist, then you would not have had the property of living on earth; but it does not follow that you would have lived somewhere else.) On the concretist view, therefore, no proposition is such that it could not have failed to be true. That is because each proposition could have failed to exist, and would have failed to be true if it had failed to exist. But then what can the concretist mean when she joins the rest of us in supposing that some propositions are necessary and others are not?

Well, perhaps she might suggest that we are asking too much when we ask that a necessary proposition be *strongly* necessary—that is, such that it could not have failed to be true. She may want instead to maintain that for a proposition to be necessarily true is for it to have the property of being true *essentially.* But that, she adds, does not require that the proposition in question be such that it can't fail to be true. What it requires is that it can't both *exist* and fail to be true: alternatively, what it requires is that it could not have been false. Compare: for me to have a property essentially, it is not necessary that I be such that I could not have lacked the property. After all, *no* property is such that I could not have lacked it, I could have failed to exist, in which case I would have had no properties at all. What is required is only that it be impossible that I *exist* and lack the property, or (equivalently) impossible that I have the *complement* of the property in question. So if I am essentially a person, then it is impossible that I be a nonperson, although it is not impossible that I fail to be a person. And the concretist suggests that we say something similar here: for a proposition *p* to be necessary, it is not required that *p* be such that it could not have failed to be true: all that's required is *weak* necessity: that *p* be such that it could not have been false.

But this suggestion has its own problems. Suppose the concretist thinks propositions are brain inscriptions: then the proposition *There are brain inscriptions* obviously enough will be such that it could not have been false. It is therefore necessary that there are brain inscriptions, and hence necessary that there are brains; what we have here is a sort of ontological argument for the existence of brains and brain inscriptions. On this account far too many propositions turn out to be necessary. And given that necessity and possibility are related as duals, we expect, of course, that the same difficulties will arise for possibility. The concretist can't say that a proposition is possible just in case it could have been true (the dual of weak necessity): for then far too few propositions are possible. It is possible, for example, that there be no human beings and no brain inscriptions; but on the concretist view, of course, this proposition could not have been true. She might therefore try retreating to the suggestion that a proposition is possible when (like *There are no human beings*) it *could have failed to be false* (the dual of strong necessity); but then on her view every proposition, including the most blatant contradiction, is possible. For take any proposition you like: it could have failed to exist, in which case it would have failed to be false. The conclusion, I think, is that propositions can't be concrete, contingently existing objects such as human mental acts, or brain inscriptions or other arrays of neural material, or sentence tokens, or anything else of that sort.

VI. Back to the Causal Requirement

If the causal requirement implies that what we know and believe are concrete representations in our brains or elsewhere, then what we have is less a remarkable discovery than a *reductio*. Here we should reason by *modus tollens* rather than *modus ponens*. But of course the causal requirement is open to many interpretations; the phrase 'the causal requirement' really hides a vast horde of possible principles. Taken vaguely, the principle certainly seems to have at least some initial intuitive support; *some* version of it, it seems, is likely to be true. But what kind of causal connection between object of knowledge and knower is required?

Could I know truths about abstract sets of concrete objects—for example, that the union of a pair of sets can't have fewer members than either of the pair—by way of standing in causal relations with their concrete members? Would *that* be enough of a causal connection with the sets? Further, sets of contingent objects are ontologically dependent[23] upon their members (more exactly, the members of their transitive closures) in that no set could have existed if one of its members had not existed. (If Quine had not existed, there would have been no such thing as his unit set.) Still further, no set could have existed at a time *before* its members exist. So in a way the fortunate event of Quine's coming into existence brings about, or causes, or produces, or is at any rate sufficient for the existence of his unit set. Is this sort of bringing about sufficient to satisfy the causal requirement? Can I know that Quine is a member of his unit set by virtue of standing in causal relation to Quine, whose existence in turn brings about the existence of that set? Aristotle thought I could grasp or apprehend a property (redness, for example) by standing in an appropriate causal relation to *exemplifications* of it (a red silo, for example): was he right? Can I grasp properties logically related to properties I grasp? If I grasp a given property *P*, is that sufficient (so far as the causal requirement is concerned) for grasping its complement −*P*, or must I also stand in the appropriate causal relation to some example of −*P*? (In some cases—cases of properties that are necessarily exemplified—this will be difficult to arrange.) And if I grasp the properties *humanity* and *mortality*, will that suffice, so far as the causal requirement goes, for grasping the proposition *All men are mortal*? Or must I stand in some causal relation with the proposition itself, as opposed to those properties?

But perhaps the fundamental question is really this: why think propositions, properties, sets, states of affairs, and their like cannot stand in causal relations? The notion of an abstract object, after all, comes from the notion of

[23]See my "Actualism and Possible Worlds," *Theoria* (1977).

abstraction; it is in origin an *epistemological* rather than an ontological category. According to the tradition, it is *properties* that are abstracted in this way; Aristotle and many others have held that when we perceive an object of a certain sort, we are able to abstract and thus grasp some of its properties.[24] So an abstract object is the sort of object we grasp by abstraction: but of course that leaves open the question what sort of a thing an abstract object *is.* One traditional view is that the things we thus abstract are outside space and time and incapable of standing in causal relations. We are told that Plato held this view; if so, he didn't hold it clearly and consistently. Plato speaks of the idea of the good as *primus unter pares* among the ideas; it is an idea par excellence; but he also speaks of it as if he thinks it has causal powers of great significance.

And in any event, the view in question—that propositions, sets, properties, and their like are outside space and time and cannot stand in causal relations— is only one view among others. Theists, for example, may find attractive a view popular among medieval philosophers from Augustine on: the view that abstract objects are really divine thoughts. More exactly, propositions are divine thoughts, properties divine concepts, and sets divine collections.[25] But then these objects can enter into the sort of causal relation that holds between a thought and a thinker, and we can enter into causal relation with them by virtue of our causal relation to God. It is therefore quite possible to think of abstract objects as capable of standing in causal relations, and in causal relations with us; hence the causal objection to *a priori* knowledge can be easily sidestepped.

[24]You may object that it is hard to conceive of this in neural terms; I reply that it is equally hard to conceive of thinking of the moon in neural terms, or to see how it is, in neural terms, that we are able to think about the null set, or the unit set of Quine. But then how exactly *does* this work? What happens when we grasp a property, and how does it happen that we can do that? Here perhaps the best answer is Aristotle's: "The soul is so constituted as to be capable of this process." *Posterior Analytics,* II, 19 100a 14.

[25]See my "How to Be an Anti-Realist," *Proceedings and Addresses of the American Philosophical Association* (1982); see also Christopher Menzel, "Theism, Platonism and the Metaphysics of Mathematics," *Faith and Philosophy* 4, no. 4 (October 1987), reprinted in *Christian Theism,* ed. Michael Beaty (Notre Dame: University of Notre Dame Press, 1990); and Christopher Menzel and Thomas Morris, "Absolute Creation," *American Philosophical Quarterly* 23 (1986), reprinted in T. V. Morris, *Anselmian Explanations* (Notre Dame: University of Notre Dame Press, 1987). Suppose you find yourself convinced that (1) there are propositions, properties, and sets, (2) that the causal requirement is indeed true, and (3) that (due to excessive number or excessive complexity or excessive size) propositions, properties, and sets can't be *human* thoughts, concepts, and collections. Then you have the materials for a theistic argument.

7

Induction

Human beings, as David Hume once pointed out, ordinarily expect (indeed, inveterately assume) that the future will resemble the past. Night has followed day for lo! these many years; it will come as no surprise that today will be followed by tonight. This fact about us and our expectations may have been known even before Hume. It was certainly known to Thomas Reid, who claimed that among the "principles of contingent truth" is that "*in the phaenomena of nature, what is to be, will probably be like to what has been in similar circumstances* (Reid's emphasis). He goes on:

> We must have this conviction as soon as we are capable of learning anything from experience; for all experience is grounded upon a belief that the future will be like the past. . . .
>
> This is one of those principles which, when we grow up and observe the course of nature, we can confirm by reasoning. We perceive that nature is governed by fixed laws, and that, if it were not so, there would be no such thing as prudence in human conduct; there would be no fitness in any means to promote an end; and what on one occasion promoted it, might as probably on another occasion, obstruct it.
>
> But the principle is necessary for us before we are able to discover it by reasoning, and therefore is made a part of our constitution, and produces its effects before the use of reason.[1]

Somewhat more specifically

> It is undeniable, and indeed is acknowledged by all, that when we have found those things to have been constantly conjoined in the course of nature, the appearance of one of them is immediately followed by the conception and belief of the other.[2]

[1] *Essay on the Intellectual Powers of Man*, in *Thomas Reid's Inquiry and Essays*, ed. R. Beanblossom and K. Lehrer (Indianapolis: Hackett, 1983) VI, 12, p. 283. A similar principle is stated by Hume: "If reason determined us, it wou'd proceed upon that principle, *that past instances, of which we have had no experience, must resemble those, of which we have had experience, and that the course of nature continues always uniform.*" *A Treatise of Human Nature*, ed. L.A. Selby-Bigge (Oxford: Clarendon Press, 1888), I, III, 6, p. 89 (Hume's emphasis). (Subsequent page references to the *Treatise* are to this edition.) He goes on to argue that one must (rationally) accept this principle in order to be rational in following inductive practice, and that in fact there is no rational support for the principle.

[2] *An Inquiry into the Human Mind on the Principles of Common Sense*, in *Thomas Reid's Inquiry and Essays*, VI, 24, p. 97.

We use the term 'induction' in both a broad and a narrow sense. Taken narrowly, it denotes our practice of extrapolating frequencies from observed sample to population generally: given that n/m observed objects of sort A have been B, we infer by the "Straight Rule" that (all else being equal) n/m As are B.[3] Broadly taken, however, the term denotes our whole nondeductive procedure of acquiring, maintaining, and discarding beliefs about what is so far unobserved or undetected or unknown. It is a complicated, multitudinous process involving inherited ideas about the ways of the world, interlocking chains of inductions in the narrow sense, views about what is essential and what accidental and about which differences are important and which not, and judgments of initial plausibility. This process of considering, examining, and evaluating hypotheses may go on unreflectively and unselfconsciously, or by way of explicit, self-conscious reflective attention; it is guided by simplicity and in other ways by what we human beings find natural and familiar. (Alpha Centaurians might proceed quite differently.)

Reid's remarks apply in the first instance to induction taken more narrowly, and he makes at least two important claims here. First, he says that having this conviction—that "in the phaenomena of nature, what is to be, will probably be like to what has been in similar circumstances"—is essential to learning from experience. This conviction is belief in a principle of the 'Uniformity of Nature'. Notorious difficulties beset the project of stating such a principle more exactly; among the chief sources of the difficulty is the enormously complicated, highly articulated nature of inductive practice. We make meta-inductions, take some differences to be important and others not, sometimes generalize to *all* the so and sos and other times only to those around here, or on earth, or in our galaxy, and so on. Stated in Reid's rough-and-ready way, it has powerful intuitive appeal. There is an important caveat, however. Must I *explicitly endorse* this principle in order to learn from experience? It is hard to see why; surely a person could learn from experience even though it never occurred to her to form any general beliefs about the future and its relation to the past (of course, if I believed the *denial* of the relevant uniformity principles, I would have a defeater for the beliefs I might nevertheless find myself forming). What learning from experience requires is the *habit* or *practice* of making inductive inferences, whether or not this habit is accompanied by metaconvictions about the general course of nature. But if we revise Reid's position in this direction (and perhaps this is no more than what he really intended), we can easily see that he is right. We are able to learn from experience—that fire will burn, that mosquito bites itch, that rock fall is dangerous, that unsupported objects near the surface of the earth will fall—only by virtue of mobilizing the habit or practice in question.

Second, says Reid, this habit characterizes our epistemic practice when we are children, before we attain the "age of reason." When we grow up, he says, we can observe the course of nature and confirm the principle; but the principle

[3]Of course the 'all else being equal' covers a multitude of sins. We don't necessarily mean to infer that n/m As are B all over the world, or through all of space and time, or in circumstances very different from the current ones, or for just any old A and B.

is "necessary for us before we are able to discover it by reasoning." Clearly we *do* change belief in this way as children. But *can* we confirm Reid's principle (taken now as a proposition) when we grow up and observe the course of nature? That is, can we confirm it noncircularly, without employing the practice or something tantamount to it? I can't see how. It is only by virtue of this way of forming, maintaining, changing belief, that I can so much as learn my language. (My parents teach me 'red'; I get the idea; unless I proceed in accord with this habit, I shall have to start over the next time they use 'red'.) And without language it is doubtful that I could formulate or entertain Reid's principle, let alone confirm it. Further, suppose I confirm a given instance of the principle: I observe that the trees I come across have leaves in the summertime, and project that this is true more generally. It is only by way of induction that I take the property I express by 'tree' to be repeatedly displayed in my experience. It is by induction that I take this next thing, which looks like a tree, to be a tree rather than, for example, a paper-mache model or a laser projection or a desertlike mirage; it is by induction that I take the tree I now see in my backyard to be the same object (or even the same kind of object) that I saw there yesterday; it is by induction that I form the belief that the backyard itself appropriately resembles (by way, for example, of containing soil under that grass rather than concrete or plastic) what was there yesterday. And finally, suppose I do note that when what was future came to pass, it resembled what was past: that is to note no more than that past futures have resembled past pasts. It is only by employing the very principle (or habit) in question, however, that I can see this as confirming that *future* futures will resemble past futures. So I can't noncircularly confirm Reid's principle.

I. The Old Riddle of Induction

Reid's claim, therefore, is that we form, maintain, and change belief in accord with the principle that the future will appropriately resemble the past. (For the force of 'appropriately', see pp. 133ff.) Hume thought he saw a philosophical problem here, a problem we have come to call 'the problem of induction'— more recently (if we have read our Goodman) 'the old riddle of induction'. But what precisely *is* this old riddle? Something like this. We make predictions: we predict that today will be followed by tonight, that the earth will not stop rotating at, say, 6:00 P.M. today, that the next ax head dropped in water will sink. What *justifies* these predictions? Or rather, what justifies *us* in making them? There are no necessary connections among matters of fact, says Hume:

> As to past *Experience*, it can be allowed to give *direct* and *certain* information of those precise objects only, and that precise period of time, which fell under its cognizance: but why this experience should be extended to future times, and to other objects, which for aught we know, may be only in appearance similar; this is the main question on which I would insist. The bread, which I formerly ate, nourished me; that is, a body of such sensible qualities was, at that time, endued with such secret powers: but does it follow, that other bread

must also nourish me at another time, and that like sensible qualities must always be attended with like secret powers?[4]

It does *not* follow; there are plenty of possible worlds (worlds run by mischievous Cartesian demons, perhaps) in which things go just as they have up to the present, but then go completely crazy; there are as many worlds like that as worlds in which induction will continue to be a reliable source of belief. So what justifies us in making *this* prediction rather than its denial? What makes this the *right* prediction? Indeed, what justifies us in making any prediction at all? Perhaps the course of wisdom is to abstain altogether from such a doubtful business.

Here Hume seems to give a double answer. On the one hand, *nothing* justifies us; these inferences are without foundation; we have no reason to make them:

> . . . two principles, *That there is nothing in any object, consider'd in itself, which can afford us a reason for drawing a conclusion beyond it;* and *That even after the observation of the frequent or constant conjunction of objects, we have no reason to draw any inference concerning any object beyond those of which we have had experience;* . . . These principles we have found to be sufficiently convincing, even with regard to our most certain reasonings from causation.

> If I ask why you believe any particular matter of fact, which you relate, you must tell me some reason; and this reason will be some other fact, connected with it. But as you cannot proceed after this manner, *in infinitum*, you must at last terminate in some fact, which is present to your memory or sense; or must allow that your belief is entirely without foundation.[5]

On the other hand, however, what makes these inferences the *right* inferences is that great guide of human life, custom. It is only because we have this inductive habit that our experience is useful to us; this habit causes us to expect, for the future, a train of events similar to those that have appeared in the past;[6] it is therefore a good thing that we have this habit. But then how shall we understand Hume here? Are these inferences right, justified, or not? My best guess is as follows. On the one hand, there is the absence of the necessary connection he mourns; this means that all such inferences are without justification and that there is no reason for making them. On the other hand, we do in fact, guided by custom, make such unjustified inferences; it is a good thing,

---

[4]*An Enquiry concerning Human Understanding* (LaSalle, Ill.: Open Court, 1956), IV, 2, p. 34.

[5]*Treatise*, pp. 139 and 48 (Hume's emphasis). Hume scholarship, of course, has long been vexed with respect to the question of the nature and extent of Hume's skepticism. Here I follow the standard interpretations, as represented, for example, by Barry Stroud: "In fact, Hume claims that, for any particular thing any human being believes about what he has not yet experienced, the person has no more reason to believe it than he has to believe its contradictory"; *Hume* (London: Routledge & Kegan Paul, 1977), p. 14. Not everyone finds Hume's skepticism here either convincing or threatening. Thus H. A. Prichard, *Knowledge and Perception* (Oxford: Clarendon Press, 1950), p. 174: "to my mind the *Treatise* is one of the most tedious of books, and close examination of it renders me not skeptical but angry."

[6]*Treatise*, p. 47.

furthermore, that we do, for, says Hume (now reasoning by way of this very inductive habit), if we didn't we wouldn't get on at all well. So the situation is ambiguous, ironic. That we make these inferences, form beliefs in these ways, is a happy circumstance; otherwise we would be in deep and immediate trouble. But our reasoning thus is deplorable; for we are not rationally justified in so doing.

Well, *are* these inferences ungrounded, unfounded, irrational, or without justification? But what, precisely, is the complaint? Is it that I am *irrational* in reasoning in this way? That seems unlikely. Here once more we meet the protean, many-sided character of 'rationality'.[7] But surely, first, I can be *Foley* rational, in reasoning thus, and with respect to both ends of the Foley spectrum: reasoning in this way is *in fact* a good way to achieve our ends, and this means to our ends is also one we *think* is a good one to achieve our ends (and one such that, even after reflection, we would *continue* to think a good way to achieve those ends). Second, I'm surely not irrational in reasoning this way, in the way in which someone suffering from the manic phase of manic-depressive psychosis is irrational. There is nothing psychotic or dysfunctional in reasoning this way; indeed, it is the person who does *not* reason inductively who requires therapy. Third, surely there is no *deliverance of reason* that one violates in reasoning thus: true, in so reasoning, one goes *beyond* the deliverances of reason (taken narrowly as *a priori* intuition and deduction) but the deliverances of reason do not include the proposition that the deliverances of reason alone are acceptable or justified. So there is nothing *irrational* about reasoning in this way.

Is the claim instead that we are *deontologically* unjustified in reasoning in this way? That seems obviously wrong: there are no intellectual duties—at any rate none any of us know of—to refrain from forming belief in this way. (We might add that your forming beliefs in this way is not a result of *past* negligence or dereliction of duty.) So what, precisely, is supposed to be the problem? Is it that we can't be *sure* when we form belief in this way? But often we *are* sure. Is it that we can't give a noncircular argument for the reliability of induction? That's true enough; but the same holds for deduction, and if it does not disqualify the latter, why should it disqualify the former? Is it that we can't have Cartesian *certainty* with respect to beliefs formed in this inductive way, that is, is it that we can't deduce the belief in question from the indubitable deliverances of experience by way of arguments we see to be self-evidently valid? Perhaps that is so, but why suppose it is an infirmity, or that as a result such beliefs are in any sense unjustified or irrational? Indeed, why suppose this lack of Cartesian certainty (whatever precisely it is) incompatible with warrant sufficient for knowledge? Here Hume owes us an argument. (It had better be a powerful argument, furthermore, since we ordinarily take it utterly for granted that no such Cartesian certainty is required for rationality, justification, or knowledge.) Is it that it is *possible* that beliefs formed this way should from now on be mistaken, possible that the actual world should turn out to be one of

---

[7]See my *Warrant: The Current Debate* (New York: Oxford University Press, 1993), pp. 132ff.

those worlds governed by a Cartesian demon, a demon who has chosen the present as the time at which induction will no longer yield true beliefs? That is of course possible; but how does it show that we are unjustified or irrational—or that these beliefs don't have high warrant for us? Here, once more, Hume owes us an argument.

This sort of reasoning doesn't lack Foley justification, isn't irrational in the sense of being pathological or psychotic or neurotic, doesn't go contrary to the deliverances of reason, and isn't deontologically unjustified. Perhaps Hume or his followers have something still different in mind when they say that inductive reasoning is unjustified or irrational; if so, they should tell us what it is. In any event, from the present perspective on warrant (contrary to Hume), inductive beliefs often achieve high warrant; for these beliefs are often firmly held, and formed by way of cognitive faculties successfully aimed at truth and functioning properly in a congenial environment. (Don't we know, for example, that pigs can't fly, that human beings are not [without auxiliary help] able to leap tall buildings at a single bound, that if you step off the top of a 3000 foot cliff, you will fall down rather than up?) Hume assumes without argument that if you don't have a deductively valid argument for the conclusion in question from propositions that indubitably report your own immediate experience, then that conclusion has no warrant for you and you have no reason to believe it. But why accept that assumption? What is the reason for supposing (what at first and even second glance seems implausible and fantastic) that if there isn't a good argument of this sort for the conclusion in question, then we have no reason at all for it? This assumption itself seems to suffer from self-referential difficulties: it is certainly not self-evident, and it is hard to see how we could produce a decent argument for it from propositions that are self-evident or appropriately about our immediate experience.

On the present account of warrant, at any rate, the absence of such an argument is no bar to an inductively formed belief's having warrant. What counts instead is whether we do *in fact* reason in this way when our faculties are functioning properly, whether we do in fact reason from correlations we have observed to correlations we have not. The answer, of course, is obvious; it is the person (if there is one) who *can't* (or won't) reason thus who displays pathology.

Is it *necessary* that beliefs formed in accordance with our ordinary inductive practices have warrant? I think not. There could be creatures who did not follow the sorts of inductive policies we follow; such creatures might be such that their practice was not encapsulable in a rule at all, or such that while encapsulable, it was not encapsulable in anything like the Straight Rule.[8] Further, creatures who reasoned in this way could be cognitively successful (in

---

[8]Of course they couldn't sensibly follow the *anti-inductive* policy: if m/n observed As have been B, infer that $1-m/n$ As are B; this quickly leads to trouble. One out of ten maple trees you have observed has been less than two feet tall; eight out of ten have been between two and sixty feet tall; one out of ten has been more than sixty feet tall. Following the anti-inductive policy, you will conclude that nine out of ten maples are less than two feet tall and nine out of ten are more than sixty feet tall: not a pretty picture.

worlds quite different from ours); they could also certainly enjoy deontological justification and Foley rationality. They could also enjoy warrant: God could have created the world in such a way that inductive (Straight Rule) policies would be unsuccessful; he could have created creatures such that when their faculties functioned properly, they did not reason in accord with the straight rule but in some other way; and he could have adjusted their mode of reasoning to the world in such a way that it would yield truth. Had such creatures, by way of some cognitive accident, begun to form beliefs in *our* inductive way, those beliefs would not have had warrant. It is therefore not a *necessary* truth that inductive reasoning is warranted. We may take comfort, however, from the happy thought that it is nonetheless a truth.

II. The New Riddle of Induction

We reason in accord with the expectation that the future will appropriately resemble the past; more generally, that sample will appropriately resemble population. The term 'appropriately', however, is of the first importance; we don't hold that sample will resemble population in *every* respect. All observed pinecones, naturally enough, have been both observed and within visual range of some human being; we don't conclude that there are no unobserved pinecones, or that no pinecones are outside visual range of human beings. All observed amoebas have been within an inch or so of the lens of a microscope; we don't draw the indicated conclusion. We don't think sample resembles population in *that* respect. Every pain such that I have determined by observation whether it was in my body, *was;* I don't draw the doleful conclusion that probably all pains are in my body. All observed explosions have occurred prior to the year 2000 A.D.; none but the pathological optimist concludes that there will be no war in the twenty-first century.

Nelson Goodman's "new riddle of induction" forcefully reminds us of these facts. Say that a thing is *grue* "if examined before 2000 A.D. and determined to be green, or is not so examined and is blue."[9] We then examine a selection of emeralds and do so, naturally enough, before 2000 A.D.; they are all determined to be green. So all the emeralds we have examined are grue. If we draw the indicated inductive conclusion that all emeralds are grue, we are committed to the unhappy view that all emeralds not examined before 2000 are blue; this conflicts with another projection we make, which is that all emeralds (whether or not examined before 2000) are green. Something is clearly amiss, and clearly

[9]*Problems and Projects* (Indianapolis: Bobbs-Merrill, 1972), p. 359. 'Grue' (and its partner in crime 'bleen') made its first appearance earlier in *Fact, Fiction, and Forecast* (Cambridge: Harvard University Press, 1955, reprint, Indianapolis: Bobbs-Merrill, 1973), where Goodman introduced it as follows: "the predicate 'grue' . . . applies to all things examined before t just in case they are green but to other things just in case they are blue" (p. 74 in the 1972 edition). That makes it look as if a thing x is grue if and only if: if it is examined before t then it is green, and if it is examined after t then it is blue. The problem with that formulation is that it isn't possible to be sure that a thing examined only before t is grue; on that formulation, whether it is grue (before t) also depends on its career after t.

enough it has to do with that predicate 'grue': but what, precisely, is wrong with it? The new riddle of induction, therefore, is this question: what makes a predicate *projectible?* More exactly, since (as I see it) it is *properties* rather than predicates that are projectible, what makes a property projectible? A projection is the drawing of an inference of the sort *n/m objects of sort A are B* from the premise that *n/m* observed objects of sort *A* have been found to be *B*. A projection, therefore, will involve two properties: the *reference* property *A* and the *projected* property *B*. It will also involve a sample class: the class of those objects that have the reference property and are such that we have determined whether they have the projected property.

Goodman calls our attention to at least three different kinds of allegedly pathological projections. First, there are those that project such a property as *having been observed* (by me, by some human being, by some observer or other). An example would be the inductive argument for epistemological idealism:

All observed physical objects have been observed.

Therefore, (probably) all physical objects have been observed.

Second, there are the grue/bleen[10] cases; and thirdly, there are projections where the reference property *A* is a disjunctive property *C or D* and one or the other of the disjuncts is such that every member of the sample class has it. (That is, either all the observed *As* have been *Cs* or they have all been *Ds*.) Say that a gruppy is anything that is either a grizzly bear or a puppy; I have examined many puppies but no grizzlies; I then argue,

All the gruppies I have examined have been cute and cuddly;

So (probably) all gruppies are cute and cuddly;

so (probably) all grizzlies are cute and cuddly. A frontiersman who reasons like this would enjoy a life like that of Achilles: exciting but short. This argument is but a special case of the Inductive Argument for Optimism: all of the *examined* enjoyable events in my life are pleasant; so all of the examined (enjoyable or future) events of my life are pleasant; so probably all of the (enjoyable or future) events of my life are pleasant; so probably all the future events of my life are pleasant.[11] Projections of this sort, we might say, involve an unsuitable reference property.

Projections may therefore suffer from at least three sorts of infirmities: projecting such properties as *being observed,* projecting such properties as

[10]An object *x* is *bleen* iff it is examined before *t* and found to be blue, or is not examined before *t* and is green.

[11]Goodman could have added the curve-fitting problem. As Leibniz points out, for any finite set of observations of the path of a comet, infinitely many different curves can be found to fit; he also points out (re Bernoulli) that given any finite set of statistics, there will be infinitely many statistical hypotheses fitting the facts. See Ian Hacking's *The Emergence of Probability* (London: Cambridge University Press, 1975), p. 164.

being grue, and having a disjunctive reference property where one of the disjuncts is had by all members of the sample class. Goodman himself suggests that what counts for projectability (and suitability as reference property) is *entrenchment;* the more frequently a predicate (Goodman displays a certain quasi-Victorian bashfulness when it comes to speaking of properties) has been projected, the more projectable it is.[12] Properties like that of having been observed, or being a bleet (being either a bagful of marbles or a fleet of naval vessels) or gruppyhood, or *being grue* have seldom or never been projected or employed as reference properties, at least in the heat of serious practical use. They are therefore ill-entrenched, and this is the source of their lack of projectability.

But is entrenchment really the key? Suppose a nuclear test goes awry and a subtle malady begins to spread through the population. Victims of this malady regularly project such properties as *being observed, being observed prior to 2000 A.D., being a horse or a horsefly, being a bleet, being a tily* (a tiger lily or a tiger), and other gruesome Goodmanian gerrymanders. Suppose I learn that this malady is invariably inherited; and suppose it vastly increases the birthrate among its victims, so that in two generations or so there will have been many more people on the face of the earth than in all the generations up to the present, and those pathological predicates will have been projected more often than their nonpathological colleagues. Would I then rightly conclude that while *now* these properties are not projectable, they will be in 50 years or so? Surely not. Suppose I learn that it was only relatively recently—10,000 years ago, let's say—that human beings began to *refrain* from projecting the pathological properties in question and that as a matter of fact they have been projected about as often as any others; have I discovered that these properties, contrary to what we have thought, are projectable after all? Again, surely not.

We must look a bit further. If entrenchment doesn't do it, what does? What distinguishes the projectable sheep from the unprojectable goats? Grue and bleen are disjunctive properties,[13] of course, but that's not the answer; we sometimes quite properly project disjunctive properties. All observed tiger lilies have been found to be (say) orange or yellow; we quite properly conclude that (probably) they are all either orange or yellow. Nor need we reject every projection where the reference property is disjunctive and our evidence confined to one disjunct. I discover that 9 out of 10 creatures who are either red-haired Frisians or non-red-haired Frisians can swim; I can properly conclude that 9 out of 10 such persons can swim, even if my sample class happens to contain only Frisians without red hair. Indeed, *all* inductive inferences with universal conclusions are equivalent to projections of that form: *all observed crows have been found to be black* is equivalent to *all observed (crows existing*

---

[12]*Fact, Fiction, and Forecast* (1973), pp. 102ff. Here I take it Goodman is restricting the relevant class of projectors to *human beings;* our discovering that some other race of creature—Alpha Centaurians, let's say—has often projected such properties as *has been observed* would presumably cut no ice.

[13]Assuming for the moment that the notion of a disjunctive *property,* as opposed to a disjunctive *predicate,* is unproblematic.

prior to 2000 A.D. or crows not existing prior to 2000 A.D.) have been found to be black, with all our evidence falling under the first disjunct of that disjunctive property. We can say, of course, that we can't properly make the projection where *A* is a disjunctive property *C or D* such that *C* and *D* are *relevantly different* from one another and our sample contains only *C*s (or only *D*s): but what constitutes a relevant difference? One sort of case is just where things that are *C* are clearly very different from things that are *D*, as in the case of tilies or bleets. But what makes things very different? Any two objects share as many properties as you please and differ in as many as you please (taking 'property' in the usual broad sense): what is it, then, that distinguishes relevantly different properties? That question is far from trivial.

We have three kinds of pathology here: but perhaps we can reduce the multiplicity. Turn to the first, the kind involving such projected properties as *being observed.* Examples would be

> All observed emeralds have been observed,
> Therefore probably all emeralds have been observed;
> All observed amoebaes have been found to be within an inch or so of the lens of a microscope,
> Therefore probably all amoebas are within an inch or so of the lens of a microscope;

and

> All observed robins have begun to exist before 2000 A.D.,
> Therefore probably all robins will have begun to exist before 2000 A.D. (so that any robins around after, say, 2080 will be octogenarians).

One thing characteristic of these cases is that it is impossible—logically impossible in the first case, impossible in other ways in the second and third—that a counterexample to the conclusion should turn up in the sample class.[14] If we generalize a bit, we can see the essential similarity of the second kind of pathology—that involving such properties as grueness and bleenhood. A thing is grue if and only if either it is examined before 2000 A.D. and found to be green, or not so examined and blue. Now all examined emeralds have been found to be grue, since all examined emeralds have been examined before 2000 A.D. and found to be green. I conclude that all emeralds are grue: is it possible that my sample class contain a counterexample to that conclusion? Well, yes; it is possible that there be nongreen emeralds, and possible that some of them should turn up in my sample class; furthermore, any nongreen emerald I observe before 2000 A.D. will be observed before 2000 A.D., thus falsifying the second disjunct of the definition of 'grue', and will be found to be nongreen, thus falsifying the first disjunct of the definition. So it is possible that a counterexample to the conclusion should turn up in the sample class.

---

[14]See my *God and Other Minds* (Ithaca: Cornell University Press, 1967; reprint 1991), pp. 258ff.

But there is a certain kind of counterexample to the conclusion that cannot turn up in the sample class—a kind such that as a matter of fact there are many examples of it. It is not possible that a *green* counterexample to the conclusion appear in the sample class—at any rate it isn't possible *now* that such a counterexample turn up in the sample class, and it won't be possible until 2000 A.D. A green counterexample to the conclusion would be a green emerald that was not examined before 2000 A.D.; no doubt there are many such emeralds, but none of them can turn up in my sample class until 2000 A.D. Although it is possible that a counterexample to the conclusion that all emeralds are grue should turn up in my sample class (it is possible that there be blue emeralds), it is not possible that a *green* counterexample to my conclusion should be a member of my sample class—not for the next few years, anyway. This is so, furthermore, even though it is possible that there *be* green counterexamples to my conclusion—indeed, we all believe that it is not just *possible* but *true* that there are green counterexamples to that conclusion.

Suppose we say, therefore, that a projection is *limited* at *t* if at *t* it is possible that there be a counterexample to the conclusion, but impossible at *t*[15] that a counterexample to its conclusion should have appeared in its sample class; and say that a projection is *limited with respect to P* at *t* if it is possible that there be a counterexample to its conclusion that has *P* (that is, possible that there be an object that both has *P* and is a counterexample to its conclusion) but impossible at *t* that such a counterexample should turn up in its sample class. Then both the first and second kinds of pathology involve projections that are limited or limited with respect to some property; both are such that even if there are counterexamples to the conclusion of the indicated type, no such counterexample can turn up in the sample class. The third kind of pathology—the sort where the reference property is a disjunctive property *C* or *D*, with every member of the sample class displaying *C* (or else every member of it displaying *D*)—involves a closely related anomaly. Suppose a projection of that sort is such that its conclusion is that everything that has *C* or *D* has *P*, and every member of the sample has *C*: then its structure precludes its sample class containing a counterexample to its conclusion that has *D*, even if there are such counterexamples, that is, even if there are things that have *D* (and hence *C* or *D*) but don't have *P*. Again, no such counterexample to the conclusion will ever turn up in the sample, whether or not there are any.

Shall we say that the problem with all these properties is just that they are limited, or limited with respect to some property *P*, so that even if there is a counterexample of a certain sort to its conclusion, that counterexample will not turn up in the sample class? But why is *that* a problem—that is, why does the fact that a projection is limited in this way disqualify it? Well, won't the sample class of such a projection be biased, that is, such that the distribution of the projected property in it differs from the distribution that property enjoys in the reference class? But that does not follow. All that follows from its being thus

---

[15]*Accidentally* impossible: that is, impossible in the way in which it is now impossible that you should not have been born. See my "On Ockham's Way Out," *Faith and Philosophy* 3, no. 3 (1986), p. 235.

limited is that we don't *know* that its sample class is not biased; and we can't find out (at least by way of inductive inference) that it isn't. And that infirmity affects many perfectly proper projections. Checking to see how the Douglas firs in the North Cascades National Park are faring under the onslaught of the dreaded Borer Beetle, I make a survey: 31 out of the 100 firs I examine show at least some damage, so I conclude more generally that about 3 out of 10 firs in the park have suffered some damage. I can't be sure my sample is fair, however, because constraints of time, distance, and terrain prevent me from examining the trees on the far side of Inaccessible Ridge. (I can't be completely sure that my sample is fair without examining *all* the North Cascade firs, so that my sample class coincides with my reference class.) Other and more dramatic cases are already familiar: all the paramecia I have examined for some property P have been close to a microscope; I can't find out inductively that those *not* near a microscope display the same distribution of P.

Indeed, all the members of our sample classes for *any* projection have been observed; we can't discover—by induction anyway—that those sample classes are fair. This means that nearly every projection is limited with respect to some property. For nearly any projection, if it is possible that there be a counter-example to the conclusion, then it is possible that there be an *unobserved* counterexample to the conclusion; but (of course) no such counterexample could turn up in the sample class. So being limited with respect to some property or other is not sufficient for being pathological.

What about being limited with respect to the *projected* property, as in, for example, the inductive argument for idealism? What shall we say there? Is that sufficient for a projection's being of no force? No. Why might one think so? Well, we know that even if the conclusion were false, the sample class would never contain a counterexample to it; no such counterexample could turn up. And that might lead us to think that the projection has no force at all. But we really have substantially the same problem with respect to *any* induction: there will be certain ways in which the conclusion could be false, certain possible kinds of counterexamples to the conclusion, such that even if there *are* counter-examples of that sort, they could never turn up in the sample class. If that doesn't disqualify projections (and it doesn't), neither should the fact that the projection is limited with respect to the projected property.

The alleged infirmity, therefore, does not as such disqualify projections. So what is it that is responsible for the pathological nature of properties such as *being grue*? The basic form of the answer is not hard to make out. The projectability of a property cannot be investigated simply by asking which properties have *in fact* been projected most frequently; nor does it seem that we can find anything like a criterion for separating the projectable sheep from the unprojectable goats in terms of the logical properties of the attributes in ques-tion. Instead, the crucial question is this: which properties are the ones a properly functioning adult human being in our circumstances will in fact project? Here I shall only gesture toward the truth, rather than develop an appropriately articulated theory; but the broad outline of the answer, in so far as the properties Goodman considers, is not hard to see. Properly functioning human beings don't typically project such properties as *having been observed* or *having been observed prior to 2000,* or *being a bleet;*[16] a schoolchild who did so (and wasn't joking or pretending to be a weird philosopher) would be admonished; if he repeated the offense he would be kept in from recess and threatened with remedial help. No properly functioning human being would form a belief about grizzlies by disjoining the property of being a grizzly with that of being a puppy, examining a bunch of puppies for that property, and attributing to the grizzlies the property found to characterize the puppies. You plot your observations of the pressure of hydrogen as a function of temperature and volume; you draw a nice smooth curve through the points on the graph but gratuitously add a few singularities: for example, the function is $p = t/v$, except at midnights on Tuesdays in the southern hemisphere during the second century A.D., when it was $p = t^3/v$. Your reasoning is seriously defective; and what makes it defective is just the fact that properly functioning human beings (in your circumstances) would never in fact reason in that way.

You might think, once more, that there is a *logical* problem with reasoning in that fashion. For take the argument about grizzlies: true enough, you have an argument for the conclusion that grizzlies are not dangerous, but obviously you can construct another similar argument for the proposition that all grizzlies *are* dangerous, at least if you know of some class of beings that all of them are dangerous. For (nearly) any inference I of this defective sort, there is another for a conclusion inconsistent with the conclusion of I; and perhaps you think *that* is the problem with them. But this can't be the answer; the fact is for (nearly) any inductive inference of *any* sort there will be another with an incompatible conclusion. Via straightforward inductive reasoning we conclude that no pigs can fly; but of course there is also the projection

> Every pig that can't fly, and which is such that it has been determined whether it has the property of being either P_1 or P_2 or P_3 or . . . or P_n (where P_i is any property unique to pig p_i), has had that property;
>
> So probably every pig that cannot fly has that property;

in which case it is likely that any unexamined pigs can fly. So that's not the answer. The answer is given, instead, by our design plan. A properly functioning human being will not make such projections; these projections are a sign of dysfunction, pathological in a more than metaphorical sense.

More exactly, a properly functioning human being will be much less strongly inclined to make those peculiar Goodmanian projections than the more standard variety. Still more exactly, where there is a conflict between projections of the first sort and projections of the second, the second wins hands down. It is not that the pathological projections have no weight at all. Even the inductive argument for epistemological idealism has *some* small force; it is just that its modest force is overwhelmed by the superior force of projections with

---

[16]Of course they *sometimes* do: we might conclude that 85 percent of the grizzly bears in Alaska have never been observed by human beings. (But we don't do it by observing a sample of grizzlies, noting that 85 percent of them have not been observed by human beings, and . . .)

incompatible conclusions. It isn't true that we get *no evidence at all* for all emeralds' being grue from the fact that all observed emeralds have been grue; it is just that we have much stronger evidence for an incompatible proposition. What makes for strength, or, alternatively, for degree of projectability? Nothing but our design plan. A properly functioning human being will find some proposed projections much weightier than others. A projection involving green will be much weightier than one involving grue; so where a green and grue projection conflict, the grue projection will gracefully give way. And of course if this were not so, we could never learn from experience— that is, we could never learn from experience about what is unobserved. For if all projections were created equal, then for any projection leading us to expect that n/m objects of a sort A are B, or that the next A will be a B, there will be another of equal weight for the conclusion that it is false that n/m As are B or that the next A will be a B: *All observed crows are black*, so *Probably all crows are black* will be countered by *All observed black crows have proved to have been observed before the present time;* so *Probably no unexamined crows are black*.[17]

By way of conclusion, note that this account can be extended to neighboring areas. Obviously we cannot so much as begin the intellectual life without gaining a mastery of a sizable repertoire of concepts. But how do we acquire these concepts? In the typical case, we learn them from others. You notice that your 18-month-old daughter is intently inspecting a red ball; you say (in that loud and rather insincere tone of excitement we use with 18-month-olds), "See the red ball! That's red!!" She gets the idea and can eventually use the word 'red' with the best of us. But why is *that* the idea she gets? After all there are plenty of others she could have gotten instead, plenty of others logically related in the same way to her experience; and as Wittgenstein reminded us, directions can always be misinterpreted. Instead of acquiring the concept *redness*, she could instead have focused on *being observed* (and perhaps she would conclude that we have many words for this property) or *observed by me*, or *red and observed by me*, or *either red and observed prior to now or observed after now and green*, or *red and smaller than Daddy* or . . . But she doesn't; that must await her reading Goodman. Similarly, she could have acquired such concepts as *undetached ball part*, or *ball stage*, or . . . But again, she doesn't; that must await her reading Quine.[18] Upon going to school and learning addition, she

---

[17]Granted: our design plan requires projecting green rather than grue. But isn't there something *objectively* right about projecting the one rather than the other? Given the actual constitution of the world, of course: if we projected those pathological properties, we would be right much less often than in fact we are. But that this is so is not a necessary truth.

[18]See Quine on the radical indeterminacy of translation, *Word and Object* (Cambridge: MIT Press, 1960), pp. 72ff. Clearly one important constraint to take into account in translation will be our design plan: human beings are unlikely to wield such concepts as *undetached rabbit part* and *rabbit stage* except in special circumstances. We know something about the concepts properly functioning human beings acquire and use in the relevant situations; clearly we should avail ourselves of that knowledge in proposing a translation.

Quine himself, of course, seems to conclude that there really aren't *different* concepts here at all; put his way, there is really no difference in meaning, in our own language, between 'rabbit',

could get the idea of *quus* rather than *plus*, quaddition rather than addition. But, once more, she doesn't; that must await her reading of Kripke.[19] The explanation in each of these cases is the same: what makes the concepts she acquires the *right* ones, what makes the others wrong, is that a properly functioning human being will acquire the first kind; acquiring the second in those circumstances will be pathological, out of accord with our design plan. So the normativity involved is the normativity that goes with proper function. It is the very sort of normativity that is involved when you say, of your balky automobile, "When you turn the key, the starter ought to engage." It is the same normativity as that involved in such generalizations as *An adult human heart at rest ought to beat at between forty and eighty beats per minute;* it is the same normativity as that involved in such psychological generalizations as *A three-year-old child ought to have a vocabulary of more than three hundred words.*

The old riddle of induction, therefore, is the question 'What makes it right or rational to follow inductive methods in forming beliefs?' Hume thought there was no solution. The new riddle of induction is the question, 'What makes a property projectable?' Goodman thought the answer was entrenchment. Both Goodman and Hume are wrong; there is an answer to each question, and it is substantially the *same* answer. What makes it right to form belief in that inductive manner is just the fact that that is how a properly functioning human being forms beliefs; and what makes projectable properties projectable is just the fact that properly functioning human beings project them. But given that these projections and beliefs meet the other conditions for warrant (given that these beliefs and projections are formed in an appropriate cognitive environment and that the modules of the design plan governing their production are successfully aimed at truth), that is sufficient for warrant. And given that the beliefs in question are held sufficiently firmly, it is also sufficient (along with truth) for knowledge.

'undetached rabbit part', and 'rabbit stage'. But this is doubly deficient. First, if this were so, we shouldn't so much as have a puzzle here; the claim of radical indeterminacy is startling only because there *is* a difference in meaning between these predicates. (See my chapter 4, n. 16.) Second, Quine's argument that there is no difference of meaning here is entirely inconclusive. Perhaps it is true, as he says, that "There is nothing in linguistic meaning, then, beyond what is to be gleaned from overt behavior in overt circumstances" ("Indeterminacy of Translation Again," *Journal of Philosophy* [January 1987], p. 5). The native says 'gavagai'; all I have to go on, in trying to understand her, is her behavior and circumstances; and there are rabbit stages and rabbit parts present just as well as rabbit. But it does not follow, of course, either that there is no diversity of meaning between 'rabbit stage', 'rabbit part', and 'rabbit', or that we don't know which meaning is attached to 'gavagai'. Given our noetic constitution, what a properly functioning human being gleans from the native's overt behavior in those circumstances is that it is the concept *rabbit*, not *undetached rabbit part*, that is attached to 'gavagai', even if examples of the latter concept are present whenever examples of the former are.

[19]See his *Wittgenstein on Rules and Private Language* (Cambridge: Harvard University Press, 1982).

8

Epistemic Probability: Some Current Views

A pervasive feature of our intellectual life is our believing a proposition *A on the evidential basis of* another or others. Sometimes we believe *A simpliciter;* other times what we believe is that *A* is likely or *probable.* I believe that my neighbor is burning leaves again on the basis of my belief that it's leaf-burning time and there is smoke billowing up from behind his house; I believe that the temperature dipped near the freezing point last night on the basis of my belief that there is frost on the roof of the house across the road; I think it likely that Feike can speak some English on the basis of my knowledge that 9 out of 10 Frisian teenagers can do so and Feike is a Frisian teenager. Where the proposition *B* on the basis of which I believe *A is evidence for A* or *evidentially supports A,* what we have is *propositional evidence.* This is the sort of circumstance in which my believing one proposition or group of propositions confers warrant (for me) upon another proposition I believe—warrant it would otherwise (typically) lack.

Propositional evidence is *second-level* evidence. We have first such sources of warrant as perception, memory, induction, reason (in the narrow sense in which it is the source of what is self-evident to one or another degree), and so on. Call these *first-level* sources of warrant. Following currently fashionable practice, we may picturesquely think of these sources of warrant as input—output devices, realized or concretized functions; they take as input situations of one sort or another (being appeared to a certain way, for example) and yield as output a belief, a belief that may have one or another degree of warrant. But when one belief gets warrant for me by way of being accepted on the evidential basis of another belief, we have a second-level source of warrant: this mechanism or faculty takes *beliefs* (alternatively, beliefs as well as other circumstances) as input, rather than nonpropositional circumstances, and yields as output another belief, or a modification of belief. In the first sort of case we have nonpropositional evidence—the evidence of the senses, perhaps, or of memory. In the second we have propositional evidence, the sort of case where what confers warrant on my belief *B* is another belief *A,* not an experience or a set of circumstances. No doubt you believe that the earth is round; and perhaps (unlike most of us, who believe this by way of testimony) you do so on the basis of the sort of evidence presented for that fact in the sixth grade. That evidence is indeed evidence; and *The earth is round* has warrant, for you, just because you believe it on the basis of that evidence. (In this kind of case, perhaps we should speak of *transfer* of warrant, rather than a *source* of warrant, since it is only if A has warrant that B can get it by way of being believed on the basis of A).[1]

Propositional warrant comes in two styles: *deductive*, and *nondeductive* or probabilistic. A proposition A can get deductive warrant, for me, by way of being believed on the basis of other propositions I already believe that have warrant for me, and that *entail* A. I have already said most of what I have to say about deductive warrant in chapter 6; here I have two brief reminders. First, A does not automatically get warrant for me, just by virtue of being entailed by other propositions I already believe. A is a complicated tautology; it therefore follows by propositional logic from anything else I believe; but if I can't see that it follows and believe it just because I find it in a comic book, it has little warrant for me. In the typical case, A gets warrant for me in the deductive way (by way of being believed on the basis of other propositions that have warrant for me and that entail it) only if I grasp the connection between A and those others, *see that* those others entail A,[2] and believe A on the basis of those others. Second, even where A entails B and I both see the connection between them and believe the latter on the basis of the former, it still is not *automatically* the case that B has as much warrant for me as A. Perhaps I see the connection between the premises of some mathematical argument and the rather complicated conclusion, but not very clearly; in such a case the premises might have maximal or near maximal warrant for me and the conclusion considerably less.

In other cases my evidence does not entail B but still supports it. I believe that the butler is innocent; my evidence is that he was 10 miles away from the scene of the crime an hour before the crime took place, that he had no means of transportation other than his own two legs, that he is middle-aged and overweight, and that middle-aged and overweight men are scarcely ever able to run 10 miles in one hour. There is evidence[3] for special relativity; this evidence supports but does not entail that theory. The same goes for the evidence for the proposition that the earth is billions of years old.

In both sorts of cases—that is, in the cases where the cited evidence entails A as well as cases where it does not—A is *probable* with respect to the evi-

---

[1] As we saw in chapter 4, *testimony* is another case where warrant gets transferred; the testifiee's belief has no warrant unless the testifier's does. (The testifiee may be *justified* in believing the testifier under those conditions; but that is a different story.) A difference is that the testifiee need not explicitly believe that the testifier testifies to what he does; that thought may never cross his mind; he may be paying attention only to the testimony. But if B gets its warrant, for me, by way of being believed on the basis of A, then I must or must have explicitly believe or believed A as well as B.

[2] In the typical case: but not necessarily in every case, for I could come to believe or know that some proposition B, which I already know, entails A, without myself seeing the entailment. I might thus come to know the conclusion of a complicated computation carried out by a computer. Here my warrant is mixed; part of it is broadly inductive, depending upon my belief that the computer is functioning properly.

[3] For example, muon decay phenomena, the null result of the Michaelson-Morley experiment, and the Haefele-Keating experiment involving high-speed transport of cesium clocks.

dence; the *epistemic conditional probability* of A with respect to that evidence is high. The term 'epistemic probability' is used variously by various authors. I shall use it to refer to the relationship between a pair of propositions A and B when A is evidence, propositional evidence, for B. More precisely, in those cases I shall say that the epistemic conditional probability of B on A is high. This conditional epistemic probability, whatever exactly it is, is the main subject of this chapter and the next. Our question is: what is the relation between a pair of propositions A and B when the epistemic conditional probability of A on B is high? What kind of account or analysis can we give of this relation? What makes it the case that P(A/B) is high? And what, precisely, is the relation between conditional epistemic probability and warrant?

That question is as hard as any in epistemology; the whole area bristles with paradox, mystery, confusion, darkness, despair. Probability, as Churchill did not say, is a riddle swathed in a mystery wrapped in an enigma. The first thing to see, in trying to grasp the general lay of the land, is to note the divide between epistemic and *statistical* or, better, *objective* probability.[4] In this chapter I shall distinguish the former from the latter and point out some debilitating problems with the main accounts of the former; in the next I shall propose what I hope is a better substitute.

I. Epistemic Probability and Statistical Probability

The most prominent kind of objective probability is statistical probability; and in my *Warrant: the Current Debate,* chapter 6, we noted the difference between such propositions as

(a)   The probability that a 30-year-old urban Australian male is a member of the Ku Klux Klan is very low,

(b)   It is unlikely that a horse will weigh more than a ton,

(c)   The probability that a two-year-old Rhode Island Red from southern Wisconsin will contract coccidiosis within the next year is .004,

(d)   The probability that a tritium atom will decay within the next 13 years is just over one-half,

on the one hand, and

(e)   The probability of the proposition *Feike can swim* on *9 out of 10 Frisians can swim and Feike is a Frisian* is high,

[4]As I see it, statistical probability is one variety (perhaps the most prominent and least controversial variety) of objective probability; another variety is logical probability. I therefore use the term 'objective' for the main nonepistemic variety of probability. There is a danger, here, however, that this usage suggests that epistemic probability is 'subjective', and in fact the term 'subjective probability' is sometimes used for epistemic probability. This seems to me infelicitous, in that it is only on certain (mistaken, as I see it) theories of probability that epistemic probabilities are subjective. As I see it (and on the account of epistemic probability in chapter 9), there is nothing characteristically subjective about epistemic probability.

(f) It is likely that special relativity is at least approximately true,

(g) Despite the Flat Earthers, it is monumentally improbable that the earth is flat,

(h) It is extremely likely that the sun will rise tomorrow, and that if it does, it will rise in the east,

(i) It is likely that Goldbach's conjecture (that every even number is the sum of two primes) is true

and

(j) The Linguistic Theory of the *A Priori* is at best unlikely,

on the other.

There are several salient differences between probabilities of the first sort and those of the second. First, as their very name indicates, those of the first sort are often or typically determined or discovered by broadly statistical means; we take what we hope is a fair sample of 30-year-old urban Australian males, determine that few of them are members of the Ku Klux Klan, and then draw the preceding conclusion. The statistics we collect are a guide to the probability we seek: we ascertain the proportion of two-year-old Rhode Island Reds from southern Wisconsin that have contracted coccidiosis within the last two years, and conclude (*ceteris paribus*) that the probability in question is close to the proportion in question. Not so for epistemic probability; it is not by statistical means that we determine that special relativity is probable with respect to our evidence. It is not by statistical means that we determine that the probability that Feike can swim is high, relative to the evidence that Feike is a Frisian teenager and 9 out of 10 Frisian teenagers can swim.

Second, statistical probabilities often change over time: the probability that a 50-year-old American female will live to the age of 80 is higher now than it was 75 years ago, as is the probability that a New Yorker will be run over by a taxicab. Epistemic probabilities, on the other hand, do not change over time;[5] the probability of special relativity on the evidence cited for it in, say, 1920, is the same now as it was then.

Third, statistical probabilities of this sort are ordinarily *general* or *indefinite:* they specify the probability that a thing of one sort is also a thing of another. Thus we have the probability that a 19-year-old heavy smoker will live to the age of 70, that a tritium atom will decay during the next 123 years, that a resident of Japan will be more than six feet tall. Such general probabilities are to be contrasted with *definite* or *specific* probabilities, such as the probability that Sam (who is among other things 19 years old and a heavy smoker), or that Sei (who is Japanese) will live to be 70. Epistemic probabilities, however, are just such definite probabilities; what is epistemically probable (or not) is a

---

[5]At any rate they do not change over time nearly as rapidly as do statistical probabilities. The account of epistemic probability I shall give in chapter 9 does not preclude change in epistemic probabilities, and if in fact there is no such change, that will be a contingent rather than a necessary truth.

proposition. It is special relativity, or *Paul is now watching television,* or *The earth is flat,* or *The butler did it,* that are epistemically probable to one degree or another. Indeed, the proposition in question could be that the statistical probability of an *As* being a *B* is .9; it is epistemically probable (for me) that the statistical probability of a horse's weighing more than a ton is low.

Fourth, statistical probability is an *objective* feature of a situation, having to do essentially with infinitary analogues of proportions of things of one kind among things of another. Therefore statistical probability is independent of what we know or believe; it is entirely possible that we should be wholly mistaken as to what the statistical probability of an *As* being a *B* is, even when we are completely rational and have done our level best, following all the proper procedures. More important, statistical probability is independent of our nature. Statistical probability is not and could not be species relative; but epistemic probability, as I shall argue, is indeed kind or species relative.

Note finally that epistemic probability displays one further feature, and an important one at that: there is a sort of *normativity* about it. What is epistemically probable in a given situation is what, in some sense, *ought* to be believed in that situation.[6] Relative to our cognitive situation, it is extremely improbable that the earth rests on the back of a turtle which rests on the back of another turtle, which rests on still another, so that it's turtles all the way down; hence there is something mistaken, improper, wrong, deplorable in that belief. If one of your grown children embraced it, you would suffer consternation and dismay. Probable beliefs are the *right* ones, the *acceptable* ones, the *approvable* ones. Because of this normative feature of epistemic probability, the contrast between the two sorts of probability is sometimes said to be that between *factual* and *normative* probability. But this too is misleading, since epistemic probabilities are also factual. It is simply a fact that *Feike can swim* is (epistemically) probable with respect to *9 out of ten Frisians can swim and Feike is a Frisian;* it is simply a fact that the denial of the former is (epistemically) improbable with respect to the latter.

Of course there are many-sided and overlapping connections between these two varieties of probability; and according to Ian Hacking, they have been run together ever since their emergence in the seventeenth century: "the probability that emerged so suddenly [in the decade around 1660] is Janus-faced. On the one side it is statistical, concerning itself with stochastic laws of chance processes. On the other side it is epistemological, dedicated to assessing reasonable degrees of belief in propositions quite devoid of statistical background."[7] As we shall see, this Janus-faced character of probability goes much further back than the seventeenth century; but Janus-faced it certainly is. There will also be interesting and complicated cases of reiterated and mixed probabilities. It is epistemically probable (with respect to our evidence) that the statistical probability of a tritium atom's decaying within the next 13 years is just over one-half;

---

[6]The normativity here (as we shall see) is not deontological; it is not that there is something *blameworthy* in accepting the wrong beliefs on the basis of your evidence; in so doing you aren't necessarily going counter to your duty.

[7]*The Emergence of Probability* (London: Cambridge University Press, 1975), p. 12.

it is statistically probable, we hope, that epistemically probable beliefs (beliefs probable with respect to someone's evidence) are true; and that epistemically probable beliefs are statistically likely to be true is epistemically probable with respect to my evidence. (So, at any rate, *I* say; the skeptic may demur.) I shall say no more about statistical probability here; in chapter 9 I shall try to give a fuller account of statistical probability and the objective probability of which it is a species.

II. Theories of Epistemic Probability

In thinking about warrant and epistemic probability, there are in particular two phenomena to bear in mind. First, there is the fact that one or more propositions can serve as a (*prima facie*) good reason for believing another proposition *A*, without entailing *A:* in such a case we have nondeductive propositional evidence (as we may call it) for *A*. In such a case, furthermore, *A* can acquire warrant, for me: nondeductive propositional warrant. And second, there is the fact that one or more propositions may make another proposition *likely* or *probable*—in the way in which the evidence for a theory—special relativity, the Linguistic Theory of the *A Priori*, the Doctrine of Transubstantiation, whatever—can make that theory probable; under those conditions, *A* will be *epistemically* probable—*conditionally* epistemically probable. What we seek is a good (or even decent) account of conditional epistemic probability.

There are substantially three theories of epistemic probability (taken as a relation among propositions): the *personalist* or Bayesian theory (see *Warrant: The Current Debate*, chapters 6 and 7), the *logical* theory of probability (pioneered by J. M. Keynes, developed by Rudolph Carnap, and, among contemporary philosophers, championed with great verve by Richard Swinburne and D. C. Stove), and what I shall call the *statistical* account, where the aim is, somehow, to derive epistemic probability from the statistical syllogism. (We might as well have called this last the *Kyburgian* theory, since Henry Kyburg has developed it with magnificent penetration and thoroughness.) I am sorry to report that none of these theories is successful.

A. Bayesianism

In *Warrant: The Current Debate*, chapters 6 and 7, I argued that Bayesianism does not provide either a good theory of warrant or a good theory of rationality; and I argued *ambulando* that it does not provide a good theory of conditional epistemic probability either. I won't repeat those arguments here, but let me briefly summarize the main problems encountered by the Bayesian intent on a theory of conditional epistemic probability. What he proposes, of course, is to give an account of conditional epistemic probability in terms of *personal* probability. Roughly (very roughly) speaking, my personal probability for a proposition *A* is the degree to which I believe *A*, or the level of confidence I invest in it, or the degree of credence I afford it. More specifically, the Bayesian proposes an account of conditional epistemic probability in terms of conditional personal probability, where my conditional personal probability for A on B ($P_{me}(A/B)$) is the quotient of my personal probability for $A\&B$ ($P_{me}(A\&B)$) by my personal probability for B ($P_{me}(B)$), provided the latter is nonzero. And here there are two possibilities. First, we might say that A is epistemically probable on B 'for me' if $P_{me}(A/B)$ is high enough; and, second, we might say that A is epistemically probable on B ('for me') if my unconditional probability for A is less than $P_{me}(A/B)$.

But each of these proposals faces daunting disabilities. First and most serious, a problem that afflicts both proposals. On the Bayesian account we need a *subscript;* we must *relativize* epistemic probability (to persons); $P_{me}(A/B)$ might be quite different from $P_{you}(A/B)$. But then, of course, we shall have to say that the conditional epistemic probability of A on B with respect to *you* may be quite different from that with respect to *me*. The problem is that conditional probability is *not* thus relative to persons. *Feike can swim* is probable with respect to *99 out of 100 Frisian lifeguards can swim and Feike is a Frisian lifeguard* no matter what you or I think and no matter what the status of our noetic structures or credence functions. That this die has come up ace on each of the last 3,000 tosses is evidence that it will come up ace on the next— again, no matter what the structure of my credence function, or yours, or anyone else's. Call the first 'A' and the second 'B'; it is not the case that A is epistemically probable, on B, relative to *me* but possibly not epistemically probable, on B, relative to *you*. This, I think, is the central problem with Bayesianism.

But even if we were to acquiesce in this unlikely relativization, our problems would be just beginning. For take the first suggestion: that A is epistemically probable on B, 'for me', if $P_{me}(A/B)$ is high enough. This must be incorrect, as an account of epistemic conditional probability; for clearly I might *know* a pair of propositions, one of which was epistemically improbable with respect to the other. I know, for example, both *99 out of 100 Americans are less than 6 foot 4 inches tall and Harry is an American,* and *Harry is 6 foot 5 inches tall.* Clearly the second is epistemically improbable with respect to the first; but since I know them both (and therefore accord great credence to each), my personal probability for the second on the first will be high.[8] But then I can't explain the epistemic improbability ('with respect to me') of the second on the first in terms of the low degree of my personal probability of the second on the first.

Turn to the second suggestion: that A is epistemically probable on B ('for me') if my personal probability for A is less than my conditional personal probability for A on B—that is, if $P_{me}(A)$ is less than $P_{me}(A/B)$. This also fails. The conditional epistemic probability of *Feike can swim* on *99 out of 100 Frisian lifeguards can swim and Feike is a Frisian lifeguard* is in fact high, and high 'for me'. But on the account in question, it could fail to be high ('for me'). Call the first proposition (*Feike can swim*) 'A' and the second (*99 out of 100*

---

[8]Say I believe each of A and B to .999; then $P_{me}(-A \vee -B)$ will be at most .002 (since it is equal at most to the sum of the probabilities of the disjuncts), in which case $P_{me}(A\&B)$ will be at least .998, so that $P_{me}(A/B)$ will be at least 998/999.

Frisian lifeguards can swim and Feike is a Frisian lifeguard) 'B'; and suppose I believe each of them to about .3, so that $P_{me}(A) = P_{me}(B) = .3$; and suppose my personal probability for the conjunction of A with B is very low—.001, say. A little calculation then reveals that $P_{me}(A)$ is greater than $P_{me}(A/B)$, so that on this second Bayesian suggestion, A would *not* be epistemically probable ('for me') with respect to B. But, of course, B *is* evidence for A and A is epistemically probable on B, no matter what else I know.

B. *The Logical Theory of Probability*

As we learn from Ian Hacking,[9] the logical theory of epistemic probability goes back to the seventeenth century; in more recent times it has been defended by J. M. Keynes,[10] Harold Jeffreys,[11] Rudolph Carnap,[12] Richard Swinburne,[13] D. C. Stove,[14] John Bigelow,[15] and others. Taken as a theory of epistemic conditional probability, such a view should have two parts. First, the heart and soul of the theory would be that for any pair of propositions, there is a definite and logically necessary relationship of probability between them, a relationship that conforms to the probability calculus. But second, epistemic probability must be grafted onto this logical probability. In the simplest case, logical probability and epistemic probability would be simply identified: no distinction would be drawn between them. And as a matter of historical fact, it is only this simplest case that has been exemplified; those who have offered a logical theory of epistemic probability have not, so far as I know, distinguished logical from epistemic probability.[16]

Suppose we think first about this relation of logical probability said to obtain among propositions. From this perspective, probability may be metaphorically considered as *partial entailment,* with entailment *simpliciter* a special case in which the conditional probability of A on B ($P(A/B)$) is equal to 1. On the logical interpretation, a probability statement of the form $P(A/B) = n$ is not first of all an epistemic statement about what is or is not sensible or rational or acceptable or warranted; it simply records a necessary, objective, quasi-logical fact about A and B. Probability thus construed has nothing to do with partial belief, or uncertainty, or lack of knowledge, or observed frequencies. The truth of a probability statement in no way depends upon what anyone knows or believes, or upon any other contingent state of affairs. God may not *need* probability; nevertheless, he knows the value of $P(A/B)$ for any propositions A and B. The relationship in question, furthermore, conforms to the

[9]*The Emergence of Probability,* chap. 17.

[10]*A Treatise on Probability* (London: Macmillan, 1921).

[11]*Theory of Probability* (Oxford: Clarendon Press, 1939).

[12]*Logical Foundations of Probability* (Chicago: University of Chicago Press, 1950).

[13] *An Introduction to Confirmation Theory* (London: Methuen, 1973).

[14]*The Rationality of Induction* (Oxford: Clarendon Press, 1986), part II.

[15]"Possible Worlds Foundations for Probability," *Journal of Philosophical Logic* (1976), pp. 299ff.

[16]Perhaps an exception is Henry Kyburg, whose view is not easy to classify. See below, section C.

calculus of probabilities; so if *A* entails *B*, then *B* has a probability of 1 on *A* and necessary truths have a probability of 1 on any evidence.

Further, each proposition will have an *a priori* or, better, *intrinsic*[17] probability: this will be its probability on any necessary truth. There will be an inverse relationship between *content* and probability: the more you say (the greater the content of your assertion), the more likely you are to be wrong (the lower its probability). What is true in every possible world has minimal content and maximal probability; what is true in no possible world has maximal content and minimal probability. What is true in no possible world, of course, is necessarily false; among *contingent* propositions what is true in just one possible world—the proposition *α is actual,* for example (where 'α' is a name of the actual world)—has maximal content and minimal probability. If we think of the content of a proposition as the (infinitary analogue of) the proportion of possible worlds in which the proposition is true, then the inverse relationship between content and intrinsic probability immediately follows:

> THE PRINCIPLE OF INTRINSIC PROBABILITY (PIP): Intrinsic probability is a monotonic decreasing function of content: for any propositions *A* and *B*, if *A* has more content than *B*, then the intrinsic probability of *A* is not greater than that of *B*.

(If *A* and *B* have the same degree of content, then perhaps other factors—simplicity [as with Richard Swinburne],[18] for example—may enter, whereby *A* is awarded more intrinsic probability than *B*, despite their enjoying the same degree of content.)

Wherein lies the appeal of the logical theory? Chiefly in the fact that for a significant range of pairs of propositions <*A,B*>, it seems to be no more than the sober truth: there *does* seem to be a relationship of probability between the propositions in question, and it also seems to be *necessary* that there is the relation in question. Principal among the logical theorist's exhibits would be statistical syllogisms: it seems intuitively obvious that the proposition *Feike can swim* is probable with respect to the proposition *9 out of 10 Frisians can swim and Feike is a Frisian.* Furthermore, *that* this relation obtains between them does indeed seem necessarily true; it is at best extremely hard to see how it could be that the first should fail to be probable with respect to the second. A second sort of exhibit, perhaps not quite so compelling but still convincing, is afforded by pairs of propositions <*A,B*> where *A* is a well-confirmed scientific theory and *B* is the evidence for it—special relativity and its evidence, for example. Here it seems clear that special relativity is more probable than not, more likely than its denial with respect to the evidence offered; and that that is so does not seem to be merely a contingent truth. Take the turtles-all-the-way-down theory: it seems clear that this is improbable, and necessarily improbable, with respect to our evidence.

---

[17]The term 'intrinsic probability' is Swinburne's; I prefer it to the more common 'a priori probability', since these probabilities, if there are any such things, are surely not for the most part determinable *a priori.*

[18]See his *An Introduction to Confirmation Theory.*

Now there are two basic problems or questions for this theory of epistemic probability. First, there is the question whether there *is* such a relationship among propositions as the logical theorist says there is: is there really any such thing as logical probability? Second, there is the question what logical probability, if there is such a thing, has to do with epistemic probability; in particular, can the latter be identified with the former? Decency and good order require that we take the first question first. According to Frank Ramsey, "A more fundamental criticism of Mr. Keynes' views, . . . is the obvious one that there really do not seem to be any such things as the probability relations he describes."[19] But Ramsey is wrong: there really do seem to be such things as the probability relations he describes. More exactly, there really do seem to be such things as *some* of those probability relations: those involved in the examples I gave earlier. Still, there is a point to Ramsey's complaint: there are many pairs of propositions $<A,B>$ such that if there is such a thing as the logical probability of A on B, we haven't the faintest idea what it might be. What, for example, is the probability of *Paul is jogging* or *San Francisco will win the Super Bowl* or *Socrates was snubnosed* on a necessary truth? That's not easy to say. Of course that is by no means conclusive; there could be such a relationship even if we were unable, in many cases, to see what the probability was.

There is another set of problems, however, that may be more serious: these have to do with infinite magnitudes of one sort or another. Formally, probability theory is a branch of measure theory, which grew out of a concern to understand and generalize our homely notions of length, area, and volume. Consider a real line segment closed at both ends. It is composed of uncountably many points—each of which, paradoxically, has no length. How do all those unextended points add up to something with length? Furthermore, the left half of the line is only half as long as the whole line, despite the fact that each contains the same (cardinal) number of points. The history of measure theory is the history of attempts to come to an account of measure that deals properly with sets of infinite magnitude and is also intuitively satisfactory.[20] As it turns out, no wholly satisfactory account is possible.[21] Analogues of the geometrical problems afflict logical probability as ordinarily construed. Clearly, if there are only finitely many possible worlds, there is no problem: the logical probability of a proposition A on a proposition B will be simply the proportion of A worlds among B worlds, the quotient of worlds in which both A and B are true by worlds in which B holds. But of course it seems unlikely that there are only finitely many possible worlds; and if there are infinitely many possible worlds, there will also be infinitely many propositions (for any possible world W there

[19]"Truth and Probability" (written in 1926), in *The Foundations of Mathematics and Other Logical Essays*, ed. R. B. Braithwaite (New York: Humanities Press, 1950), p. 161.

[20]See Bas van Fraassen's *Laws and Symmetries* (Oxford: Oxford University Press, 1989), pp. 325–31, for a brief but instructive account (with further references) of this history.

[21]Thus H. L. Royden in *Real Analysis* (New York: Macmillan, 1968), pp. 53–54: "Ideally, we should like m (the measure) to have the following properties: that m is defined for every set of real numbers, that the measure of an interval is its length, that the measure is countably additive, and that it is translation invariant. Unfortunately," he goes on to say, "as we shall see . . . , it is impossible to construct a set function having all of these properties."

will be the proposition that W is actual). And now we get problems. For example, suppose propositions form a set,[22] a countable set.[23] Then it will not be possible that logical probability both be connected in the set of propositions and also countably additive (that is, such that for a countable family of propositions mutually exclusive in pairs, the probability that a member of that set is true is the sum of the probabilities of the members of the set.)

But is this a real problem for logical probability? Consider countable additivity: we are already accustomed to the claim that points have zero length, yet somehow manage to clump together in such a way as to compose something that *does* have length. Why is it any more upsetting to think that a countable set of propositions may be such that each has zero probability, although the probability that some member of the set is true, is 1? True, the set of points in question is uncountable and the set of propositions countable; but is that a difference worth worrying about?

Even if we learn to accept the loss of countable additivity, however, don't we still have problems? I used to think so. I formerly argued that there is good reason to think there *isn't* any such relation among propositions;[24] but my arguments seem less persuasive to me now than they did then. The principal problem is presented by infinite classes of propositions mutually exclusive in pairs: here, I said, there is no function that assigns intrinsic probability in such a way as to satisfy both the probability calculus[25] and intuition. The argument went as follows. Consider a countably infinite set D of possible propositions with the same degree of content that are jointly exhaustive and mutually exclusive in pairs: for example, let D be the set {*there are no flying donkeys, there is just 1 flying donkey, there are just 2 flying donkeys, . . . there are just n flying donkeys, . . .* }. Each of these propositions is maximally specific about the number of flying donkeys there are; thus it seems plausible to suppose that they all have the *same* degree of content. If so, then (given PIP) it can't be that some of them have an intrinsic probability of 0 and others a nonzero intrinsic proba-

---

[22]That they do so isn't at all obvious: for any set S of propositions, there is presumably the proposition that S is distinct from the Taj Mahal; but then the set of propositions (supposing there is one) will be as large in cardinality as its power set; and this conflicts with the theorem of ordinary set theories to the effect that the power set of a set S always exceeds S in cardinality.

[23]This isn't at all obvious either: for presumably for each distinct positive real number r there is a distinct proposition r *is greater than* 0 and for each real number r between 71 and 73 it is possible that I should be r inches tall. If so, there will be at least continuum many propositions.

[24]"The Probabilistic Argument from Evil," *Philosophical Studies* (1979) and "Epistemic Probability and Evil," in *Archivo di Filosofia,* ed. Marco Olivetti (Rome: Cedam, 1988).

[25]Since our subject is conditional probability, suppose we consider a set of axioms (adapted from Richard Swinburne) for the Probability Calculus that take conditional probability as primitive:

   (1) $P(A/B) = r$, r a real number between 0 and 1 inclusive
   (2) If A entails B, then $P(B/A) = 1$
   (3) If C is possible and $(A\&B\&C)$ is not possible, then $P((A v B)/C) = P(A/C) + P(B/C)$ (Additive Axiom)
   (4) $P((A\&B)/C) = P(A/C) \times P(B/(A\&C))$ (Multiplicative Axiom)
   (5) If necessarily (A iff B), then $P(A/C) = P(B/C)$ and $P(C/A) = P(C/B)$ (Equivalence Axiom).

From *An Introduction to Confirmation Theory,* pp. 34–35.

bility; for then any proposition p that has a nonzero intrinsic probability will have both more content and greater intrinsic probability than the disjunction of those propositions which have 0 intrinsic probability.[26] Nor, for the same reason, can it be that intrinsic probability gets assigned via a function that asymptotically approaches 0. (For example, the first member of the set gets probability .5; the second probability .25; the third probability .125, and so on.) For take any member m_1 of D. There will be a pair of members m_2 and m_3 (further out in the series) such that the intrinsic probability of each of them is less than one-half that of m_1. But then their disjunction will have less intrinsic probability than that of m_1, and also less content; and this violates (PIP). So all the members of D must have the same intrinsic probability.

Now the only way to assign them all the *same* probability, obviously, is to assign them all probability 0. This gives us two problems. First, we lose countable additivity, for whatever that's worth: each of these propositions has a probability of 0; so the sum of their probabilities is zero; but the probability of their (infinite) disjunction is 1. Second, we must face other consequences that initially, at any rate, seem unhappy. Thus Carnap[27] and many of his followers manfully accepted the consequence that each proposition in such a set as D must thus have 0 intrinsic probability. But then such universal propositions as *no donkeys can fly* (which is equivalent to *there are no flying donkeys,* the first member of a set like D) get an intrinsic probability of 0, as do most of the sorts of universal generalizations to be found in science.

Initially this may not seem unduly unpalatable, but it has consequences that may be at least unsettling. If *no donkeys can fly* has an intrinsic probability of 0, then its denial, *there are some flying donkeys,* has an intrinsic probability of 1. In fact, for any number n you please, the intrinsic probability that there are more than n flying donkeys on this showing, is 1. Of course, this peculiar consequence is not limited to flying donkeys and other broadly speaking equestrian-style animals. The same goes for any kind of object such that, (1) for any number n, it is possible that there be just n such objects (flying donkeys, to be sure, but also Homeric gods, French-speaking Siberian cheese hounds, and evil demons), and (2) the propositions in the relevant set D all have the same content. I went on to say that if the intrinsic probability of such a proposition is 1, then its probability on any evidence will also be 1, so that no matter how much negative evidence we acquired, the proposition that there are evil demons

---

[26] p will have more content than the disjunction, since the latter will have less content than any of its disjuncts, each of which has the same content as p; p will have more intrinsic probability than the disjunction, since the probability of the disjunction will be the sum of the probability of its disjuncts, which is 0.

[27] See his *Logical Foundations of Probability.* In that work Carnap recommended a single confirmation function ('c*') as appropriate or correct; c* has the consequence that universal generalizations over (countably) infinite classes have an intrinsic probability of zero. He later came to think c* too restrictive and proposed an uncountable magnitude of c functions, any of which is acceptable from a formal point of view; these functions share the above feature with c*. See Carnap's *The Continuum of Inductive Methods* (Chicago: University of Chicago Press, 1952) and John Kemeny's "On Carnap's Theory of Probability and Induction," in *The Philosophy of Rudolph Carnap,* ed. P. A. Schilpp (LaSalle, Ill.: Open Court, 1963).

(or flying donkeys) would have a probability of 1 on our evidence—and this despite the fact that we know there aren't any flying donkeys! I added that it won't help to suppose that each of the members of D gets an *infinitesimal* intrinsic probability—a probability greater than zero but closer to zero than any real number; for then the proposition that there are at least *n* flying donkeys, say, for any number *n* you please, while it won't be 1, will be closer to 1 than any real number is; and that's an improvement hardly worth mentioning.

But this argument against the notion of intrinsic probability leaves a lot to be desired. First, it isn't really clear that intuition demands that the members of D all have the *same* content. True: they are equally specific—maximally specific—about how many flying donkeys there are; so one possible relevant difference among them is ruled out; but that fails to show that there isn't *any* relevant difference among them. We can't *see* a relevant difference among them—fair enough: but that doesn't show that in fact there isn't any. It is one thing to fail to see a relevant difference; it is quite another to see that there isn't any relevant difference. (It is one thing to fail to see that a proposition is impossible; it is quite another to see that it is possible.) So perhaps they don't all have the same content.

But even if they do (and even if (PIP) is true), no really untoward consequences obviously follow. The problem was that if they all have the same intrinsic probability, then they all have an intrinsic probability of 0, and a consequent probability of 0 on any evidence: and then we seem committed to holding that the probability of there being ghosts, flying donkeys, and their ilk on any evidence is 1. But that is not as distasteful as it might initially seem. For even if the intrinsic probability of a proposition is 1 (or infinitesimally close to 1), we might still have very good reason to think it false. Perhaps the intrinsic probability that I should be standing just here just now is 0; I still have good reason to think I am standing here now, and in fact *know* that I am. Suppose it is true that for any number *n*, the diameter of the universe could be *n* light years: then there will be infinitely many disjoint (real) intervals within which the diameter of the universe could fall, so that the probability that the diameter of the universe falls within a given interval is 0 or infinitesimally close to 0; we might still have good reason for thinking, of just one of those intervals, that the diameter of the universe falls within it.

Finally, perhaps we do know that there aren't any flying donkeys. But what we know, when we know that, isn't that there aren't any *anywhere at all,* in any part of the universe. (What we know is that there aren't any anywhere around *here.*) According to one contemporary cosmological theory, during the early moments of the Big Bang there was enormous and nearly instantaneous expansion, resulting in enormously many different subuniverses (as we may call them) that share a common origin but are now such that communication among them is impossible. In some of these, so the speculation goes, the values of physical constants are quite different from what they are in our subuniverse; and who knows what sorts of creatures might lurk in those subuniverses? Indeed, who knows what sorts of creatures lurk in remote parts of *our* subuniverse?

Still another, more general difficulty with the argument is that it relies too heavily upon difficulties in thinking about infinite magnitudes. The fact is we don't know how to think to very good purpose about such magnitudes (recall H. L. Royden's remark in n. 21). The probability calculus applies neatly and easily to the finite case, the case of proportions in finite classes. It is harder to see how things go in the case of infinite magnitudes, and the greater the cardinality, the harder it is to see how things go. But perhaps this is just a reflection of the more general truth that infinite magnitudes present real problems of understanding. Cantor's Paradise is indeed seductive; but that paradise, like others, is not well understood. If so, the fact that infinite magnitudes present problems for the logical theory of probability isn't much of an argument against it. Pinning a problem with a life of its own to a theory doesn't much damage the theory.

Still further, why must the logical theorist dig in his heels and insist that *all* pairs of propositions fall within the field of logical probability? (Why insist that the relation is connected?) We have clear intuitions, after all, only in a very restricted area here. It seems clear that there is a probability relation between *Feike can swim* and *9 out of 10 Frisians can swim and Feike is a Frisian;* but the same does not go for *Feike can swim* and, say, *China is a large country.* If there is a probability relation between these two, it is not one revealed by intuition. The same goes for *Feike can swim* and, for example, *2 + 1 = 3:* we certainly don't have much by way of an intuition that the first has some probability—0 or any other—on the second. Why can't the logical theorist just agree that the relation in question isn't connected among propositions? Even if there is no such thing as an intrinsic probability of *there are exactly three flying donkeys,* there could still be a logical probability in the sorts of cases where there seems to be one: statistical syllogisms and the relation between a well-confirmed scientific theory and its evidence, for example. On balance, therefore, it seems to me that the best course is to acquiesce in intuition and suppose that there is indeed such a thing as logical probability. So there are at least two varieties of *objective* probability: logical and statistical.

The first part of the logical theory of epistemic probability, therefore, is at least plausible: there is such a thing as logical probability. But the logical theory of epistemic probability has another part as well: the construction of epistemic probability on the basis of logical probability. Here the usual procedure has been to *identify* the two: and this is hopelessly inadequate. Suppose there *is* such a relationship among propositions as the logical theorist says there is: how does that constrain the way we ought to think? Or rather, since from one perspective what I ought to believe about anything is the truth, how does it go beyond any other truth in constraining the way we ought to think? We can best approach this matter by considering entailment (more exactly, strict implication). Suppose a set of axioms for arithmetic—axioms all of which I see to be true—entails the denial of Goldbach's conjecture (according to which every even number is the sum of two primes); of course, none of us human beings knows this, or is able to see the connection between the axioms and the conjecture. Does the second have a very high epistemic probability with respect to the first? Is the first good evidence, for me, for the second? I know the first; is there a relevant sense in which I ought, in consequence, to believe the second? Is it the rational thing to believe? I think not; neither I nor any of the rest of us can see any relevant connection between the two; we can't see the entailment or give an argument from what we do see to the conclusion that it is there.

It is equally apparent that the first confers no *warrant,* for me, on the second, in these conditions. Suppose (by virtue of cognitive malfunction) I believed the second on the basis of the first, despite the fact that I can see no connection whatever between them: I would not know the second (if it is true), despite its being entailed by the first. So what probabilistically supports what, for us, depends upon our noetic capabilities and situation. We can't sensibly *identify* epistemic probability with logical probability, and can't do so even for the special case of entailment. Indeed, the father (the modern father) of the logical theory himself saw this point with lucid clarity:

> Probability is, *vide* Chapter II (%12), relative in a sense to the principles of *human* reason. The degree of probability which it is rational for *us* to enter-tain, does not presume perfect logical insight, and is relative in part to the secondary propositions which we in fact know; and it is not dependent upon whether more perfect insight is or is not conceivable. It is the degree of proba-bility to which those logical processes lead, of which our minds are capable; or, in the language of Chapter II, which those secondary propositions justify, which we in fact know. If we do not take this view of probability, if we do not limit it in this way and make it, to this extent, relative to human powers, we are altogether adrift in the unknown; for we cannot ever know what degree of probability would be justified by the perceptions of logical relations which we are, and must always be, incapable of comprehending.[28]

Even if (more accurately, even though) there is such a thing as this alleged logical probability, therefore, we cannot sensibly identify epistemic probability with it. Of course it does not follow that epistemic probability doesn't crucially involve logical probability; and in chapter 9 I shall argue that it does.

C. Kyburgian Probability

Henry Kyburg's continued and ever more subtle concern with epistemic probability—in particular with the problems of direct inference—has extend-ed over a period of thirty years and more. As he points out, one source of epistemic probability is statistics: *known* statistics, anyway. I have conducted a survey; 9 out of 10 of the Australians I survey like Scotch whiskey; if my survey is done reasonably well and if I know no more about Jack than that he is an Australian, it will be epistemically probable, for me, that Jack likes Scotch. This seems a promising place to start, in explaining epistemic probability; Kyburg thinks that it is also a promising place to end. His idea is that this sort of knowledge of frequencies is the *only* source of epistemic probability; if a belief has any degree at all of epistemic probability, it is by way of some such knowl-edge, and nothing else is really relevant.

---

[28]Keynes, *A Treatise on Probability,* p. 32.

1. Kyburg Explained

From one perspective, it is fair to say, I think, that the main thrust of Kyburg's work is the effort to derive epistemic probability from known statistics; and his work is by far the most powerful and subtlest version of such efforts.[29] From another perspective, Kyburg's views are close to those of the logical theorists. A statement of the form *the probability of A (with respect to some rational corpus C) is r,* he says, is necessarily true if true at all; here he joins forces with the logical theorists. So perhaps we should think of him as marrying statistics with logical probability, hoping that this apparently improbable union will issue in a viable theory of epistemic probability.[30]

Kyburg's view differs from that traditional logical view in several respects. First and relatively unimportant: epistemic probability, as he sees it, is *interval* valued rather than point valued; perhaps the epistemic probability (relative to what I know) that the Tigers will win tomorrow's game is the interval $<.24, .31>$ rather than some point in that interval. Second and perhaps less unimportant: Kyburg's conditional probabilities don't always satisfy the probability calculus. Sometimes the conditional probability of A given B ($P(A/B)$) will not be equal to the quotient of the unconditional probability of A&B by that of B.[31] Third and still more important: for Kyburg there isn't any such thing as $P(A/B)$ *simpliciter;* what there is is $P(A/B)$ with respect to a *rational corpus,* a set of beliefs meeting certain conditions. $P(A/B)$ might be high relative to one rational corpus and low relative to another, even if both corpora contain only truths: perhaps the first contains the information that *a* is an *A,* that all As are Bs, that 9 out of 10 Bs are C, and nothing else relevant, while the second contains the information that *a* is an *A,* that all As are Ds, that 1 out of 10 Ds are Cs (and nothing else relevant). Fourth, on Kyburg's view it is not the case that every pair of propositions is such that the first has a nontrivial probability[32] (relative to a given rational corpus) with respect to the second. Epistemic probability essentially originates in the statistical syllogism; so if a given rational corpus contains no statistical syllogism with respect to a given proposition A, then A has no nontrivial probability with respect to that corpus.

"The essential idea," he says,

> is this: every probability statement contains an implicit reference to a real or hypothetical body of knowledge or rational corpus, which may be construed as a set of statements in a certain language. Probability statements are not

[29] For another (and earlier) effort, see Wesley Salmon's *The Foundations of Scientific Inference* (Pittsburgh: University of Pittsburgh Press, 1967), pp. 108ff. (For critical animadversions on Salmon's attempt, see my "The Probabilistic Argument from Evil."

[30] We can see a different sort of rapprochement between logical and statistical views of probability: if the statistics in question concern *possible worlds,* more exactly, the ratio of possible AB worlds to B worlds, then the two coincide.

[31] More precisely (since Kyburg's probabilities are interval valued rather than real valued) sometimes his probabilities do not conform to the interval form of conditionalization. See, for example, William Harper, "Kyburg on Inference," in *Henry E. Kyburg, Jr. & Isaac Levi,* ed. Radu J. Bogdan (Dordrecht: D. Reidel, 1982), and see Kyburg's reply in the same volume, pp. 159ff.

[32] Any proposition A will of course have a probability of one sort or another on any proposition B: if all else fails, its probability on B will be, trivially, the whole unit interval.

directly empirical; they are logically true statements of the metalanguage, if true at all. Two conditions must be satisfied to insure the truth of a probability statement: first, there must be a frequency statement in the rational corpus which mentions a number or interval corresponding to the value of the probability; second, the set which is the subject of that frequency assertion must be singled out by appropriate epistemological considerations as the correct and relevant reference class for that statement.[33]

Still informal but a bit more specific:

Roughly speaking, we shall say that a statement has the probability p (in general p will be an interval i of reals) relative to a body of knowledge, when (a) it is known in that body of knowledge that the statement is equivalent to (has the same truth value as) a statement of the form a ϵ b; (b) it is known in that body of knowledge that a belongs to c; (c) that body of knowledge contains the statistical knowledge that the proportion of objects in c that belong to b fall in the interval i and (d) there is nothing in our body of knowledge that conflicts with this assignment of probability.[34]

So "The subject of that frequency assertion must be singled out by appropriate epistemological considerations"; and "there is nothing in our body of knowledge that conflicts with this assignment of probability." Here we have perhaps the most important topic for a program like that of Kyburg's: the dreaded *problem of the reference class*. In essence the problem is simplicity itself. Suppose you are trying to determine the epistemic probability, relative to your body of knowledge, of the proposition *Feike can swim*. According to Kyburg, this probability will have to originate in some relevant known frequencies. So perhaps we know that Feike is a Frisian, and that 5 out of 10 Frisians can swim; we know that he is a Frisian North Sea dweller and that 7 out of 10 Frisian North Sea dwellers can swim; and finally, we know that he is 81 years of age, and that 3 out of 10 octogenarians can swim. If we know nothing else relevant to the question, what shall we say is the epistemic probability that Feike can swim?

Perhaps it is clear that as between the first two statistical statements, the second should have preference: the reference class in the second is a proper subset of that in the first. But what about the second and third? If this is what we know, what is the epistemic probability (for us) that he can swim? And what about Goodmanian gerrymanders as reference classes? I propose to estimate the epistemic probability that the next toss of this coin will turn up heads: I take as the reference class the union of the set of tosses that have so far turned up heads with the unit class of the next toss of this coin; I hopefully conclude that it is very likely that the next toss will come up heads. What shall we say about a case like that? Kyburg neither has nor claims to have a principled way to exclude such classes. His whole enterprise is like that of the classical Chisholm: the project is to find a criterion that, when applied to given cases, yields the results we intuitively think correct. He believes his efforts in this

---

[33]Self-Profile, in *Henry E. Kyburg, Jr. & Isaac Levi*, p. 12.
[34]*The Logical Foundations of Statistical Inference* (Dordrecht: D. Reidel, 1974), p. 156.

direction are on the right track but have not yet succeeded. The difficulty of this project has turned out to be absolutely appalling[35] (and, as I see it, the difficulty of the task is another testimony to the enormous articulation, complication, and subtlety of this part of our cognitive design plan).

The first thing to see about Kyburg's project, therefore, is that it essentially involves offering a criterion for separating the sheep from the goats, correct direct inferences from incorrect, proper uses of the statistical syllogism from improper. And his essential idea, contrary to classical Bayesianism, is that there are constraints on rational degrees of belief that go far beyond probabilistic coherence, conditioning, and the others suggested by Bayesians.[36] You have noted that 3 out of 10 *As* are *Bs*; you know nothing special about the next *A*, but believe to degree .9 that it will be *B;* you can do this without violating any of the Bayesian constraints, but (as Kyburg quite properly points out) you are nonetheless irrational or defective in some way. (Kyburg does not *argue* that such a corpus of beliefs is defective; he simply takes it for granted that it is, and that this is a difficulty for Bayesianism.) The central Kyburgian project is that of finding a criterion to distinguish correct from incorrect uses of direct inference; so in a way there is no attempt here to say what epistemic probability *is*. Or rather, there is no *new* attempt to do so; Kyburg is content to accept the logical view, according to which probability statements are noncontingent propositions specifying logical or quasi-logical relations among propositions.

Following Reichenbach, Kyburg insists that any respectable epistemic probability arises by way of inferences from knowledge of the relevant relative frequencies. But clearly this raises a problem: what about the *premises* of a direct inference? Doesn't the notion of epistemic probability apply to them? Aren't they too epistemically probable or improbable to some degree or other? If so, however, how do *they* acquire that probability? I see a bear, and know that most bears are dangerous; I therefore infer that what I see is probably dangerous. How do we construe the epistemic probability of my belief *that's a bear?* This belief certainly seems epistemically probable; its probability does not seem to originate in any sort of direct inference; Kyburg's basic idea is that all epistemic probability comes by way of direct inference; so there seems to be a problem. Kyburg sees this problem as crucial for his program. If he falls into Bayesianism here, he says, there is nothing to prevent the infection from spread-

---

[35] "All probabilities . . . I take to be based on direct inference—that is, the statistical syllogism. What is required to make the statistical syllogism work is an appropriate epistemological notion of randomness. As all of my commentators . . . have noted, my treatment of randomness is a mess. . . . The version printed in LFSI [*The Logical Foundations of Statistical Inference*] I noticed to be defective even before the book was published, and was corrected on an *errata* sheet included in copies of the book. No sooner was that circulating than new difficulties emerged, and I circulated the 1977 letter. . . . The version of the definition incorporated in the 1977 letter was . . . also defective. Since then I have attempted various other ploys" (*Henry E. Kyburg, Jr.,* & *Isaac Levi,* p. 159). Undaunted, Kyburg goes on to add "I do not think the general approach is wrong—I think we have some very clear intuitions about what interferes with applications of the statistical syllogism or direct inference."

[36] For an account of the Bayesian constraints, see *Warrant: The Current Debate* (New York: Oxford University Press, 1993), chap. 6.

ing: "If I am entitled to be ninety percent sure there is a rabbit in the corner of my library, just because I feel that way, why shouldn't I be entitled to be fifty percent sure that the next toss of this coin will land heads, just because I feel that way? Or 20%, if I happen to feel *that* way instead?" (*Henry E. Kyburg, Jr. & Isaac Levi*, p. 135)

Here he makes an ingenious suggestion. Consider what we may call, broad-.ly, *observation* statements: *that is a bear, this is red,* and (with a microscope and alittle practice) *that is an amoeba.* Under a variety of conditions we find ourselves more or less strongly inclined to accept such statements: they are, we might say, *prima facie* acceptable. But some of these statements turn out to be erroneous, says Kyburg, in the sense that we find that conjunctions of them conflict with necessary truths. (I am holding a marble between two fingers in such a way that it *feels* like two marbles; it *looks* as if there is only one marble, however, so one or the other of the two observation statements must be rejected.) To resolve the conflict in such cases, says Kyburg, we apply two principles:

> *The Minimum Rejection Principle:* We want to maximize the content of our body of knowledge—we want to know as much as we can. Thus we want to reject or regard as erroneous, as few of these statements as possible.

> *The Distribution Principle:* Given the satisfaction of the first principle, we should suppose that the errors among various statements are distributed as evenly as possible among various sorts of statements. (*Henry E. Kyburg, Jr. & Isaac Levi* p. 136)

On the basis of these two principles, he says, "we can assign *approximate* error frequencies to the various kinds of statements that will (or even 'might') be among those we are initially inclined to accept" (p. 137). But then if the probability that a statement S will have to be rejected is sufficiently low, we may accept as a moral certainty the proposition that S will not have to be rejected; and this "is about the same thing" as to accept S itself as a moral certainty (p. 137). So observation statements themselves get into a Kyburgian rational corpus by way of the statistical syllogism;[37] in this way Kyburg cleverly assigns epistemic probabilities to observation statements without violating his empiricist principles, according to which, he thinks, any assignment of epistemic probability must be done on the basis of broadly statistical experience.

There are real problems here; for example, the problem of the reference class (error frequencies are to be assigned to *kinds* of statements) returns with a vengeance. But it is worth noting that if this procedure will work at all, it will work as well for memory as for perception; we can follow the same procedure there. And of course the same goes for beliefs about other minds, and for ethical or moral beliefs; again, we can follow the same procedure there. The same goes for religious beliefs; I might note the religious beliefs I am initially

[37]Of course, that still leaves us with *some* statements that don't obviously get into the corpus in that way: statements to the effect that a given statement is *prima facie* acceptable for me, that is, statements to the effect that a given statement is such that (on the basis of perception, perhaps) I am inclined to accept it.

inclined to accept, note the proportion of such beliefs that (as it turns out) I am obliged to reject (in that conjunctions of them conflict with necessary truths), and thus assign a probability to them, which should then be (on Kyburgian terms) the degree to which I accept or believe them.

2. Kyburgian Probability and Conditional Epistemic Probability

Kyburg's views on probability have been growing and deepening over a period of many years, culminating first in his monumental *The Logical Foundations of Statistical Inference* and more recently in his and Levi's *Profiles* volume; and a formidable technical literature has grown up around them.[38] This is not the place for detailed and technical investigation of the inner workings of Kyburg's system; but even without that, we can see something important here. Our topic is epistemic probability: a relation among propositions whereby a proposition can acquire warrant for me by standing in that relation to another that already has warrant for me.[39] Kyburg speaks, of course, of epistemic probability: but he says little about how he sees its connections with justification, or rationality, or warrant. So suppose we begin by asking whether Kyburgian probability is a good candidate for a species of warrant; that is, suppose we ask whether what Kyburg offers can be seen as a viable account of epistemic probability, where the latter is seen as a warrant-conferring relation. I think the answer is clear: it cannot.

Note that what got defined in the earlier quotation is *absolute* or *unconditional* epistemic probability with respect to a rational corpus. Now our concern, of course, is epistemic *conditional* probability, the sort of case where a proposition gets warrant for me by virtue of being accepted on the basis of another belief that already has warrant for me. Kyburg has an account of conditional epistemic probability to go with the account of epistemic probability *tout court;* indeed, he has two different accounts. Here we need not enter the details;[40] but briefly, the matter is as follows. Given the above account of unconditional probability, what shall we take to be the conditional probability $P(A/B)$ with respect to a given rational corpus K? There are two possibilities. First, we could take it to be the quotient of $P(A\&B)$ (with respect to K) by $P(B)$ (with respect to K); call this 'the classical Kyburg conditional probability'. Second, we could take it to be the probability of A with respect to K augmented by B—that is, with respect to the conjunction of B with K; call this 'the

---

[38]As one example, consider the Kyburg–Levi debate over conditionalization: Levi's, "Direct Inference," *Journal of Philosophy* 74, and "Confirmational Conditionalization," *Journal of Philosophy* 75; Kyburg's "Randomness and the Right Reference Class," *Journal of Philosophy* 74; and chapter 10 of Levi's *The Enterprise of Knowledge: An Essay on Knowledge, Credal Probability and Chance* (Cambridge: MIT Press, 1980). Teddy Seidenfeld joined the discussion in "Direct Inference and Inverse Inference," *Journal of Philosophy* 75, as did William Harper in "Kyburg on Direct Inference" in Kyburg and Levi's *Profiles* volume, pp. 114–124.

[39]We could also inquire whether there is a relation among propositions whereby a proposition can acquire *justification* for me, by way of standing in that relation to another proposition that already has it; and indeed it is possible that the same relation should fill both bills.

[40]For those details, see Kyburg's reply to his critics in the *Profiles* volume, pp. 159ff.

nonclassical Kyburg conditional probability of *A* on *B'*. That these two do not always yield the same result has been the occasion of a good deal of spirited criticism; Kyburg, however, remains unrepentant.[41]

Neither of these, however, offers decent prospects for an account of conditional epistemic probability. We can see this by considering first Kyburg's suggestion as to how it is that observation beliefs (or other spontaneous beliefs) acquire an epistemic probability relative to a rational corpus. As you recall, his idea is that we find ourselves accepting a variety of such beliefs, some of which we later have to reject because we see that conjunctions of them conflict with necessary truths; and the epistemic probability of such a belief, for me, will be something like the reciprocal of the proportion of beliefs of that kind (however 'that kind' is to be explained) that I am thus obliged to reject. It is clear, however, that a belief may have a great deal of probability of *that* sort with respect to my rational corpus even if it has very little by way of warrant for me. For perhaps (by way of cognitive malfunction or deficiency) I am inclined to accept the wrong observation statements. Perhaps (to echo examples in *Warrant: The Current Debate*) whenever I am appeared to redly, I form the belief that no one else is then appeared to redly, or that I alone am ever appeared to redly, or that everyone in North Dakota is now being appeared to redly, or that I am appeared to that way by something that is green. Clearly an experimentally inclined Alpha Centaurian scientist or Cartesian evil demon could tinker with my noetic powers in such a way that my cognitive response to experience becomes wholly distorted; and perhaps I never discover any inconsistencies between conjunctions of these statements and necessary truths (or truths of other sorts). On Kyburg's suggestion, my belief that I alone am appeared to redly will have a good deal of epistemic probability for me: but surely it will have little by way of warrant. Even if it is extremely probable, indeed, morally certain (following Kyburg's method) with respect to my corpus, it won't have much by way of warrant for me. If by some wild chance it happens to be true, I certainly won't know that it is. I may be within my rights in accepting these beliefs; but they won't have warrant for me. Kyburg's suggestion has no plausibility with respect to warrant.[42]

And this problem is inherited by the account of conditional probability. For it might be that I have much warrant for a proposition *B*, that *A* is Kyburg probable with respect to *B*, and that *A* nonetheless (again, by virtue of noetic malfunction) has very little warrant for me. Due to a brain lesion, I am pathologically suggestive; as a young man I read Washington Irving's "The Legend of Sleepy Hollow"; consequently whenever I see a horse I form the belief that there is a tiny headless horseman on its back—one too small to see without a microscope. Naturally enough, I also form the belief that nearly all horses are accompanied by tiny headless horsemen on their backs. As it happens, I never encounter contradictions between these statements and others; on the Minimum Rejection Principle they therefore have high epistemic probability for me.

[41]Ibid., p. 162.

[42]Perhaps it does better with respect to justification, particularly if the latter is deontologically conceived.

On a given occasion I see something *a* which I take to be a horse. The Kyburg probability of

(A)   *a* is a horse and there is a headless horseman riding *a*

(with respect to my rational corpus) will be nearly as great as that of

(B)   *a* is a horse;

so the classical Kyburg conditional probability of *there is a headless horseman riding a* on *a is a horse* is high. So is the nonclassical Kyburg conditional probability; for if I add B to my rational corpus the Kyburg probability of A on the augmented corpus will be high. Further, it may be that B has a great deal of warrant for me. A, however, does not. Perhaps I am *justified* in accepting it, within my rights, violating no epistemic obligations; perhaps from my (warped) perspective it is the right thing to believe; perhaps it is the Foley rational thing to believe; but it has little or no warrant for me. B, therefore, has warrant for me; the conditional Kyburg probability of A with respect to B is very high; but A has very little warrant for me. So we don't have here an acceptable account of epistemic conditional probability. Despite its great sophistication, this account of epistemic conditional probability clearly needs an addendum of some sort. Some of what it needs, I think, can be supplied by thinking, once again, in terms of the notion of proper function, as we shall see in the next chapter.

9

Epistemic Conditional Probability:
The Sober Truth

. . . a probability is a reputable proposition . . . .
A probability is that which happens for the most part.
—Aristotle

We saw in chapter 8 that the current theories of epistemic probability are not satisfactory; and it isn't as if with a little more Chisholming they would do the trick. We can therefore no longer postpone the project of giving a decent account of epistemic conditional probability. As I said at the beginning of the chapter, this is an assignment that is far from trivial (to put it mildly); on the Yosemite rock-climbing scale of difficulty it's a clear 5.15 (which means it's so hard it probably can't be done). Still, why should that deter us?

I. The Two Faces of Epistemic Probability

Start by returning to the distinction between epistemic probability and objective probability. According to Ian Hacking, as we saw, our modern concept of probability emerged around the 1660s and is Janus-faced: "On the one side it is statistical, concerning itself with stochastic laws of chance processes. On the other side it is epistemological, dedicated to assessing reasonable degrees of belief in propositions quite devoid of statistical background."[1] I doubt that Aristotle would be impressed by this claim about our 'modern' concept of probability. At any rate he already saw probability as Janus-faced, as the epigraphs indicate; the faces he saw, furthermore, closely resemble the faces that, according to Hacking, are presented by our modern concept of probability.

On the one hand, a probable proposition is one that is reputable, as Aristotle says, or *approvable* or *worthy of* belief, or such that it is rational or sensible to believe it, or to afford it a high degree of confidence. For example, it is probable that the sun will rise tomorrow and improbable that the earth rests on the back of a turtle, which rests on the back of another turtle, . . . , so that it's turtles all the way down. On the other hand, a probability, as Aristotle also

---

[1] *The Emergence of Probability* (Cambridge: Cambridge University Press, 1975), p. 12.

says, is "a thing that happens for the most part"; for example, it is probable that an adult human being will be more than 5 feet tall.

Aristotle adds that not just any old thing that happens for the most part is a probability: "not, however, as some definitions would suggest, anything whatever that so happens, but only if it belongs to the class of what can turn out otherwise."[2] In the typical case, therefore, a probability is neither necessary nor necessary with respect to what we know; *All bachelors are unmarried* is not a probability, and the same goes for *New York City is larger than Peoria*. In the paradigm cases, a proposition is (epistemically) probable when we have evidence for it, but evidence that falls short of being logically conclusive. It is extremely probable that the earth is round; here we have evidence, and very good evidence, but not evidence that entails the proposition in question. Similarly for special relativity: we have good evidence for it, but the evidence falls short of being logically conclusive. According to Aristotle, therefore, a probability is what it is rational or reasonable to believe; it is also what happens for the most part. Presumably it is the former because it is the latter: what happens for the most part is such that it is rational or sensible to believe it, or to afford a high degree of confidence to it. The sun always rises in the east, it is therefore rational to believe that it will do so tomorrow, and irrational to believe that it will rise in the west.[3]

Aristotle is right: there are these two sides to probability. I don't mean to say merely that there are the two kinds of probability—objective and epistemic—I distinguished before, although that is also true. What I mean is that epistemic probability *itself* is Janus-faced. Suppose we begin by considering those paradigm examples of epistemic probability judgments I mentioned earlier on:

(a)   The probability of the proposition *Feike can swim* on *9 out of 10 Frisians can swim and Feike is a Frisian* is high.

(b)   It is likely that special relativity is at least approximately true.

(c)   Despite the Flat Earthers, it is monumentally improbable that the earth is flat.

(d)   It is extremely likely that the sun will rise tomorrow, and that if it does, it will rise in the east.

(e)   It is probable (but not maximally probable) that Goldbach's conjecture (that every even number is the sum of two primes) is true.

(f)   The Linguistic Theory of the *A Priori* is at best unlikely.

(g)   Given the existence of a wholly good, omniscient, and omnipotent God, it is not unlikely that there should be the distribution of pain and suffering the world in fact displays.

[2]*Rhetoric*, I, 2 (1357 a 35, p. 2157, in J. Barnes, ed., *The Complete Works of Aristotle* (Princeton: Princeton University Press, 1984).

[3]Of course 'what always happens' and 'what happens for the most part' must be taken with a grain of circumspection. Emeralds have always been grue; it does not follow that the rational thing to believe is that they will continue to be so. See chapter 7, pp. 128ff.

(Some of these claims, of course, will be disputed; those who offer a probabilistic atheological argument from evil will no doubt dispute (g),[4] certain skeptics will dispute (b) and (d), linguistic theorists and Flat Earthers will dispute (f) and (c) respectively, and those endorsing the logical theory of epistemic probability will dispute (e).) Consider, for example, the assertion that special relativity is probable with respect to the evidence cited for it. Such an assertion, I think, typically comprises two subclaims. First, there is the objective component, the claim that special relativity is *objectively* probable on the evidence cited. The second claim is that given this evidence and no other source of warrant for or against the theory in question, the sensible or rational propositional attitude to take toward the proposition in question is to believe it, or to be at least fairly confident of it; this is the *normative*[5] component. A typical probability judgment has both an objective and a normative component. Let me elaborate.

First, a proposition is epistemically probable, in the typical case, when it is the rational thing to believe, or to which to afford a high degree of confidence, in circumstances where we have some but less than entailing evidence for it. When I say that relativity theory is probable with respect to the evidence and that the theory that it's turtles all the way down is improbable with respect to the evidence, I mean to say that it is rational or reasonable to bestow a high degree of confidence on the first belief but irrational or unreasonable to do the same with respect to the second. But is that *all* I mean? I don't think so: I also mean to say, in the first case, that special relativity is *objectively* probable on the evidence. I mean to attribute to relativity theory and the evidence for it a certain relation that holds independently of human beings, their constitutions and dispositions, and what they think.[6] *Feike can swim* is probable with respect to *99 of 100 Frisian lifeguards can swim and Feike is a Frisian lifeguard;* in asserting this I claim not merely that the rational propositional attitude, given just that evidence about Feike's swimming ability, is one of considerable confidence; I also mean that it is objectively probable. It is epistemically probable that the sun will rise tomorrow; the rational propositional attitude, then, toward that proposition is one of considerable confidence. But that proposition is also objectively probable on our evidence, and that it is, is part of what I assert when I assert that it is epistemically probable.

A. The Objective Component

In these typical cases, then—cases like the relation of relativity theory to the evidence or of the theory that it's turtles all the way down—*two* things get

[4]See my "Epistemic Probability and Evil," in *Archivo di Filosofia*, ed. Marco Olivetti (Rome: Cedam, 1988), and the chapters on the problem of evil in my forthcoming *Warranted Christian Belief.*

[5]But here we must be wary; in contrasting the normative component with the objective component, I don't for a moment mean to suggest that the former is merely subjective, or a mere matter of opinion, or anything of the sort. On the contrary: the normative component is itself perfectly objective.

[6]Here I was helped by Stephen Wykstra.

asserted: that the proposition is objectively probable (improbable) with respect to the evidence, and that the belief in question is rational (irrational), given the circumstances of having as evidence what in fact we do have as evidence. But how shall we understand this objective component?

Is it simply logical probability? In some cases, yes: cases like the first case above, cases involving a statistical syllogism. In other cases, no; cases like the second and third, cases involving induction and/or abduction. We can see this as follows. Consider the proposition that the sun will rise tomorrow (call it 'S') and the evidence (call it 'E') for it. The objective probability, here, is no doubt not just (say) the logical probability of S on E, not just the proportion of possible S worlds among worlds in which our evidence holds. There are all those counterinductive possible worlds, where things go just as they have up till now, whereupon everything goes crazy. There are all those gruesome Goodmanian worlds where t is the present. For all we know, the proportion of S worlds among E worlds is much lower than the objective probability of S on E. Consider such a theory as special relativity ('SR') and its evidence ('E'). SR is objectively probable on E; but it is by no means clear that this objective probability is just the *logical* probability of SR on E. There are all those possible worlds where E holds, but SR does not, being supplanted by some Goodmanian gerrymander; again, for all we know the proportion of SR worlds among E worlds is much lower than the objective probability of SR on E.

But then what sort of objective probability do we have in those cases? In brief, the answer, I think, is in the following neighborhood: the objective probability in question is indeed a logical probability, but it isn't one conditional just on the evidence. It is also conditional on other propositions: such propositions, perhaps, as that *The future will relevantly resemble the past* (the world is not, for example, a grue world) and perhaps *Simpler theories are more likely to be true than complex ones.* Alternatively, the relevant set of possible worlds is not just the worlds in which the evidence is true, but some narrower class of worlds, perhaps specifiable in part in terms of similarity to what we think the actual world is like. This problem of saying precisely what it is that the relevant objective probability is conditional upon is both tantalizing and difficult (and perhaps it is relative to context); I shall leave it to the reader and hurry on.

In the typical probability judgment, therefore, there is both a normative and an objective component. In the typical probability judgment, furthermore, these two components *coincide,* in that a high degree of confidence is rational or appropriate where there is high objective probability on the relevant evidence. More exactly, the degree of confidence that is rational or appropriate with respect to a proposition A will be a function of the *known* or (rationally) *believed* objective probability of A on the evidence (provided there is no other source of warrant for A or $-A$). For example, the epistemic probability that Feike can swim on the proposition *Feike is a Frisian lifeguard and the objective probability that a Frisian lifeguard can swim is .99,* is high; if all I know about Feike's swimming ability is that he is a Frisian lifeguard and that the objective probability of a Frisian lifeguard's being a swimmer is .99, then the right propositional attitude for me to take toward Feike's being able to swim is one of substantial confidence. This is sometimes put more precisely (perhaps *too* precisely) as follows: the epistemic conditional probability of a proposition A on the supposition that the objective probability of A is x, is x.[7]

In judgments of epistemic probability both of these components are typically involved—typically, but not always.[8] Here (as in many other areas, including that of warrant itself) there are important analogical extensions of the central kind of judgment involved—or perhaps we should say that there is a paradigmatic central core sort of judgment, with analogically related kinds of judgments occupying a penumbral area surrounding the central core. Thus judgments of epistemic probability, or their near neighbors, often display only one of the two components typically involved. I believe that Goldbach's Conjecture is probable with respect to our evidence (it has been confirmed for ever so many even numbers). Of course, I also know that it is either necessarily true or necessarily false; therefore (if we assume that objective probability conforms to the calculus of probability), its objective intrinsic probability is either 1 or 0; but then its probability conditional on our (or any) evidence is also 1 or 0. In fact, however, it has neither maximal nor minimal epistemic probability on our evidence. My judgment that the conjecture is probable with respect to our evidence, therefore, doesn't involve a judgment of objective probability. Philosophical theses, for another example, are typically necessarily true if true at all; hence their objective probability on any evidence will be 0 or 1; but their epistemic probability on our evidence is often neither 0 nor 1. I claim it is rather likely that there are individual essences but rather unlikely that there are qualitative individual essences. My claim is not one of objective probability; for each of *There are individual essences* and *There are no qualitative individual essences* is either necessarily true or necessarily false; the objective probability of each, therefore, is either 0 or 1; but in neither case is the epistemic probability (so it seems to me) either maximal or minimal. So here the objective probability drops out, leaving just the other element, the claim that the view in question is the rational one, given our evidence. Consider an analysis of warrant, or the view that nominalism is false and there exist universals, or consider existentialism, the view that the individual essences of contingent objects are ontologically dependent upon those objects. These claims are noncontingent; but their epistemic probability on our evidence is certainly neither maximal nor minimal. Here again the objective component of the judgment of epistemic probability drops out, leaving only the claim that the reasonable or rational degree of confidence, in the judgment in question, is r.[9] And of course it is also

---

[7]Often called "Miller's principle" and first stated in D. Miller's "A Paradox of Information," *British Journal for the Philosophy of Science* (1966). Fascinating questions arise with respect to Miller's principle, questions I can't enter here. Probing discussion of this principle and the qualifications may be found in David Lewis'"A Subjectivist's Guide to Objective Chance," in *Ifs*, ed. W. Harper, R. Stalnaker, and G. Pearce (Dordrecht: D. Reidel, 1981), pp. 271ff.; Bas van Fraassen's *Laws and Symmetries* (Oxford: Clarendon Press, 1989), pp. 82–83 and 195–201; and van Fraassen's "Belief and the Will," *Journal of Philosophy* 81, no. 5 (May 1984), pp. 247ff., where the connection between Miller's principle and van Fraassen's (Reflection) is briefly explored.

[8]Here I was helped by a comment by Robin Collins.

[9]This phenomenon may suggest that judgments of epistemic probability really involve only the normative claim, with an appropriate objective probability claim intimately related (in many or

quite possible to separate out the normative component of the epistemic probability judgment, leaving just the objective component.

B. The Normative Component

But how shall we understand this normative component: how shall we understand the *rationality* or *reasonability* involved? The basic idea is simple enough: it is Aristotle's idea that a probability is a *reputable* proposition. More exactly, the probable belief is the *right* belief, the *correct* or *approved* belief: in a word: the *rational* belief. But what is the force of *rational* here? Our concern here, first of all, is not with Foley rationality, the appropriateness of chosen means to chosen ends. Nor is it with rationality in the sense in which one who has recovered from a bout with the manic phase of manic-depressive psychosis is said to have regained rationality (although it is closer to that notion than to Foley rationality). To see what kind of rationality *is* involved, we must start by returning to that remark of J. M. Keynes, who, though the modern father of the logical theory of probability, nevertheless pointed out that

> Probability is, *vide* Chapter II (%12), relative in a sense to the principles of *human* reason. The degree of probability which it is rational for *us* to entertain, does not presume perfect logical insight . . . ; and it is not dependent upon whether more perfect insight is or is not conceivable. . . . If we do not take this view of probability, if we do not limit it in this way and make it, to this extent, relative to human powers, we are altogether adrift in the unknown.[10]

We must add a remark made by Thomas Reid: "in most cases, we measure the degrees of evidence by the effect they have upon a sound understanding, when comprehended clearly and without prejudice."[11] According to Keynes, "probability is relative to human powers"; according to Reid, we measure the degree of evidence (and here I think he might as well have said 'probability') by its effect on a sound understanding. Evidence is intimately related to what we human beings *see* as evidence; conditional probability is intimately related to what *we take* to support what. According to Reid, "we measure the degree of evidence [or the degree of epistemic probability] by the effect it has on a sound understanding": that is (presumably) we measure the degree of support offered a proposition *A* by a proposition *B* by considering what sort of effect belief in *B* has, in a sound understanding, on belief in *A*. A "sound understanding," says Reid; what he means, I think, is that what counts here is (at least in part) the effect of believing *B* with respect to believing *A* for someone who suffers from no cognitive defect, or deficiency, or dysfunction; someone whose (relevant) noetic faculties are functioning properly.

What we are concerned with, therefore, is rationality in the sense of *the*

---

most cases, *via* a Miller-like principle). Such an account could certainly be correct; I don't see that the difference between it and what I propose is significant.

[10]J. M. Keynes, *A Treatise on Probability* (London: Macmillan, 1921), p. 32.

[11]*Essays on the Intellectual Powers of Man*, in *Thomas Reid's Inquiry and Essays*, ed. R. Beanblossom and Keith Lehrer (Indianapolis: Hackett, 1983), VII, 3. This remark is not reflected in his own discussion of probability; Reid didn't take the hint he himself offered toward developing a satisfactory way of thinking about probability.

deliverances of reason. Among the deliverances of reason, as we saw in chapter 6, are some of the truths of mathematics and logic. Also among them, however, are certain judgments of probability—for example, that, given our evidence, it is likely that the earth has existed for more millions of years, or that given that Feike is a Frisian and 9 out of 10 Frisians can swim, it is likely that he can swim. In asking after the normative component of such a probability judgment, we are asking what someone of "sound understanding," someone whose rational faculties are functioning properly, would believe, for example, about Feike's ability to swim, given that evidence. But that is not exactly right: it is not just *absence of cognitive dysfunction* that is relevant here; we aren't asking about what would be thought by someone whose only intellectual distinction here is that he is not of subnormal perspicacity. Consider a concrete case: we say that special relativity is probable with respect to the evidence, or that it is probable, with respect to the evidence, that the butler did it. What we mean (in addition to the claim of objective probability) is that in those circumstances, someone who is trained at this sort of thing, and does it well, would hold the belief in question or at any rate afford it a pretty high degree of confidence. While we may not be thinking of a veritable Mozart of probabilities, we are not thinking of your average probability duffer either.[12] When it comes to the deliverances of reason, what counts is the best, or nearly the best, that human beings can do.

What makes it the case, therefore, that *B* is evidence for *A* (what makes *A* epistemically probable with respect to *B*) is the effect *B* has on the degree of belief enjoyed by *A* in a sound understanding—a sound *human* understanding, that is; things might go quite differently for Alpha Centaurians or angels. This is the basic intuitive idea; the problem is to fill out these intuitions into an explanation of conditional epistemic probability that will furnish real insight and understanding. Here I shall have to be content with outlining the basic idea, making little more than a gesture or two in the direction of a complete and satisfying theory.[13]

II. An Account of the Normative Component

We seek to understand the normative component of the conditional epistemic probability of a proposition *A* on a proposition *B*. Recall first the connection between epistemic probability and warrant: where *A* is epistemically probable on *B*, *A* can acquire warrant for *S* by way of *S*'s believing *B* on the basis of *A*. And instead of giving an account of the normative component of epistemic conditional probability, we could give an account of a proposition *A*'s having

---

[12]In *The Fragmentation of Reason* (Cambridge: MIT Press, 1990), pp. 4ff., Stephen Stich reports research (by Nisbett, Nisbett and Ross, Tversky and Kahneman) suggesting that your average probability duffer makes many mistakes with respect to probability, falling into the Gamblers' Fallacy, for example, and sometimes judging that a conjunction is more probable than one of its conjuncts.

[13]In coming to this account of epistemic probability, I have learned much from Richard Otte: see his "A Theistic Conception of Probability," *Faith and Philosophy* 4, no. 4 (October 1987), pp. 427ff.

conditional warrant for a person S by virtue of being believed on the basis of some other proposition B. That would have had a strange and alien look, however, and in the interests of familiarity and smoothness I shall give an account of the former kind; still, the intertranslatability of epistemic warrant and (the normative component of) epistemic conditional probability reminds us that the general conditions of warrant apply here too. Accordingly, call someone who does the best or nearly the best that human beings can do, in this area, 'rationally perspicacious'—'rational' for short. We are interested in the degree of confidence afforded a proposition A, by a rational person S, whose evidence for A is B, in circumstances where the conditions of warrant apply; that is, circumstances where S's belief that A (or her degree of confidence in A) is formed by way of properly functioning cognitive faculties, in an epistemically congenial environment, according to a design plan whose relevant modules are successfully aimed at truth.

We do need a qualification here: in the general account of warrant, the only propositional attitude in which we are interested is *belief;* in the case of epistemic probability, however, we are indeed interested in belief, but also in such propositional attitudes as *having considerable confidence in.* If you have a one in a thousand chance of winning a lottery, your degree of confidence in the proposition that you won't win will be high, perhaps very high; but no doubt it will not be true that you *believe* you won't win. (If you do, why did you buy the ticket?) Degrees of confidence get expressed, in English, in at least two ways: on the one hand, one says something like "I am fairly confident that it will snow tomorrow"; and, on the other, "I think it fairly probable that it will snow tomorrow." (Here there lurks opportunity for confusion; for you can use that same locution to express your belief that the *objective* probability of snow [relative to the appropriate body of evidence] is fairly high.) For present purposes we can think of belief as the upper limit of degree of confidence. But this means that the third and fourth components of the basic account of warrant must be *generalized* to apply properly to the case of probability. We must say, here, that the design plan is successfully aimed at an appropriate correlation between the objective conditional probability of a proposition A on a proposition B, and the degree of confidence invested by S in A on the basis of B. A good or successful design plan P, then, will be one such that there is a substantial statistical probability that a propositional attitude formed in accordance with P (in a favorable cognitive environment) toward a proposition A, on the basis of a proposition B, will match or approximate the objective probability of A on B.

Given these preliminaries, we might initially say (following Reid's lead) that the normative component of the epistemic conditional probability of a proposition A on a proposition B is something like *the degree of confidence a rational person (in circumstances in which the conditions of warrant are fulfilled) would have in A, given that she accepted B.*[14] But of course this is not even a

---

[14]Reid's qualifications that the person in question *understand* A and B, and that they are "considered without prejudice" (her judgment is not clouded or skewed by avarice, lust, love for her children, or other distractions), get absorbed into the condition that the circumstances are such that the conditions for warrant are satisfied.

decent beginning, not even a zeroeth approximation as it stands; obviously there is no such thing as *the* degree to which a rational person will accept *A*, given that she accepts *B*. How much confidence she invests in *A* will depend upon the rest of her circumstances. For example, I believe that garages seldom contain pythons; I am in your garage and am amazed to see a python; the degree of confidence I afford to the proposition that your garage contains a python, given that I believe no more than one out of a million garages harbor pythons, will then be very different from what it would have been if I were not looking at that python. In this case the crucial circumstance is my perceiving a python—more broadly, my experience. In other cases, the rest of what I *believe* is a crucial circumstance. *A* is the proposition that you perceive an oak tree; *B* is the proposition that 99 out of 100 trees around here are elms. You believe *B;* how much confidence you display in *A* given that you believe *B* will depend not just on what the tree you are examining looks like, but also on, for example, whether you believe you can distinguish oaks from elms on sight. Alternatively, you believe that 1 out of a 100 trees in the county you are visiting is an elm; if you also believe that you are on an estate where most of the trees are elms, then of course your degree of confidence that the tree you're looking at is an elm will be quite different from what it would have been otherwise.

Our interest, here, is clearly in cases where you believe *B*, believe *A* on the basis of *B*, and have no other source of warrant for *A* or for its denial; and we must add that you have no *undercutting defeater* for the warrant *A* gets by virtue of being believed on the basis of *B*. Of course there is no reason to think there will be a specific real number registering your degree of confidence in *A*, given that you believe *B* in those circumstances. First, it may be that there is no sensible way of assigning real numbers to degrees of confidence; perhaps we shall have to remain content with a comparative rather than a quantitative conception of epistemic probability. Second, even if we could plausibly represent those degrees of confidence by way of real numbers, it would typically be impossible to say precisely what degree of confidence you have in a proposition: precisely how confident are you that the next American president will be a Democrat? Third and more important, even if we can quantify degrees of confidence, it seems likely that there is a certain *range* associated with the probability of *A* on *B*. Different rational (that is, properly functioning) persons who believed *B* might display different degrees of confidence in *A*, perhaps substantially different degrees, even in relevantly similar epistemic circumstances. So I shall represent both degree of confidence and conditional epistemic probability by real intervals rather than real numbers. (Of course it is vaguely silly to speak, here, of real numbers and intervals thereof [it's a bit like doing high-powered mathematics on extremely crude statistics]; but I shall follow current custom and persevere.)

The rough initial idea, then, is that the normative component of the conditional epistemic probability of *A* on *B* is the interval containing the degrees of belief a rational person could have in *A*, provided she believed *B* and was aware that she believed *B*, considered the evidential bearing of *B* on *A*, had no other source of warrant for *B* or its denial, and had no defeater for the warrant, if any, accruing to A or its denial by virtue of being thus believed on the basis of B.

Here I say S *believes B;* but for obvious reasons we should not construe this as *maximal* belief, belief to the highest degree. We believe many propositions, and believe them to various degrees. I believe that $2 + 1 = 3$, that I live in Indiana, that Glasgow is the largest city in Scotland, and much else as well; and I believe these propositions to different degrees. I do not merely believe these propositions *probable;* nor is it the case that I am merely very *confident* of them; I *believe* them. On the other hand, while it is false that I *believe* that you will not win the Illinois lottery, I am confident that you will not win (you hold only one of a million tickets) and I also believe it very probable that you won't win. I am also confident and believe it probable that the Detroit Tigers will not win next year's World Series (last year they had a dismal record and have made no improvements during the off-season); but it would be wrong to say that I *believe* they won't win. (I do believe that they didn't win the series *last* year.) The border between believing probable and believing *simpliciter* is hazy and vague, as is the border between the latter and having a high degree of confidence short of belief. Here we don't have the space to explore these matters with the care they deserve; but what counts for the account of conditional epistemic probability is that S believes B. To a first approximation, therefore:

> (CEP) $P(A/B) = <x,y>$ iff $<x,y>$ is the smallest interval which contains all of the intervals which represent the degree to which a rational human being S (for whom the conditions necessary for warrant hold) could believe A if she believed B, had no undercutting defeater for A, had no other source of warrant either for A or for $-A$, was aware that she believed B, and considered the evidential bearing of B on A.[15]

III. Replies and Comments

Now for some comments, qualifications and replies to objections: I shall be agreeably brief and dogmatic.

A. *The van Fraassen Objection*

First, according to Bas van Fraassen,

> We sometimes see the conditional probability of A on B (given B, on the supposition that B) explained as the probability which A would have for me if I were given B as total new evidence. This explanation is totally flawed as an interpretation of conditional probability (in part because some propositions could never be anyone's total evidence and in part because some which admittedly could be true could never be ones one could believe to be true).[16]

[15]Compare Richard Otte's (n. 13) account:

(Otte) $P_C(A/B) = <x, y>$ iff $<x, y>$ is the smallest interval which contains all of the intervals which represent the degree to which a properly functioning cognizer in circumstances C could believe proposition A if she fully believed proposition B.

[16]*Images of Science*, ed. P. Churchland and C. Hooker (Chicago: University of Chicago Press, 1985), p. 250.

And isn't my account subject to this stricture, or something like it? No doubt there are plenty of propositions no properly functioning human being could so much as grasp; these, clearly enough, will be propositions no human person could believe. There are others we can grasp, all right, but which are still such that no rational human being could believe them—*There aren't any people*, perhaps, or *No one believes anything*, or *There is nothing (contingent) at all*. What, on my account, is the epistemic conditional probability of a proposition *A* on a proposition *B* we can't so much as believe? The answer, clearly enough, is that such propositions—propositions rational human beings can't believe— will not be in the field of the relation of epistemic conditional probability. (To put it in a way that is at least mildly misleading, epistemic conditional probability is not defined for such propositions.) Some propositions are such that no rational creatures could believe them; others are such that *human beings* can't believe them (but perhaps other creatures could). Those propositions would not be in the field of *our* epistemic conditional probability; it would not follow that they were not in the field of epistemic conditional probability for any rational creatures at all.

Epistemic probability is species relative; perhaps there are other kinds of persons—angels, Alpha Centaurians, what have you—with quite different design plans for whom the structure of epistemic probability is also quite different. (Perhaps they can grasp propositions we can't; perhaps their degrees of confidence are more finely tuned than ours; and perhaps the normative component of epistemic conditional probability for them tracks objective probability more faithfully than it does for us.) But that is not our present concern. We are concerned with the *human* design plan, and with the latter as it in fact is. The above account therefore needs amendment: we must restrict it to pairs of propositions such that rational human beings can believe both members of the pair. (Of course, the propositions excluded from the field of epistemic conditional probability may still be in the field of *objective* probability.)

Second, what about the case of pairs of propositions <*A*, *B*> such that it is possible that a rational person believe both *A* and *B*, but not possible for *B* to be the *sole* source of warrant for *A*, for her?[17] For example, what is the epistemic probability, for me, of the proposition *I believe that London is larger than Peoria* conditional on the proposition *London is larger than Peoria*? If I am rational, it will not be possible for the first proposition to be such that the only source of warrant for it (or its denial), for me, will be the second; for once I consider the evidential bearing of the second on the first, I will find myself believing the first (or its denial). This belief, furthermore, will have *introspective warrant* for me—the sort of warrant enjoyed by my beliefs about how I am appeared to, whether I am in pain, what I believe. The second, therefore, can't be the sole warrant, for me, for the first.

But here the problem is only apparent: although *I* can't entertain the first proposition (a proposition about what I believe) without forming a belief about it, a belief that has introspective warrant, *you* can. So here the account applies straightforwardly: it *is* possible that the second be the sole source of warrant,

---

[17]Here I am indebted to Richard Foley.

for a rational person, for the first (even though there is a person for whom it is not possible that the second be the sole source of warrant, for *him,* for the first).

This pair of propositions <*A, B*>, therefore, does not meet the condition of being such that it is possible that a rational person believe both *A* and *B,* but not possible for *B* to be the sole source of warrant for *A,* for her. Other pairs <*A, B*>, however, do meet this condition; what shall we say about them? Let *A* be *2 + 1 = 3,* or *People sometimes believe things,* or *There are or have been people,* or *Some things are colored,* or *People are sometimes appeared to in one way or another,* or *Something has happened at some time or other.* Here it seems that no proposition *B* could be a rational person's sole source of warrant for the proposition in question. In some cases (*2 + 1 = 3,* for example) this is because it is not possible that a rational person have no *nonpropositional* warrant for the proposition in question. Setting aside cases of that sort, however, how could it be that, say, the proposition *I am now being appeared to redly* should be my sole source of warrant for the proposition *People are sometimes appeared to in one way or another?* For one thing, any rational person will either *be* being appeared to in one way or other, or will *remember* having been appeared to in one way. For another, any rational person for whom the conditions of warrant are satisfied (for that proposition) will be in an epistemically congenial environment and will know that other people are sometimes appeared to in one way or another. What shall we say about propositions of this sort?

Here there are two important subcases. On the one hand, *A* might automatically, so to speak, have *maximal* warrant, and may therefore be such that it can't receive additional warrant by way of being believed on the basis of some proposition *B.* Perhaps the corresponding conditional of *modus ponens, 2 + 1 = 3,* and *I am now being appeared to redly* (when I am) are of that sort. Here the right thing to say, I think, is that no pair whose first member is one of those propositions is in the field of conditional epistemic probability; more generally, a pair <*A, B*> is in the field of that relation only if *A* can have less than maximal warrant for a rational human being.

But there is also the more difficult kind of case, the case where no rational person can be such that a proposition *B* is the sole source of warrant for *A,* for her, but *A* can nonetheless have less than maximal warrant for her. Perhaps certain moral or ethical propositions are of this sort. Perhaps the proposition *It is wrong to hurt people just because it affords you a certain mild pleasure* is like that. Perhaps it gets a certain degree of warrant from the operation of something like a moral sense, but the warrant it thus gets for you can be smothered by the wrong kind of environment (you are brought up in a society of sadists), or enhanced and reinforced by the right kind of environment (one in which your natural tendency to believe the proposition is reinforced by precept and example). Even if this example is not universally persuasive, it still seems clearly *possible* that there should be propositions of this sort: that is, it seems possible that there should be propositions that automatically have *some* warrant for a rational person, but not *maximal* warrant. Such propositions, one thinks, could receive an access of warrant, for *S,* by way of being believed (in part) on the basis of other propositions. What shall we say about *these?*

Here I am pulled in two directions. On the one hand, pairs $<A, B>$ such that B can't be the sole source of warrant for A (or its denial) really don't meet the conditions of epistemic probability; in these cases B has no contribution to make strictly of its own. In a way, there really *isn't* any such thing as the epistemic conditional probability of A on B—B *alone*, so to speak. (Of course, it may still be the case that B contributes to the *total* warrant possessed by A, for S, and of course there is the *objective* conditional probability of A on B.) This suggests that the right course here is the same as in the cases of those pairs $<A, B>$ such that B can't be the sole source of warrant for A because A already enjoys maximal warrant apart from any relation to B: such pairs are not in the field of the relation of epistemic conditional probability.

On the other hand, in these cases B does (or can) contribute to the total warrant possessed by A, for S; B is (or can be) part of S's total evidence for A; it can be part of S's total case for A. That suggests that conditional epistemic probability *is* defined for such cases. If we are persuaded by the latter consideration, we must make a qualification: we must say, for these pairs, that the epistemic probability of A on B is a function of the difference between the degree of confidence S would have in A if she had only the sources of warrant for A necessary for rationality, and the degree of confidence she would have in A if she had those sources of warrant and also B. I leave as homework the project specifying this function.

B. The Kyburg Connection

There is obviously an intimate connection between *known frequencies* and epistemic probability. For example, the epistemic probability that Feike can swim on the proposition *Feike is a Frisian and among the Frisian lifeguards I have heard about, the proportion of those that can swim is about .99*, is high. So statistical information is one source of epistemic conditional probability. *Pace* Kyburg, however, it is not the *only* nondeductive source: that is, it is not the case that whenever a statement A is nondeductive evidence for another statement B—whenever a statement B is epistemically probable with respect to another statement A that does not entail it—then the only relevant factor is known (or believed) frequencies. Other factors clearly enter as well. Given Newton's evidence, an inverse square law

(a) $\quad F = \dfrac{m_1 m_2}{d^2}$

is no doubt epistemically more probable than

(b) $\quad$ Either $F = \dfrac{m_1 m_2}{d^{2.000000000004}} \quad$ or $\quad F = \dfrac{m_1 m_2}{d^{1.999999999996}}$;

but this difference is not a reflection of statistical knowledge in his evidence. What is involved instead is something like simplicity and naturalness. As Leibniz (and a thousand others since) pointed out, it is possible to draw any number of curves through data plotted on a graph; you will reject most of these on grounds of adventitious complication. Hence, the epistemic conditional probability of the simpler hypotheses on the data is greater than that of the more complex hypotheses. (What we hope, of course, is that in fact simplicity and naturalness, properly understood, will be objectively relevant to truth, so that a simple hypothesis is objectively more likely to be true than a complex one.)

More generally, consider ordinary cases where a theory is probable with respect to the relevant evidence: special relativity, or *The earth is billions of years old,* or *There are individual essences;* it is at best monumentally difficult to see how these probabilities could arise by way of statistical knowledge of any sort.

C. Epistemic Probabilities Are Contingent

It is not the case, *pace* the logical theorists (and again, *pace* Kyburg), that a statement of epistemic probability is noncontingent, necessarily true, or necessarily false. (a) is epistemically more probable than (b) on Newton's evidence; a rational human being with Newton's evidence will invest greater confidence in (a) than in (b); but that this is so is not a necessary truth. Clearly we could have been so constructed, for example, that we preferred complexity to simplicity in cases of this sort; and the world could have been such as to vindicate that preference.

Furthermore, *induction* is for us a source of warrant and a source of epistemic conditional probability. For example,

(c)   The next Frisian I come across will be able to swim

is, for us, epistemically probable with respect to

(d)   9 out of 10 Frisians I have encountered can swim;

but is it a *necessary* truth that this is so? Couldn't we, or to beg no questions, rational creatures a lot like us (Alpha Centaurians, let's say), be such that (d) should fail to be evidence for (c)? It certainly seems so. These Alpha Centaurians, rational creatures that they are, are nonetheless such that, when apprised of (d) (and meeting the conditions for warrant), they are no more inclined to believe (c) than its denial. Indeed, they might be such that (d) is evidence, for them, *against* (c); they might be such that in these conditions they would be strongly inclined to believe the *denial* of (c). Further, their world might be such as to vindicate this way of forming belief. For it might be statistically likely that an Alpha Centaurian who is such that nine out of ten *A*s he has come across are *B*s, is also such that the next *A* he comes across will *not* be a *B*. Perhaps these Alpha Centaurians are furnished by a benevolent creator with inclinations to form, in such contexts, the belief that the next *A* will not be a *B;* and perhaps this inclination leads them to form true beliefs on most occasions. Under these conditions (d) would not be epistemically probable, for them, with respect to (c).

Perhaps you will point out that this shows only that epistemic probability is species relative; it does not really show that (c) could fail to be evidence, *for us,* for (d). Fair enough; strictly speaking, this is correct; and indeed it *isn't* possible, both that we should display the design plan we *do* display and that (c) should fail to be epistemically probable, for us, with respect to (d). So we must divide the question. One question is whether *we* could have had a somewhat different design plan—that is, the question is whether it is possible that *human beings* should have had a design plan different along just these lines, so that (d) would not have been epistemically probable, for human beings, with respect to (c). I am inclined to think that is indeed possible (and even more inclined to think it is possible *de re,* with respect to you and me and the rest of us, that we should have had a design plan of that sort). The more important question, however, is whether there could be or could have been *rational creatures* for whom (d) is not epistemically probable with respect to (c). Here the answer is clear: indeed there could.

D. Epistemic Probabilities and the Probability Calculus

Conditional epistemic probability does not conform to the calculus of probabilities. First, there is the fact already noted that there may be no sensible way to assign real numbers to degrees of confidence; perhaps we must be satisfied with a comparative conception of epistemic probability. This is only mildly significant, however, as is the fact that epistemic probability is interval-valued rather than real-valued. More important: contrary to the probability calculus, it will not be the case that if A entails B (or even if *if A then B* is a theorem of first-order logic), then the epistemic probability of B on A will be maximal. Even if A entails B, a rational person who knew A might not bestow the maximal degree of confidence on B. Indeed, she might display very little confidence in B, or even display more confidence in −B than in B. Perhaps B is extremely complicated, for example, so that she can't see that A entails it; or B might not be particularly complicated, but nonetheless such that it isn't just obvious, even to a rational person, that it is entailed by A. Consider Peirce's Law: $((A>A)>A)>A$. According to propositional logic, this is entailed by just any proposition (more exactly, any conditional with this proposition as consequent is a tautology); but a rational person could be considerably less confident of Peirce's Law than of, say, the corresponding conditional of *modus ponens.* Consider the proposition that there are not any nonexistent objects. *Pace* Meinong, the early Russell, H. Castañeda, and others, this proposition (as I see it) is necessarily true and hence entailed by just any proposition. A rational person, however, may fail to see the entailment (or may see it dimly, through a glass, darkly) and may thus accept the proposition with considerably less enthusiasm than, say, *There is such a country as China.* But then conditional epistemic probability will not conform to the probability calculus.

By way of concluding this chapter I turn to a related question. It is obvious, I think, that *rationality* does not require coherence: that is, rationality does not require that your degrees of confidence conform to the calculus of probability.[18] To recycle the above example, clearly you can be perfectly rational and still invest considerably less confidence in Peirce's Law than in the law of excluded middle; you can invest more confidence in such contingent truths as *There was such a thing as the American Civil War* than in such necessary truths as *There exist individual essences,* or Goldbach's Conjecture (if it is true) or its denial (if it is not). I believe that there are 9 planets; I therefore believe with considerable firmness that there are at least 3^2 planets; but (being a little slow with sums) I believe much less firmly that there are at least $\sqrt[3]{729}$ planets. I am therefore incoherent. To try to achieve coherence, furthermore, would be foolish and irrational. I should not try to bring it about that I bestow the same degree of confidence on all necessary truths (or all the truths I think are necessary, or all the necessary truths I have encountered): I ought to be extremely confident of *obvious* necessary truths, but less confident of those that are less obvious. Given my epistemic condition, I ought to believe the corresponding conditional of *modus ponens* with maximal firmness; I would be irrationally opinionated, however, to believe as firmly that there are individual essences.

Nevertheless, there are areas in which conformity to the probability calculus is a sort of ideal for us. This is once more a reflection of the enormously elaborate and highly articulate nature of our noetic design plan. There are areas where we *ought* not to conform to the probability calculus, and *will* not if we are functioning properly. In these areas (believing all necessary truths to the same degree, for example), coherence is not an ideal I should aim at even as I regretfully realize that I won't achieve it; nor is it merely Quixotic, as it would be to aim to run as fast as a cheetah, or swim as far as a shark; it is positively irrational. In other areas, however, rationality and even proper function *do* require conformity to the calculus: if you believe each of *All men are mortal* and *It is false that all men are mortal* to the maximal or near maximal degree, then you are probably subject to some kind of cognitive disorder. (Perhaps you think it is not even possible [in the broadly logical sense] to do that. Very well, adjust the example to suit.)

In still other restricted areas of the design plan, proper function dictates neither coherence nor incoherence; but coherence is nevertheless an appropriate sort of ideal or goal for creatures with our sort of design plan—or perhaps for those who emphasize and develop one aspect or part of the design plan. (In the same way, an athlete might develop certain areas of her functioning; attaining a certain state—being able to swim 25 miles, for example—might serve as an appropriate goal for her, even though it is not required by proper functioning and even though it would be a ridiculously unventuresome goal for a whale and a wholly unrealistic one for an pigeon.) This is just as it is with deductive logic. People often make mistakes in logic even if they not only function properly, from a cognitive standpoint, but meet the more stringent condition of being rational. We could hardly claim that Frege was irrational (let alone cognitively dysfunctional) merely because his axioms for set theory are incon-

[18]See *Warrant: The Current Debate* (New York: Oxford University Press, 1993), chap. 7, pp. 138ff.

sistent. But when the inconsistency was called to his attention, then, naturally enough, he gave up the axioms.

Something similar holds, in some areas, for probabilistic coherence. If you come to see that you believe a contingent conjunction more firmly than you believe one of the conjuncts, you will no doubt mend your ways. Less trivially, consider

(1) there is an omnipotent, omniscient and perfectly good God,

(2) There are 10^{13} turps of evil

and

(3) Possibly, for any possible world W which is as good as the actual world, but contains less than 10^{13} turps of evil, it is not within the power of God to actualize W, despite his omnipotence and omniscience.

I might argue that the probability of (1) on (2) is not as low as you might think by pointing out that (2) is equivalent to (2)&(3) (because (3) is necessarily true).[19] According to the probability calculus, therefore, the probability of (1) on (2) is equivalent to that of (1) on ((2)&(3)). Coherence therefore demands that $P_S((1)/(2)) = P_S((1)/((2)\&(3)))$. Coherence therefore demands that $P_{you}((1)/(2)) = P_{you}((1)/((2) \& (3)))$. But of course a person S could be perfectly rational even if her degrees of confidence do not conform to this demand. Perhaps she doesn't realize that (3) is necessary; then

(a) $\dfrac{P_S((1)\&(2)\&(3))}{P_S((2)\&(3))}$

might well differ from

(b) $\dfrac{P_S((1)\&(2))}{P_S((2)\&(3))}$.

If S *is* rational, however, once she sees that (3) is indeed necessarily true, so that (2) is equivalent to ((2) & (3)) (and reflects a bit on the situation) (a) and (b) will no longer differ, or they will differ to a smaller degree. Here the point is that the probability calculus functions as a sort of ideal; rationality requires modification of S's degrees of confidence in the direction of conformity to the probability calculus. True: rationality in general does not require coherence; still, arguments of this sort are effective just because S would be less than rational if (a) and (b) remained different (or very different), once she saw that (2) and ((2)&(3)) are indeed equivalent.

[19]As I argue in chapter 9 of *The Nature of Necessity* (Oxford: Clarendon Press, 1974).

10

Coherence, Foundations, and Evidence

In chapters 3 through 9 we examined some of the main structural divisions of our design plan: memory, our knowledge of ourselves, and of others, testimony, *a priori* knowledge, induction, and epistemic probability. All of these are sources of warrant; and all but the last are *first*-level sources of warrant.[1] Conditional epistemic probability, however, is a second-level source of warrant, taking *beliefs* as input, and hence taking as input what is the output of other sources of warranted belief. Conditional epistemic probability brings us to *evidence;* and evidence brings us to two important questions about broader, systemwide, structural features of the design plan: (1) How shall we understand the alleged contrast between foundationalism and coherentism? (2) What *is* evidence, and what is its connection with warrant? In particular, is it true, as the *evidentialist* claims, that any proposition or belief that has warrant for me is one for which I have evidence of one sort or another?

In this chapter I begin by examining this contrast. I believe coherentism is ordinarily misconstrued, and misconstrued in such a way as to make it entirely implausible. Fortunately there is a better way to understand it: coherentism, as I see it, is really a very special variety of foundationalism, a variety according to which the only source of warrant is coherence. So understood, coherentism is vastly less implausible than under the usual misconstrual. Even so, however, it remains mistaken: coherence is by no means the *only* source of warrant, and is indeed neither necessary nor sufficient for it. I shall therefore reject coherentism and endorse foundationalism. There is one particular variety of foundationalism which is of enormous historical importance: the modern classical foundationalism emanating from Descartes and Locke. I shall briefly argue *ambulando* (given the desuetude into which classical foundationalism has fallen, no more is warranted) that modern classical foundationalism is mistaken. Here, however, I face an organizational embarrassment: for the sake of structural integrity and reasonable completeness, these points need to be made here; unfortunately, however, I have already said most of what I have to say about some of them in chapter 4 of *Warrant: The Current Debate.* (They also needed

---

[1] Induction, as I briefly argued in note 1 of chapter 7, is both first-level and second-level. You can explicitly form the belief *All the As I've seen so far have been Bs* and conclude *Therefore, probably the next one will be;* you can also form the expectation that the next A will be B without forming or considering any belief about the proportion of As that have so far been Bs.

to be made there.) I shall therefore adopt the following palliative maneuver: to spare the reader a trip to the library I briefly recapitulate what I said there about ordinary foundationalism, coherentism, and classical foundationalism; then I go on to say something about the brand of foundationalism that seems to me to be correct. Finally (and at slightly greater length), I shall consider (and reject) evidentialism, a special variety of foundationalism that stands in an interesting relation to modern classical foundationalism.

I. Coherence and Foundations
A. *Ordinary Foundationalism*

Coherentism is best understood, I think, by way of contrast with foundationalism—*ordinary* foundationalism, since the crucial contrast is usually thought to be between coherentism and almost any brand of foundationalism. According to the current lore, the crucial difference between foundationalist and coherentist lies in their attitudes toward *circular reasoning:* the foundationalist rejects it, but the coherentist accepts it, "provided the circle is large enough." (Indeed [so the usual view goes] she revels in it; for it is in just such circles that warrant arises.) Now *why* does the foundationalist reject circular reasoning?

To answer this question and to understand coherentism we must first note the importance, to the foundationalist, of *evidence*, of the idea of accepting one proposition on the evidential basis of another. This is *propositional* evidence, and propositional evidence is perhaps most familiar to philosophers; but of course there are other kinds. At a trial, the evidence—it might be called the 'physical' evidence—may consist not in propositions, but in tagged items displayed on a table: a pistol, perhaps, together with a torn garment and the cast of a heel print. Indeed, according to J. L. Austin, this latter use of the term is the more 'proper' one:

> The situation in which I would properly be said to have *evidence* for the statement that some animal is a pig is that, for example, in which the beast itself is not actually on view, but I can see plenty of pig-like marks on the ground outside its retreat. If I find a few buckets of pig food, that is a bit more evidence, and the noises and smell may provide better evidence still.[2]

In an older use, there is also the *evidence of the senses;*[3] and Thomas Reid also speaks of "the evidence of memory, the evidence of consciousness, the evidence of testimony, the evidence of axioms, the evidence of reasoning."[4]

It is propositional evidence, however, that is crucial to understanding the contrast between coherentism and foundationalism. According to the foundationalist, there is a *basic* or foundational level of beliefs or propositions that are not accepted on the evidential basis of other beliefs: self-evident beliefs will fall here, as well as, for example, beliefs about how one is appeared to and whether

---

[2]*Sense and Sensibilia* (Oxford: Oxford University Press, 1962), p. 115.

[3]See, for example, the passage from John Stuart Mill quoted on pp. 65–66.

[4]*Essays on the Intellectual Powers of Man*, in *Inquiries and Essays*, ed. R. Beanblossom and K. Lehrer (Indianapolis: Hackett, 1983), II, 20, p. 200.

one is in pain. Other beliefs—beliefs not in the foundations—will be accepted *on the evidential basis* of foundational beliefs; and these beliefs, if things are going properly, will be *evidentially supported* by the foundational beliefs. That is to say, the basic beliefs serve as *propositional evidence* for the nonbasic beliefs. (Propositional evidence may come in different varieties: different foundationalists may for example endorse any or all of deductive, inductive, and abductive propositional evidence.)

According to the foundationalist, the basis relation, in a proper noetic structure, is finite and terminates in the foundations. That is to say, in such a structure a given nonbasic belief will be accepted on the basis of other beliefs, which may be accepted on the basis of still others, which may be accepted on the basis of still others; and in principle this chain can be as long as you like. Given that we hold only finitely many beliefs, however, the chain must terminate, and must terminate in beliefs that are not accepted on the evidential basis of other beliefs. On the other hand, if there is a *circle* in the basis relation—that is, a case where a belief A_0 is accepted solely on the evidential basis of a belief A_1, which is accepted solely on the evidential basis of $A_2, \ldots$, which is accepted solely on the evidential basis of A_n, which is accepted on the evidential basis of A_0—then, says the foundationalist, the noetic structure in question is improper. The reason, in brief, is that warrant cannot be generated just by warrant transfer. A belief B can get warrant from another belief A by way of being believed on the basis of it, but only if A already *has* warrant. No warrant *originates* in this process whereby warrant gets transferred from one belief to another.[5] If so, however, circular reasoning will be improper. If my sole warrant for A_0 arises by virtue of my accepting it on the evidential basis of a belief A_1, which I accept solely on the basis of $A_2, \ldots$, which is based for me solely on A_n, which is based solely on A_0, then none of these beliefs has any warrant for me at all.

B. Coherentism

Now it is just here that (according to current lore) the coherentist demurs: he is said to approve of circular reasoning (provided that the circle is big enough); in fact he thinks that it is precisely in such circles that warrant arises. But this can't be right; if this is what he thinks, he is surely mistaken.[6] One can't get warrant for a belief just by bringing it about that it is a member of a large circular chain of this sort. (Couldn't you make any chain as long as you like by appropriately interpolating items?) But why saddle him with anything so silly? The fact is there is a vastly more plausible way of construing the coherentist. He should be seen, not as approving of circular reasoning or holding that warrant arises by way of warrant transfer, but as saying instead that *it is coherence that is the source of warrant*. Not warrant transfer, but coherence—coherence with the rest of one's noetic structure, or with some favored *part* of it, or with some

---

[5]For a fuller account (as well as an account of the notion of a noetic structure), see *Warrant: The Current Debate* (New York: Oxford University Press, 1993), chap. 4, pp. 74ff.

[6]See ibid., pp. 77ff.

improvement of it (for example, the result of removing all false beliefs, substituting their negations, and making other required changes) or with some part of some improvement of it. Coherence is the sole source of warrant. The *pure* coherentist eschews warrant transfer, holding that no belief will be accepted on the evidential basis of any other belief; instead, each belief will be accepted in the basic way, the warrant accruing to it (if any) arising by way of coherence. The *impure* coherentist, on the other hand, will allow that there can be warrant transfer, all right, but the warrant transferred arises originally by way of coherence.

So construed, therefore, the central coherentist tenet is that the sole source of warrant is coherence. And while this is more plausible than the claim that warrant arises just by way of warrant transfer, it is still, so it seems to me, clearly mistaken. For coherence is neither necessary nor sufficient for warrant. I gave several examples to show this point in chapter 4 of *Warrant: The Current Debate;* I shall repeat one of them (a counterexample to sufficiency) here. (If you remain unconvinced, I implore you to turn to my fuller discussion.) A central reason for the insufficiency of coherence for warrant is that coherence is a *doxastic* relation: a relation that holds just among beliefs. But the warrant of a belief does not depend merely upon its relation to other beliefs; the relation in which it stands to experience is also important. To see this, consider the Case of the Epistemically Inflexible Climber. Ric is climbing Guide's Wall (on Storm Point in the Grand Tetons). He has just led the next to last pitch and is seated on the relatively capacious belay ledge at the end of this pitch. Enjoying the mountain sunshine and idly looking around, he forms the beliefs that Cascade Canyon is down to his left, that the cliffs of Mount Owen are directly in front of him, that there is a hawk gliding in lazy circles 200 feet below him, that it is broad daylight, that the sun is wonderfully warm and pleasant, that he is wearing his new *Fire* rock shoes, and so on. His beliefs, we may stipulate, are coherent. Now add that Ric is struck by an errant burst of high-energy cosmic radiation, causing subtle but pronounced brain damage. As a result, he is subject to cognitive malfunction: his beliefs become *fixed,* no longer responsive to changes in his experience. No matter what his experience, his beliefs remain the same. This makes it difficult to communicate with him, but at the cost of great effort his partner gets him down. That evening, in a desperate last-ditch attempt at therapy, his partner takes him to the opera in nearby Jackson, where the New York Metropolitan Opera on tour is performing *La Traviata.* Ric's experience is the same as everyone else's; he is inundated by wave after wave of golden sound. The effort at therapy unhappily fails; Ric's beliefs remain fixed and wholly unresponsive to his experience; he still believes that he is on the belay ledge at the top of the next to last pitch of Guide's Wall, that Cascade Canyon is down to his left, that the sun is shining on him, that there is a hawk sailing in lazy circles 200 feet below him, that he is wearing his new *Fire* rock shoes, and all the rest. Furthermore (since he believes the very same things he believed when seated on the ledge), his beliefs are coherent. But surely they have little or no warrant for him. The reason is cognitive malfunction; his beliefs are not appropriately responsive to his experience. He may be (deontologically) *justified* in accepting those beliefs; they may also have Foley justification; they may display still other epistemic virtues. But they have no warrant for him. Clearly, then, coherence is not sufficient for positive epistemic status.

So coherentism is mistaken: coherence is not the only source of warrant. It does not follow that coherence is not *a* source of warrant—one source among others. All that follows is that it is not the *sole* source. The ordinary foundationalist can hold in perfect consistency that many beliefs get at least some warrant by way of coherence, and even that *some* beliefs get *all* their warrant solely by coherence.

Two final questions about coherentism. First, is coherence an *independent* source of warrant? Or does it have the parasitic character of testimony?[7] If I come to form some belief by way of testimony, the degree of warrant enjoyed by that belief will not depend merely upon me and the condition of my epistemic faculties; much will also depend upon how things stand with my source, the person(s) whose testimony I accept. You are a sixth-grader in an experimental school run by Alpha Centaurians; you are taught much falsehood about the size and shape of the earth, but also (by accident, so to speak) a few truths. These truths, I think, have little warrant for you, despite the fact that your cognitive faculties are in perfect working order. The warrant of a proposition I come to believe by way of testimony will depend (among other things) upon the warrant enjoyed by the same belief on the part of my source (and not conversely). We may therefore say that testimony is a sort of parasitic faculty: if you tell me that you spent your summer vacation in the Tetons, the warrant that belief has for *me* depends upon the warrant it has for *you*.

Does something similar hold for coherence? Suppose we agree that a group of beliefs each of which has a certain degree of warrant from another source, can acquire still more warrant by virtue of coherence with each other. Suppose we agree further that a belief that has no other source of warrant may nonetheless acquire warrant by virtue of coherence with other beliefs that enjoy an independent source of warrant. Should we go still further and hold that beliefs each of which has no independent source of warrant may nonetheless all acquire warrant by virtue of coherence with each other? (This would be to suppose that for some subset of my beliefs, coherence is the only source of the warrant *they* enjoy.) Or is it rather the case that coherence resembles testimony in that it either transfers warrant from beliefs that get warrant in some other way, or else enhances the warrant a belief already has from some other source? Or is it perhaps the case that beliefs that get no warrant elsewhere *can* get warrant from coherence, but only the minimal degree of warrant, so that the warrant generated in that way can never overcome warrant from other sources? If my cognitive faculties are nondefective, could I accept some proposition P such that I had some noncoherence warrant for its denial, and nothing going for it except coherence with beliefs none of which had noncoherence warrant for me? I shall leave these questions as another exercise for the reader.

Second question. I have been taking coherentism to be a *doxastic* theory:

[7]See pp. 87ff.

one according to which the only thing that counts for warrant is relationships among beliefs. This certainly seems just with respect to Lehrer, BonJour, and other prominent contemporary coherentists, who say the same thing about themselves. However it also leads directly to the fatal problem: obviously, as we have seen, a set of beliefs can be as coherent as you please but (due to cognitive malfunction of one sort or another) have entirely the wrong relation to experience and hence have little or nothing by way of warrant. But can't we construe coherence more broadly, so that its field isn't just beliefs but also includes experiences? Can't we follow F. H. Bradley, surely as respectable a coherentist as any, in seeing coherence as a relation that can hold between belief and experience, not merely between beliefs? As Bradley construes the matter, however, there is no real distinction to be made between experience and belief (judgment). There is no real distinction between my *being* appeared to thus and so and my *judging* that I am appeared to thus and so; my being appeared to thus and so just *is* my believing thus and so. But this seems clearly wrong: clearly there *is* such a distinction, if only because on many occasions I am appeared to thus and so but do not form the belief that I am thus appeared to, or any other belief with which my being appeared to thus and so could plausibly be identified. At *t* I see a large London bus bearing down on me as I try to cross the street; I form rather hasty and panic-stricken beliefs about the bus, but none about how I am appeared to. At *t + n*, after a quick sprint to the opposite side, I can perhaps remember how I was appeared to and, if of a sufficiently reflective turn of mind, may form beliefs about how I was then appeared to. (It looked as if an enormous red apartment building moving at tremendous speed were coming right *at* me!) But at *t*, when I am being thus appeared to, I need form no beliefs about it at all. Furthermore, the way in which I am appeared to is often much too complex and variegated, much too detailed and articulate for any belief I hold to be identical with that way of being appeared to. Often I can't so much as give a good description of the way in which I am being appeared to.

If so, however, we can't construe coherence between beliefs and experience as coherence among *contents,* among propositions; for being appeared to in a certain way is not the same thing as holding a belief of some sort. Furthermore, the notion of coherence among *propositions* is difficult enough; but (supposing we had a good idea as to what *that* was) what would it be for a proposition or belief to be coherent with an *experience,* a way of being appeared to, perhaps, or some other sort of experience? This looks initially formidable, but perhaps there is a fairly easy answer. Consider the case of the Epistemically Inflexible Climber. Here the problem was an unfortunate lack of fit between the way in which Ric was appeared to—'operatically' as we may say—and the beliefs he held about his surroundings. What sort of lack of fit is this? Well, at any rate it is lack of a sort of fit necessary for warrant. And from my perspective as to the nature of warrant, the answer is easy enough: what is required is that experience and belief fit together in a way permitted by proper function. The problem with the Epistemically Inflexible Climber was just that the relation between his experience and belief was pathological, not to be found in human beings whose cognitive faculties are functioning properly. So perhaps the coherentist can specify a coherence relation between belief and experience as follows: a proposition *P* is coherent with a given evidence-base[8] *E* if and only if a properly functioning human being could believe *P* and display *E*. We can also see coherence as a matter of degree here: the more firmly a properly functioning human being can believe *P* when displaying *E,* the greater the coherence between *P* and *E.* The coherentist can then quite properly see the warrant of at least some beliefs—perceptual beliefs, for example—as dependent upon the degree of coherence between that belief and the rest of S's evidence-base. Of course his views may then become indistinguishable from those of the ordinary foundationalist; but this, as I see it, is no more than a step in the right direction.

C. Classical Foundationalism

Coherentism, therefore, is mistaken; foundationalism is the truth of the matter. What sorts of beliefs, according to the foundationalist, *are* properly basic, get warrant in this basic way? As we have already seen, different foundationalists give different answers. One historically important answer is that of the *modern classical foundationalist:* a belief is properly basic for me, he says, if and only if it is either *self-evident* for me or *immediately about my experience,* in the way in which such a belief as *I am being appeared to redly* is immediately about my experience. This view was subjected to devastating criticism by Thomas Reid, who pointed out that if it were true, very few of our beliefs would have warrant, and that the restriction of proper basicality to these two classes of beliefs is at best arbitrary. We may add that classical foundationalism appears to be self-referentially incoherent; it does not meet the conditions for justification that it lays down. For according to a slightly fuller statement of classical foundationalism, a belief is justified for me if and only if either it is properly basic (that is, self-evident or appropriately about my experience) for me or accepted on the evidential basis of beliefs that are properly basic and support it. But this belief itself is not properly basic (it is neither self-evident nor appropriately about my experience); and it is at the least extremely hard to see that it is evidentially supported by beliefs that do meet that condition.

Reid criticized classical foundationalism to powerful effect; it has remained for the twentieth century, however, to see it into well-deserved retirement, and at the moment the air is full of announcements of the death of classical foundationalism. That is fair enough; but the announcers often conclude that the demise of classical foundationalism means that we must reject all of epistemology, or even the very notion of truth itself. This is a whopping *non sequitur.* Perhaps *Cartesian certainty* must follow classical foundationalism into the limbo reserved for false and extravagant philosophies; but nothing follows for epistemology generally (let alone for the notion of truth). To think otherwise is

---

[8]See chapter 2 of *Warrant: The Current Debate,* on post-classical Chisholmian internalism. Chisholm, of course, defines 'evidence-base' in such a way that it includes *all* purely psychological properties, including beliefs. For present purposes it is more convenient to take 'evidence-base' as including all purely psychological properties *except* for beliefs.

to confuse species with example; it would be like announcing the demise of the nation-state upon noting a civil war in Yugoslavia. Nor does it follow that there is no such thing as truth; it follows at best only that we don't have Cartesian certainty that we have attained truth, even when we have. Indeed, those who intemperately draw these radical conclusions from the problems with classical foundationalism betray deep concurrence with it: the only security or warrant for our beliefs, they and the classical foundationalists both think, must arise by way of evidential relationship to beliefs that are certain—that is, self-evident or about immediate experience.

D. Reidian Foundationalism

If classical foundationalism is mistaken, what sorts of beliefs *are* properly basic? From the present perspective, this translates into the following question: when a person's faculties are functioning properly, what sorts of propositions will she take as basic? What sorts of propositions will she accept without or apart from the evidential support of other propositions? I've already argued that *many* kinds of beliefs can be properly basic, in addition to those that the classical foundationalist countenances: for example, perceptual beliefs, memory beliefs, beliefs about the mental states of other persons, inductive beliefs, and testimonial beliefs. There are others that I have not mentioned: moral beliefs, for example, such as the belief that it is wrong to cause someone great suffering just because that affords you a certain mild pleasure. And in *Warranted Christian Belief,* the sequel to this work, I shall argue that, from a theistic perspective, it is plausible to follow John Calvin in thinking belief in God can also be properly basic.[9]

The modern classical foundationalist holds that when I believe propositions about the past, or about other persons, or about external objects, I must have propositional evidence for these beliefs if they are to have warrant for me: and the stronger the evidence, the greater the warrant. Just here is the crucial contrast between classical modern foundationalism and the sort of foundationalism I mean to defend—'Reidian Foundationalism', as I shall call it, because the point in question was first put clearly by Thomas Reid. The relevant difference between classical and Reidian foundationalism is encapsulated in an elementary but important point. Reidian and classical foundationalist will concur, of course, in holding that the question how I am appeared to is crucial to the question whether a given perceptual judgment has warrant for me. They will agree that if I am appeared to in a certain familiar way, I will be warranted in the belief that I see a tiger lily; if instead I am watching football on television (no tiger-lily-appearances are in the offing) but through some odd chance form this belief, it will have little or nothing by way of warrant for me. The difference between the two positions comes into view when we ask how the experience in question must be related to the belief in question, if the latter is to have warrant.

[9]Here we see an intimate connection between epistemology and metaphysics. The nose of the ontological camel pokes into the epistemological tent; for what you take to be properly basic will depend, in part, upon what sort of creatures you think human beings are.

Such a belief has warrant for me, says the classical foundationalist, if and only if I believe it on the basis of experiential propositions that support it (by way of deduction, induction, or abduction); on this view it is required (1) that I believe those experiential propositions, (2) that I believe the proposition in question on the evidential basis of those experiential propositions, and (3) that the experiential propositions in fact offer evidential support for the proposition in question. The Reidian view, by contrast, disputes each of these three points. On the Reidian view, when I am appropriately appeared to and the other conditions for warrant (cognitive capacities functioning properly in an appropriate environment according to a design plan successfully aimed at truth) are satisfied, then my belief that I see a tiger lily will have warrant for me. But it isn't necessary that I *believe* that I am appeared to in this way (or that those conditions are met). Clearly I can be thus appeared to without believing that I am. It is perhaps impossible that I *pay attention* to my phenomenal field, and fail to believe that I am appeared to in this way (when I am); but I need not pay attention to my phenomenal field; I have other things to think about. What counts for the warrant of the belief in question is not my *believing* that I am appeared to in such and such a way, but simply my *being* appeared to in that way. But if it is not necessary (for warrant) that I believe the experiential propositions in question, then (*contra* (2)) it will not be necessary that I believe the perceptual proposition on the evidential basis of the experiential propositions.

Finally and most important, it is not necessary (*contra* (3)) that the experiential propositions, whether or not I believe them, offer a good inductive, deductive, or abductive argument for the perceptual proposition. What confers warrant upon that proposition is not (*pace* the classical foundationalist) that it is certain or probable with respect to the experiential proposition; rather it has warrant simply by virtue of being formed in those circumstances— circumstances that include both being appeared to in that way and the satisfaction of the other conditions for warrant.[10]

Returning to the central idea of foundationalism, we recall that (as the foundationalist sees things) warrant accrues to a proposition in a rational noetic structure in either of two ways: either by virtue of transfer from some other proposition that already has warrant or by virtue of proper basicality. We may therefore say that proper basicality, in contrast to the basis relation, is a *source* of warrant. In seeing beliefs as properly basic, the foundationalist holds

---

[10]A compromise position is possible here. It might be held that the perceptual proposition requires to be believed on the basis of the experiential proposition, but that the latter, while it must support the former, need not do so by way of inductive, deductive, or abductive relations. It could be held that there is a relation between the propositions in question similar to the *criterial* relation that, according to Wittgensteinian philosophers (see, for example, Rogers Albritton, "Wittgenstein's Use of 'Criterion,'" *Journal of Philosophy* [1958]), holds between, say, behavioral propositions and propositions about mental states, and in virtue of which the latter receive warrant. It could also be held, in the spirit of post-classical Chisholmian internalism, that what is required is not that there be an inductive, deductive, or abductive relation between the relevant propositions, but some other relation such that the state of affairs consisting in a pair of propositions standing in that relation has the right kind of intrinsic value. See *Warrant: The Current Debate*, chap. 2.

that they receive warrant in a way different from the way in which a prop
receives warrant from another when it is (rightly) believed on the basis
other. In the typical case of perception or memory or *a priori* knowledg-, ᴜᴇ
proposition in question will receive warrant just by virtue of being accepted in
the presence of certain conditions—conditions that do not themselves directly
involve other beliefs at all. These circumstances will often include having a
certain characteristic sort of experience: thus my belief that I see a fine oak will
have warrant for me only in circumstances including my being appeared to in a
certain characteristic way. Other properly basic beliefs don't seem to involve
much by way of experience, or at any rate *sensuous* experience, as I argued in
chapters 3 and 6.

Of course, a foundationalist is not obliged to hold that the *only* conditions
conferring warrant are conditions that do not involve other beliefs. He could
consistently hold that, in some cases, what confers warrant on a proposition
that is properly basic for me is a set of circumstances that includes other beliefs
of one sort or another. Perhaps the belief that Sam is in pain is properly basic
for me in circumstances that include my being appeared to in a certain characteristic way, but also include the belief that I see Sam, or at any rate see
someone. In such a case, I do not accept the belief in question *on the evidential
basis of* the belief that I see Sam (or see someone); that belief is in no way my
evidence or part of my evidence for the proposition that Sam is in pain. It is,
nonetheless, an element in the set of circumstances that confers warrant, for
me, on the belief in question. Another example: I see what looks like a fine
bunch of tulips on your table; a whimsical bystander tells me that as a matter of
fact there aren't any tulips there but only a cleverly contrived laser image; you
tell me that there really *are* tulips there and that the whimsical bystander is only
having his (rather lame) little joke. Then my circumstances include my being
appeared to in that characteristic tuliplike way, having a defeater for the belief I
initially form (that is, that I see some tulips), and a defeater for that defeater.
The defeater-defeater isn't part of my *evidence* for the proposition that there are
indeed tulips there; it is nonetheless a proposition I believe, which is such that if
I hadn't believed it (or something similar), then in those circumstances the
belief that I see tulips would not have had warrant for me. The foundationalist,
accordingly, can sensibly hold that a belief A can be part of the warrant-
conferring condition for a belief B, even if B is not accepted on the basis of A—
even if, indeed, B is properly basic.

II. Evidentialism

The classical foundationalist insists that perceptual beliefs, when properly
formed, are formed on the basis of *evidence*. The Reidian can concur; but he
adds that the evidence need not be *propositional* evidence. For there is certainly
a broader notion of evidence lurking in the neighborhood. For example, there is
such a thing as what Reid calls the evidence of the senses; a peculiarly rigid and
doctrinaire sort of person may sometimes ignore the evidence of his senses. (I

am wedded to a theory according to which cacti are to be found only in the southwest; you show me a fine prickly pear in Michigan's upper peninsula; I stubbornly refuse to believe that it is a cactus, claiming that it is really a peculiar variety of thistle.)[11] What sort of evidence is this? It isn't, of course, propositional evidence; it is (or includes) a way of being appeared to, rather than a belief; nevertheless it shares certain salient features with propositional evidence. For this evidence is something *on the basis of which,* or *in response to which* we accept the belief in question. Second, it is in each case also something like an indication of the truth of the belief in question, in that (if things are going properly) there will be an appropriate relation of objective probability between the truth of the belief in question and the evidence on the basis of which we accept it.

Now it is initially not implausible to suppose that *whenever* a belief has warrant for me, then I have evidence for it—either propositional evidence, or testimonial evidence, or the evidence of the senses, or perhaps evidence of still another sort. This is the basic idea of an approach to warrant that has both plausibility and widespread contemporary appeal. Thus Richard Feldman and Earl Conee:

> Doxastic attitude D toward proposition p is epistemically justified for S at t if and only if having D toward p fits the evidence S has at t.[12]

Feldman and Conee's term is 'justification' rather than 'warrant'; however I believe they mean to use that term in much the way I am using 'warrant' (that is, to denote that quantity, whatever exactly it is, enough of which is sufficient to distinguish knowledge from mere true belief). In any event what I am interested in here is their suggestion taken as an account of warrant. Since William Alston[13] adopts a similar view, I shall call this view 'AFC'. Even if it isn't ordinarily put with the exemplary explicitness it enjoys at the hands of Alston, Feldman, and Conee, this general *sort* of view has and has had extremely wide currency. Indeed, the traditional 'justified true belief' analysis of knowledge has often been stated with 'S has *adequate evidence* for p' replacing 'S is justified in believing p'.

[11]Of course there are many other kinds of evidence, some explored in previous chapters. What do they all have in common? Here it is hard to do better than Reid, who says: "I confess that, although I have, as I think, a distinct notion of the different kinds of evidence above-mentioned, and, perhaps, of some others, which it is unnecessary here to enumerate, yet I am not able to find any common nature to which they may all be reduced. They seem to me to agree only in this, that they are all fitted by Nature to produce belief in the human mind, some of them in the highest degree, which we call certainty, others in various degrees according to various circumstances." *Essays on the Intellectual Powers of Man,* II, 20, pp. 200–201.

[12]"Evidentialism," *Philosophical Studies* (1985), p 15.

[13]See *Warrant: The Current Debate,* pp. 184ff. Alston speaks of *grounds* rather than evidence: "S is J_{eg} ["$_e$" for evaluative and "$_g$" for grounds] justified in believing that p iff S's believing that p, as S did, was a good thing from the epistemic point of view, in that S's belief that p was based on adequate grounds and S lacked sufficient overriding reasons to the contrary." ("Concepts of Epistemic Justification," *Monist* [January 1985], p. 71) Alston requires, as Conee and Feldman do not, that the evidence or grounds in question be a *reliable indicator* of the truth of the belief in question. Note also that Alston requires that the belief in question be *based on* the evidence in question, while Conee and Feldman require only that it *fit* that evidence. What I say will fit both suggestions.

Is the AFC view correct? From the present perspective, that question becomes the question whether, when my faculties are functioning properly, all of my beliefs will be such that I have evidence for them ('evidence' broadly construed so as to include ways of being appeared to as well as propositional evidence). Is this right? Note first that over a wide range of propositions or beliefs, a person whose faculties are subject to no malfunction will indeed accept the belief in question only if she has evidence for it. Take the case of testimony. You are in the sixth grade; your teacher tells you that the population of China exceeds that of India; you believe him. Now conceivably you could believe him on the basis of propositional evidence, reasoning as follows: "Teacher says the population of China exceeds that of India; in most of the cases where I have checked to see whether what he says is true, it was; so probably it is true in this instance; so probably the population of China exceeds that of India." You *could* come to that belief in this way; but typically you would not (it would be a peculiar sixth-grader who regularly formed beliefs in that fashion). In the typical case you would simply find yourself believing your teacher, just as, from days of earliest youth, you have always been inclined to believe your elders. (And even that suggests too much by way of reflection and self-consciousness about the formation of the belief—for example, you would not suddenly notice that you now have this new belief.) It isn't only sixth-graders, of course, who form beliefs in this way. Consider the neo-Darwinian hypothesis that all of contemporary life arose from unicellular life forms by way of random genetic variation of some sort together with natural selection, genetic drift, and the like. Those who believe this typically take it on the say-so of others (others who are thought to be in the know); they have testimonial evidence for it and can have warrant for it.[14]

Testimonial evidence is not (typically) propositional evidence; nevertheless it is evidence. And for a wide variety of propositions, a properly functioning person will come to believe them only if she has some evidence—either testimonial evidence, or propositional evidence, or the evidence of the senses, or evidence of some other sort. If I somehow come to entertain the neo-Darwinian hypothesis but have no testimonial evidence for it (and haven't developed any evidence of my own for it), then if my faculties are functioning properly, I will not accept it. Perhaps I will think of it as a sort of interesting idea that deserves further exploration; perhaps I will begin to *look for* evidence, testimonial or

[14]But only if someone *else* in the community has or has had nontestimonial evidence for it (see pp. 82ff.). This is the sort of proposition which is such that, if no one anywhere in the community has nontestimonial evidence for it, then something has gone seriously wrong from the point of view of warrant; it has little warrant for anyone. Suppose by some weird and implausible set of circumstances this theory (like Piltdown man) in fact originated in undergraduate highjinks in Victorian England; suppose there is no nontestimonial evidence for it at all in the appropriate scientific community. Then those who trustingly take it on authority are certainly justified from a deontological perspective; they also have Foley justification, as well as that broader sort of justification that ensues when everything 'internal' is going properly; nevertheless this belief will have at any rate *less* warrant for them than it otherwise would. (If the belief turns out, as it happens, to be true, we don't know that it is; we would have a communitywide semi-Gettier case.) See *Warrant: The Current Debate*, pp. 31ff.

otherwise, for or against it; but I won't afford it much credence. If I *did* believe it firmly under those conditions it would be by virtue of a sort of cognitive glitch; I would have a *thing* about that belief; I wouldn't be quite rational on that topic.

The AFC suggestion, therefore, works especially well for cases where we have propositional evidence, or testimonial or perceptual evidence. There is an enormous range of perfectly ordinary cases, however, where it is vastly less plausible. Consider the phenomenology of memory.[15] You ask me whether I have ever visited the Great Barrier Reef; I reply that I have, and tell you about the giant clams (about the size of a large overstuffed chair) I saw while snorkeling there—the kind that used to show up in grade B movies and clap shut on the ankle of an unwary pearl diver. I clearly remember visiting the reef; but what is my *evidence?* What plays the role here of propositional or testimonial evidence (or being appropriately appeared to)? Of course there are scraps of imagery that float through my mind—a partial, indistinct, intermittent, fitful image as of a boat, of bright blue sky and blue water, perhaps a fragmentary image as of an enormous clam being palpitated and slowly closing (anyone so inattentive as to get his foot caught in one of these clams would have to be very unwary indeed). Or *is* there really an image here, a being appeared to brightly and bluely, a blue and bright phenomenal image, as opposed to the *memory* that it was indeed bright and blue? In any event, even if there is imagery (and apparently people differ widely here), it is far too fragmentary and indistinct, far too partial, far too fitful, to be anything like that on the basis of which I form the belief. It is more like a sort of decoration, an evidentially irrelevant accompaniment of some kind; it isn't at all like propositional or perceptual evidence.

I remember having seen a friend a year ago in California; I can't now really think what he looks like, and I certainly don't remember that it was *he* I saw then on the basis of anything like noting that the phenomenal imagery involved looks a lot like an image of Paul. I certainly don't note the phenomenal imagery, and then see the resemblance to Paul, thus forming the belief that it is Paul I saw there in California. There is a phenomenal imagery involved; but my memory belief isn't formed *on the basis of* that imagery. The relation between that imagery and the belief is wholly different from that between perceptual imagery and perceptual belief. There is nothing like that sort of highly articulate, detailed mapping from sensuous imagery to perceptual belief. Here there is nothing we can sensibly think of as evidence on the basis of which the memory belief is formed.

The same goes for *a priori* knowledge and belief. You consider or entertain an instance of *modus ponens;* there is a bit of imagery: perhaps you catch a fleeting glimpse of a sentence. (That is, your experience is as if you caught a fleeting glimpse of a fragment of a sentence, perhaps one that expresses the proposition in question.) There is a sort of scrappy and indistinct, partial and vague image (auditory or visual) of a sentence expressing the proposition, but

[15]See pp. 57–61.

surely this image is not *evidence*. Here too, it looks difficult indeed to find anything approximating evidence on the basis of which one might be said to form such beliefs.

Still another example, and one interesting in its own right: in chapter 3 I argued that such beliefs as *I am now being appeared to in that tiger-lily way* and *I am not identical with that tiger-lily experience* are beliefs that have or can have high warrant for me. Now it is obvious, I think, that I don't hold such beliefs on the basis of *propositional* evidence. But do I believe them on the basis of *experiential* evidence, in the way in which I believe, on the basis of such evidence, that there is a tiger lily in my backyard?

Suppose we look into the question. In neither case, of course, am I *directly* aware (in the sense of chapter 3, p. 53) of the object in question. When I believe that I am not identical with the tiger-lily experience but am instead the *subject* of that experience, the one who is aware of it, I am not directly aware of myself. But of course the same goes for the tiger lily: to be aware of it I must be aware of something else, namely the tiger-lily appearances; the latter, not the former, is what I am directly aware of. (Of course, in another and perfectly good sense of 'directly aware of', I *am* directly aware of the tiger lily.) So far, therefore, there is no contrast between perceptual beliefs and these beliefs about myself.

If we take another step, however, we can see an important difference. My perceptual beliefs respond *differentially* to changes in my experience: *now*, looking at the tiger lily, I have perceptual beliefs about it—the belief, for example, that it is indeed a fine tiger lily. A moment ago, however, I was appeared to differently, and held a different belief (that large brown squirrel leapt a distance of at least eight feet—all the way from *that* tree to *that* tree!) Not so with the belief that it is *I* who see the tiger lily and saw the squirrel. According to Kant, the *I think* accompanies all of my judgments. This isn't exactly right; often I make a judgment or form a belief without (explicitly, anyway) judging or believing that it is *I* who am forming or holding the belief. (I note that the oak trees are almost fully leafed out, but I don't note further that it is I who am noting that. Having made a false move rock-climbing, I note with alarm that I am falling; I don't note that it is indeed I who note that.) But perhaps I may properly be said to make that addition implicitly or virtually; and in any event whenever I *do* note who it is that is making the judgment, what I note, naturally enough, is that it is I who do so. So Kant is right or nearly right. And *that* judgment—that it is I who judge these things—does not vary with changes in experience.

Suppose we try to put this a bit more exactly. I mean to contrast perceptual beliefs with the associated beliefs about myself; I say that the former but not the latter are responsive to changes in experience. But of course as it stands that isn't right. On those occasions when I form a perceptual belief of the sort *I see the squirrel leaping* (rather than simply *That squirrel is leaping*), my beliefs are indeed responsive to changes in experience: appeared to one way I believe *I see a squirrel leaping;* appeared to another I believe *I see tiger lilies bending in the breeze*. But there is a constant element in all of them: the part of the belief according to which it is *I* who perceive these things. *That* part of the judgment does not change in response to experience. (I don't, in these situations, respond to differences in my experience by sometimes judging that it is *I* who am thus appeared to and sometimes that it is *you* who are—although by way of pathology that would perhaps be possible.)

Accordingly, add a further refinement to our notion of evidence. There is propositional evidence, where we believe a proposition on the basis of another; obviously this sort of evidence is sensitive to differences in the relevant input. (We believe, for example, that Feike can't swim on the evidential basis of our belief that nine out of ten Frisians can't swim and Feike is a Frisian; we would not believe it on the evidential basis of the belief that nine out of ten Frisians *can* swim and Feike is a Frisian.) There is also the sort of evidence we have in perception; it is on the basis of being appeared to like *that* that I form the belief that the sprinkler is going in my backyard, and that way of being appeared to is or is part of my evidence. Here too there are different responses to different experiential inputs. So add that it is part of the idea of evidence that there be this sort of differential response to different input. Then such beliefs as that it is *I* who perceive thus and so will have an element that is not based on evidence. When on one occasion I form the belief that I see a tiger lily, and on another that I see a squirrel, and on a third that I see how Gödel's theorem is proved, it isn't that I believe that it is I who do each of these things because of some shared element or some similarity in the *experiences* I have on those occasions. Take all those beliefs I form or judgments I make that are of the form *I believe (see, judge, and so on) that A:* it isn't by virtue of some similarity among the experiences prompting them that I judge that it is *I* who do those things. It isn't as if, had my experience been appropriately different, I would have judged that it is someone *else* who sees the squirrel.[16] So the *I think* element in beliefs in which it occurs, does not respond differentially to different experiential inputs; accordingly, if we think of evidence in this way, that part of these judgments is not formed on the basis of evidence; in this it resembles memory and *a priori* beliefs. (Of course, we can perfectly properly add that beliefs of this sort are nonetheless formed *in response* to experience.)

The AFC suggestion, therefore, works well for perception, testimony, and propositional evidence; but not at all well, so it seems, for memory, *a priori* knowledge, and such knowledge as that it is *I* who see the squirrel leaping from tree to tree. In these cases there is indeed sensuous imagery, but it isn't evidence. But perhaps we aren't looking in the right place for the evidence here. This sensuous imagery isn't all there is by way of phenomenal accompaniment of memory. There is also something else: the memory proposition has a certain *felt attractiveness* about it. You remember that it was *California* where you met Paul, not New York; and that it was *Paul* you met, not Sam. You remember: *that was Paul there in California.* That proposition has about it a sense of rightness, or fittingness, or appropriateness—as opposed, say, to the proposi-

---

[16]This is not to deny that I might sensibly judge, on a given occasion, that *you* see something *I* don't (you are unsuccessfully trying to point out to me the mountain goat you see on a distant crag).

tion that it was Tom there on that occasion. Perhaps the thing to say is that there is a sort of felt push or impulse or inclination to accept the one proposition, as opposed to the other. So here there are really two quite different sorts of experience: the fleeting, indistinct, unstable, sometimes random sensuous imagery, on the one hand, and, on the other, the felt inclination to believe *that* proposition, as opposed to others that might be suggested or suggest themselves.

The same goes for *a priori* knowledge. Consider your apprehension of an instance of a simple logical law: *if Sam is happy, then someone is happy.* On considering or entertaining the proposition, perhaps you find a certain imagery; perhaps it is as if you hear parts of a sentence expressing it, or see an indistinct incomplete written version of the sentence. This sensuous imagery, again, is fleeting, indistinct, fragmentary, hard to get clearly in focus; and it apparently varies greatly from person to person. It is not at all plausibly thought of as your evidence, as something on the basis of which you form the *a priori* belief in question. You do indeed *see* that if Sam is happy, then someone is, but not by virtue of this imagery. Or think of some philosophical proposition you think obvious and obviously necessary—that no sets are cats, for example. Perhaps here the most you will have by way of imagery will be a fleeting glimpse of a cat, or maybe of a cat within braces. You do see that the proposition is true, all right, but not by virtue of the sensuous imagery that is present. In each of these cases, however, there is something else. You *see* that the proposition is true: and that involves an inclination or impulse toward believing the proposition[17]—an inclination that is either experienced or such that it can be brought to consciousness by paying attention to it. Perhaps we should say instead that the proposition in question has a sort of attractiveness, or perhaps inevitableness about it, or perhaps a sort of perceived fittingness; the phenomenology is hard to describe, but familiar to us all.

So in both these cases—memory and *a priori* beliefs—there is something in addition to the sensuous imagery: there is also that felt inclination toward believing the proposition in question (or its necessity). And of course the same really goes for perception as well: here too there are two sorts of experience, two sorts of phenomenal involvement. There is the obvious being-appeared-to sensuous imagery; but there is also that felt inclination. Upon being appeared to the familiar way that goes with perceiving a tree, I form the belief that what I see is a tree. Here too that belief has a certain felt attractiveness, a certain naturalness, a certain sort of fittingness; I feel a kind of inclination or impulsion or disposition to form *this* belief as opposed to others—for example, that I am perceiving a cliff, say, or the ocean. In all these cases, therefore, there are at least two kinds of phenomenology: there is the sensuous being-appeared-to type of phenomenology, but also the perceived or felt inclination to believe. Indeed, the same distinction holds throughout the length and breadth of our noetic structure and across all the sorts of beliefs we form: in nearly all cases

[17]As I argued in chapter 6, the inclination is really toward the belief that the proposition in question is *necessary,* couldn't be false.

there will be both sensuous imagery of a certain kind—at its most vivid and compelling in the case of sense perception—but also a sort of felt inclination or impulsion toward a certain belief.

Now suppose we return to AFC, the suggestion that whenever we form beliefs (and things are going properly) they will always be formed on the basis of evidence. This is not true if we are thinking of propositional evidence; for many beliefs—perceptual beliefs, for example—are basic. But it is also false if what we are thinking of is propositional evidence together with sensuous imagery. *That* suggestion will accommodate perception; it will not accommodate much of the rest of what we accept in the basic way. But suppose we add this inclination to believe, this perceived attractiveness, or inevitability, or fittingness of the proposition in question in the situation in question: suppose we think of *that* as evidence as well. If we think of it this way, then whenever it seems to you that something is so, you do indeed have evidence for it. By virtue of that very fact, you have evidence for it, and the stronger the seeming, the stronger the evidence.

Of course, it is *also* sometimes quite right to say that someone who has this kind of impulsional experience has *no* evidence. A person may be irrationally convinced that the rest of us are out to do him in, even though, as we say, he has no evidence at all for this paranoid belief; nor would we suppose we were wrong in thinking he had no evidence if it were pointed out that in fact he has a strong inclination to accept the proposition in question. But this just reflects our belief that in the case of believing *this* sort of proposition (as opposed to some others), if this inclination to believe is *all* you have by way of evidence, then your belief is irrational[18] and evinces pathology. It does not follow that this kind of evidence is not really evidence. And if we do take it to be evidence, then no doubt it will be true that in a well-formed noetic structure, belief is always on the basis of evidence. Indeed, how could it be otherwise? Could it really be that you should believe a proposition, even though it had none of this phenomenal attractiveness, this seeming-to-be-true—even if, that is, there was no felt or feelable inclination to believe it on your part?

So if we construe evidence in this broad fashion, including the inclination to believe as well as propositional evidence and sensuous phenomenology, then part of the AFC suggestion is true: then it is indeed true that we always or nearly always form beliefs upon the basis of evidence (at least when there is no cognitive pathology). But of course no amount of evidence of *this* sort is by itself sufficient for warrant. First, some kinds of beliefs as we have already noted, require evidence of another sort, if they are to have warrant: perceptual beliefs, for example, but also the sorts of beliefs that require testimonial or propositional evidence, such as the belief that China is larger than Australia. But this inclination-to-believe sort of evidence—call it, for want of a better term, 'impulsional evidence'—is not sufficient for warrant even in the case of beliefs that are properly basic and do not require evidence of some other sort.

---

[18]Here the irrationality in question is not Foley irrationality; it is the sort displayed by someone who seems sensible enough on most topics, but is utterly convinced that she will be the next pope, despite the fact that she is a lifelong Baptist.

Memory beliefs are of that sort; but memory can malfunction. Suppose it does: I seem to remember being present at a gathering; I seem to remember this with vivid clarity and have an extremely strong inclination to believe that I was there; it hardly needs to be said that this belief might nonetheless (by virtue of my memory's malfunction) have no warrant for me. Even if I was in fact present there (but was brought there unconscious and remained unconscious throughout my stay), I would not know that I was. So this kind of evidence, if evidence it is, is indeed present with memory beliefs; but it isn't at all sufficient for warrant. Something similar could be said for *a priori* beliefs.

In the case of memory and *a priori* belief, then, there is evidence all right—impulsional evidence—but no amount of this sort of evidence is sufficient for warrant: there must also be proper function. Obviously this also holds for perception, testimony, and the rest. My being appeared to in that characteristic fashion, together with my inclination to believe that what I see is a fine stand of alfalfa, constitutes evidence for that belief; but obviously my forming a belief on the basis of this evidence is not sufficient for warrant. If my perceptual faculties are malfunctioning (so that for example, I am always, or at ten-minute intervals, appeared to in this way, no matter what my surroundings), then my belief has no warrant. Even if, by some serendipitous circumstance, it is true, it certainly does not constitute knowledge for me. What is required here for warrant, obviously enough, is proper function, absence of cognitive pathology.

So the evidentialist is right: where there is warrant, there is evidence. Having this evidence, however, or having this evidence and forming belief on the basis of it, is not sufficient for warrant: proper function is also required. And given proper function, we also have evidence: impulsional evidence, to be sure, but also whatever sort is required, in the situation at hand, by the design plan; and that will be the evidence that confers warrant.

11

Naturalism versus Proper Function?

We have come to the end of our whirlwind tour of the design plan and it is nearly time to draw this book to a close. I quite understand that what I have said on most topics is woefully incomplete; much more must be said for any reasonably complete treatment, and indeed each of the topics of the past few chapters, treated properly, would obviously require an entire book. Still further, there are many additional topics crying out for discussion, topics I have not so much as broached. Most shall have to continue to cry unsatisfied; life is short, even if philosophy is long. One topic, however, cries out with particular insistence; in these two concluding chapters I aim to say something about it. As we noted in chapter 2 (pp. 45ff.), the account of warrant I propose is an example of *naturalistic* epistemology: it invokes no kind of normativity not to be found in the natural sciences; the only kind of normativity it invokes figures in such sciences as biology and psychology. I went on to add, however, that naturalism in epistemology can flourish only in the context of supernaturalism in metaphysics; in this chapter and the next, I want to begin to explain why. A proper treatment, once more, would require another book; I can only point to what I take to be promising lines of inquiry, a promising research program; there is no space for a complete account.

According to the central and paradigmatic core of our notion of warrant (so I say) a belief B has warrant for you if and only if (1) the cognitive faculties involved in the production of B are functioning properly (and this is to include the relevant defeater systems as well as those systems, if any, that provide *propositional* inputs to the system in question); (2) your cognitive environment is sufficiently similar to the one for which your cognitive faculties are designed; (3) the triple of the design plan governing the production of the belief in question involves, as purpose or function, the production of true beliefs (and the same goes for elements of the design plan governing the production of input beliefs to the system in question); and (4) the design plan is a good one: that is, there is a high statistical or objective probability that a belief produced in accordance with the relevant segment of the design plan in that sort of environment is true. Under these conditions, furthermore, the degree of warrant is given by some monotonically increasing function of the strength of S's belief that B. This account of warrant, therefore, depends essentially upon the notion of proper function.

But isn't this a substantial liability for my account? While the notions of proper function and design plan are clear enough when it is *artifacts* of which we speak, they do not apply as clearly to natural organisms and their parts. What is it, after all, for a natural organism—a tree, for example, or a horse—to be in good working order, to be functioning properly, to be functioning the way it ought to, to be functioning in accord with its design plan? Isn't a trout decomposing in a hill of corn functioning just as properly, so far as nature herself goes, as one happily swimming around chasing minnows? A chunk of reality—an organ or organism or garden patch or ecosystem—'functions properly' it might be thought, only with respect to a sort of grid *we* impose on nature, a grid that incorporates or depends on our aims and needs and desires.

Now it must be conceded that the notions of purpose, design plan, proper function, damage, and their colleagues are most at home in thought about artifacts, machines, and other devices that have been designed and constructed by such conscious, purposeful agents as human beings. Think of some of the distinctions drawn in chapter 2. Begin with the distinction between the *design* plan and the *max* plan, for example: an element of the design plan specifies how the thing will respond to certain conditions and what the purpose or function of its so responding is. The design plan does not cover *all* the circumstances the thing might be in; it is restricted to the ones the design plan 'takes account of'—the ones, we want to say, the designer had in mind. There will be plenty of conditions of which the designer takes no account: in the case of a radio, for example, its being smashed by a large boulder, or being vaporized in a nuclear explosion. The *max* plan specifies how the thing will respond in those conditions, but the design plan says nothing about them. It is easy to understand this in terms of the forethought and intention of a conscious and purposeful agent, and hard to understand it in any other way. The same goes for the distinction between what, as we say, an organ or artifact is *supposed* to do (designed to accomplish), on the one hand, and unintended byproducts of its working on the other; and the same holds for the distinction between what such a thing is designed to do (its purpose, say) and how it is designed to accomplish that purpose (how it functions when it functions properly). The same goes also for the feature of trade-offs and compromises; this too is most naturally thought of in terms of the choices between competing aims on the part of a conscious agent. Similarly for the fact that different parts of a design plan may be aimed in different directions and embody different purposes. Thus one part of our cognitive design plan may be aimed at the production of true beliefs, another (the optimistic overrider) at survival of illness, still another at the possibility of loyalty, and still another at concern for one's fellows. All of these features of design plans are redolent of intentional design on the part of a conscious agent, one who takes thought and aims to accomplish a purpose of one sort or another by designing something to work in a certain way.

Naturally enough, there are complications here. It may be hard to say precisely *how* conscious design and purposeful designers enter in: must there be, for any given device, some one person whose intentions determine what proper function is for that device? Presumably not: some artifacts are the results of the work of committees; and others—Indian arrowheads and canoes, for example—are such that their design plans grow or evolve over time, with each of many different people offering a bit of streamlining here or small improvement there. Further, perhaps I could trick you into designing a thing such that *you* didn't at all intend it to do what it does when it functions properly. I commission you to design a machine that does x; I really want one that does y, and I know that a machine that does x can be used to do y; then it is not the case that the purpose of the machine has anything special to do with the aims of its designer.[1] All this is quite correct; but there is nonetheless no denying that intention and conscious design crucially enter into what it is that determines the function(s) of an artifact and whether a given way of functioning is or is not proper functioning.[2]

Our paradigm cases of design and proper function, therefore, are artifacts, things designed by conscious agents. This is the ancestral home of these notions; this is where they apply most naturally and easily. Still, we certainly do apply this whole family of concepts to the natural world. We think a hawk's heart that beats only twenty-five times a minute is not functioning properly, that AIDS damages the immune system and makes it function poorly, that multiple sclerosis causes the immune system to malfunction in such a way that white blood cells attack the nervous system, and that the purpose or function of the heart is to pump blood, not to make that thumpa-thumpa sound. The notions of proper function, disease, and damage apply here and in a thousand other contexts; thinking in these terms is natural and apparently unavoidable for human beings.

Of course the compelling character of this sort of thought does not prove it coherent; nor does it show that these notions can in fact be correctly applied, not just to artifacts, but also to natural organisms. Noting the connection between *functional generalizations* (in, for example, biology and psychology) and the idea of proper function, John Pollock gloomily entertains the depressing thought "that functional and psychological generalizations about organisms are just false and the whole enterprise arises from confusing organisms with artifacts (the latter having explicit designs and designers)."[3] It isn't easy to see how we could be as confused as all *that,* however: few of us have much difficulty distinguishing (human) artifacts from organisms. And, as Pollock goes on to remark, "that conclusion seems excessively skeptical. Surely there is some point to the kinds of high level generalization that we formulate throughout the social and biological sciences."

The bulk of mankind, however, has applied the notions of purpose and proper function to natural organisms, and has done so without any confusion

---

[1]Here I am indebted to a comment by Andrew Hsu.

[2]As we saw in chapter 2, intention isn't by itself *sufficient:* you can't bring it about that this book is a washing machine simply by somehow (absurdly) intending that it wash your clothes. It must also *perform* that function to at least *some* degree, even if badly.

[3]"How to Build a Person," in *Philosophical Perspectives, 1, Metaphysics, 1988,* ed. James Tomberlin (Atascadero, Calif.: Ridgeview, 1988), p. 149.

or incoherence at all: for most human beings have thought that natural organisms and their parts *are,* in fact, designed. Most human beings *now* think so; certainly theists of all stripes do. And from a theistic point of view, of course, there is no problem here at all. From a theistic perspective there is no problem in applying these notions to natural organisms, for (from that perspective) natural organisms have indeed been designed by a conscious and intentional designer: God. From a theistic point of view, human beings, like cathedrals and Boeing 747s, have been designed; we might say that they are divine artifacts. According to Jewish, Moslem, and Christian ways of looking at the matter, furthermore, God has created us human beings "in his own image"; in certain crucial and important respects, we resemble him. God is an actor, a creator, one who chooses certain ends and takes action to accomplish them. He is therefore a *practical* being. But God is also, crucially, an *intellectual* or *intellecting* being. He apprehends concepts, believes truths, has knowledge. In setting out to create human beings in his image, then, God set out to create *rational* creatures: creatures with reason or *ratio;* creatures that reflect his capacity to grasp concepts, entertain propositions, hold beliefs, envisage ends, and act to accomplish them. Furthermore, he proposed to create creatures who reflect his ability to hold *true* beliefs. He therefore created us with that astonishingly subtle and articulate battery of cognitive faculties and powers discussed in the preceding chapters. From this perspective it is easy enough to say what it is for our faculties to be working properly: they are working properly when they are working in the way they were intended to work by the being who designed and created both them and us.

But suppose you don't think natural organisms and their organs and systems are designed by God or any other conscious rational being? Suppose you agree with Richard Dawkins:

> All appearances to the contrary, the only watchmaker in nature is the blind forces of physics, albeit deployed in a very special way. A true watchmaker has foresight: he designs his cogs and springs, and plans their interconnections, with a future purpose in his mind's eye. Natural selection, the blind, unconscious automatic process which Darwin discovered, and which we now know is the explanation for the existence and apparently purposeful form of all life, has no purpose in mind. It has no mind and no mind's eye. It does not plan for the future. It has no vision, no foresight, no sight at all. If it can be said to play the role of watchmaker in nature, it is the *blind* watchmaker.[4]

Suppose you concur with Dawkins: can you then properly employ the notion of proper function in epistemology? If you can't, you've got a problem; and you'll have the same problem with much of contemporary science. For most of the disciplines falling under biology, psychology, sociology, economics, and the like essentially involve those functional generalizations of which we have spoken,[5] and those generalizations, in turn, essentially involve the notions of proper function, damage, malfunction, purpose, design plan, and others of that family.

[4]Richard Dawkins, *The Blind Watchmaker* (New York: Norton, 1986), p. 5.
[5]See pp. 46ff., chap. 2, for argument and illustration.

But what, precisely, is the problem? Can't anyone, theist or not, see that a horse, say, is suffering from a disease, is displaying a pathological condition? Can't anyone see that an injured bird has a wing that isn't working properly? That an arthritic hand does not function properly, or that a damaged rotator cuff doesn't work as it ought? Wright seems right: "it seems to me that the notion of an organ having a function—both in everyday conversation and in biology—has no strong theological commitments. Specifically, it seems to me consistent, appropriate, and even common for an atheist to say that the function of the kidney is elimination of metabolic wastes."[6] So what, exactly, is the alleged problem?

Surely it *is* common for an atheist to say that a kidney or other organ has a function; we all, theist and nontheist alike, naturally and inevitably think this way. But there are those who object from a naturalistic stance to the notion of proper function in epistemology. They do not deny that atheists *use* this notion; what they deny is that they *correctly* use it. They mean to question whether the notions of proper function, purpose, damage, design plan, and the like can be coherently understood and endorsed from a naturalistic perspective. If, as a matter of fact, natural organisms have *not* been designed, what sense can we make of the notions of design plan and proper function as applied to them? The question is whether the claim that our faculties can function properly or improperly (the claim that our faculties have a design plan)—the question is whether this claim entails that we really *have* been designed by some personal rational being such as God. The question is whether, on my account of warrant, the proposition that some belief has warrant for you or someone entails theism or something like it. Of course, the question isn't *exactly* that: for such a proposition might *trivially* entail theism, by virtue of the fact that (as the theist thinks) theism is a necessary truth. (If so, then *any* proposition will entail theism, just as any proposition entails that there are prime numbers greater than 1000.) Alternatively, perhaps theism itself is not a necessary truth, but (as the theist may also think) it is a necessary truth that all contingent beings (God apart) have been created directly or indirectly by God. (Then any proposition predicating knowledge or any other property of someone distinct from God would entail theism.)

The real question here is something different—something not at all easy to state clearly. Perhaps we can put it like this. It looks initially as if the notion of proper function *entails* that of design, so that necessarily, anything that functions properly has a design plan. And it also looks as if necessarily, if a thing has a design plan, then either that thing or some ancestor of it was designed by a rational being. The real question is whether these appearances are deceiving; the real question is whether there is a satisfactory *naturalistic* explanation or analysis of the notion of proper function. I turn now to some representative attempts to give just such an analysis of that notion.

[6]Larry Wright, "Functions," *Philosophical Review* (1973), p. 82; reprinted in *Conceptual Issues in Evolutionary Biology: An Anthology,* ed. Elliot Sober (Cambridge: MIT Press, 1984), p. 350.

I. Naturalistic Analyses of Proper Function

Now the proposed naturalistic analyses with which I am acquainted are analyses of what it is for an organ or system to *have a function;* they are not analyses of what it is for an organ or system to *function properly,* to work the way it ought to work. They try to tell us what it is, for example, for it to be the case that the function of the heart is to pump blood, and the function of the telephone is to enable rapid, convenient vocal communication. They don't try to tell us what it is for a heart or telephone to function properly, to work the way it ought to. And the transition from the one to the other isn't quite as easy as it might seem. We can't say, for example, that a thing is functioning properly just if it is performing its function, whatever that is; for to be functioning properly, at least in the fullest sense, it must be functioning in the way it was designed to. A radio that continues to translate electromagnetic radiation into sound waves after being dropped in the bathtub is not necessarily still functioning properly—in particular if it now gets only one station and that one only with a lot of interference.[7] But perhaps we can regard these efforts to provide a naturalistic analysis of *function* as a first step toward providing a naturalistic analysis of *proper function.* As we shall see, even this first step is fraught with enormous difficulties.

A. Pollock

I turn first to an account that is widely popular in the oral tradition and is suggested but not explicitly endorsed by John Pollock. The focus of Pollock's concern is not proper function as such but *functional generalizations*—the sorts of generalizations to be found in biological and psychological descriptions of the way in which human beings or other organic creatures work. As Pollock points out, such generalizations seem to involve an implicit presupposition: when we formulate similar generalizations about machines,

> The generalizations we formulate are really about how machines work when they "work properly" or when they "are not broken." Similarly it seems that generalizations about organisms should be understood as being about the way they work when they are 'working normally'.

Here 'working normally' and 'not being broken' mean something like 'subject to no dysfunction' or 'working properly' or 'not malfunctioning'. Functional generalizations about organisms, therefore, say how they work when they are functioning properly. Pollock notes next that there is no difficulty in saying what it is for a *machine* to function properly: "The obvious way to interpret such qualifications in generalizations about machines is by appeal to the intentions of the designers. . . . They work properly when they work as they were

---

[7]As we saw in chapter 2, it is also possible that a thing be damaged (and so fail to function in the way it was designed to), but perform its function even better than before; this is a sort of borderline case where one doesn't know whether to say it is functioning properly or not.

designed to work."[8] Now this suggestion, clearly enough, is not available for a *naturalistic* account of proper function in natural organisms; so what can be put in its place?

> What is important in the formulation of these generalizations, and what makes it useful to formulate them, is that the disruptive happenings are *unusual*. It is pretty *uncommon* to be hit on the head by a meteorite or have a heart attack or suffer a stroke. It is the *improbability* of such occurrences that leads us to formulate functional descriptions that hold only in their absence.

He then proposes that $(x)(Ax \rightarrow Bx)$ is a true functional generalization just if

> There is a structure type S such that (1) A's tend to have a structure of that type, and (2) anything having a structure of that type will conform to the generalization $(x)(Ax \rightarrow Bx)$ just as long as it retains that structure.[9]

Thus (according to Pollock) the functional generalization *Human hearts circulate the blood* is true just if there is a structure type human hearts tend to display, and anything having that structure type circulates the blood.

The suggestion seems to be as follows. Functional generalizations about organisms are to be understood as being about the way these organisms and their parts work when they are functioning properly or 'working normally'; but what makes a given way of working a *normal* way of working is that it is the usual, common, or statistically most probable way for a thing of the sort in question to work. I say this is what Pollock's words *suggest;* perhaps it doesn't represent his settled thinking on the matter. Whether or not this is what Pollock intends, however, it isn't satisfactory. There is more than one problem with the account.[10] Perhaps the most obvious one is that it clearly won't do to equate a thing's functioning *properly* with its functioning the way in which a thing of that sort *ordinarily* or *most frequently* functions. It won't do, for example, to suggest that a human organ or system S works properly when it conforms to the functional generalizations that hold for organs or systems of which S is an example—given that these functional generalizations are thought of as containing an implicit restriction to *statistically normal* conditions.

Such an account is nowhere nearly either necessary or sufficient. Most 60-year-old carpenters have lost a finger or thumb; it is not the case that those who

---

[8]Pollock, "How to Build a Person," pp. 146ff. for his discussion; the quotations are from p. 148.

[9]Ibid., p. 150; in the first quotation, the emphasis is mine. Pollock's proposal can't be quite right: in saying that a human heart works in a certain way (circulates the blood, for example) we mean to restrict ourselves to *properly functioning* human hearts, as Pollock suggests; but we also mean to restrict ourselves to human hearts *in the right sort of environment* (the sort of environment for which the heart is designed). Thus there must be blood for the heart to circulate; the arteries must not contain large holes and they must be neither too constricted nor too elastic; for earth creatures, gravity can't exceed some value close to what it is on earth, and so on.

[10]For example, as Kenneth Konyndyk points out, there are problems with the notion of *structure* here: the heart of someone who has just died may display the same structure as it did shortly before death, but fail to conform to the generalization *human hearts pump blood*. We need something like a clause specifying that the organism in question is *healthy;* but isn't health just another of that interdefinable set of notions of which the naturalist needs a naturalistic explanation?

have not have hands that are not normal and not capable of proper manual function; and the same would hold even if we were all carpenters. Perhaps most male cats have been neutered; it hardly follows that those that haven't are abnormal and can't function properly. The vast majority of sperm don't manage to fertilize an egg; the lucky few that do can't properly be accused of failure to function properly, on the grounds that they do things not done by their colleagues. Most baby turtles never reach adulthood; those that do are not on that account dysfunctional. Obviously you can function properly even if you don't function the way most of your peers do. Statistical preponderance is not necessary for proper function.

It isn't sufficient either. Due to high-energy radiation from a nuclear holocaust (so we can imagine), most human beings are born with damaged optical nerves, so that they are nearly blind and nearly always in severe pain. The number of people with the new style visual system vastly exceeds the number of human beings (going all the way back to the beginning of the human race) who displayed the old style. Then the new style visual system would be the statistically normal one. It is clear, however, that the new visual systems would not be functioning properly. Hence (statistical) normal function is also insufficient for proper function. (And those lucky enough to have visual systems that still functioned the old way would have properly functioning visual systems, but not ones that worked the way most human visual systems work in the conditions in which most human visual systems are found.) Another example: suppose early human beings began breaking the left leg of newborn children (in order to propitiate the gods); the result is that they could walk and run only with difficulty. Suppose this went on for a hundred thousand years, so that the vast majority of human beings have been treated in this way; and suppose a few parents, out of carelessness or neglect or impiety, didn't bother to follow this custom. On the Pollockian suggestion, those with broken legs would have had properly functioning legs; and those lucky few whose legs work like ours would have had malfunctioning legs. But this is obviously wrong.

B. Millikan

"Having a proper function," says Ruth Millikan, "is a matter of having been 'designed to' or of being 'supposed to' (impersonal) perform a certain function. The task of the theory of proper functions is to define this sense of 'designed to' or 'supposed to' in naturalist, nonnormative, and nonmysterious terms" She immediately issues a *caveat*, however: " 'Proper function' is intended as a technical term. It is of interest because it can be used to unravel certain problems, not because it does or doesn't accord with common notions such as 'purpose' or the ordinary notion 'function'."[11] Strictly speaking, of course, if her aim is not to give an account of the common notion of function, then her project is not as it stands directly relevant to the question at issue: the question whether there is available a naturalistic understanding or analysis of proper function. It is of

[11]*Language, Thought, and Other Biological Categories* (Cambridge: MIT Press, 1984), pp. 17, 18.

course the *common* notion of proper function (the common notion of what it is for an organ or system to work properly) that is involved in my account of knowledge; the question, therefore, is whether there is a naturalistic analysis or account of that common notion. The fact that some *special* or *technical* sense of the words 'proper function' is susceptible to a naturalistic explanation won't bear on *that* question, interesting or useful as that technical sense may be. Millikan's account, however, is subtle and challenging (and formidably difficult), and it is worth looking to see whether in fact it provides the materials for an adequate or accurate naturalistic analysis of the notion of proper function. It may still cast light on that project, even if in the end it does not enable us to find such an account.

Since Millikan's account *is* so difficult (since it is so difficult to get a clear view of the logic of her chain of definitions) we should start with the basic idea. According to Peter Godfrey-Smith, on Millikan's view, "Most simply, the functions of a thing are those of its powers or properties which account for its survival and proliferation. Hearts have proliferated because they pump blood, so pumping blood is the heart's function." This seems right, as an account of Millikan (and according to the grapevine it has her blessing). We might make it just a shade more explicit: an organ or system or organism O is working properly in working a certain way, if it has ancestors, and its ancestors' working in that way contributed to the survival of those ancestors, and hence to the existence and character of O.

Millikan's official definition of proper function goes as follows:

> Where *m* is a member of a reproductively established family R and R has the reproductively established or Normal character C, *m* has the function F as a direct proper function iff:
>
> (1)   Certain ancestors of *m* performed F.
>
> (2)   In part because there existed a direct causal connection between having the character C and performance of the function F in the case of these ancestors of *m*, C correlated positively with F over a certain set of items S which included these ancestors and other things not having C.
>
> (3)   One among the legitimate explanations that can be given of the fact that *m* exists makes reference to the fact that C correlated positively with F over S, either directly causing reproduction of *m* or explaining why R was proliferated and hence why *m* exists.[12]

This definition requires some stage setting: we need the notion *reproductively established family* as well as the notion *having the reproductively established or Normal character C*. "Reproductively established family" is recursively defined, and the definition presupposes the defined term 'B's being a reproduction of A'. Millikan's whole definitional schema is complex; it involves both several chains of definitions ('reproduction', 'reproductively established property', 'reproductively established family', 'reproductively established character', for example) and several recursive definitions, some of which appar-

---

[12]Ibid., p. 28. Godfrey-Smith's comments appear in his review of *Language, Thought, and Other Biological Categories*, in *Australasian Journal of Philosophy* 66, no. 4 (December 1988), pp. 556ff.

ently require double recursions. The logical relations between some of the notions aren't at all clear to me. Further, I think there are logical problems with the definitions: for example, 'being a reproduction of' is defined in terms of 'proper function', but 'proper function' is defined in terms of 'reproductively established family' and 'reproductively established or Normal character C', which, in turn, are themselves defined in terms of 'being a reproduction of'.

I don't think this account is at all successful. In trying to criticize or evaluate it, however, it is difficult to separate the problems that have to do just with its complicated and messy logic—the complex and apparently circular definitions, for example—from difficulties with the basic idea. Still, I think we can see what needs to be seen without recounting and examining all the details of the logical machinery. (I do run some risk of misrepresentation, however, particularly since certain aspects of the whole definitional structure remain obscure to me.) Of course Millikan's definition is not a definition of 'x is functioning properly' or 'x is functioning properly in doing A', but instead of 'an object m's having F as a direct proper function'. But perhaps there will be some fairly simple relation between the two; in any event, there will be the materials for a good naturalistic definition or account of *functioning properly* here only if the account of *proper function* is satisfactory.

Sadly enough, it isn't. First, isn't it obvious that a thing need not have *ancestors* to have a proper function, direct or otherwise? And isn't it clearly possible that a thing—an organ or organism or artifact—have a function and function properly even if it had no ancestors? It is clear that Millikan intends her theory to apply to the cases, not just of natural organs like hearts and lungs, but also to artifacts (p. 20 ff.). But surely the first telephone, say, could have had a proper function and could have been capable of proper functioning even if it had no ancestors at all. Whether or not in fact it *had* ancestors isn't crucial; Alexander Graham Bell being the sort of person he was, no doubt it did. But he could have been even more creative and original than he was: he could have created the first telephone *de novo*. If he had, the telephone would still have had the proper function of transmitting sound the way a telephone does; and doubtless it would still have been capable of proper function and malfunction (no doubt it would not have worked properly if dropped off the roof or immersed in a pail of cold water).

But the same goes for natural organisms. Whether or not God *did* create Adam and Eve instantaneously out of the dust of the earth, he *could* have; and if he had, wouldn't Adam's heart have had a function—the same function served by your heart and mine? And wouldn't it therefore have been capable of functioning *properly?* So the proposed necessary and sufficient condition is clearly not necessary. The offending feature of the definition, furthermore—the feature according to which a thing has a proper function only if it has ancestors—is not easy to remove from a Millikan-style account; it seems essentially involved in conditions (2) and (3). It is therefore hard to see how to repair the definition.

The proposed necessary and sufficient condition is clearly unnecessary: it is also insufficient. A Hitler-like madman gains control: as part of his Nietzschian plan to play God, he orders his scientists to induce a mutation into selected non-Aryan victims. Those born with this mutation can't see at all well (their visual field is a uniform shade of light green with little more than a few shadowy shapes projected on it). When they open their eyes and use them, furthermore, the result is constant and severe pain, so severe that it is impossible for them to do anything except barely survive. They are unable to listen to music, or read (or write) poetry or literature; they can't do mathematics or philosophy or evolutionary biology; they can't enjoy humor, play, adventure, friendship, love, or any of the other things that make human life worthwhile. Their lives are poor, nasty, brutish, and short. Hitler and his henchmen also begin a systematic and large-scale program of weeding out the non-Aryan nonmutants before they reach reproductive maturity. The mutation spreads; it gets out of control; after a few generations the bulk of the world's population displays it and the number of nonmutants dwindles. But then consider some nth generation mutant m. He is a member of a reproductively established family and has a certain reproductively established character C (the relevant part of which involves his visual system). He has ancestors, and among his ancestors, there was a causal connection between that character and the way their visual systems performed, which accounts for the positive correlation of that character with that way of functioning among his ancestors. Condition (3) is also met; one among the legitimate explanations of his existence makes reference to the fact that this character C is correlated positively with this way of functioning: for this way of functioning conferred a survival advantage, in that Hitler, his thugs and their successors were selectively eliminating those who do not display it. But wouldn't it be wrong to say that m's visual system is functioning properly? Or that its function is to produce both pain and a visual field that is uniformly green? Or that the resistance medical technicians who desperately try to repair the damage are interfering with the proper function of the visual system?

Another case: adapt the previous leg-breaking example. Imagine that things go as in that example, and that, further, those whose left legs aren't broken have a difficult time reproducing (it is considered impious to mate with them). Now consider someone whose leg, in accordance with this superstition, has been broken: a little reflection shows that the leg meets the Millikan conditions for proper function. But surely it would not be functioning properly.

There is still another problem here, and a serious one at that: this sort of account is implicitly circular. (More exactly, it suffers from a sort of defect that can be removed only at the cost of circularity.) This point will emerge most naturally in connection with Bigelow and Pargetter's account of functions, to which I now turn.

C. Bigelow and Pargetter

John Bigelow and Robert Pargetter's account of functions has a title as terse as it is elegant: "Functions."[13] "The way to construe functions," they say, ". . . is (roughly) to construe them in the manner of dispositions." (p. 189) More fully,

[13]*Journal of Philosophy* (1987), pp. 181ff. The quotations in this section are from pp. 189, 192–94.

What confers the status of a function is not the sheer fact of survival-due-to-a-character, but rather, survival due to the propensities the character bestows upon the creature. The etiological theory describes a character *now* as serving a function, when it *did* confer propensities that improved the chances of survival. We suggest that it is appropriate, in such a case, to say that the character *has been serving that function all along*. Even before it had contributed . . . to survival, it had conferred a survival enhancing propensity on the creature. And to confer such a propensity, we suggest, is what constitutes a function. Something has a (biological) function just when it confers a survival enhancing propensity on a creature that possesses it.

What sorts of things are they, precisely, that *have* functions, on this view? The first and last sentences suggest that it is an *organ* or *system* or perhaps an *organism* that has a function.[14] An organ, system or organism has a function when it has a character or set of properties by virtue of which it does something A—circulates the blood, for example, or prevents food from going down the windpipe—which confers upon its possessor a survival-enhancing propensity; and under these conditions doing A is a function of that organ or system. So a heart, for example, has a biological function—circulating the blood—if and only if it has a certain structure by virtue of which it circulates the blood, and its circulating the blood confers a survival-enhancing disposition or property on its possessor.

Bigelow and Pargetter go on to make explicit four features of this "propensity account of biological functions." First, the account must be relativized to an environment: "When we speak of the function of a character, therefore, we mean that the character generates propensities that are survival-enhancing in the creature's natural habitat" (189). How shall we understand "natural habitat"?

> In its most obvious use, the term 'habitat' applies to the physical surroundings of a whole organism. But we can also extend its usage, and apply the term 'habitat' to the surroundings of an organ within an organism. Or to the surroundings of a cell within an organ. In each case, the natural habitat of the item in question will be a functioning, healthy, interconnected system of organs or parts of the type usual for the species in question. When some of the organs malfunction, then other organs, which go on performing their natural function, may no longer be contributing to survival. We still say they are performing their natural function, even though this does not enhance the chance of survival. Why? Because it would enhance survival if the other organs were performing the way they do in healthy individuals. (pp. 192–193)

So an organ or system has a function if and only if it has a property or character that confers a survival-enhancing propensity (to save space, call it a 'sep') upon its owner *in the latter's natural habitat*. (Bigelow and Pargetter recognize that disputes may arise as to precisely what a creature's natural habitat *is;* but they are content with the resulting vagueness.) Second, functions "are to be specified subjunctively: they *would* give a survival-enhancing propensity to a creature in an appropriate manner, in the creature's natural hab-

---

[14]As Del Ratzsch points out, this is already problematic: a genetic characteristic (for example, the gene for sickle-cell anemia) can have a function, even if it doesn't confer a survival-enhancing propensity upon a creature that possesses it.

itat" (p. 193). Third, they suggest that in a precise theory of this kind "it will be necessary to spell out the notion of a 'survival-enhancing propensity' in formal terms, employing the rigors of the probability calculus" (p. 194). Fourth, they raise but don't answer the question whether this account, which is explicitly addressed to *biological* functions, will also suffice for functions of artifacts.

This is an interesting suggestion, and Bigelow and Pargetter make many instructive comments along the way. It is easy to see, however, that their account does not succeed as a naturalistic *account* or *analysis* of proper function. (It must be added, of course, that they nowhere acknowledge this project as one of their aims.) For first, any analysis of proper function erected on the basis of their account of biological function will be circular. This is because the account relies upon the notion of the *natural habitat* of an organ or system; but in specifying what the natural habitat of an organ or system *is*, Bigelow and Pargetter employ concepts that patently involve the notion of proper function: "In each case, the natural habitat of the item in question will be a functioning, healthy, interconnected system of organs or parts of the type usual for the species in question" (p. 192). A *functioning* system of organs, one supposes, is a *properly* functioning system; here, clearly 'functioning' means 'properly functioning'. (This suggestion is reinforced by their term 'healthy'.) As far as I can see, furthermore, this feature is essential to the account. My heart's carrying on in its accustomed way does confers a sep on me, all right—but only if the other parts of my circulatory system are themselves functioning properly, functioning the way they do in a healthy human being. There could be tiny elastic holes in my aorta which are such that if my heart functions normally (beats at a normal rate with normal intensity so as to produce normal blood pressure) there will be extensive hemorrhaging leading to debilitation and death. If, on the other hand, it beats much more gently and at the rate of fifteen beats per minute, I will survive. Suppose I have such aortic perforation: under those conditions my heart is still functioning properly if it proceeds in the ordinary way, despite the lethal consequences in this situation.

So the account is circular. But, second, I think it is easy to see that the proposed necessary and sufficient condition for a thing's having a (biological) function is neither necessary nor sufficient. Consider first sufficiency, and return to the example I used in connection with Pollock and Millikan. Hitler and his thugs induce that visual mutation into selected non-Aryan victims; it results in near blindness and constant pain. He and his henchmen also begin a systematic and large-scale program of weeding out the non-Aryan nonmutants before they reach reproductive maturity. Then consider some unfortunate whose visual system works the new way. Its working that way will confer a sep upon its owner all right (in view of the intentions of the Nazis), but it surely won't be the case that her visual system is functioning properly, or that its function is to produce pain and a visual field displaying nothing but a uniform expanse of green.

So even if we ignore the circularity, this account does not yield a naturalistic sufficient condition of proper function. But the condition is also unnecessary. According to Bigelow and Pargetter, an organ or system has a function provided it has a character that confers a sep on its owner in the natural habitat of that organ or system—where the natural habitat, they say, involves the *healthy* or *proper* function of the *other* organs and systems connected with the one in question. In some cases this stipulation yields the right result: thus my heart may be functioning properly, even if by virtue of malfunction elsewhere (a perforated aorta, for example) its functioning in that way does not confer a sep upon me. In other cases, however, it does not. Bigelow and Pargetter overlook systems or organs whose function is *damage control* or *repair* (healing, for example) or *troubleshooting;* these systems properly come into play only when there is *loss* of proper or healthful function elsewhere. For these systems, the appropriate "natural habitat" would be a state of the organism in which there is *malfunction* in connected systems or organs. Scabs form over damaged portions of the skin; if they formed in what Bigelow and Pargetter say is the natural habitat of the scab-forming system (a healthy, properly functioning, undamaged organism), they would form when there was no damage. That would hardly confer a survival-enhancing propensity on the organism in question. (If you turn up with a lot of adventitious and unnecessary scabs, your fellows may shun you, leading to depression, declining health, and an early grave.) On this account, then, the scab-producing system would not have a function, or at any rate would not have a function by virtue of forming scabs, and when it did form scabs, it would not be performing a function.

Similarly for other systems. If you are perfectly healthy, but your immune system works the way it works when you have a virulent infection, you may be in trouble. In a healthy human being, bodily temperature varies from about 97.3° to 99.1° F, and this system's thus regulating temperature (by way of perspiration, shivering, adjusting metabolism, and expansion and contraction of blood vessels) no doubt confers a sep upon its owner. When the body is invaded by bacteria or a virus, however, the temperature may rise, perhaps to 104° F or higher, causing dizziness, weakness, hot flashes and chills, visual impairment, and other unhappy conditions. Still, the temperature-regulating system is functioning perfectly properly, despite the fact that if it functioned *that* way (causing temperature to rise to 104°) in a healthy person, its so functioning would certainly not confer a sep. There are various bodily systems and organs whose function is to repair damage of various sorts; if these things did what they do best in a *healthy* organism, they might lead to an early demise rather than confer a sep; but then, on Bigelow and Pargetter's account, they don't have a function.

As a matter of fact, there could be damage-control systems attached to damage-control systems *ad libitum*. It might be that a given damage-control system S works only when there is damage to some part of the organism, and another damage-control system S* works only when there is damage to S; in principle this could go on as far as you please. It is extremely hard to see how properly to accommodate this complexity on Bigelow and Pargetter's scheme. We might start off as follows: an organ has a function if either (a) it has a character that confers a sep on a healthy organism, or (b) there is a certain way of malfunctioning such that the organ's character confers a sep on an organism that is malfunctioning in *that* way. But no hope here; a thing's having a way of working that confers a sep on a *malfunctioning* organism is not sufficient for the exercise of that way of working's being (one of) its function(s). Consider again the perforated aorta case. My aorta is riddled with tiny holes; therefore my heart's beating very gently and at a rate of only fifteen beats per minute would confer an enormous sep; but that is not sufficient for its being one of the functions of my heart to beat at that rate. If it *does* beat at that rate, it is malfunctioning, no matter what the state of the rest of my body. So this suggestion won't work. Of course there are other strategies to try; but it is extremely difficult to see how to accommodate this sort of complication without reference to a design plan. The condition suggested by Bigelow and Pargetter is accordingly unnecessary (as well as insufficient), and repair looks difficult.

Here perhaps sufficient ingenuity could win the day. There are other problems that go deeper, however. According to contemporary evolutionary theory, we human beings along with the rest of the multifarious forms of life on this planet arose by way of natural selection (and perhaps such other processes as random genetic drift) working on some form of genetic variation—random genetic mutation is a prominent candidate. This view has currently achieved the status of orthodoxy;[15] still, as Bigelow and Pargetter point out (p. 188), it is at best *contingently* true. It is *possible,* in the broadly logical sense, that the view is flatly false. It is possible, for example, that each of the main forms of life was created by God (or by some other powerful and knowledgeable being) *ex nihilo,* or by instantaneous modification of previous life forms, or in some other way incompatible with mechanisms proposed by contemporary evolutionary theory. If so, however, no correct account of proper function can *presuppose* the truth of contemporary evolutionary theory—that is, presuppose it in the sense that if the account is correct, then any case of proper function must be related in some fairly strong way to survival. Thus, suppose the human race was created by a Cartesian demon who delights in deception, and takes great pleasure in creating beings who think of themselves as the epistemic lords of the universe, but are in fact absurdly mistaken in their most confident opinions. Then our cognitive systems and their modules would indeed *have functions* (functions quite different from the ones we think they have), but it need not be the case that these systems and modules conferred on us a survival-enhancing propensity. Perhaps some parts of the system would be there, not because they promoted survival, but because they contributed to the satisfaction of this demonic whim.

More realistically, suppose we have been created by God, and (as Christians, Jews, and Moslems hold) created in his image. This means (among other things) that he intended to create us in such a way as to reflect, to some degree, his epistemic powers. Suppose you grasp Gödel's argument for the incompleteness of arithmetic, or Cohen's for the independence of the Continuum Hypoth-

---

[15]According to the 1979 edition of the *New Encyclopedia Britannica,* vol. 7, "evolution is accepted by all biologists and natural selection is recognized as its cause. . . . Objections . . . have come from theological and, for a time, from political standpoints."

esis from the rest of ordinary set theory; or suppose you achieve the sort of insight into the human condition conferred by a truly great novel; or suppose you come finally to understand quantum theory. Then the beliefs you form will no doubt be a result of some epistemic structure or system or power; it is *possible,* furthermore, that the system in question has a function and is functioning properly here, even if its so functioning has nothing to do with survival and confers upon you no survival-enhancing propensity at all. Again, perhaps God wanted creatures who could appreciate the beauty of the earth and the power of art and poetry; the relevant modules of our cognitive systems might then have a function, all right, and function perfectly properly, whether or not that part conferred an advantage with respect to survival.

More generally, from a theistic perspective it could be true that many subsystems of our cognitive and affective systems have functions, and function properly, not because their functioning in that way promotes survival, but because it serves other ends: the possibility of a certain sort of knowledge, or of morality, or loyalty, or love, or a grasp of beauty, or something else. It is therefore obviously possible that such a system have a function that confers no survival-enhancing propensity at all. Indeed, it could be that its functioning properly should put its owners at something of a *disadvantage* with respect to survival. Since this state of affairs is clearly possible, it is possible that a thing have a function (and function properly) even if that way of functioning confers no sep upon its owner. This proposal therefore fails as a naturalistic analysis of proper function, and fails resoundingly. (It is not as if the problem is a technical bug or two that we could work out with a little chisholming.)

Indeed, none of the suggestions we have considered shows any real promise of providing a naturalistic analysis of that notion. Since none of the candidates is anywhere nearly successful, perhaps the sensible view is that the prospects for a naturalistic account of proper function look dim.[16] Before we draw that conclusion, however, we might consider one further suggestion. Richard Foley[17] suggests that perhaps the naturalist can make progress, here, by suggesting a *disjunctive* account of proper function, one of the disjuncts specifying how it goes in the case of artifacts and the other how it goes in the case of nonartifacts. Consider a sort of rough-and-ready prototype of such an analysis:

---

[16]Of course these three are by no means all of the attempts to give a naturalistic account of proper function; there are many more. For example, there are earlier efforts by Carl Hempel ("The Logic of Functional Analyses," in *Symposium on Sociological Theory,* ed. Llewellyn Gross (Evanston, Ill.: Row, Peterson, 1959), and Ernest Nagel, "The Structure of Teleological Explanations," in *The Structure of Science* (New York: Harcourt, Brace and World, 1961), pp. 398–428. Neither of these is at all satisfactory. There is in addition the account by Larry Wright mentioned in n. 8; this account is also subject to counterexamples, some of which are provided by Christopher Boorse in "Wright on Functions," *Philosophical Review* (1976), pp. 70ff. Boorse provides an account of his own, but the account proceeds in terms of the *goals* of a system or organ or organism—a notion that is as much in need of explanation, from a naturalistic point of view, as that of proper function itself. Still further, accounts of function are offered by Karen Neander, "The Teleological Notion of 'Function'" *Australasian Journal of Philosophy* (1991) LXIX, 4: 454–468, Paul Griffiths, "Functional Analysis & Proper Functions," *British Journal for the Philosophy of Science,* forthcoming; these accounts also succumb to the counterexamples on pp. 203–4.

[17]Private communication.

x functions properly in doing *A* if and only if if *x* is an artifact, then it functions in the way in which it was designed to function[18] and if *x* is a nonartifact, then doing *A* has or had survival value.

This analysis needs a lot of work: but doing the work won't be necessary for what I want to say about it. Now first, this sort of analysis implies that the notion of proper function is really ambiguous; it means one thing when applied to artifacts and something else when applied to nonartifacts. Is this really correct? Or is this suggestion better understood as the claim (see the next section) that the notion of proper function does not really apply to nonartifacts, so that our applications of it in that realm really involve something like useful (or useless) fiction?

Setting aside that question, however, we can still see that the suggestion won't do the job. For first, it is hard to see how any such proposed necessary and sufficient condition could be sufficient. Suppose human beings are not artifacts; they aren't created by God or anyone else. Examples like those of Hitler and his henchmen show that a way of functioning's having or having had survival value isn't anywhere nearly sufficient for proper function. But there is a deeper debility here: this is the one that I said (see pp. 204ff.) applies to the Millikan account and also applies much more broadly. For suppose *x* is a nonartifact—an equine heart, for example. And suppose *x* malfunctions: as in the perforated aorta example, it beats at only fifteen strokes per minute. Due to the perforated aorta on the part of *x*'s owner, however, *x*'s functioning in that way has survival value for its owner. As a matter of fact, many of *x*'s ancestors had the same aortal problem (although not nearly all of their peers did). Then *x* meets the suggested condition for proper function, but surely doesn't function properly. (More generally, there can be complementary pairs of malfunction or deformity, complementary in the sense that one of them confers survival value by compensating for the damage that would otherwise be done by the other. Then that one confers survival value, but would not do so in a healthy organism.) And in the same way, of course, an organ could be functioning perfectly properly, but fail to confer survival value because of malfunction elsewhere; and this could be so not only for a given organ or organism, but also for its ancestors.

The way to effect a repair, obviously enough, is to stipulate, as Bigelow and Pargetter do, that *x* is functioning in the context of an organic system that is healthy, functioning properly. But then of course our proposed analysis becomes circular. I don't see any way around this difficulty for a naturalistic analysis of proper function, and tentatively conclude that no such analysis can be provided.

Following Kornblith, I argued (in chapter 2) that 'naturalized epistemology' is best seen as the claim that the only sort of normativity involved in warrant is the sort to be found in the natural sciences. On the view of warrant I propose, that *is* the only sort of normativity involved: the functional generalizations to be found in biology, psychology, sociology, and so on have recourse to the normative notion of proper function, and that notion (along with notions

---

[18]Here of course we need some of the qualifications mentioned previously at pp. 195ff.

interdefinable with it, such as the notion of a design plan), on my account, is the only normative notion involved in warrant. Therefore, if, as it looks, it is in fact impossible to give an account of proper function in naturalistic terms, then metaphysical naturalism and naturalistic epistemology are at best uneasy bedfellows. The right way to be a naturalist in epistemology is to be a supernaturalist in metaphysics.

II. So What's a Poor Naturalist to Do?

But even if the naturalist can't suppose that there is literally such a thing as proper function in nature, perhaps she can still help herself to some of the benefits of thinking there is. She does not believe that we human beings have been designed and created by God, a being with maximal power and knowledge and goodness, who proposed to endow us with the ability to achieve true beliefs on a wide variety of topics. That idea is a mere fiction. Still, fiction has its uses; fiction can help us to achieve a level of understanding we can't easily achieve otherwise. We can learn much by thinking about frictionless surfaces, true vacuums, human beings with coherent credence functions. Perhaps we think the evidence for evolution (taken as the thesis of universal common ancestry) is a bit slim: we remain agnostic about it.[19] Even so, the theory can serve as a kind of unifying hypothesis, enabling us to see connections we might otherwise miss; it can also serve as the source of other hypotheses and conjectures, the exploration of which advances our understanding of the subject matter. Alternatively: perhaps you think the fact is there are no intentions (no desires and beliefs), or that the question whether there are has no answer. Nonetheless you can adopt *the intentional stance* toward other persons and some machines (that is, you can treat them and think of them *as if* they did possess desire and belief, make with respect to them the predictions and predications you would make if you thought they did possess those properties); if you do so, your predictions will go much more easily and smoothly.[20]

Agreed: it requires a certain sophistication to see how a fiction can help us gain genuine understanding; but the thought that it *can* goes back at least to Hobbes and Locke (if not to Plato), with their fictional notion of an aboriginal contract signed and sealed by our remote progenitors hoping for relief from their miserable lives in the state of nature. Perhaps the prime modern source of the notion is Kant.[21] There are his regulative ideas (or ideals) of reason: the ideas of a personal God, of the soul as substance, and of the world as the totality of causally related appearances in space and time. The status of these

[19]See my "When Faith and Reason Clash: Evolution and the Bible," *Christian Scholars Review,* Sept., 1991 (XXI:1).

[20]Another reason for adopting the intentional stance: perhaps for reasons of your own you want to preserve verbal agreement with those with whom you really disagree; you may want to speak with the vulgar but think with the learned.

[21]Although the notion is also to be found in Leibniz, who thought the idea of atoms a useful fiction, a pleasant story that has its uses in helping us understand, but not to be taken as part of the real truth. See his letter to Remond, July 1714, in *Philosophical Papers and Letters,* ed. L. E. Loemker (Dordrecht: D. Reidel, 1970), 2:656–57.

ideas (as with much in his thought) in Kant's overall view is uncertain, but at any rate Kant apparently believed they serve an important cognitive function even if they are not to be thought of as specifying the sober truth. Indeed, Kant speaks of something like useful fiction with respect to the very constellation of ideas under consideration (purpose, goal, design plan, proper function, and their colleagues):

> There can be, then, purposiveness without purpose, so far as we do not place the causes of this form in a will, but yet can only make the explanation of its possibility intelligible to ourselves by deriving it from a will. Again, we are not always forced to regard what we observe (in respect of its possibility) from the point of view of reason. Thus we can at least observe a purposiveness according to form, without basing it on a purpose (as the material of the *nexus finalis*), and remark it in objects, although only by reflection.

And:

> An object, or state of mind, or even an action is called purposive, although its possibility does not necessarily presuppose the representation of a purpose, merely because its possibility can be explained and conceived by us only so far as we assume for its ground a causality according to purposes, i.e. in accordance with a will which has regulated it according to the representation of a certain rule.[22]

Kant's idea, therefore, is that there are natural phenomena of which we can gain proper understanding only by way of such notions as purpose and function—despite the fact that nature itself can't properly be seen as displaying (or even covertly harboring) purpose or function.

In *Die Philosophie des Als Ob,* Hans Vaihinger enthusiastically builds an entire philosophy on these felicitous fictions; indeed, he claims that Kant "reached the high-watermark of his critical philosophy" when he hit on the idea that *purpose in nature* is just such a fiction.[23] So perhaps the naturalist can join Kant and Vaihinger here, and explain or understand proper functioning in terms of this fiction (as he sees it); perhaps he could say that our faculties are working properly when they are working the way they *would* work if the theistic story *were* true.[24] He may therefore treat this story the way correspond-

---

[22]*Critique of Judgment,* trans. and introd. J. H. Bernard (New York: Hafner Press, 1951), 55/6, pp. 54–55. These quotations are both to be found in Christel Fricke's "Explaining the Inexplicable. The Hypotheses of the Faculty of Reflective Judgement in Kant's Third Critique," *Nous* (March 1990), pp. 52–53.

[23]Translated under the title *The Philosophy of 'As if'* by C. K. Ogden (New York: Harcourt, Brace, 1925), pp. 293, 23.

[24]But here he must be careful. If theism were true, then probably there would be something like Calvin's *Sensus Divinitatis,* a many-sided disposition to accept belief in God (or propositions that immediately and obviously entail the existence of God) in a wide variety of circumstances. See my "Reason and Belief in God," in *Faith and Rationality: Reason and Belief in God,* ed. A. Plantinga and N. Wolterstorff (Notre Dame: University of Notre Dame Press, 1983), pp. 80–82. But then our faculties would be functioning properly when we form such beliefs in the basic way—that is, immediately, without believing on the evidential basis of other propositions. And then such basic belief in God would have warrant—a conclusion the nontheist may wish to avoid.

ing stories are treated by some who accept ideal observer theories in ethics, or social contract theories in political philosophy, or possible worlds theories in metaphysics, or Peircean theories of truth. I may be able to gain insight into rightness for action or goodness for character by considering what an ideal observer would approve; perhaps I need not add that in fact there exists an ideal observer. I can see possible worlds theory as a source of insight into the structure of modality; perhaps I need not add that possible worlds theory is the sober metaphysical truth of the matter.[25] Perhaps you can even explain what it is for a proposition to be true in terms of what an ideally rational scientific community would endorse. (But again: you must be wary; if this view is not put carefully, you may wind up committed to the *necessary existence* of an ideally rational scientific community.)[26] And perhaps the naturalist can take the same attitude toward proper function and its confreres. Adopting the intentional stance enables us to gain understanding: so say those who think intention ultimately a fiction. Perhaps those who think proper function ultimately fictitious can similarly recommend adopting the *functional* stance.

As a special case, there is the stance Bas van Fraassen takes toward possible worlds, modality, and unobservables in science. Possible worlds and their ilk, says van Fraassen, are *pictures* that guide our inference, *models* of a certain sort, but *fictional* models not to be taken seriously as part of the real truth of the matter. "Such fictions," he says, "are useful in giving an account of the surface phenomena—and there is in reality, nothing below the surface."[27] So modality (for example) is a feature of the models we make and use for one purpose or another; it is not to be found in reality *an sich*. In the same or similar spirit Nancy Cartwright claims that the fundamental laws of physics govern, not objects in reality, but models we make in quest of understanding.[28] And perhaps in one of these ways a nontheist can accept the present account of positive epistemic status, even if he thinks there is no good way to understand proper function and allied notions from a nontheistic perspective. This is another way in which he may propose to speak with the vulgar but think with the learned.

Now these antirealist stances are refined and highly sophisticated—in fact, a bit contorted. And, like all unnatural stances, they become awkward and uncomfortable if held for any length of time. If in one way a fiction can help

[25]Of course I am not advocating this attitude toward possible worlds theory; *I* think it is indeed the sober truth. See "Two Concepts of Modality: Modal Realism and Modal Anti-Realism," in *Philosophical Perspectives, I, Metaphysics, 1987,* ed. James Tomberlin (Atascadero, Calif.: Ridgeview, 1987).

[26]As is Hilary Putnam in two presidential addresses: "Reason and Realism," *Proceedings and Addresses of the American Philosophical Association* (August 1977), and "Models and Reality," *Proceedings of the Association for Symbolic Logic* (1980). For the argument, see my "How to Be an Anti-realist," *Proceedings and Addresses of the American Philosophical Association* (September 1982).

[27]"Probabilities of Conditionals," in *Foundations of Probability Theory, Statistical Inference, and Statistical Theories of Science, I* , ed. W. L. Harper and C. A. Hooker (Dordrecht: D. Reidel, 1976), p. 267.

[28]*How the Laws of Physics Lie* (Oxford: Clarendon Press, 1983).

you understand a phenomenon, in another it can harm your understanding of it. You think the fact is there is no such thing as intention (or modality, or proper function, or right and wrong); you find yourself nonetheless ineluctably compelled, in your nonphilosophical life, to adopt the intentional stance. Indeed, no one, I suspect, really *adopts* the intentional stance, any more than you adopt your parents; we all take it utterly for granted from earliest consciousness that others have desires and beliefs. Similarly, we all take it for granted that there is such a thing as proper function for the heart, or kidney, or lung. More poignantly, there is such a thing as *malfunction* for these things. The functionalist stance is awkward: to adopt it you are to think that George's heart isn't *really* malfunctioning (or that there isn't any truth of the matter as to whether it is), but you are to treat it and think about it, somehow, as if it *were* malfunctioning. Can you really avoid doublethink? Alternatively, can you avoid what from your own perspective is illusion and error? Illusion, as Freud and Marx tell us, has its uses; but helping to achieve straightforward understanding is not among them.

So suppose you are a naturalist, and are convinced that there is no way to make sense of the notion of proper function from a naturalistic perspective; and suppose you are unwilling to take refuge in The Philosophy of As If. Then you do have a serious objection to the analysis of warrant I propose and you will have to reject it. Indeed, you will have to reject the notion of proper function as well. If you are dead certain naturalism is true, you will have to accept the cost, not only of rejecting this account of warrant, but of rejecting the very idea of proper function. A high price, no doubt—but no more than what a serious naturalism exacts.

But suppose, on the other hand, you are convinced (as most of us are) that there really is such a thing as warrant and really are (for natural organisms) such things as proper function, damage, design, dysfunction, and all the rest. You think there really are these things and are unwilling merely to take the functionalist stance: then if you also think there is no naturalistic analysis of these notions, what you have is a powerful argument against naturalism. Given the plausible alternatives, what you have, more specifically, is a powerful theistic argument; indeed, what you have is a version of Thomas Aquinas's Fifth Way:

> The fifth way is taken from the governance of the world. We see that things which lack knowledge, such as natural bodies, act for an end, and this is evident from their acting always, or nearly always, in the same way, so as to obtain the best result. Hence it is plain that they achieve their end, not fortuitously, but designedly. Now whatever lacks knowledge cannot move towards an end, unless it be directed by some being endowed with knowledge and intelligence; as the arrow is directed by the archer. Therefore some intelligent being exists by whom all natural things are directed to their end; and this being we call God.[29]

[29]*Summa Theologiae*, I, Q. 2, a. 3.

"Whatever lacks knowledge cannot move towards an end, unless it be directed by some being endowed with knowledge and intelligence"; we may construe this as the claim that there is no naturalistic explanation or analysis of proper function. If this claim is correct (and we have seen that it is supported by a consideration of the main attempts to produce such an analysis), then indeed the way to be a naturalist in epistemology is to be a supernaturalist in ontology.

12

Is Naturalism Irrational?

I. The Problem

In the preceding chapter we saw that the notion of proper function provides the resources for an argument against metaphysical naturalism. More specifically: suppose you believe that there really is such a thing as proper function for our cognitive faculties (or for any natural organs or systems), and suppose you also believe (as is suggested by chapter 11) that there is no naturalistic account, reduction, or analysis of the notion of proper function: then you have the materials for a powerful argument against metaphysical naturalism. This is an argument for the *falsehood* of naturalism: if your premises are true, naturalism is false. In this chapter I propose to develop two epistemological arguments against metaphysical naturalism: the main one, however, is not for the falsehood of naturalism, but for the conclusion that it is irrational to accept it. The difference between them is like the difference between arguing, by way of the argument from evil, that theism is *false,* versus arguing, by way of the evidentialist objection to theistic belief, that whether or not theism is true, at any rate it can't be rationally accepted.[1]

Most of us think (or would think on reflection) that at least *a* function or purpose of our cognitive faculties is to provide us with true beliefs. Moreover, we go on to think that when they function properly, in accord with our design plan, then for the most part they do precisely that. Qualifications are necessary, of course. There are various exceptions and special cases: visual illusions, mechanisms like forgetting the pain of childbirth, optimism about recovery not warranted by the relevant statistics, unintended conceptual by-products, and so on. There are also those areas of cognitive endeavor marked by enormous disagreement, wildly varying opinion: philosophy and Scripture scholarship come to mind. Here the sheer volume of disagreement and the great variety and contrariety of options proposed suggest that either not all of us are such that our cognitive faculties *do* function according to the design plan, in these areas, or that it is not the case that the relevant modules of the design plan are aimed at truth, or that the design plan for those areas is defective.

Nevertheless over a vast area of cognitive terrain we take it both that the purpose (function) of our cognitive faculties is to provide us with true or

---

[1] See my "Reason and Belief in God," in *Faith and Rationality: Reason and Belief in God,* ed. A. Plantinga and N. Wolterstorff (Notre Dame: University of Notre Dame Press, 1983), pp. 17ff.

verisimilitudinous beliefs, and that, for the most part, that is just what they do. We suppose, for example, that most of the deliverances of memory are at least approximately correct. True, if you ask five witnesses how the accident happened, you may get five different stories. Still, they will agree that there was indeed an *accident,* and that it was an *automobile* accident (as opposed, say, to a naval disaster or a volcanic eruption); there will usually be agreement as to the number of vehicles involved (particularly if it is a small number), as well as the rough location of the accident (Aberdeen, Scotland, as opposed to Aberdeen, South Dakota), and so on. And all this is against the background of massive and much deeper agreement: that there are automobiles; that they do not disappear when no one is looking; that if released from a helicopter they fall down rather than up, that they are driven by people who use them to go places, that they are seldom driven by three-year-olds, that their drivers have purposes, hold beliefs, and often act on those purposes and beliefs, that few of them (or their drivers) have been more than a few miles from the surface of the earth, that the world has existed for a good long time—much longer than ten minutes, say—and a million more such Moorean truisms. (Of course, there is the occasional dissenter—in the grip, perhaps, of cognitive malfunction or a cognitively crippling philosophical theory.)

We think our faculties much better adapted to reach the truth in some areas than others; we are good at elementary arithmetic and logic, and the perception of middle-sized objects under ordinary conditions. We are also good at remembering certain sorts of things: I can easily remember what I had for breakfast this morning, where my office was located yesterday, and whether there was a large explosion in my house last night. Things get more difficult, however, when it comes to an accurate reconstruction of what it was like to be, say, a fifth century B.C. Greek (not to mention a bat), or whether the axiom of choice or the continuum hypothesis is true; things are even more difficult, perhaps, when it comes to figuring out how quantum mechanics is to be understood, and what the subnuclear realm of quark and gluon is really like, if indeed there really is a subnuclear realm of quark and gluon. Still, there remains a vast portion of our cognitive terrain where we think that our cognitive faculties do furnish us with truth.

But isn't there a problem, here, for the naturalist? At any rate for the naturalist who thinks that we and our cognitive capacities arrived upon the scene after some billions of years of evolution (by way of natural selection, genetic drift, and other blind processes working on such sources of genetic variation as random genetic mutation)? Richard Dawkins (according to Peter Medawar, "one of the most brilliant of the rising generation of biologists") once leaned over and remarked to A. J. Ayer at one of those elegant, candle-lit, bibulous Oxford college dinners that he couldn't imagine being an atheist before 1859 (the year Darwin's *Origin of Species* was published); "although atheism might have been logically tenable before Darwin," said he, "Darwin made it possible to be an intellectually fulfilled atheist."[2]

[2]*The Blind Watchmaker* (New York: Norton, 1986), pp. 6, 7.

Now Dawkins thinks Darwin made it possible to be an intellectually fulfilled atheist. But perhaps Dawkins is dead wrong here. Perhaps the truth lies in the opposite direction. If our cognitive faculties have originated as Dawkins thinks, then their ultimate purpose or function (if they *have* a purpose or function) will be something like *survival* (of individual, species, gene, or genotype); but then it seems initially doubtful that among their functions— ultimate, proximate, or otherwise—would be the production of true beliefs. Taking up this theme, Patricia Churchland declares that the most important thing about the human brain is that it has evolved; hence, she says, its principal function is to enable the organism to *move* appropriately:

> Boiled down to essentials, a nervous system enables the organism to succeed in the four F's: feeding, fleeing, fighting and reproducing. The principle chore of nervous systems is to get the body parts where they should be in order that the organism may survive. . . . Improvements in sensorimotor control confer an evolutionary advantage: a fancier style of representing is advantageous *so long as it is geared to the organism's way of life and enhances the organism's chances of survival* [Churchland's emphasis]. Truth, whatever that is, definitely takes the hindmost.[3]

Her point, I think, is that (from a naturalistic perspective) what evolution guarantees is (at most) that we *behave* in certain ways—in such ways as to promote survival, or survival through childbearing age. The principal function or purpose, then, (the 'chore' says Churchland) of our cognitive faculties is not that of producing true or verisimilitudinous beliefs, but instead that of contributing to survival by getting the body parts in the right place. What evolution underwrites is only (at most) that our *behavior* be reasonably adaptive to the circumstances in which our ancestors found themselves; hence (so far forth) it does not guarantee mostly true or verisimilitudinous beliefs. Of course our beliefs *might* be mostly true or verisimilitudinous (hereafter I'll omit the 'verisimilitudinous'); but there is no particular reason to think they *would* be: natural selection is interested not in truth, but in appropriate behavior. What Churchland says suggests, therefore, that naturalistic evolution—that is, the conjunction of metaphysical naturalism with the view that we and our cognitive faculties have arisen by way of the mechanisms and processes proposed by contemporary evolutionary theory—gives us reason to doubt two things: (a) that a *purpose* of our cognitive systems is that of serving us with true beliefs, and (b) that they *do*, in fact, furnish us with mostly true beliefs.

W. v. O. Quine and Karl Popper, however, apparently demur. Popper argues that since we have evolved and survived, we may be pretty sure that our hypotheses and guesses as to what the world is like are mostly correct.[4] And Quine says he finds encouragement in Darwin:

> What does make clear sense is this other part of the problem of induction: why does our innate subjective spacing of qualities accord so well with the functionally relevant groupings in nature as to make our inductions tend to come

---

[3] *Journal of Philosophy*, 84 (October 1987), p. 548.
[4] *Objective Knowledge: An Evolutionary Approach* (Oxford: Clarendon Press, 1972), p. 261.

out right? Why should our subjective spacing of qualities have a special purchase on nature and a lien on the future?

There is some encouragement in Darwin. If people's innate spacing of qualities is a gene-linked trait, then the spacing that has made for the most successful inductions will have tended to predominate through natural selection. Creatures inveterately wrong in their inductions have a pathetic but praiseworthy tendency to die before reproducing their kind.[5]

Indeed, Quine finds a great deal more encouragement in Darwin than Darwin did: "With me," says Darwin,

the horrid doubt always arises whether the convictions of man's mind, which has been developed from the mind of the lower animals, are of any value or at all trustworthy. Would any one trust in the convictions of a monkey's mind, if there are any convictions in such a mind?[6]

So here we appear to have Quine and Popper on one side and Darwin and Churchland on the other. Who is right? But a prior question: what, precisely, is the issue? Darwin and Churchland seem to believe that (naturalistic) evolution gives one a reason to doubt that human cognitive faculties produce for the most part true or beliefs: call this 'Darwin's Doubt'. Quine and Popper, on the other hand, apparently hold that evolution gives us reason to believe the opposite: that human cognitive faculties *do* produce for the most part true or beliefs. How shall we understand this opposition?

II. Darwin's Doubt

One possibility: perhaps Darwin and Churchland mean to propose that a certain objective conditional probability is relatively low: the probability of human cognitive faculties' being reliable (producing mostly true beliefs), given that human beings *have* cognitive faculties (of the sort we have) and given that these faculties have been produced by evolution (Dawkin's blind evolution, unguided by the hand of God or any other person). If metaphysical naturalism and this evolutionary account are both true, then our cognitive faculties will have resulted from blind mechanisms like natural selection, working on such sources of genetic variation as random genetic mutation. Evolution is interested, not in true belief, but in survival or fitness. It is therefore unlikely that our cognitive faculties have the production of true belief as a proximate or any other function, and the probability of our faculties' being reliable (given naturalistic evolution) would be fairly low. Popper and Quine, on the other side, judge that probability fairly high.

---

[5] "Natural Kinds," in *Ontological Relativity and Other Essays* (New York: Columbia University Press, 1969), p. 126.

[6] Letter to William Graham, Down, July 3, 1881, in *The Life and Letters of Charles Darwin Including an Autobiographical Chapter*, ed. Francis Darwin (London: John Murray, Albermarle Street, 1887), 1:315–16.

The issue, then, is the value of a certain conditional probability: P(R/ (N&E&C)).[7] Here N is metaphysical naturalism. It isn't easy to say precisely what naturalism *is*, but perhaps that isn't necessary in this context; prominent examples would be the views of (say) David Armstrong, the later Darwin, Quine, and Bertrand Russell. (Crucial to metaphysical naturalism, of course, is the view that there is no such person as the God of traditional theism.) E is the proposition that human cognitive faculties arose by way of the mechanisms to which contemporary evolutionary thought directs our attention; and C is a complex proposition whose precise formulation is both difficult and unnecessary, but which states what cognitive faculties we have—memory, perception, reason, Reid's sympathy—and what sorts of beliefs they produce. R, on the other hand, is the claim that our cognitive faculties are reliable (on the whole, and with the qualifications mentioned), in the sense that they produce mostly true beliefs in the sorts of environments that are normal for them. And the question is: what is the probability of R on N&E&C? (Alternatively, perhaps the interest of *that* question lies in its bearing on *this* question: what is the probability that a belief produced by human cognitive faculties is *true,* given N&E&C?) And if we construe the dispute in this way, then what Darwin and Churchland propose is that this probability is relatively low, whereas Quine and Popper think it fairly high.

A. Stich versus Pangloss

Well, what sorts of considerations would be relevant to this question? Consider the sort of argument implicit in the passage from Quine: "Creatures inveterately wrong in their inductions have a pathetic but praiseworthy tendency to die before reproducing their kind," he says; humankind, happily enough, has not died before reproducing its kind; so probably we human beings are not inveterately wrong in our inductions. This claim is specified to inductions, of course; but presumably the same would go for some or all of our other characteristic beliefs. (According to J. Fodor, "Darwinian selection guarantees that organisms either know the elements of logic or become posthumous."[8]) The claim seems to be that the selection processes involved in evolution are likely to produce cognitive faculties that are reliable, given that they produce cognitive faculties at all.

Stephen Stich attempts to set out the argument implicit in Quine's and Popper's brief and cryptic remarks. (He notes that versions of this argument circulate widely in the oral tradition, but are seldom if ever developed in any detail.) As he sees it, this argument essentially involves two premises: (a) that "evolution produces organisms with good approximations to optimally well-

---

[7]We could think of this probability in two ways: as a conditional *epistemic* probability, or as a conditional *objective* probability. Either will serve for my argument, but I should think the better way to think of it would be as objective probability; for in this sort of context epistemic probability, presumably, should follow known (or conjectured) objective probability.

[8]"Three Cheers for Propositional Attitudes," in *Representations* (Cambridge, Mass.: MIT Press, 1981), p. 121.

designed characteristics or systems,"[9] and (b) that "an optimally well-designed cognitive system is a rational cognitive system," where (on one of the two understandings of 'rational' he considers) a *rational* cognitive system, in turn, is a *reliable* cognitive system, one that produces a preponderance of true beliefs. Stich proposes "to make it clear that there are major problems to be overcome by those who think that evolutionary considerations impose interesting limits on irrationality";[10] what he shows, I think, is that the denials of (a) and (b) are wholly compatible with contemporary evolutionary theory, and not implausible with respect to it.

By way of attack on (a) he points out that natural selection is not the only process at work in evolution; there is also (among others) random genetic drift, which "can lead to the elimination of a more fit gene and the fixation of a less fit one." For example, a genetically based and adaptively favorable trait might arise within a population of sea gulls; perhaps six members of the flock enjoy it. Being birds of a feather, they flock together—sadly enough, at the site of a natural disaster, so that all are killed in a tidal wave or volcanic eruption or by a large meteorite. The more fit gene thus gets eliminated from the population. (There is also the way in which a gene can be fixed, in a small population, by way of random walk.) He points out further, with respect to (a), that there is no reason to think it inevitable that natural selection will have the *opportunity* to select for optimal design. For example, an adaptively positive trait might be linked with an adaptively negative trait by pleiotropy (where one gene codes for more than one trait or system); then it could happen that the gene gets selected and perpetuated by virtue of its link with the positive trait, and the negative trait gets perpetuated by way of its link with the gene. A truly optimal system— one with the positive trait but without the negative—may never show up, or may show up too late to fit in with the current development of the organism.[11]

With respect to (b), the claim that an optimally designed cognitive system is rational (that is, reliable), Stich observes, first, that optimal design, presumably, is to be understood in terms of fitness: "From the point of view of natural selection, it is plausible to say that one system is better designed than a second if an organism having the first would be more fit—that is, more likely to survive and reproduce successfully—than a conspecific having the second. A system is optimally well designed if it enhances biological fitness more than any alternative" (p. 57). He then argues that reliable cognitive systems are not necessarily more fitness-enhancing than unreliable ones; it is not the case, he

[9]Here I assume that (a) is to be understood as "evolution *always* or *nearly always* produces organisms with good approximations."

[10]*The Fragmentation of Reason* (Cambridge: MIT Press, 1990), p. 56.

[11]Ibid., p. 64. He also makes more fanciful suggestions as to how it is that natural selection may never get to select for truly optimal systems: "Modern technology builds prosthetic limbs out of space age alloys and communications systems that transmit messages with the speed of light. It seems very likely indeed that certain organisms would have a real competitive edge if they were born with such limbs, or with nerves that conduct impulses at the speed of light. The fact that there are no such creatures surely does not indicate that the imagined changes would not enhance fitness. Rather, we can be pretty confident natural selection never had the chance to evaluate organisms that utilize such materials" (p. 65).

argues, that for any two cognitive systems S_1 and S_2, if S_1 is more reliable than S_2, then S_1 is more fitness-enhancing than S_2. S_1, for example, might cost too much by way of energy or memory capacity; alternatively, the less reliable S_2 might produce more by way of false beliefs but nonetheless contribute more to survival.[12]

So Stich's point is this: as far as contemporary evolutionary theory is concerned, there is little reason to endorse either (a) or (b). But has he correctly identified the conclusions (or the premises) of those he sets out to refute?[13] "We now have a pair of arguments," he says, "for the claim that evolution and natural selection *guarantee* at least a close approximation to full rationality in normal organisms, ourselves included" (p. 59, my emphasis) and "An essential component in both arguments sketched in 3.1, aimed at showing that evolution will *insure* rationality, is . . ." (p. 63, my emphasis). If his aim is to cast doubt on these arguments, taken as arguments for the claim that evolution and natural selection *guarantee* or *insure* rationality, then he has certainly fulfilled his aim. But perhaps Quine and Popper and their allies do not mean to argue anything quite so strong. Perhaps what they mean to argue is only that it is fairly or highly *probable*, given that we and our cognitive faculties have evolved according to the processes endorsed by contemporary evolutionary theory, that those faculties are reliable; perhaps they mean to argue only that P(R/(N&E&C)) is fairly high. What Stich shows is that it is perfectly possible both that we and our cognitive faculties have evolved in the ways approved by current evolutionary theory, and that those cognitive faculties are not reliable. But that does not address Quine's argument taken as an implicit argument for the claim that P(R/(N&E&C)) is fairly high, and *a fortiori* it does not serve as an argument for Darwin's Doubt, that is, for the claim that P(R/(N&E&C)) is fairly low.

B. The Doubt Developed

Can we assemble an argument for Darwin's Doubt from (among other things) the materials Stich presents? In order to avoid irrelevant distractions, suppose we think, first, not about ourselves and our ancestors, but about a hypothetical

---

[12]"a very cautious, risk-aversive inferential strategy—one that leaps to the conclusion that danger is present on very slight evidence—will typically lead to false beliefs more often, and true ones less often, than a less hair-trigger one that waits for more evidence before rendering a judgment. Nonetheless, the unreliable, error-prone, risk-aversive strategy may well be favored by natural selection. For natural selection does not care about truth; it cares only about reproductive success" (p. 62). The point seems correct, but its relevance is not wholly obvious. The claim he proposes to refute is that an optimally fit system would also be reliable (and maybe even optimally reliable); but this claim is compatible with the existence of a pair of systems one of which is both more fitness-enhancing but less reliable than the other. By way of analogy, consider the ontological argument: maximal greatness, no doubt, would require, say, maximal excellence with respect to knowledge; but it does not follow that if x is greater than y, then x is more excellent with respect to knowledge than y.

[13]Of course, it would be easy to misunderstand the arguments of those he tries to refute, given their authors' reluctance to state them explicitly.

population of creatures a lot like ourselves on a planet similar to Earth. (Darwin proposed that we think about another species, such as monkeys.) Suppose these creatures have cognitive faculties, hold beliefs, change beliefs, make inferences, and so on; and suppose these creatures have arisen by way of the selection processes endorsed by contemporary evolutionary thought. What is the probability that their faculties are reliable? What is P(R/(N&E&C)), specified not to us, but to them? According to Quine and Popper, the probability in question would be rather high: belief is connected with action in such a way that extensive false belief would lead to maladaptive behavior, in which case it is likely that the ancestors of those creatures would have displayed that pathetic but praiseworthy tendency Quine mentions.

But now for the contrary argument. First, perhaps it is likely that their *behavior* is adaptive; but nothing follows about their *beliefs*. We aren't given, after all, that their beliefs are so much as causally connected with their behavior; for we aren't given that their beliefs are more than mere epiphenomena, not causally involved with behavior at all. Perhaps their beliefs neither figure into the causes of their behavior, nor are caused by that behavior. (No doubt beliefs would be caused by *something* in or about these creatures, but it need not be by their behavior.) You may object that as *you* use 'belief', beliefs just *are* among the processes (neural structures, perhaps) that (together with desire, fear, and the like) *are* causally efficacious. Fair enough (you have a right to use that word as you please); but then my point can be put as follows: in *that* use of 'belief' it may be that things with propositional contents are not beliefs, that is, do not have causal efficacy. It can't be a matter of definition that there are neural structures or processes displaying both propositional content and causal efficacy with respect to behavior; and perhaps the things that display causal efficacy do not display the sort of relation to content (to a proposition) that a belief of the proposition *p* must display toward *p*. You say that in that case the things, if any, that stand in that relation to a proposition would not be beliefs (because, as you see it, beliefs must have causal efficacy). Well, there is no sense in arguing about words: I'll give you the term 'belief' and put my case using other terms. What I say is possible is that the things (mental acts, perhaps) that stand in that relation to content (to propositions) do not also enjoy causal efficacy. Call those things whatever you like: *they* are the things that are true or false, and it is about the likelihood of *their* truth or falsehood that we are asking. If these things, whatever we call them, are not causally connected with behavior, then they would be, so to speak, *invisible* to evolution; and then the fact that they arose during the evolutionary history of these beings would confer no probability on the idea that they are mostly true, or mostly nearly true, rather than wildly false. Indeed, the probability of their being for the most part true would have to be estimated as fairly low.

A second possibility is that the beliefs of these creatures are not among the *causes* of their behavior, but are *effects* of that behavior, or effects of proximate causes that also cause behavior. Their beliefs might be like a sort of decoration that isn't involved in the causal chain leading to action. Their waking beliefs might be no more causally efficacious, with respect to their behavior, than our dream beliefs are with respect to ours. This could go by way of pleiotropy: genes that code for traits important to survival also code for consciousness and belief; but the latter don't figure into the etiology of action. Under these conditions, of course, their beliefs could be wildly false. It *could* be that one of these creatures believes that he is at that elegant, bibulous Oxford dinner, when in fact he is slogging his way through some primeval swamp, desperately fighting off hungry crocodiles. Under this possibility, as under the first, beliefs would not have (or need not have) any purpose or function; they would be more like unintended by-products. Under this possibility as under the first, the probability that their cognitive faculties are reliable, is low.

A third possibility is that beliefs do indeed have causal efficacy with respect to behavior, but not by virtue of their *content;* put it in currently fashionable jargon, this would be the suggestion that while beliefs are causally efficacious, it is only by virtue of their *syntax,* not by virtue of their *semantics.* Indeed just this thesis is part of a popular contemporary view: the computational theory of mind.[14] I read a poem very loudly, so loudly as to break a glass;[15] the sounds I utter have meaning, but their meaning is causally irrelevant to the breaking of the glass. In the same way it might be that these creatures' beliefs have causal efficacy, but not by way of the content of those beliefs. A substantial share of probability must be reserved for this option; and under this option, as under the preceding two, the likelihood that the beliefs of these creatures would be for the most part true would be low.

A fourth possibility: it could be that belief is causally efficacious— 'semantically' as well as 'syntactically'—with respect to behavior, but *mal-adaptive.* As Stich points out, it is quite possible (and quite in accord with current evolutionary theory) that a system or trait that is in fact maladaptive— at any rate less adaptive than available alternatives—should nonetheless become fixed and survive. Perhaps the belief systems of these creatures are like the albinism found in many arctic animals, or like sickle-cell anemia: maladaptive, but connected with genes coding for behavior or traits conducive to survival. They could be maladaptive in two ways. First, perhaps their beliefs are a sort of energy-expensive distraction, causing these creatures to engage in survival-enhancing behavior, all right, but in a way less efficient and economic than if

[14]See, for example, J. Fodor's "Methodological solipsism considered as a research strategy in cognitive psychology," *Behavioral and Brain Sciences* (1980) p. 68; see Stephen Stich's *From Folk Psychology to Cognitive Science* (Cambridge: MIT Press, 1983), chap. 8 and elsewhere. See also P. Churchland, "Eliminative Materialism and Propositional Attitudes," *Journal of Philosophy* 78 (1981); Fred Dretske, *Knowledge and the Flow of Information* (Cambridge: MIT Press, 1981); J. Fodor, *Psychosemantics* (Cambridge: MIT Press, 1987); B. Loar, *Mind and Meaning* (Cambridge: Cambridge University Press, 1981); and Z. Pylyshyn, *Computation and Cognition* (Cambridge: MIT Press, 1984). Robert Cummins goes so far as to call this view—the view that representations have causal efficacy only with respect to their syntax, not with respect to their semantics or content—the 'received view', in *Meaning and Mental Representation* (Cambridge: MIT Press, 1989), p. 130. In *Explaining Behavior* (Cambridge: MIT Press, 1988), Fred Dretske takes as his main project that of explaining how it could be that beliefs (and other representations) play a causal role by virtue of their contents.

[15]The example is Dretske's.

the causal connections by-passed belief altogether. Second, it could be that beliefs in fact produce maladaptive behavior. Perhaps a mildly maladaptive belief-behavior structure is coded for by the same genetic structure that produces some adaptive behavior. Suppose these creatures' beliefs do not for the most part produce adaptive behavior: the mechanisms that produce them might nonetheless survive. Perhaps on balance their behavior is sufficiently adaptive, even if not every segment of it is. Some probability, then, must be reserved for the possibility that these creatures have cognitive faculties that are maladaptive, but nonetheless survive; and on this possibility, once more, the probability that their beliefs would be for the most part true is fairly low.

A fifth (and final) possibility is that the beliefs of our hypothetical creatures are indeed both causally connected with their behavior and also adaptive. Assume, then, that our creatures have belief systems, and that these systems are adaptive: they produce adaptive behavior, and at not too great a cost in terms of resources. What is the probability (on this assumption together with N&E&C) that their cognitive faculties are reliable; and what is the probability that a belief produced by those faculties will be true?

Not as high as you might think. For, of course, beliefs don't causally produce behavior *by themselves;* it is beliefs, desires, and other things that do so together. Suppose we oversimplify a bit and say that my behavior is a causal product just of my beliefs and desires. Then the problem is that clearly there will be any number of *different* patterns of belief and desire that would issue in the same action; and among those there will be many in which the beliefs are wildly false. Paul is a prehistoric hominid; the exigencies of survival call for him to display tiger-avoidance behavior. There will be many behaviors that are appropriate: fleeing, for example, or climbing a steep rock face, or crawling into a hole too small to admit the tiger, or leaping into a handy lake. Pick any such appropriately specific behavior B. Paul engages in B, we think, because, sensible fellow that he is, he has an aversion to being eaten and believes that B is a good means of thwarting the tiger's intentions.

But clearly this avoidance behavior could be a result of a thousand other belief-desire combinations: indefinitely many other belief-desire systems fit B equally well. (Here let me ignore the complication arising from the fact that belief comes in degrees.) Perhaps Paul very much *likes* the idea of being eaten, but whenever he sees a tiger, always runs off looking for a better prospect, because he thinks it unlikely that the tiger he sees will eat him. This will get his body parts in the right place so far as survival is concerned, without involving much by way of true belief. (Of course we must postulate other changes in Paul's ways of reasoning, including how he changes belief in response to experience, to maintain coherence.) Or perhaps he thinks the tiger is a large, friendly, cuddly pussycat and wants to pet it; but he also believes that the best way to pet it is to run away from it. Or perhaps he confuses running *toward* it with running *away* from it, believing of the action that is really running away from it, that it is running toward it; or perhaps he thinks the tiger is a regularly recurring illusion, and, hoping to keep his weight down, has formed the resolution to run a mile at top speed whenever presented with such an illusion; or perhaps he thinks he is about to take part in a sixteen-hundred-meter race, wants to win, and believes the appearance of the tiger is the starting signal; or perhaps. . . . Clearly there are any number of belief-cum-desire systems that equally fit a given bit of behavior where the beliefs are mostly false. Indeed, even if we fix desire, there will still be any number of systems of belief that will produce a given bit of behavior: perhaps Paul does not want to be eaten, but (a) thinks the best way to avoid being eaten is to run toward the tiger, and (b) mistakenly believes that he is running toward it when in fact he is running away.

But these possibilities are wholly preposterous, you say. Following Richard Grandy, you point out that when we ascribe systems of belief and desire to persons, we make use of "principles of humanity," whereby we see others as resembling what we take ourselves to be.[16] You go on to endorse David Lewis's suggestion that a theory of content requires these "principles of humanity" in order to rule out as "deeply irrational" those nonstandard belief-desire systems; their contents involved are "unthinkable," and are hence disqualified as candidates for someone's belief-desire structure.[17] Surely you (and Grandy and Lewis) are right: in ascribing beliefs to others, we *do* think of them as like what we think we are. (This involves, among other things, thinking that the (a) purpose or function of their cognitive systems, like that of ours, is the production of true beliefs.) And a theory of content ascription does indeed require more than just the claim that the content of my beliefs must fit my behavior and desires: that leaves entirely too much latitude as to what that content, on a given occasion, might in fact be. These principles of humanity will exclude vast hordes of logically possible belief-desire systems as systems (given human limitations) no human being *could* have; thus such principles will exclude my attributing logical omniscience (or probabilistic coherence) to Paul, or even a system involving the *de re* belief, with respect to each real number in the (open) unit interval, that it is indeed greater than 0. These principles will also exclude some systems as systems we think no properly functioning human being *would* have: accordingly, I will not attribute to Paul the view that emeralds are grue, or the belief that it would be good to have a nice saucer of mud for lunch (Elizabeth Anscombe, *Intention,* sec. 38).

These points are quite correct; but they do not bear on the present question. It is true that a decent theory of content ascription must require more than that the belief fit the behavior; for a decent theory of content ascription must also respect or take for granted what we ordinarily think about our desires, beliefs, and circumstances and the relations between these items. But in the case of our hypothetical population, these "principles of humanity" are not relevant. For we are not given that its members are human; more important, we are not given that those principles of humanity, those commonsense beliefs about how their behavior, belief, and desire are related, are true of them. We can't assume that their beliefs, for given circumstances, would be similar to what we take it *we*

[16]"Reference, Meaning and Belief," *Journal of Philosophy* 70 (1973), pp. 443ff.
[17]*On the Plurality of Worlds* (Oxford: Basil Blackwell, 1986), pp. 38ff., 107–8.

would believe in those circumstances. We must ask what sorts of belief-desire systems are *possible* for these creatures, given only that they have evolved according to the principles of contemporary evolutionary theory; clearly these gerrymanders are perfectly possible. So perhaps their behavior has been adaptive, and their systems of belief and desire such as to fit that adaptive behavior; those beliefs could nonetheless be wildly wrong. There are indefinitely many belief-desire systems that fit adaptive behavior, but where the beliefs involved are not for the most part true. A share of probability has to be reserved for these possibilities as well.

Our question was this: given our hypothetical population along with N&E&C, what is the probability that the cognitive systems of beliefs these creatures display is reliable? Suppose we briefly review. First, on the condition in question, there is some probability that their beliefs are not causally connected with behavior at all. It would be reasonable to suppose, on that condition, that the probability of a given belief's being true would not be far from $1/2$, and hence reasonable to suppose that the probability that their cognitive faculties are reliable (produce a substantial preponderance of verisimilitudinous beliefs) is very low. Second, there is some probability that their beliefs are causally connected with behavior, but only as epiphenomenal effect of causes that also cause behavior; in that case too it would be reasonable to suppose that the probability of their cognitive systems' being reliable is very low. Third, there is the possibility that belief is only 'syntactically', not 'semantically', connected with behavior; on this possibility too, there would be a low probability that their cognitive faculties are reliable. Fourth, there is the possibility that their beliefs are causally connected ('semantically' as well as 'syntactically') with their behavior, but maladaptive; again, in this case it would be reasonable to suppose that the probability of R is low. Fifth, there is also some probability that their beliefs are causally connected with their behavior, and are adaptive; as we saw, however, there are indefinitely many belief-desire systems that would yield adaptive behavior, but are unreliable. Here one does not quite know what to say about the probability that their cognitive systems would produce mainly true beliefs, but perhaps it would be reasonable to estimate it as somewhat more than $1/2$.[18] These possibilities are mutually exclusive and jointly exhaustive; if we had definite probabilities for each of the five cases and definite probabilities for R on each of them, then the probability of R would be the weighted average of the probabilities for R on each of those possibilities—weighted by the probabilities of those possibilities. (Of course we don't have definite probabilities here, but only vague estimates; it imparts a spurious appearance of precision to so much as mention the relevant formula.)

---

[18]Of course it might be, with respect to this fifth case, that the relevant probabilities differ with respect to different cognitive faculties. Perhaps the probabilities are highest with respect to, say, perception and other sources of belief coming into play in situations crucial to survival; perhaps the probabilities are considerably lower with respect to the sorts of intellectual pursuits favored by people past their reproductive prime: such pursuits as philosophy, literary criticism, set theory, and evolutionary biology. See pp. 232ff.

Trying to combine these probabilities in an appropriate way, then, it would be reasonable to suppose that the probability of R, of these creatures' cognitive systems being reliable, is relatively low, somewhat less than ½. More exactly, a reasonable posture would be to think it very unlikely that the statistical probability of their belief-producing mechanisms' being reliable, given that they have been produced in the suggested way, is very high; and rather likely that (on N&E&C) R is less probable than its denial.

Now return to Darwin's Doubt. The reasoning that applies to these hypothetical creatures, of course, also applies to *us;* so if we think the probability of R with respect to *them* is relatively low on N&E&C, we should think the same thing about the probability of R with respect to *us*. Something like this reasoning, perhaps, is what underlay Darwin's doubt—although Darwin did not have the benefit of pleiotropy, random genetic drift, gene fixation by random walk, and the other bells and whistles that adorn current evolutionary theory. So taken, his claim is that P(R/N&E&C) (specified to us) is rather low, perhaps somewhat less than ½. Arguments of this sort are less than coercive; but it would be perfectly sensible to estimate these probabilities in this way.

III. A Preliminary Argument against Naturalism

Suppose you do estimate these probabilities in roughly this way: suppose you concur in Darwin's Doubt, taking P(R/(N&E&C)) to be fairly low. But suppose you also think, as most of us do, that in fact our cognitive faculties *are* reliable (with the qualifications and nuances introduced previously). Then you have a straightforward probabilistic argument against naturalism—and for traditional theism, if you think these two the significant alternatives. According to Bayes' Theorem,

$$P((N\&E\&C)/R) = \frac{P(N\&E\&C) \times P(R/(N\&E\&C))}{P(R)}$$

where P(N&E&C) is your estimate of the probability for N&E&C independent of the consideration of R. You believe R, so you assign it a probability near 1 and you take P(R/(N&E&C)) to be no more than ½. Then P((N&E&C)/R) will be no greater than ½ times P(N&E&C), and will thus be fairly low. You believe C (the proposition specifying the sorts of cognitive faculties we have); so you assign it a very high probability; accordingly P((N&E)/R) will also be low. No doubt you will also assign a very high probability to the conditional *if naturalism is true, then our faculties have arisen by way of evolution;* then you will judge that P(N/R) is also low. But you do think R is true; you therefore have evidence against N. So your belief that our cognitive faculties are reliable gives you a reason for rejecting naturalism and accepting its denial.

The same argument will not hold, of course, for traditional theism; on that view the probability that our cognitive faculties are reliable will be much higher than $1/2$; for, according to traditional (Jewish, Christian, Moslem) theism, God created us in his image, a part of which involves our having knowledge over a wide range of topics and areas.[19] So (provided that for you the prior probabilities of traditional theism and naturalism are comparable) P(traditional theism/R) will be considerably greater than P(N/R).

IV. The Main Argument against Naturalism

A. *The Doubt Developed Again*

Still, the argument for a low estimate of P(R/(N&E&C)) is by no means irresistible. In particular, our estimates of the various probabilities involved in estimating P(R/(N&E&C)) with respect to that hypothetical population were (of necessity) both extremely imprecise and also poorly grounded. You might reasonably hold, therefore, that the right course here is simple agnosticism: one just does not know (and has no good way of finding out) *what* P(R/(N&E&C)) might be. It could be very low; on the other hand it could be rather high. With our limited cognitive resources, you say, the proper course is to hold no view about what that probability might be; the proper course is agnosticism. This also seems sensible; accordingly, let's suppose, for the moment, that the proper course *is* agnosticism about that probability. What would then be the appropriate attitude toward R (specified to that hypothetical population)? Someone who accepts N&E and also believes that the proper attitude toward P(R/(N&E&C)) is one of agnosticism clearly enough has good reason for being agnostic about R as well. She has no other source of information about R (for that population); but the source of information she does have gives her no reason to believe R and no reason to disbelieve it. The proposition in question is the sort for which one needs evidence if one is to believe it reasonably; since there is no evidence the reasonable course is to withhold belief.

But now suppose we again apply the same sort of reasoning to ourselves and our condition. Suppose we think N&E is true: we ourselves have evolved according to the mechanisms suggested by contemporary evolutionary theory, unguided and unorchestrated by God or anyone else. Suppose we think, furthermore, that there is no way to determine P(R/(N&E&C)) (specified to us). What would be the right attitude to take to R? Well, if we have no further information, then wouldn't the right attitude here, just as with respect to that hypothetical population, be agnosticism, withholding belief?

Compare the case of a believer in God, who, perhaps through an in-

---

[19]Thus, for example, Thomas Aquinas:

Since human beings are said to be in the image of God in virtue of their having a nature that includes an intellect, such a nature is most in the image of God in virtue of being most able to imitate God. (*Summa Theologiae*, Ia, q. 93, a. 4)

Only in rational creatures is there found a likeness of God which counts as an image . . . . As far as a likeness of the divine nature is concerned, rational creatures seem somehow to attain a representation of [that] type in virtue of imitating God not only in this, that he is and lives, but especially in this, that he understands. (*Summa Theologiae*, Ia, q. 93 a. 6)

judicious reading of Freud, comes to think that religious belief generally and theistic belief in particular is almost always produced by wish fulfillment. Such beliefs, she now thinks, are not produced by cognitive faculties functioning properly in a congenial environment according to a design plan successfully aimed at truth; instead they are produced by wish fulfillment, which, while indeed it has a function, does not have the function of producing true beliefs. Suppose she considers the objective probability that wish fulfillment, as a belief-producing mechanism, is reliable. She might quite properly estimate this probability as relatively low; alternatively, however, she might think the right course, here, is agnosticism; and she might also be equally agnostic about the probability that a belief should be true, given that it is produced by wish fulfillment. But then in either case she has a defeater for any belief she takes to be produced by the mechanism in question. Consider the first case: she thinks the probability that wish fulfillment is reliable is low, and the probability that a belief should be true, given that it is produced by wish fulfillment not far from $1/2$. Then she has a straightforward defeater for any of her beliefs she takes to be produced by wish fulfillment. Her situation is like that of the person who comes into a factory, sees an assembly line carrying apparently red widgets, and is then told by the shop superintendent that these widgets are being irradiated by a variety of red lights, which makes it possible to detect otherwise undetectable hairline cracks. She should take it that the probability that a widget is red, given that it looks red, is fairly low; and she then has a reason, with respect to any particular widget coming down the line, to doubt that it is red, despite the fact that it looks red. To use John Pollock's terminology (and since I am already filching his example, why not?), she has an *undercutting* defeater (rather than a *rebutting* defeater). It isn't that she has acquired some evidence for that widget's being nonred, thus rebutting the belief that it is red; it is rather that her grounds for thinking it red have been undercut. And, indeed, upon hearing (and believing) that the widgets are being thus irradiated, she will probably no longer believe that the widget in question is red.

Consider, on the other hand, a second kind of case: here she does not come to believe that the probability of a widget's being red, given that it looks red, is low; instead, she is agnostic about that probability. As before, the shop superintendent tells her that those widgets are being irradiated by red light; but then a vice-president comes along and tells her that the shop superintendent suffers from a highly resilient but fortunately specific hallucination, so that he is reliable on other topics even if totally unreliable on red lights and widgets. Still, the vice president *himself* doesn't look wholly reliable: there is a certain shiftiness about the eyes. . . .

Then she doesn't know *what* to believe about those alleged red lights. What will she properly think about the color of the widgets? She will presumably be agnostic about the probability of a widget's being red, given that it looks red; she won't know what that probability might be; for all she knows it could be very low, but also, for all she knows, it could be high. The rational course for her, therefore, is to be agnostic about the deliverances of her visual perception (so far as color detection is concerned) in this situation. But then she also has a good reason for being equally agnostic about the proposition *a is red*, where *a* is any of those red-appearing widgets coming down the assembly line. She has an undercutting defeater for the proposition *a is red*; this defeater gives her a reason to be agnostic with respect to that proposition. If she has no defeater for that defeater, and no further evidence for the proposition, then on balance the right attitude for her to take toward it would be agnosticism.

By parity of reason, the same goes, I should think, for the believer in God of a couple of paragraphs back. She too has an undercutting defeater for belief in God; if that defeater remains itself undefeated and if she has no other source of evidence, then the rational course would be to reject belief in God. That is not to say, of course, that she would in fact be *able* to do so; but it remains the rational course.

But now suppose we return to the person convinced of N&E who is agnostic about P(R/(N&E&C)): something similar goes for him. He is in the same position with respect to any belief B of his, as is that believer in God. He is in the same condition, with respect to B, as the widget observer who didn't know what or who to believe about those red lights. So he too has a defeater for B, and a good reason for being agnostic with respect to it. If he has no defeater for that defeater, and no other source of evidence, the right attitude toward B would be agnosticism. That is not to say that he would in fact be able to reject B. Due to that animal faith noted by Hume, Reid, and Santayana (but so-called only by the last-named), chances are he would not; still, agnosticism is what reason requires. Here, then, we have another way of developing Darwin's Doubt, a way that does not depend upon estimating P(R/(N&E&C)) as low, but requires instead only agnosticism about that probability.

B. The Argument

By way of brief review: Darwin's Doubt can be taken as the claim that the probability of R on N&E&C is fairly low; as I argued, that is plausible. But Darwin's Doubt can also be taken as the claim that the rational attitude to take, here, is agnosticism about that probability; that is more plausible. Still more plausible is the disjunction of these two claims: either the rational attitude to take toward this probability is the judgment that it is low, or the rational attitude is agnosticism with respect to it. But then the devotee of N&E has a defeater for any belief B he holds. Now the next thing to note is that *B might be N&E itself*; our devotee of N&E has an undercutting defeater for N&E, a reason to doubt it, a reason to be agnostic with respect to it. (This also holds if he isn't agnostic about P(R/(N&E&C)) but thinks it low, as in the preliminary argument; he has a defeater either way.) If he has no defeater for this defeater and no independent evidence—if his reason for doubting N&E remains undefeated—then the rational course would be to reject belief in N&E.

And here we must note something special about N&E. So far, we have been lumping together all of our cognitive faculties, all of our sources of belief, and all the sorts of beliefs they produce. But perhaps these different sorts of faculties should be treated differentially; clearly the argument can be narrowed down to specific faculties or powers or belief-producing mechanisms, with possibly different results for different cases. And surely the argument does apply more plausibly to some cognitive powers than to others. If there are such differences among those faculties or powers, presumably *perception* and *memory* would be at an advantage as compared with the cognitive mechanisms whereby we come to such beliefs as, say, that arithmetic is incomplete and the continuum hypothesis is independent of ordinary set theory. For even if we evaluated the probabilities differently from the way I suggested, even if we thought it likely, on balance, that evolution would select for reliable cognitive faculties, this would be so only for cognitive mechanisms producing beliefs relevant to survival and reproduction. It would not hold, for example, for the mechanisms producing the beliefs involved in a logic or mathematics or set theory course. According to Fodor (as we saw), "Darwinian selection guarantees that organisms either know the elements of logic or become posthumous"; but this would hold at most[20] for the most elementary bits of logic. It is only the occasional assistant professor of logic who needs to know even that first-order logic is complete in order to survive and reproduce.

Indeed, the same would go generally for the more theoretical parts of science.[21]

> Evolution suggests a status for the distinctions we naturally make, that removes them far from the role of fundamental categories in scientific description. Classification by colour, or currently stable animal-mating groups is crucial to our survival amidst the dangers of poison and fang. This story suggests that the ability to track directly certain classes and divisions in the world is not a factor that guides scientists in theory choice. For there is no such close connection between the jungle and the blackboard. The evolutionary story clearly entails that such abilities of discrimination were 'selected for', by a filtering process that has nothing to do with successful theory choice in general. Indeed, no faculty of spontaneous discrimination can plausibly be attributed a different status within the scientific account of our evolution. Even

---

[20]"At most" because, as I argued, if Darwinian selection guarantees anything, it is only that the organism's *behavior* is adaptive: there isn't anything in particular it needs to *believe* (or, *a fortiori*, to know).

[21]This hasn't been lost on those who have thought about the matter. According to Erwin Schrödinger, the fact that we human beings can discover the laws of nature is "a miracle that may well be beyond human understanding," (*What is Life?* [Cambridge: University of Cambridge Press, 1945], p. 31). According to Eugene Wigner, "The enormous usefulness of mathematics in the natural sciences is something bordering on the mysterious, and there is no rational explanation for it" ("The Unreasonable Effectiveness of Mathematics in the Natural Sciences," in *Communications on Pure and Applied Mathematics,* [13, p. 2]) and "It is difficult to avoid the impression that a miracle confronts us here, quite comparable in its striking nature to the miracle that the human mind can string a thousand arguments together without getting itself into contradictions, or to the two miracles of the existence of laws of nature and of the human mind's capacity to divine them" (p. 7). And Albert Einstein thought the intelligibility of the world a "miracle or an eternal mystery" (*Lettres à Maurice Solovine* [Paris: Gauthier-Villars, 1956], p. 115).

if successful theory choice will in the future aid survival of the human race, it cannot be a trait 'selected for' already in our biological history.[22]

So even if you think Darwinian selection would make it probable that certain belief-producing mechanisms—those involved in the production of beliefs relevant to survival—are reliable, that would not hold for the mechanisms involved in the production of the theoretical claims of science, such beliefs, for example as E, the evolutionary story itself. And of course the same would go for N.

What we have seen so far, therefore, is that the devotee of N&E has a defeater for any belief he holds, and a stronger defeater for N&E itself. If he has no defeater for this defeater, and no independent evidence, then the rational attitude toward N&E would be one of agnosticism.

But perhaps he will claim to have independent evidence. "True," he says, "if N&E were all I had to go on, then the right cognitive stance would be agnosticism about R and in fact about any proposition produced by my belief-producing faculties, including N&E itself. But why can't I reason inductively as follows? My cognitive faculties must indeed be reliable. For consider A_1, any of my beliefs. Naturally enough, I believe A_1; that is, I believe that A_1 is true. So A_1 is one of my beliefs and A_1 is true; A_2 is one of my beliefs and A_2 is true, A_3 is one of my beliefs and A_3 is true, and so on. So, by induction, I argue that all or nearly all of my beliefs are true; I therefore conclude that my faculties are probably reliable (or at any rate probably reliable *now*) because as a matter of fact it is probable that each of the beliefs they have presently produced is true."

This argument ought to meet with less than universal acclaim. The friend of N&E does no better, arguing this way, than the theist who argues that wish fulfillment must be a reliable belief-producing mechanism by running a similar argument with respect to the beliefs he holds that he thinks are produced by wish fulfillment. He does no better than the widget observer who, by virtue of a similar argument, continues to believe that those widgets are red, even after having been told by the building superintendent that they are irradiated by red light. Clearly this is not the method of true philosophy.

Accordingly, the friend of N&E can't argue in this way that he has independent evidence for R. Of course, she isn't likely to argue in *that* way; she is more likely to suggest that we consult the scientific results on the matter: what does science tell us about the likelihood that our cognitive faculties are reliable? But this can't work either. For consider any argument from science (or anywhere else) he might produce. This argument will have premises; and these premises, he claims, give him good reason to believe R (or N&E). But note that he has the very same defeater for each of those premises that he has for R and for N&E; and he has the same defeater for his belief that those premises constitute a good reason for R (or N&E). For that belief, and for each of the premises, he has a reason for doubting it, a reason for being agnostic with respect to it. This reason, obviously, cannot be defeated by an ultimately undefeated defeater. For

[22]Bas van Fraassen, *Laws and Symmetry* (Oxford: Clarendon Press, 1989), pp. 52–53.

every defeater of this reason he might have, he knows that he has a defeater-defeater: the very undercutting defeater that attached itself to R and to N&E in the first place.

We could also put it like this: any argument he offers, for R, is in this context delicately circular or question-begging. It is not *formally* circular; its conclusion does not appear among its premises. It is instead (we might say) *pragmatically* circular in that it purports to give a reason for trusting our cognitive faculties, but is itself trustworthy only if those faculties (at least the ones involved in its production) are indeed trustworthy. In following this procedure and giving this argument, therefore, he subtly assumes the very proposition he proposes to argue for. Once I come to doubt the reliability of my cognitive faculties, I can't properly try to allay that doubt by producing an *argument;* for in so doing I rely on the very faculties I am doubting. The conjunction of evolution with naturalism gives its adherents a reason for doubting that our beliefs are mostly true; perhaps they are mostly wildly mistaken. But then it won't help to *argue* that they can't be wildly mistaken; for the very reason for mistrusting our cognitive faculties generally will be a reason for mistrusting the faculties generating the beliefs involved in the argument.

But (someone might say) isn't there a problem with this argument for pragmatic circularity? The devotee of N&E begins (naturally enough) by accepting N&E; upon being apprised of the previous argument (so I say), he comes to see that he has an undefeated undercutting defeater for R and hence an undefeated reason for doubting N&E; hence (so I say) it is irrational for him to accept N&E, unless he has other evidence; but any purported other evidence will be subject to the same defeater as N&E. But now comes the rejoinder: as soon as our devotee of N&E comes to doubt R, he should also come to doubt his *defeater* for R; for that defeater, after all, depends upon his beliefs, which are a product of his cognitive faculties. So his defeater for R (and N&E) is also a defeater for that defeater, that is, for *itself.* But then when he notes *that,* and *doubts* his defeater for R, he no longer *has* a defeater (undefeated or otherwise) for N&E; so how is it irrational for him to accept N&E?

What we really have here is one of those nasty dialectical loops to which Hume calls our attention:

> The skeptical reasonings, were it possible for them to exist, and were they not destroy'd by their subtlety, wou'd be successively both strong and weak, according to the successive dispositions of the mind. Reason first appears in possession of the throne, prescribing laws, and imposing maxims, with an absolute sway and authority. Her enemy, therefore, is oblig'd to take shelter under her protection, and by making use of rational arguments to prove the fallaciousness and imbecility of reason, produces in a matter, a patent under her hand and seal. This patent has at first an authority, proportioned to the present and immediate authority of reason, from which it is deriv'd. But as it is suppos'd to be contradictory to reason, it gradually diminishes the force of that governing power, and its own at the same time; till at last they both vanish away into nothing by a regular and just diminution. . . . 'Tis happy, therefore,

that nature breaks the force of all skeptical arguments in time, and keeps them from having any considerable influence on the understanding.[23]

When the devotee of N&E notes that he has a defeater for R, then at that stage he also notes (if apprised of the present argument) that he has a defeater for N&E; indeed, he notes that he has a defeater for anything he believes. Since, however, his having a defeater for N&E depends upon some of his beliefs, what he now notes is that he has a defeater for his defeater of R and N&E; so now he no longer *has* that defeater for R and N&E. So then his original condition of believing R and assuming N&E reasserts itself: at which point he again has a defeater for R and N&E. But then he notes that *that* defeater is also a defeater of the defeater of R and N&E; hence . . . So goes the paralyzing dialectic. After a few trips around this loop, we may be excused for throwing up our hands in despair, or disgust, and joining Hume in a game of backgammon. The point remains, therefore: one who accepts N&E (and is apprised of the present argument) has a defeater for N&E, a defeater that cannot be defeated by an ultimately undefeated defeater. And isn't it irrational to accept a belief for which you know you have an ultimately undefeated defeater?

Hence the devotee of N&E has a defeater D for N&E—a defeater, furthermore, that can't be ultimately defeated; for obviously D attaches to any consideration one might bring forward by way of attempting to defeat it. If you accept N&E, you have an ultimately undefeated reason for rejecting N&E: but then the rational thing to do is to reject N&E. If, furthermore, one also accepts the conditional *if N is true, then so is E,* one has an ultimately undefeated defeater for N. One who contemplates accepting N, and is torn, let's say, between N and theism, should reason as follows: if I were to accept N, I would have good and ultimately undefeated reason to be agnostic about N; so I should not accept it. Unlike the preliminary argument, this is not an argument for the *falsehood* of naturalism and thus (given that naturalism and theism are the live options) for the truth of theism; for all this argument shows, naturalism might still be true. It is instead an argument for the conclusion that (for one who is aware of the present argument) accepting naturalism is irrational. It is like the self-referential argument against classical foundationalism: classical foundationalism is either false or such that I would be unjustified in accepting it; so (given that I am aware of this fact) I can't justifiably accept it.[24] But of course it does not follow that classical foundationalism is not *true;* for all this argument shows, it could be true, though not rationally acceptable. Similarly here; the argument is not for the falsehood of naturalism, but for the irrationality of accepting it. The conclusion to be drawn, therefore, is that the conjunction of naturalism with evolutionary theory is self-defeating: it provides for itself an undefeated defeater. Evolution, therefore, presents naturalism with an unde-

---

[23]*A Treatise of Human Nature,* with an analytical index, ed. L. A. Selby-Bigge (Oxford: Clarendon Press, 1888), I, IV, i, p. 187.

[24]See my "Reason and Belief in God," in *Faith and Rationality: Reason and Belief in God.*

feated defeater. But if naturalism is true, then, surely, so is evolution. Naturalism, therefore, is unacceptable.

The traditional theist, on the other hand, isn't forced into that appalling loop. On this point his set of beliefs is stable. He has no corresponding reason for doubting that it is a purpose of our cognitive systems to produce true beliefs, nor any reason for thinking that $P(R/(N\&E\&C))$ is low, nor any reason for thinking the probability of a belief's being true, given that it is a product of his cognitive faculties, is no better than in the neighborhood of $1/2$. He may indeed endorse some form of evolution; but if he does, it will be a form of evolution guided and orchestrated by God. And *qua* traditional theist—*qua* Jewish, Moslem, or Christian theist[25]—he believes that God is the premier knower and has created us human beings in his image, an important part of which involves his endowing them with a reflection of his powers as a knower.[26]

Of course he can't sensibly *argue* that in fact our beliefs are mostly true, from the premise that we have been created by God in his image. More precisely, he can't sensibly follow Descartes, who started from a condition of general doubt about whether our cognitive nature is reliable, and then used his theistic belief as a premise in an argument designed to resolve that doubt. Here Thomas Reid is surely right:

> Descartes certainly made a false step in this matter, for having suggested this doubt among others—that whatever evidence he might have from his consciousness, his senses, his memory, or his reason, yet possibly some malignant being had given him those faculties on purpose to impose upon him; and therefore, that they are not to be trusted without a proper voucher. To remove this doubt, he endeavours to prove the being of a Deity who is no deceiver;

[25]Things may stand differently with a *bare* theist—one who holds only that there is an omnipotent, omniscient, and wholly good creator, but does not add that God has created humankind in his own image.

[26]Of course, God's knowledge is significantly different from human knowledge: God has not been designed and does not have a design plan (in the sense of that term in which it applies to human beings). When applied to both God and human beings, such terms as 'design plan', 'proper function', and 'knowledge', as Aquinas pointed out, apply *analogously* rather than univocally. What precisely is the analogy in this case? Multifarious (for example, divine knowledge as well as human knowledge requires both belief and truth); but perhaps the central analogy lies in the following direction. God has not been designed; still, there is a way in which (if I may say so) his cognitive or epistemic faculties work. This way is given by his being essentially omniscient and necessarily existent: God is essentially omniscient, but also a necessary being, so that it is a necessary truth that God believes a proposition A if and only if A is true. Call that way of working 'W'. W is something like an *ideal* for cognitive beings—beings capable of holding beliefs, seeing connections between propositions, and holding true beliefs. It is an ideal in the following sense. Say that a cognitive design plan P is *more excellent than* a design plan P^* just if a being designed according to P would be epistemically or cognitively more excellent than one designed according to P^*. (There will be environmental relativity here; furthermore, one thing that will figure into the comparison between a pair of design plans will be stability of its reliability under change of environment.) Add W to the set to be ordered. Then perhaps the resulting ordering will not be connected; there may be elements that are incomparable. But there will be a *maximal* element under the ordering: W. W, therefore, is an ideal for cognitive design plans, and it is (partly) in virtue of that relation that the term 'knowledge' is analogically extended to apply to God.

whence he concludes, that the faculties he had given him are true and worthy to be trusted.

It is strange that so acute a reasoner did not perceive that in this reasoning there is evidently a begging of the question.

For, if our faculties be fallacious, why may they not deceive us in this reasoning as well as in others?[27]

Suppose, therefore, you find yourself with the doubt that our cognitive faculties produce truth: you can't quell that doubt by producing an argument about God and his veracity, or indeed, any argument at all; for the argument, of course, will be under as much suspicion as its source. Here no argument will help you; here salvation will have to be by grace, not by works. But the theist has nothing impelling him in the direction of such skepticism in the first place; no element of his noetic system points in that direction; there are no propositions he already accepts just by way of being a theist, which together with forms of reasoning (the defeater system, for example) lead to the rejection of the belief that our cognitive faculties have the apprehension of truth as their purpose and for the most part fulfill that purpose.

Once again, therefore, we see that naturalistic epistemology flourishes best in the garden of supernaturalistic metaphysics. Naturalistic epistemology conjoined with naturalistic metaphysics leads *via* evolution to skepticism or to violation of canons of rationality; conjoined with theism it does not. The naturalistic epistemologist should therefore prefer theism to metaphysical naturalism.[28]

We must draw this book to a close. I have argued that the best way to construe warrant is in terms of proper function: a belief has warrant, for a person, if it is produced by her cognitive faculties functioning properly in a congenial epistemic environment according to a design plan successfully aimed at the production of true or verisimilitudinous belief. We have seen something of how this view applies in a number of areas of our cognitive life. We have also seen that this view of warrant is a *naturalistic* one, but one that requires, for its best flourishing, to be set in the context of supernatural theism. It is therefore time to turn more directly to the question of theistic belief. In the sequel, *Warranted Christian Belief,* I propose to apply what (as I hopefully think) we have learned about warrant, justification, and rationality to questions about Christian beliefs.

[27]*Essays on the Intellectual Powers of the Human Mind,* in *Inquiries and Essays,* ed. R. Beanblossom and Keith Lehrer (Indianapolis: Hackett, 1983), V, 7, p. 276.

[28]Victor Reppert reminds me that the argument of this chapter bears a good bit of similarity to arguments to be found in chapters III and XIII of C. S. Lewis' *Miracles;* the argument also resembles Richard Taylor's argument in Chapter X of his *Metaphysics.*

Index